THE WAR THAT CHANGED THE COURSE OF HISTORY

GALLIPOLI
1915

VAHDETTİN ENGİN
MUZAFFER ALBAYRAK

REPUBLIC OF TURKEY MINISTRY OF CULTURE AND TOURISM
DIRECTORATE OF GALLIPOLI HISTORIC SITE PUBLICATIONS

© **Republic of Turkey Ministry of Culture and Tourism**
Directorate of Gallipoli Historic Site
3481

Pocket Books - 4

ISBN: 978-975-17-3836-3

catab.kulturturizm.gov.tr
e-mail: tarihialanbaskanligi@kultur.gov.tr

Writers
Vahdettin Engin, Muzaffer Albayrak

Translated by
Murat Kazancı

Proof Reading
Nazan Tutaş

Cover Design
Yunus Karaaslan

Page Design
Çelebi Şenel

Production
Yeditepe Basım Yayın Dağıtım Ltd. Şti.
Çatalçeşme Sok. No: 52/1
Cağaloğlu - Fatih / İstanbul
Tel: (0212) 528 47 53

Print Run
5.000

Publication Place and Date
İstanbul, 2016.

Albayrak, Muzaffer, Engin, Vahdettin
   The War That Changed The Course of History GALLIPOLI 1915 / Vahdettin Engin, Muzaffer Albayrak- Ankara: Ministry of Culture and Tourism, 2016.
   228 p.: coll. ill.; 21 cm.- (Minstry of Culture and Tourism publications; 3481, Directorate of Gallipoli Historic Site pocket books; 4)
      ISBN: 978-975-17-3836-3
      Maps and Photographs included.
      I. title II. Engin, Vahdettin. III. series

THE WAR THAT CHANGED THE COURSE OF HISTORY

GALLIPOLI
1915

VAHDETTİN ENGİN
MUZAFFER ALBAYRAK

REPUBLIC OF TURKEY MINISTRY OF CULTURE AND TOURISM
DIRECTORATE OF GALLIPOLI HISTORIC SITE PUBLICATIONS

CONTENTS

FOREWORD

B attle of Gallipoli is the brightest page in the history of Turkish nation which is full of glory and honour of numerous victories. From the political standpoint, it was a battle where many aspirations, passions and dreams were deadlocked; militarily it was a history made by man's power, perseverance and faith.

The Battle stands out as a matchless section in world history where a nation, without falling into despair over the impossibilities, fought shoulder to shoulder against the enemy with their hearts hitting for the same purpose and bravely resisted the enemy's latest war technologies to reach the highest rank that can be achieved.

Undoubtedly, the Battle was not an ordinary military campaign or an ordinary war. In terms of world history, it had a direct influence on the course, duration and result of WWI. For the Turkish nation and Islamic world, it was a struggle for independence. The victory at Gallipoli was achieved with self-confidence and morality and it ensured confidence and hope for the future. Indeed, those who brought the victory in the War of Independence inherited the spirit and self-confidence of Gallipoli.

Directorate of Gallipoli Historic Site was founded to serve on the lands where one of the greatest legends of Turkish history had been written. The aim of the Directorate is to cherish the memories of tens of thousands of martyrs and veterans involved in the Battle and to work for preserving the history, culture, values and natural tissue of the area as well as maintaining, improving, promoting and transferring these to the future generations.

Because our past enlightens our future; it brings benefits at individual, social and universal levels. In this way, individuals learn how to live in peace, leaving aside such attributes as religion, language, race and looking out for common values. An individual who learns the history of his own nation gains national awareness by recognising national values and national culture. He develops a sense of civic responsibility. Thus societies give direction to their future by taking lessons from their history.

To this end, we have published this book, which covers the Battle of Gallipoli as part of WWI in general and as naval and land battles ended with one of the greatest victories of Turkish history in particular, for the youth and the future generations. We also aimed to remember the heroic struggle of our beloved martyrs and veterans who fought for the sake of religion and homeland and to pay –to some extent- our debt of gratitude to them.

Our dear martyrs, at their final resting place, should feel that; this holy land they irrigated with their blood will always be defended and protected by our youth and the entire nation as the most sacred inheritance as in the past.

Hereby, I remember once again with mercy and gratitude all those who gave us the honour of this great victory, particularly including Mustafa Kemal Atatürk and his comrades; all the brave members of our great army who participated in this struggle and all the martyrs who sacrificed their lives for the sake of their homeland. May God bless their souls.

Mahir ÜNAL
Minister of Culture and Tourism

PREFACE

attle of Gallipoli is one of the most significant episodes of not only Turkish history but also of world history. The Battle symbolises the great resistance of the Ottoman Empire in a period of break-up against the most powerful armies of the world. Europe's imperialist states which strived to wipe Turks out of the Balkans and Anatolia suffered a devastating defeat at Gallipoli.

In terms of history, properly understanding the Battle of Gallipoli is very important for the Turkish society. Because the Battle revealed that the Turkish nation had been capable to fight against the greatest powers of the world in a way to remind the brightest victories of its history. The victory at Gallipoli saved the future of Turkish nation as well.

After the onset of WWI, the Allied Powers aimed to end the war in a short time by opening a front at Gallipoli. To them, capturing the Strait of the Dardanelles was equal to capturing İstanbul. And the fall of İstanbul would mean knocking the Ottoman Empire out of the war, which would expectedly pave the way for the Allies, make their struggle against Germany easier, and bring victory in a short time. The British, who had the greatest naval power of the world, believed that they would pass through the Dardanelles without much effort. Winston

Churchill, the British First Lord of Admiralty, masterminded a plan to force the Dardanelles to reach İstanbul. He thought that the Ottoman Empire, who was defeated by the Balkan states a couple of years ago, would easily surrender and Turkish soldiers would flee in front of cannons of their battleships.

But thing did not happen as the Allies had expected. Turkish troops, whom they considered to flee the front seeing the armoured ships, bravely defended their homeland. The Allied navy, attacking the Dardanelles with all its power to get a final result on 18 March 1915, had to withdraw suffering great losses. The British navy, described as invincible, had suffered a historic defeat despite the support from the French.

Afterwards they implemented plans to invade Gallipoli. On 25 April 1915, landing operation on Gallipoli began. As in the naval war, the heroic struggle of Turkish soldiers and officers came to the fore. During the war, morality of Turkish soldiers was always at the top level. They attacked the enemy without any fear and hesitation, believing that they would go to Jannah, and ultimately saved their homeland. The Allies, who lost the land battles after the defeat at the sea, quietly withdrew from Gallipoli with the shame of successive defeats.

Therefore, it is an obligation to teach the Battle of Gallipoli, with its historically high values, to the young generations. It will be a source of motivation for the youth to learn properly how their ancestors had successfully fought against the great powers. On the other hand, grasping with this opportunity that no success would be earned without sacrifice, the young generations will realize that they should never refrain from any sacrifice for their country to be worthy of their ancestors. The Battle of Gallipoli, with all these aspects and samples, is an important lesson for our young people.

This book has been written with all these considerations. It is easy to read. Besides, we tried to include the information that best gives the spirit of Çanakkale. Therefore, after every section on the naval and land battles, an evaluation follows. In addition, many anecdotes related to the heroes and the course of the war and examples demonstrating the human aspect will ensure a more vivid picture of the war.

In the first chapter, the road to the First World War is covered. And the next chapter depicts the outbreak of WWI, the Ottoman entry into the war and opening of the Gallipoli front. Then the sections about naval war and land battles, with special mention of every front, follow. The final part of the book presents a general evaluation.

It is certain that to elaborately narrate each phase of a war that started in February 1915 and continued until the end of January 1916 requires writing many volumes. However, our aim was to write a readable book that would give in the best way the spirit of and truth about Gallipoli to young generations in a single volume. Maximum effort has been expended to achieve this.

Our final word is for the Çanakkale heroes, whom we try to recall with this book. We remember with respect and mercy all those martyrs and veterans of Çanakkale although we know that we owe an unpayable debt of gratitude to every member of Turkish army from privates to officers, who fought for the sake of religion and homeland and made history. God rest their souls.

January 2016
Vahdettin ENGİN
Muzaffer ALBAYRAK

THE ROAD TO WORLD WAR I

Gallipoli was one of the most important fronts of the First World War where the world's great powers clashed for about one year between February 1915 and January 1916. The Peninsula was a scene of fierce fighting, with more than one million soldiers involved in land, sea and air battles.

Britain and France's naval attacks on the Peninsula, followed by land invasion, encountered the Ottoman Empire's resistance with the help from its ally, Germany. Both sides suffered heavy casualties. The British and French forces were decisively defeated and the Ottoman Empire eventually emerged victorious from the Battle of Gallipoli, also known as the Battle of Dardanelles or the Battle of Çanakkale, which is regarded as one of the greatest victories in Turkish history.

Why did the Battle start? Why did the Great Powers launch the campaign at Gallipoli? To answer these questions, one must look at the developments that led up to the WWI.

In the 19th century, the foremost European powers, energized by the industrial revolution, had launched a new period of colonial expansion in Asia, Africa and America. Most notably Britain and France colonized millions square kilometres of land. The industrialized countries of the West sought to expand their economies by securing regular flow of cheap raw materials from colonies. And what is more, Europe's industrialization relied almost exclusively on slave labour imported from colonies. France and Britain had maintained a fragile but working balance in the colonial period until the late 19th century, during which Germany, a comparatively latecomer to the system of nation states, threw a spanner into the works. It began to actively seek colonies when unification of German state was achieved in 1870 following their victory over France. As Germany had largely completed the industrialization by the end of the century, its need for rapid colonial expansion was desperate.

Towards the end of the 19th century, much of the world -about 85 percent- had been colonized by European Powers, who were all competing for colonies and trade around the world. The First World War was indeed the result of this prolonged rivalry which was exacerbated by a tangled network of alliances formed across Europe: Germany, Austria-Hungary and Italy formed the Central Powers. Against German threat, France first turned to Russia and established a military alliance. Britain joined the group after it signed a series of agreements, first with France in 1904 and with Russia in 1907, thereby forming the Entente Powers.

While unresolved conflicts and clash of interests between the Great Powers in the 19th century had led to the outbreak of WWI, the Ottoman Empire, finding itself in a cleft stick and finally participating in the showdown, was obliged to pay a heavy price for the tragic end; the break-up of the Empire.

Should Turkey have joined WWI? In point of fact, the world system had become polarized in the last quarter of the century, the inevitable outcome of which was to be faced in an unprecedented global conflict. Ottoman Sultan, Abdülhamid

II, who saw where the things were heading, was working on his own plans as Europe was divided into rival camps. He first formed a powerful land army to stand out against the threats that might emerge if Europe plunged into the war. He was expecting to stay out and take advantage of a possible war. Abdülhamid II aimed at reviving and underlining the status of the Ottoman Empire as a global power by keeping the Ottoman territories in Rumelia, Anatolia as the center, as far as Thessaloniki, the Hejaz and Palestine regions, Kirkuk and Mosul at Ottoman hands,. Although it is somewhat debatable whether he was able to achieve all these, what is certain about him is that he directed the Empire towards such an aim.

However, things did not go quite as planned. The 31 Mart Incident gave the Committee of Union and Progress (CUP), a group composed of mainly army officers and civil servants, the opportunity to take control of the country. Abdülhamid was deposed following the coup that came in 27 April 1909. The floundering of the CUP rule was due to lack of experience in running the government and unfamiliarity with state affairs. The country was severely traumatised by the failure of the CUP to prevent the outbreak of the Balkan Wars and the loss of all the territories in Rumelia. The following year, the country found itself being dragged into a hastily launched war.

As WWI was the outcome of the rivalry between the imperialist countries and their greed for resources in the Ottoman territories, the Ottoman Empire should not have gotten involved in the war. Even if they had to, they should have taken side with the more powerful bloc. But Britain, France and Russia had refused the CUP's offer of alliance as their eyes lingered on the Ottoman territories and oil reserves across the country. Thereupon, the Ottoman Empire entered the war with the Central Powers with the help of a little bit of encouragement from Germany, the CUP leaders assuming that after major defeats and severe losses there might be some advantages to be gained in the war.

During the four years of warfare fought against the Allied Powers, auxiliary machinery and equipment of the Turkish army were provided by Germany, whose missions dominated Turkey's effective military ranks. The country's crippled economy was already incapable of carrying the burden of a global war, which worsened the military and social effects of WWI across Turkey.

Arms competition among the principal European Powers prior to 1914 heated up, with each side growing its military strength and improving military technology. Both blocs were thinking themselves superior. As a result of this, even tiny problems would be able to mount international tension, which in turn exacerbated the arm race. The growing tension between the two sides worsened in the summer of 1914 and an unprecedented war that the world had ever seen was triggered; when a Serbian anarchist assassinated Archduke Franz Ferdinand, the heir to the throne of Austria-Hungary, on 28 June. The Austrian-Hungarian Empire declared war on Serbia, which was followed by subsequent declarations of war by other countries involved in the Great War.

The Ottoman Empire Joining the Great War

What was it that dragged the Ottoman Empire into the Great War essentially caused by the rivalry among the European Powers? Was it necessary? The story of why the Ottoman Empire entered the First World War can only be properly understood by looking at, as Europeans put it, "the Eastern Question" that dominated the politics and diplomacy in Europe.

The centuries-long rivalry between the Europeans and the Turks had started after the latter's settling down to Anatolia. The Turks had an edge over Europe for so long that the image of 'invincible Turk' was not erased from the memories of the Europeans for centuries. European Powers sought ways to get rid of Turks, making use of any opportunity when it arises. Especially, internal and external efforts to topple the Ottoman Empire had begun by the 19th century. "The Eastern Question" was a term coined by the Europeans to systematize these efforts. The Great Powers also started to call the Ottoman Empire as 'sick man' to easily solve the question in their own favour. They ended up in more aggressive policies towards the once-great Empire to 'throw it into the dustbin of history', waiting for the dead man's shoes.

Despite all their efforts, the Ottoman Empire was the only domain that escaped European colonization throughout the 19th century. They failed to bring the 'sick man' to his knees. What they really failed to realize was that the Ottoman Empire had recovered considerably thanks to reform measures taken by the end of the 19th century, especially during the reign of Sultan Abdülhamid II, after it experienced a period of decline in political, economic and military power at the beginning of the century. Once again, it became an important actor of international politics who was challenging the Great Powers, or *Düvel-i Muazzama* as it was called in Ottoman Turkish.

Throughout the 19th century, the Ottoman territories had been the scene of clash of interests between the Great Powers. The power struggle was exacerbated during Sultan Abdülhamid's reign and the Great Powers had their greedy eyes fixed on the Ottoman lands. France's lust for the Middle East was evident. In addition to its long-standing commercial activities across the Middles East, France was taking lead on protecting the

Christians of the region. Britain had a new interest in the Middle East due to its presence in India and became concerned over the control of the routes to its colony. The British strategy in the region thus centred around extending the domain of influence by getting support of Arab sheiks; so they preferred to cooperate with local sheiks or leaders instead of direct invasion if they wanted to take control of an area, i.e. in the Persian Gulf. For some time, they would not intervene in the business of local governors. Conversely, they would protect them against possible threats. The British rule would be established over time in case of adaptation of the locals to foreign protection. Another major power, Russia, had always been interested in the Ottoman territories due to its traditional strategy of reaching the 'hot seas' (Mediterranean). Russia lay claim to rights of protection over the Ottoman Empire's Orthodox subjects and wanted to increase its regional influence by taking advantage of them.

On the other hand, the Ottoman Empire possessed major oil reserves whose control became an important issue of conflict between the Great Powers. Britain tried to provoke the Arabs inside the Ottoman Empire; in its propaganda often claiming that the Arabs must have held the title of Caliphate and the Ottomans had exploited them.

Amid this state of growing international tension, Abdülhamid II successfully strived to keep the Empire intact, sometimes by forming alliances for good reason as it was almost impossible to withstand the major powers of the time, namely Britain, France and Russia.

In this context of war, Germany, as a major player in international politics with its rising power by the last quarter of the 19th century, seemed to be a natural ally to Abdülhamid II in his fight against the Entente Powers. When Wilhelm II became emperor of Germany in 1888, he adopted an expansionist foreign policy called 'weltpolitik' (world policy), which marked a decisive break with former 'realpolitik' of Otto von Bismarck, as Germany had long lagged far behind other European countries in finding new resources and markets. In a rush to make up for the lost time, Germany struggled to implement its long-term ambition to build a world empire stretching from the Baltic to the Persian Gulf. Therefore Germany's eyes also lingered on the Ottoman territories.

Abdülhamid II took advantage of Germany's keen interest on the region as he pursued a foreign policy aimed at provoking the competition between the Great Powers. Germany as a new powerful actor strengthened Abdülhamid's hand, in this sense, against Britain and France, from which he benefited quite as much as his empire continued to survive and even gained strength.

Abdülhamid attempted to play France off against Britain in Egypt while inciting rivalry between Germany and Britain in the Persian Gulf and Mesopotamia, thereby preventing any of these countries from dominating the region. Furthermore, he extended the state's authority with the Hejaz Railway. Abdülhamid's Empire incisively resisted the British attempts to dominate the Persian Gulf and Yemen, increasing the Arab sheiks' loyalty to the state by sending them gifts. Equally important was incorporation of Mosul's oil fields into *Hazine-i Hassa*, the Sultan's individual estate or Privy Treasury.

British and French politicians were of the opinion that the Ottoman Empire, situated on the passageway of the colonies and possessed rich resources, had been on the verge of disintegration and they had waited enough for their share of the inheritance. This was indeed one of the reasons that dragged the Turks into the war.

Although aware of their intentions, the Ottoman Empire had initially sought to side with Britain and France. In a futile attempt, the CUP leaders communicated with these countries, indicating that they favoured an alliance, which was turned down by the Entente. At the end of the day, Germany turned out to be a correct partner.

When the conditions compelled the Ottoman Empire to consider partnership with Germany (as Turkey was driven into an alliance), Gemany's proposal to form an alliance came. The Grand Vizier Said Halim Pasha negotiated the course of events with the German Ambassador Wangenheim and upon consensus, later on 28 July 1914, he presented the Ottoman Empire's conditions of alliance. As a matter of fact, the Ottoman government, especially Minister of Interior Talat Pasha, had already known that Germany offered alliance since it was on the brink of war against Russia. However, they predicted that the conflict would end in the short term and thought they would guarantee the survival of what remained of the Empire with the alliance of Germany.

Drafted by the Grand Vizier Said Halim Pasha, Minister of War Enver Pasha, Minister of Interior Talat Pasha, and the Head of Parliament Halil Bey, the Germany Ambassador Wangenheim signed the treaty on 2 August 1914, according to which the Ottoman Empire pledged to enter the war on the side of the Central Powers and commissioned a German delegation for the command and control of its armed forces.

Just one day before the signing of the Turco-German alliance, Germany declared war on Russia. On 2 August 1914 the Ottoman Empire ordered general mobilization. On the same day, Britain seized two Ottoman dreadnoughts *Sultan Osman* and *Sultan Reşad* under construction in the British shipyards, which had been ordered and paid in full by the Ottoman Empire.

The situation grew much worse when Germany launched attack on France on 3 August and on Belgium on 4 August, due to which Britain declared war on Germany. It became apparent that the situation was escalating out of control and the conflict was spreading across Europe, contrary to what the CUP leaders predicted.

Despite it all, the Turks were still avoiding a formal declaration of war although they began mobilisation and speeded up their preparations for the war.

Meanwhile, two German cruisers, *Goeben* and *Breslau*, which had been in the Mediterranean since July under the command of Rear Admiral Wilhelm Souchon, were allowed by the Ottoman government safe passage through the Dardanalles on 11 August. In a very critical time, the cruisers had been ordered to reach İstanbul while being tracked by the British navy. The cruisers evaded the British fleet and reached İstanbul. Britain protested against the arrival of the German ships and claimed that they should have been sent back according to the international law. But the Grand Vizier Said Halim Pasa declined the Britain's request informing that the ships had been purchased from Germany. *Goeben* and *Breslau* were immediately given new Turkish names; *Yavuz* and *Midilli* respectively. The officers and crews of the ships, wearing the Ottoman fez, were commissioned to the Ottoman navy.

Ambassadors of the Entente, however, were seeking ways to delay the Ottoman involvement in the war siding with the Central Powers. The Ottoman government, too, was not advocating an immediate entry as the general mobilization was not complete. This did not prevent Germany from exerting pressure on the Ottoman Empire to end neutrality and to join the war as soon as possible. Especially, Ambassador Wangenheim and Liman von Sanders were trying to convince the Turkish side at all costs. Souchon was very willing to undertake an offensive on Russian ships in the Black Sea while the German officers, uneasy of remaining passive, were threatening to turn back to Germany.

As Said Halim Pasha was unenthusiastic about fighting against Britain, he alleged that the Ottoman Empire was unable to join the war due to the lack of arms, munitions, clothes and especially funds. Rejected by the Grand Vizier, Wangenheim then negotiated with the CUP leaders, namely Talat, Enver and Cemal Pashas and persuaded them to enter the war on condition that Germany would provide war indemnity and war material requirement.

Subsequently, a Turkish fleet under the command of Souchon set sail off the Black Sea, sank several Russian vessels and launched attacks on the Russian ports of Odessa, Sevastopol and Novorossiysk on 29 October. This provoked Russia into a declaration of war on the Ottoman Empire on 1 November. Russia's declaration was followed by Britain and France on 5 November. The Ottoman Empire's formal declaration of war on the Entente came on 12 November, after which the Caliph Sultan Reşad, proclaimed holy war on 14 November.

THE GALLIPOLI FRONT

The Gallipoli Front had been another theatre of fighting opened after the outbreak of the First World War. To the Allied Powers, seizing the Dardanelles would have brought about capturing İstanbul, which in turn would have meant knocking the Ottoman Empire out of the war. This would have supposedly helped in some ways: competing with Germany would be easier and they would win the war in a short time. Britain, enjoying its status as the world's dominant naval force, assumed that they would pass without difficulty through the Dardanelles. It was Winston Churchill, the First Lord of the Admiralty at the time, who masterminded the British fleet's forcing its way through the Dardanelles and reaching İstanbul. The Ottoman weakness demonstrated in the war against the Balkan states a while back caused Britain to think that it would be defeated in two ticks.

The Strait of the Dardanelles: Historical Significance

It was a known fact that the defence of İstanbul depended on the defence of the Strait of the Dardanelles. That's why Sultan Mehmed the Conqueror, following the conquest of İstanbul, had two fortresses built, for the defence of the Dardanelles, facing one another at the narrowest point of the Strait. The fortress on the Rumelian side was named as *Kilitbahir*, while the one on the Anatolian side was called *Kala-i Sultâniye*.

These structures were not only very strong, they were well-equipped with heavy artillery as well. And they were thusly able to protect the Strait from enemy fleet, which was tested in 1464 when the Venetian naval force failed in the attack on the Dardanelles.

Köprülü Mehmed Pasha, during the reign of Sultan Mehmed IV, built two more castles further south than *Kilitbahir* and *Kala-i Sultaniye* for the defence of the Strait of the Dardanelles. The castle on Rumelia was named *Seddülbahir* and the castle on Anatolia was named *Kumkale*. Sultan Mehmed IV personally visited these castles in September 1659 and ensured that they were also equipped well with artilleries.

It was only after the Russian ships burned the Ottoman fleet at *Çeşme* and started pounding the Strait during the Turkish-Russo War of 1768 that the Ottoman government turned to a European adviser, Baron de Tott, and assigned him to oversee the fortification of the Strait. Baron de Tott ordered the placement of a line of redoubts along the Anatolian shore from *Naraburnu* to *Kumkale* and improved the artillery capacity in *Kumkale* and *Seddülbahir*, after which a Russian fleet hit the buffers at the entrance to the Strait despite attempts to blockade.

The redoubts survived down to the early 19th century, but were in poor condition. Sultan Selim III (1789-1807), having a special interest in the Dardanelles throughout his reign, charged the French officer M. Juchereau de St. Denys, who was on active duty in the Ottoman army, with preparing a report on the condition of the castles in the Strait. In his report, St.

Denys specified that the castles in the Strait were incapable of defence and a moderate fleet could pass through the Strait easily. He suggested that *Naraburnu* should be strengthened with reinforcements.

The report's recommendations were right on target. A British fleet was able to pass the Strait without much difficulty on 19 February 1807, whereupon Selim III refocused on the fortification of the Strait and ordered building new bastions on both shores. New forts (also officially called bastion or redoubt) were immediately erected in *Naraburnu*, several others in the area between *Seddülbahir* and *Kilitbahir* Castles close to the Aegean Sea and around Gallipoli close to the Sea of Marmara.

However, it was during the reign of Sultan Abdülhamid II that the Strait came under a complete system of fortification because never before had the defence of İstanbul been as crucial as it was at that time. Especially, following the Ottoman-Russo War of 1877-78, the Great Powers had intensified their aggressive policies against the Ottoman Empire. To avert this, the defence of İstanbul, capital of the Empire, was of vital importance, which was increasing the significance of protecting the Dardanelles.

Well aware of this significance, Sultan Abdülhamid II, on various occasions, had several reports prepared on actions to be taken to strengthen the Strait and ordered building strong fortresses in line with these reports. First steps were taken in 1880 and lines of defence of the Strait were identified in accordance with the report prepared by Asaf Pasha, inspector and minister of construction for the Strait of *Bahr-i Sefid* (Mediterranean). Asaf Pasha then concentrated his attention on strengthening *Seddülbahir* and *Kumkale*.

Bastions built on the shores of the Strait included *Mecidiye,* *Hamidiye, Mesudiye, Namazgâh, Yıldız, Ertuğrul* and *Orhaniye.*

Meanwhile, the government was following a policy of Muslim resettlement to areas of non-muslim population around the bastions to establish a type of balance.

The Fortifications of the Dardanelles before the Naval Operations

Following the Balkan Wars, the CUP government had set out to reorganize the Turkish army and appointed German officers to that end. The request for German military instructors was made in May 1913 during the grand viziership of Mahmud Şevket Pasha. General Liman von Sanders, along with some other officers, resigned from the German army and took service with the Ottoman Empire to lead the military reforms. A military board was formed with 41 German officers, 10 of whom arrived in İstanbul in December 1913 and the rest landed in the first months of 1914. Due to the increasing need, many German officers were assigned to train the Ottoman army until the Great War, members of the board rising to 71. German influence in the Ottoman army was to increase when Enver Pasha became Minister of War (3 January 1914) and the Deputy Commander-in-Chief.

It must be noted that the German officers had participated in the preparations of fortifications in the Dardanelles, initiated prior to the Ottoman Empire's entry into the war, while contributing to the reorganisation of the Turkish army.

Before the mobilisation in August 1914, the existing fortifications in Çanakkale were concentrated in two main groups. The first group was observing the 3,5 km wide entrance to the Aegean Sea. The second group was located to block the passageway between *Kepez* and *Naraburnu* at the narrowest point of the Strait. The 25 km zone between the two groups of fortifications and the 35 km of the Strait a little beyond Nara up to the Marmara Sea, however, were not fortified. The fortifications at the entrance of the Strait consisted only of *Seddülbahir* and *Ertuğrul* forts on the European side and *Kumkale* and *Orhaniye* on the Anatolian side.

Fortifications at the Strait started very quickly with all available opportunities: six bastions and seven heavy batteries were stationed on the European shore while eight bastions and three heavy batteries protected the Anatolian shore. The entrance was blockaded with twenty artilleries and some 103 more were scattered along the Strait. Twenty two howitzers whose ranges changing from 7,000 to 14,000 metres were also emplaced.

Besides, two lines of sea mine were laid at the entrance following *Yavuz* and *Midilli*'s entry on 10 August 1914. Two illumination projectors required for night warfare were placed as well.

Eight field howitzers were deployed on the hills that lie between the *Karanlık* Harbour, located at the entrance, and the inland fortifications. These howitzers, that would change positions if necessary, were to fire at the enemy ships which could escape the heavy bombardment of Turkish guns and start shooting inland bastions.

Unused, quick-firing, 15-cm diameter modern artilleries were removed from Turkish warships and emplaced on both sides of the Strait.

For reinforcement, three old vessels, named *Mesudiye*, *Barbaros Hayreddin* and *Turgut Reis*, in small tonnage range were first stationed behind the *Kepez* Cape and later off Çanakkale and *Nara*. The vessels had been tasked with keeping an eye on enemy fleet passing through the Strait and patrolling *Saros* Bay.

To delude the enemy, fake cannons, which were supposed to misdirect the enemy bombardments, were installed on various points of the waterway along the coast.

Except for two lines of mine planted earlier, nine new lines were added. Detection and removal of the mines by enemy minesweepers were hindered by light batteries surrounding the minefields on both shores of the Strait.

Eight searchlights were located for illuminating the minefields at night, increasing the number of searchlights to ten.

To block the passage of submarines, a net barrage was deployed off *Nara* 30 m below sea level.

The battle-ready 7th and 9th Infantry Divisions along with six Gerdermarie Battalion, tasked with guarding the *Saros* Bay and Anatolian coastline across *Bozcaada*, were to prevent a probable enemy landing.

The command of the fortifications of the Strait devolved upon Captain Cevat Bey (later Cevat Pasha) as from 10 August 1914 under the title of 'Çanakkale Fortified Area Command'. Cevat Pasha collaborating with German Commanders Usedom and Merten, worked on the defence strategy of the Strait.

Çanakkale after the Ottoman Entry into the War

The Allied attack on the Ottoman territories began right after the Ottoman entry into WWI. In reply to the attack on the Russian ports in the Black Sea on 29 October, Russia declared war on 1 November and launched an offensive across the Caucasus. Two days later, on 3 November, the British and French battleships began long-range bombardment on *Seddülbahir* and *Kumkale*, thus ending up siding with Russia and waging war against the Ottoman Empire.

In the attack, the British battlecruisers *Indefatigable* and *Inflexible* cannonaded *Seddülbahir* and *Ertuğrul* redoubtss while the French battleships *Bouvet* and *Suffren* bombarded Turkish forts on the Anatolian side, namely *Kumkale* and *Orhaniye*.

Turkish side could not resist the violent attacks from the enemy battleships that had quick-firing guns shooting from a range of 12-14 km as the battleships stayed outside the range of Turkish artilleries. The first enemy attacks of the incipient war caused heavy losses. Five officers and 81 privates, including the Commander of the *Seddülbahir* Castle Şevki Bey, died and became first martyrs of the war before the Çanakkale front opened.

After the attack on 3 November, the Allied Navy chose the island of Limni (Lemnos) as the base. In this way, the entrance to the Dardanelles was kept under constant control. They did not launch a new attack, but there was an expectation that a new front would be opened up there.

In the following days, the Allies tried to carry out a submarine attack on the Dardanelles. The British submarine B-11 attacked the Turkish battleship *Mesudiye* which was anchored in *Sarısığlar* Bay, 10 km south of Çanakkale, and was intended to guard minefields. On 13 December 1914, B-11 torpedoed twice and sank *Mesudiye*. 10 officers and 25 privates of the crews were martyred and 5 officers along with 3 privates were trapped in the engine room.

The search for the survivors started and the rescuers hammered the hull of the capsized battleship. This was heard and answered by the men inside.

Rescuers needed oxy-acetylene welding kit and corkscrew to save the survivors. Immediate action was taken to bring these materialsfrom İstanbul. Meanwhile, moral support was vital for the trapped crew members. The rescuers continued hammering the hull to give support to the crew lying on bunk beds in the water. The next day, with the equipment brought from İstanbul, a small hole was drilled for insiders to get some air. The rescuers also tried to talk with them and poured some milk right into the hole to feed them. Eventually, after the 36-hour effort, the crew was rescued through a big hole.

Then, guns removed from *Mesudiye* were reinstalled in Rumelia as *Baykuş* (*Mesudiye*) battery and used for the fortification of the Strait. Fire from the battery on 18 March was quite effective.

On 15 January 1915, the soldiers in Nara noticed that the wire web hanging down from the police post had been broken by force. Nearby batteries were informed immediately of the situation. The French submarine Safir, surfacing from below, was sunk by Turkish forces. The submarine's captain and crew, recued and taken captive, were sent to İstanbul.

The incidents were foreshadowing the forthcoming major offensive by the Allies on the Dardanelles. The Turkish General Staff received the news from its intelligence services in Egypt, Athens, Italy and London that Britain was planning an operation on the Strait. Details of the operation were yet to be known but it was thought to be a large-scale attack and measures were taken accordingly for intercepting it.

After the bombardment of 3 November, 3rd Corps Headquarters commanded by Esat Pasha departed Tekirdağ for Gallipoli on 4 November.

Çanakkale Fortified Zone Command, with the 9th Division at its command, had been connected directly to the Commander-in-Chief.

In addition to these measures, the Turkish army placed greater emphasis upon the coastal and underwater fortifications of the 9th Division zone in the Gallipoli Peninsula from north to south. Also, deployment of artilleries from units outside Çanakkale strengthened the defence of the Strait. As an additional precaution, some vessels were commissioned in the Strait against enemy submarines that could infiltrate. Before the war, for the purpose of protecting İstanbul, there were thirty two batteries in the Dardanelles and three in the Independent Heavy Artillery Battalion. In that period, due to the lack of officers and privates for these thirty five batteries, Heavy Artillery Inspector General Posseldt and Combat Engineer Inspector General Weber, both German, proposed that the number of batteries be decreased to twenty two and the number of staff be increased to peacetime complement, which was approved and implemented.

Turkish High Command put above-water reconnaissance and surveillance services under German Delegate Merten Pasha's order. For the training of artillery officers and sergeants in the Fortified Zone Command, coastal artillery specialist German Lieutenant Colonel Wossidlo was appointed as Commander of Anatolian Hamidiye bastion.

In this way, the Dardanelles were being prepared against a possible enemy attack. Meanwhile, Lieutenant Colonel Mustafa Kemal Bey was appointed as the commander of the

19th Division on 20 January 1915. As the Ottoman Empire entered the war, Mustafa Kemal Bey did not want to stay in the military attaché's office in Sofia and had demanded to be given the task in the front. Thereupon, he was brought to the Commandership of the 19th Division, then located in Tekirdağ. Meanwhile Çanakkale Naval Wars had not yet begun. Mustafa Kemal Bey, on 24 January, started his career in Tekirdağ and having completed the task about the 19th Division, was transferred to Maydos (Eceabat), on 25 February. The Allies had been forcing the Strait of the Dardanelles from the sea since 19 February 1914. Fortified Zone Command gave the duty of defending against the possibility of enemy landing to the 19th Division.

Allies Open the Gallipoli Front

After the First World War began, all the violence had reigned in the summer months of 1914, and it had turned to intense trench warfare towards autumn. Soon after, countries at war needed new battlefields to break the stalemate.

With an aim to alleviate the burden of the war and prevent the enemies from bringing fresh forces into the battlefield, Germany began to exert pressure on the Ottoman Empire, calling for action against Russia and Britain.

As a result of these pressures, *Sarıkamış* and Canal operations were performed, and both have resulted in failure. Although unsuccessful, Germany was partly relieved by the operations because Russia and Britain had to allocate part of their forces to these fronts.

Quite concerned about the Sarıkamış operation, Russia vehemently asked its Allies to open a front in the West to tie up the Ottoman Army. Britain, too, was unsettled by the Ottoman attempt of threatening the Suez Canal which was vital to the British interests as this sea route was connecting India to the Mediterranean. Consequently, Russia's request was found appropriate and opening a new front was considered useful.

Churchill had planned forcing the Strait from the sea to pass through the Dardanelles as early as September 1914. The Allies turned back to this plan. However, Churchill was despising the Ottoman Empire due to the crushing defeat in the Balkan Wars and was suggesting that the British fleet would pass the Strait easily. He was sure that the Ottoman soldiers would immediately flee the front in the face of heavy artillery fire from the British battleships.

However, no consensus was reached among the British about opening a front at Gallipoli. Lord Fisher, First Sea Lord, roughly estimated that an army of 75,000 soldiers would be required to open a new front. Commander-in-Chief of British naval forces, Admiral Carden, stated, in his report, that it might be possible, though it may last a bit longer, to pass through the Dardanelles with an adequate number of ships.

British War Council convened on 5 January 1915. At the meeting, the Secretary of War, Kitchener, defended the opening of the Gallipoli front, which was supported by Churchill. The opinion of the Council was weighted in favour of opening the front at the meeting on 13 January. Kitchener asserted that the campaign would not pose danger and that the navy would return in case of a failure. Contrarily, Lord Fisher pointed out that there were not enough sea and land forces to go round.

The council, at the meeting on 28 January, reviewed its resolution on the Gallipoli front. As a result, it was decided that a naval attack should be launched on the Strait of Dardanelles, thus opening a new front. As the campaign, if successful, was expected to change the fate of the war because of possible gains and accompanying political developments, preparations for the campaign accelerated with the participation of France.

Envisaged gains of opening the Gallipoli front:

-As the Arctic Ocean froze and Baltic Sea was sealed off by the Germans, supporting Russia seemed beyond the bounds of possibility. If the Dardanelles fell, the British and French would have a direct contact with Russia and support it.

-Opening of the Gallipoli front would eliminate the Ottoman pressure on the Suez Canal and India route, a potential attack on Egypt would be averted.

-İstanbul would be invaded and the Ottoman Empire would be kicked out of the war. Left alone, Germany could be defeated more easily and the war could end sooner.

-Balkan states hesitating to join the war would side with the Allied Powers.

-Ottoman influence on the Muslim communities of the British colonies would be weakened.

-Keeping the Ottoman army at Gallipoli would prevent troop reinforcements to the existing fronts at the Caucasus, Egypt and Iraq.

Besides the general motives to open the Gallipoli front, each of the Entente Powers (Britain, France and Russia) had its own specific reason to launch the attack on the Strait.

Britain: Drawing the attention of the Turkish army to the Strait, Britain aimed to eliminate the threat against Egypt and the Suez Canal, to prevent reinforcements to the Turkish army based in Iraq, to get into İstanbul before Russians and retain it, to support Russia with weapons and ammunitions so as to enable it to prolong the war.

France: France's plan was to support Russia and crush the Germans, besides abiding by the requirements of political and military agreements with its Allies.

Russia: Its aims included capturing İstanbul, establishing fast and secure contact with its Allies, thus getting desperately needed weapons and ammunitions from them, keeping the Caucasus away from the Turkish threat.

However, all three had a common reason too: International propaganda for the 'holy war' was continuing and 'unity of Islam' was emerging as a threatening movement. Considering the fact that most of colonies of the Allied Powers were Muslims, this threat would endanger all the colonies. Threatening İstanbul, the centre of the Islamic world, and capturing it would eliminate that potential movement. On the other hand, neutral Balkan states, namely Romania, Bulgaria and Greece, would side with the Entente if the Strait fell and the Ottoman Empire was knocked down. Thus, the Central Powers (Germany and Austria-Hungary) would be besieged.

NAVAL WARS

The Entente had opened the Gallipoli front relying on the above-mentioned grounds and pursuant to the scheme pioneered by Churchill.

The Allied navy was commanded by the British Carden. Admiral Guepratte was in charge of the French fleet. The Allied forces, gathered at the entrance of the Dardanelles, consisted of the following:

British fleet: 14 battleships, 5 cruisers, 16 destroyers, 1 aircraft carrier, 5 submarines, 21 minesweepers.

French fleet: 4 battleships, 6 destroyers, 1 aircraft carrier, 2 submarines.

As for the land forces, two British infantry battalions and an Australian brigade were assembled on the Island of Limnos at the beginning of March with an aim to completely destroy and invade the forts silenced by the navy.

Admiral Carden's attack plan for forcing the Dardanelles was composed of four successive phases:

1-Destruction of the outer forts at the entrance of the Strait

2-Destroying the defensive arrangements inside the Strait down to *Kepez*

3-Destruction of the forts at the narrows between *Kilitbahir* and *Çanakkale*

4-Removing the mine fields and passing through the Sea of Marmara

On the opposite side, the Commander of the Fortified Zone, Cevat Pasha had contemplated defensive measures.

The most effective weapon of the defence, mines had been planted in ten lines and the number of mines was increased to 400 in February 1915. Defence strategy of the Strait composed of four phases:

1-At the entrance, *Seddülbahir* and *Ertuğrul* forts on the Rumelia side and *Kumkale* and *Orhaniye* forts on the Anatolia side of the Dardanelles would try to prevent the enemy from entering the Strait.

2-If the enemy fleet entered the Strait, howitzers based on Erenköy-Tenkerdere line would start the bombardment and hinder the enemy fleet manoeuvring in this zone.

3-Located in the middle of the Strait, artillery barrages comprising light ship guns and howitzers were utilized to guard the mine fields and to obstruct the enemy efforts to sweep mines.

4-Forts on both flanks of the Strait across Çanakkale-*Kilitbahir* zone, the most important and effective defence line for the defence of the Strait, constituted the intermediate defence which was designed to hamper the passage of the enemy ships through the Sea of Marmara.

Commander of the Allied Naval Forces, Admiral Carden opted for the attack on 19 February 1915, which was not a randomly selected date. As mentioned above, it was the anniversary of a historic event. In 1807, the Ottoman Empire had been fighting with Russia, an ally of Britain. The latter had sent naval support to Russia.

During the Russo-Turkish war in 1807, Britain had sent a naval support to its ally, Russia. Commanded by Admiral Duckworth, the British fleet had passed the Strait of Dardanelles, through the unwariness of Turkish guards, and had steamed into İstanbul. The fleet had anchored off the Prince's Islands for about two weeks and İstanbul had been threatened with imminent Allied invasion. Having realized that it could do nothing more thanks to the measures taken by the Ottoman Empire, the enemy had resorted to escaping; however, this time encountered by the guards on its way back home, the fleet had a hard time getting out of the Strait, suffering some casualties.

As for the attack on 19 February 1915, Britain, before all else, aimed to destroy the outer forts of the Dardanelles, namely *Seddülbahir (Helles), Ertuğrul, Orhaniye* and *Kumkale*. At the second stage, according to the plan, first line of mines would be cleared, which would be succeeded by the major attack. To that end, forts on both sides up to *Kepez* would be destroyed by the naval strike. It would open a path in the further lines of mines and clear the way for İstanbul. After the navy's passing through the Strait, the Allied troops would seize the forts ashore and fully control the Strait. Accordingly, a few enemy ships began shelling the Turkish forts at the entrance of the Dardanelles on 19 February.

The Battle in the Strait from 19 February to 18 March

Six battleships had been commissioned with a duty to destroy the fortifications at the entrance of the Strait. The ships would start bombarding the forts before entering their range, proceed steadily and finally destroy the forts completely firing all the shells at hand.

The offensive began at 09.50 in the morning of 19 February. *Seddülbahir* and *Ertuğrul* forts on the Rumelia side and *Kumkale* and *Orhaniye* forts on the Anatolian side came under heavy fire. Turkish bastions initially failed to respond to the enemy ships as they were out of range. As the ships approached, Turkish forts were able to strike back.

The Allied attack on 19 February could not achieve its objective of destroying the Turkish forts. Damage to the forts was insignificant compared to the intensity of the bombardment throughout the seven-hour fighting. Turkish side suffered fifteen casualties, four soldiers martyred and eleven wounded in the clashes.

The next day, due to a heavy storm, the enemy fleet was forced to suspend the attack until 25 February. The Allied attack, restarted on 25 February, utterly destroyed the forts at the entrance of the Strait with short-range bombing. Turkish casualties were heavier than the previous attack, 13 martyred and 19 wounded.

The Allied fleet entered the Strait on 27 February after destroying the fortifications at the entrance. However, they had to withdraw because the howitzers located in the intermediate defence began to damage the enemy ships.

Turkish artillerymen in the damaged forts at the entrance drew back and *Seddülbahir* and *Kumkale* forts were evacuated to avoid the bombardment. To take immediate advantage of the situation, the Allied Naval Command dispatched battalions to *Seddülbahir* and *Kumkale*. The battalion in *Kumkale* encountered Turkish troops and retreated. The one in *Seddülbahir*, however, managed to damage four out of six artilleries. When it reached at *Ertuğrul* fort, it had to retreat due to relentless heavy fire.

In 1st and 3rd of March, naval vessels entering the Strait wanted to collect mines. But with effective howitzer fire in the intermediate fortifications, little progress was made and they could not succeed it.

The Allied forces, on 4 March, landed once again at *Seddülbahir* and *Kumkale* to complete the unfinished destruction. A unit of 150 infantry soldiers and a destruction team, operating under the protection of the entire fleet, turned to *Kumkale* and *Orhaniye* forts. In the face of heavy fire by Turkish troops, they withdrew unsuccessfully.

The infantry squadron and destruction battalion landed at *Seddülbahir*, taking advantage of cover, moved toward the forts but had to retreat facing heavy fire by Turkish troops defending the region. Turkish forces repulsed the attack of the British squad landed at *Seddülbahir* with bayonet charge, which was harbinger of the epic to be written by *Mehmetçik* – literally Little Mehmet, a general term used affectionately to refer soldiers of the Turkish Army - in Çanakkale.

Allied navy was passing through the Dardanelles from 5 to 18 March nearly every day and exchanging artillery fire with Turkish forts. Minesweepers were trying to collect sea mines. Nonetheless, artillery barrages on both sides of the Strait were not allowing them. With effective fire, Turkish artilleries were inflicting casualties for the enemy minesweepers and their staff.

On the night of 8 March, the Fortified Zone Command commissioned Nusret Mine Ship to Erenköy Bay, where the enemy ships used to manoeuvre, to lay 26 mines at hand. Commander of Nusret, Captain Hakkı Bey of Tophane, and Mine Commander, Captain Nazmi Bey, fulfilled this dangerous and important task successfully. 26 mines, placed by Nusret and constituted the 11th line of mines at the Strait, were to bring great damage to the enemy fleet on historic 18 March clashes and two warships hitting these mines were to sink.

Allied navy commander, Admiral Carden was having difficulties in implementing his four-step plan. He was not able to silence Turkish guns and collect the mines. As of 15 March, only one line of mine was swept. Turkish forts in the centre stood intact in front of him. Carden had to leave his post after suffering a nervous breakdown due to the failure in the naval attacks and was replaced by Rear Admiral De Robeck on 17 March. The new commander was expected to launch the last major offensive immediately.

The Allies decided to deploy new infantry forces to the Dardanelles to support naval operations and to take control of the forts on the coastal area. As part of the new plan, General Hamilton, who was assigned to the British Land Forces Command, reached Çanakkale on 17 March. General d'Amade, French commander who joined the Allied land forces with a division, came to Çanakkale.

New commander of the Allied navy, Admiral De Robeck gathered a war council in the battleship Queen Elizabeth. The council, comprised commanders of land and naval forces present in Çanakkale, decided to start the all-out attack on 18 March.

The Naval Battle of 18 March

Naval battles that started on 19 February had continued for about a mount and fierce clashes had occurred between Turkish artillerymen at the forts and the Allied warships. Prior to the major battle on 18 March, overall position of the two parties was as follows:

Turkish forces: Fortified Zone Command, with the fall of outer fortifications on 25 February, was trying to resist unceasing offensive and minesweeping operations of the enemy fleet across the Strait, taking new measures. Commander of the Fortified Zone, Cevat Pasha, tried to increase the number of artilleries on both sides of the Strait as much as possible and kept the Allied navy pinned down with reorganized batteries. At night, against the minesweeping activities of the enemy fleet, the number of searchlights illuminating the sea was raised to 23. Available mines were landed where necessary. On the night of 8 March, Nusret Mine Ship laid 26 mines to Erenköy Bay.

Allied forces: As of 18 March, the situation looked bleak for the Allied navy. The Allied forces had lagged behind Admiral Carden's plan to pass through the Strait. Damage to Turkish artillery by the naval bombardment had been less than expected, which was not enough to silence the skilfully concealed artillery barrages on the Turkish side. Minesweepers were not able to collect sea mines. On the other hand, it became clearthat the Dardanelles campaign would not be prolonged without ground forces. Hence, Britain and France deployed new ground troops to Çanakkale. By 17 March 1915, an army of 60,000 troops were gathered on the Island of Limnos to take joint action with the Allied fleet. Admiral Carden, down in the dumps due to the failure to make adequate progress in accordance with his plan, specifically in silencing Turkish forts and minesweeping activities, stepped down as Commander of the Allied fleet on 16 March, using his health condition as an excuse. His replacement was the British Admiral De Robeck to command the Allied naval force. Churchill, First Lord of the Admiralty, asked De Robeck whether he thought the Dardanelles campaign was right and implementable. De Robeck found the campaign achievable and stated that the offensive would be launched on 18 March under favourable weather conditions.

The Battle at the Strait: 18 March 1915

On 17 March, Admiral De Robeck put finishing touches on his plan at the meeting held with all the admirals and general who had been serving in the Allied fleet. According to the plan, the fleet composed of 18 battleships was divided into three groups:

First group consisted of British battleships *Queen Elizabeth, Inflexible, Agamemnon, and Lord Nelson*

Second group comprised French warships *Suffren, Bouvet, Charlemagne, Gaulois and British Triumph and Prince George*

Third group was composed of British battleships *Ocean, Vengeance, Albion, Cownwallis, Irresistible, Canopus, Swiftsure* and *Majestic.*

After the battleships silenced the Turkish forts on the coastline, sea mines were to be swept and a safe-passage corridor was to be opened up for the fleet. 18 battleships were carrying 250 gun-barrels, in total, of various calibres, including the battleship *Queen Elizabeth* with 38cm guns with the ability to fire about 500-kg shell..

The Fortified Zone Command was withstanding the brunt of the enemy's attack with patience and resoluteness. Forts and artillery barrages were showing maximum effort and persevering with fulfilling the assigned duties.

Fortified Zone Command had reserved 74 coast artilleries, 82 mortars and howitzers and 58 small cannons of various calibres in the forts and batteries for defence against the Allied force on 18 March. Compared with the enemy fleet,

Turkish forces were significantly disadvantaged in terms of number and quality of available guns and most importantly the ammunition reserves.

On 18 March, Commander Cevat Pasha had been scheduled to conduct inspection on the Peninsula side. He was informed, by the Chief of Staff of the Fortified Zone Command Lieutenant Colonel Selahaddin Adil Bey, of the news that a large naval task force was approaching the Strait. Adil Bey, instantly alerting the guards of the Strait, commanded the army until Cevat Pasha's arrival at 2 pm.

Four battleships in the first group of the Allied fleet began bombardment at 11.30 am of intermediate forts, including *Hamidiye* on Anatolia, *Mecidiye* on *Rumelia, Namazgah, Çimenlik* and *Dardanos*. At first, Turkish forts did not fire back due to the long distance. As the enemy fleet came nearer, the forts began shooting back at 12 pm, inflicting damage to the battleships with the shots on target. At 12.30 pm, De Robeck ordered the second line of battleships to move forward. French battleships that comprised the second line were trying to accomplish the task with heavy guns by 8-9 km approaching the Turkish forts. Intense bombardment of ten warships that entered the Strait began to shatter the forts; in some bastions, guns were covered with soil while some bastions ceased fire.

Effective bombardment helped the enemy's minesweepers move forward to clear the passageway for the Allied navy. Turkish forts and battery barrages defending the minefields were struggling to prevent minesweeping of the enemy battleships.

By 1.30 pm, it became apparent that the French battleships, defiantly moving forward, had been severely affected by the fire of the Turkish artillery, particularly *Gaulois* and *Suffren* battleships had suffered heavy damage. Hereupon, Admiral De Robeck, decided to move the third group of battleships forward.

The decisive moment that changed the course of the war arose when the British battleships entered the Strait. While damaged French warships sailed out of the Strait, another French pre-dreadnought Bouvet was rocked by a huge explosion, as it manoeuvred back following *Gaulois* and *Suffren*, at 2 pm. The warship, hitting one of the mines landed by *Nusret*, overturned and sank in just two minutes. More than 600 crew members got drowned.

The incident, occurred at a time that the Turkish forts had been overwhelmed by intense bombardment, bolstered the Turkish artillery's morale. And all the batteries started to open fire on the Allied fleet. Entering the Strait, British warships had also begun bombardment with all their strength. The battle at the Strait had turned to a fierce fighting. Turkish forts, namely *Hamidiye, Mecidiye* and *Namazgah*, had been severely damaged under heavy bombardment.

At 3.30 pm, the British vessel *Irresistible* careened, losing steerage after a huge explosion. After half an hour, the vessel, hitting another mine, heeled over to one side and sank. The crew were evacuated by the rescue ships. Another British battleship *Ocean*, under heavy bombardment of the Turkish artillery, failed in its task of rescuing the stricken *Irresistible* and set back. On its way back, *Ocean* hit an underwater mine at 6 pm and was abandoned to its fate after the crew were rescued. *Irresistible* and *Ocean* fully sank after dark.

Admiral De Robeck ordered a withdrawal after the sinking of three ships and destruction of three others.

As it got dark on 18 March, the Allied fleet, having lost around a third of the vessels it had at the beginning, was leaving the Strait while the Turkish side was claiming a historic victory.

The bastions had suffered minor repairable damage considering the thousands of shells fired from the enemy fleet. Only eight artilleries were destroyed. Eight lines of mine out of eleven were still intact, which made it impossible for the enemy fleet to pass through the Strait before sweeping them totally.

Casualties of the victorious Turkish artillerymen on 18 March included 26 martyrs and 53 wounded. Three German soldiers serving in the forts were dead while fifteen others were injured. However, allied casualties exceeded 800.

An Evaluation of the Battle of 18 March

The British-French joint attack on the Dardanelles as part of an attempt to capture İstanbul fizzled out on 18 March, which marked a historic victory for the Turkish army beyond any doubt.

Naval attack on the Dardanelles, driven by the perception that the Turkish artillerymen would surrender or flee their positions upon seeing the Allied fleet at the entrance of the Strait was an unreasonable campaign carried out with such impudence. It was apparent that no fleet without the support of powerful land force would pass through the Dardanelles and seize İstanbul.

The strength of the navy in front of Çanakkale was evident to all. Turkish army command had taken some measures thinking that the enemy fleet would cross the Strait. The measures included preparations for moving the seat of government and the sultan's palace from İstanbul to Anatolia. While the enemy attack on the Dardanelles continued, two trains were kept ready at the *Haydarpaşa* station in case they were needed. If the enemy managed to pass through the Dardanelles, the trains would take the government seat to Eskişehir and the Sultan along with the Courtiers to Konya. İstanbul would not surrender, contrary to what the British had anticipated, and it would be defended to death. Artilleries had been deployed along the coastline of Marmara, from *Sarayburnu* to *Bakırköy* and further defence measures had been taken. On 18 March, a phone line was connected between İstanbul and Çanakkale, transferring information about the battle every ten minutes.

Turkish army command responded to the Allied attack with opportunities at hand: Sea mines were used extensively against the powerful battleships. Mines that lay in wait for the enemy in the Strait constituted the backbone of Turkish defence. On 18 March, Turkish artillery fearlessly and faithfully fulfilled the duty of defending with extraordinary effort and devoutness despite enemy shells falling like rain. Turkish army's morale was extremely high as they believed in the victory, one of the most striking examples of which was seen when Corporal Seyit (*Seyit Onbaşı*) carried a shell weighing 215 kg to the gun whose crane had been damaged.

There is no doubt that the victory of Turkish artillery on 18 March was a prelude and harbinger of the history written by *Mehmetçik* in the Çanakkale Land Wars to be commenced on 25 April 1915 and to last about eight and a half months.

A Hero at Seddülbahir: Sergeant Mehmet Bigalı

Turkish artilleries had abandoned Seddülbahir fort after naval bombardment on 25 February 1915 destroyed their cannons. The fort was very important for surveillance against the enemy's advancing navy. That's why 3rd Battalion of the 27th Regiment of the 9th Division was tasked with the defence of Seddülbahir sector. The battalion was under the command of Maydos Sector Commander Lt. Col. Mustafa Kemal and was mainly responsible for coastal defence.

A detachment from the 3rd Battalion would provide surveillance in and around the areas located just below the fort. This platoon was under the control and command of Sergeant Mehmet Bigalı.

Sergeant Mehmet placed his team in a wider area across the seaside in order to let them see the other side clearly. They had only rifles and hand grenades. He personally counted the bullets and gave all of them to the soldiers. They all performed bayonet drill. There were only 30 soldiers but they all knew how important their tasks were. They were undeterred and never fell for intimidation. Morale of the team was extremely high. Sergeant Mehmet was told that the enemy could only attack through the sea. They did not expect a land operation. So, he placed only five soldiers for night watch and positioned the remaining men in trenches along the fort.

On 4 March 1915, British soldiers got on motorboats from war ships and gunboats. There were machine guns in front of the motorboats. They fired both from the ships and the boats. However, the Turkish soldiers did not respond to these attacks. With supports from five armoured and seven torpedo boats, the motorboats eventually arrived at the beach one after the other. Soldiers then stepped ebulliently from the motorboats onto the land, thinking that there would not be any attack from the fort.

However, they were suddenly met with excessive gunfire from the Turkish soldiers stationed at the fort. Enemy soldiers retreated back with some of them taking covers behind the rocks, some jumping into the sea whist some went back to the motorboats.

Aside from the warships, which were firing away from the sea, the soldiers on the land could not counter the attacks from the Turks. However, this firing did not yield any result because the warships could not identify the exact locations of the Turkish soldiers. This is because the gunfire from the Turkish soldiers stationed at the fort was coming from different locations as the soldiers were changing positions. The British assumed that the number of the soldiers at the fort was more. As a result, the soldiers waiting in the boats did not want to move inland despite several forceful attempts by their commanders. After all, they also saw that whoever approached or stepped on the beach was shot at once.

Sergeant Mehmet was among those who were firing rapidly and changing positions. Soon he realized that his gun had stopped working properly. He furiously threw away the gun towards the enemy and started pelting them with stones. Then he started to throw whatever he found. These actions motivated his team members who stepped up their gunfire on the enemies. In the middle of these shootings, one of the bullets touched Sergeant Mehmet's head softly but he did not even realize it. Then suddenly, a second bullet hit him on the right chest, by which time the British ships had already begun leaving.

Mustafa Kemal, the sector commander, giving accounts of this event, narrates that:

'Sergeant Mehmet is from Biga. I met him when he came to Biga for sick leave a few months after the war ended. I listened to the story of the war from him. He narrated the story like this :

'I was on duty with my team when the enemy aboard the ships, after shooting the coastline for some long hours, they started getting off the ships and moving into the land with a very heavy force. We also came out from where we hid, lied on the ground and started to fire. The enemy soldiers lied down too. We were very close to each other. In the course of action, the mechanism of my gun stopped working. So, I threw away my gun in anger. An enemy soldier aimed at me and shot. I grabbed the paddle and attacked him. I don't remember how many of them I hit. When I opened my eyes I was in the health tent.'

Mustafa Kemal proposed that a medal be rewarded to Sergeant Mehmet Bigalı for his display of extraordinary courage and heroism in defeating the enemy that invaded Seddülbahir:

"The enemy forces that came inland were repelled by bayonet charge under the command of the son of Mustafa, Mehmet, who fought under the 10th Squadron of the 27th Regiment of the 9th Division. This sergeant had to fight with just a rock because his gun's mechanism was broken. He fought very bravely , being an example to all his team but unfortunately got shot in the head and on his right chest. I would like this sergeant to be rewarded accordingly."

Sergeant Mehmet Bigalı was therefore awarded with 'Silver Combat Prerogative Medal' on 12 April 1915.

Sergeant Mehmet's incomparable heroism was heard in İstanbul in a short while, articles describing him had appeared in newspapers. As a result of Sergeant Mehmet's heroism, Müdafa-i Milliye Magazine's lead writer, Mr. Mehmet Zeki, sent him 10 liras as a form of appreciation for his heroism and love for his country and its people. A golden watch was also put on Sergeant Mehmet's chest by the people of Kayseri.

Çanakkale Fortified Zone Chief of Staff Selahaddin Adil Bey is talking about 18 March Battle at the Strait

Lt. Col. Selahaddin Adil Bey, as Vice Chief of Staff of Çanakkale Fortified Zone, played an important role in the defence of the Dardanelles. Selahaddin Adil personally led the war in the absence of Cevat Pasha, who was Çanakkale Fortified Zone Chief of Staff on 18 March. In his memoirs, this is how he narrated the event of the 18 March 1915:

"In the early hours of 18 March 1915, the Allied navy gathered near Bozcaada was seen to be moving and later begun movements towards the Strait. Yenişehir lookout point notified this and it was understood that a war was about to start."

All troops were notified and they were ordered to get ready for the war as instructed earlier. Officers took their places in the lookout points. Carrying their weapons, each and every soldier stood waiting with great perseverance, belief and the honour of fighting for their country. From different directions, ezan was heard starting with "Allahu Akbar".

Earlier, Cevat Pasha headed towards Gelibolu to visit Esat Pasha of Yanya, 3rd Army Corps Commander, and to inspect the Bolayır fortifications. News was sent to him via telegraph stating that a war was about to begin. Ministry of War was also briefed on the situation. The ministry gave the instruction that the prime ministry was to be informed of the situation of enemy forces and the fortified zone every ten minutes, he got telegraphs stating the recent updates. Understandably, the government may have had to make important decisions like whether or not the troops should draw back to the Anatolia.

In Selahaddin Adil's own words:

"After I was informed that the enemies were heading towards the Strait I took my place in the lookout point, a few hundred

meters away from the fort, with my binoculars to watch out on the troops.

The enemy fleet "Triumph" made the first shot at 11.15.

On 18 March, from 11.15 in the morning till 14:00, the situation went on smoothly. I could personally feel this. Unfortunately, our commander had gone to Gelibolu and had not yet returned, which is why all of the responsibilities were on my shoulders and I was waiting for the return of Cevat Pasha.

At 14 o'clock, it was seen from our place that Bouvet was sinking. A smile of hope appeared on our faces and our hearts were relieved a little. . This coincided with the return of Cevat Pasha from Rumelia to the Anatolia. His return came with luck. When this occurred there was a long silence in the battle line. The French ships Suffren and Charlemagne that followed the Rumelia coast came to Bouvet's rescue. The French completely ended their fire whilst the English gave a break for about five minutes.

As for me, the load of being in charge had suddenly been lifted and I was proud to give good news to Cevat Pasha as he took back his position after a couple of minutes. I was pleased to see that the general situation was promising and was happy to be relieved of the heavy responsibility.

The most important part of the victory on 18 March is the dedication of the soldiers and officers. German and Turkish soldiers at Anatolian Hamidiye, men at the Rumelian Hamidiye, Mecidiye and Namazgah forts and the central group, all stayed in their positions and discharged their duties. Even some old soldiers who could not be of much help carried water to soldiers and gave them moral supports through prayers. Mecidiye fort changed soldiers under fire three times.

It is possible to reach success if there is strong faith, perseverance and judicious use of limited resources. The Battle of 18 March is a good example which shows that those who keep their morale and faith high will win."

Corporal Seyit and the 215kg Bullet

As far as Çanakkale is concerned, one of the most well-known heroes is Corporal Seyit. Almost everyone knows how he carried a 215 kg bullet on his back when the crane of the cannon got broken when he was working in the Rumelian Mecidiye fort during the Battle of 18 March. There is a monument of him describing this event in Kilitbahir near the Mecidiye Fort today.

The extraordinary story of an artillery soldier, Corporal Seyit, who was working in the Mecidiye fort and defending the Dardanelles during the battle on 18 March 1915 is a great example of the will and courage the Turkish soldiers demonstrated in the war.

Corporal Seyit had described this unbelievable story in 1936 to a journalist with a very modest wording:

"I was able to find Seyit from Edremit, born in 1889, and make him speak of the Battle of 18 March with great difficulty.

'I didn't do anything?' he said. 'Only if you should have seen it. Yet he could not resist my insistence, so he began to tell:

In the last days of February, the enemy ships forced their way into the Strait but could not succeed. On 18 March, I was managing the third long cannon in Kilitbahir Mecidiye fort. It was early dawn when the watchmen reported that the enemy ships were increasing at the entrance of the Strait. We were all following the orders that had been given. At eight o'clock, we heard a rumble in the Strait but this one was nothing like the ones before. This time we were under heavy fire and up in response. Our redoubt nearly got hit. At first, few cannon balls flew past us and landed in the water. We were left in the smoke and the dust for some time. Then I noticed that a 38 cm artillery gun had damaged our ball crane heavily and overturned the reserve gun lane. The main road was rugged but covered with sand.

Thankfully, our cannon was not damaged. We cleared the way immediately and saved our sergeant there. There was no hope of him, he was just breathing and that was it, we sent him back immediately. After things got a bit settled, I looked around and then saw our commander staring at the broken crane and the enemy ships slowly crossing the Strait. I looked at the same way and saw the enemy ships entering the Strait. I rushed to the cart with cannon balls and looked at my desperate friends. I tried lifting the ball once but it slipped because it was oily. I cleaned my hands with some dirt, put my knee on the floor and lifted the ball. I found myself in the cannon; I don't remember how I climbed the stairs to the cannon. I jumped back down and kept on carrying the balls to the cannon. After a short silence, our cannon was up and running again. After a little while, we shot the fourth ball, the surveillance post reported that we have two hits on the enemy ships. After hearing the news, I was feeling like the cannon balls were sacks of hay.

Our commander approached me and said:

- That's it, you're tired Seyit. Come see the enemy on the run, he called me into the surveillance position.

- I will join you after I finish carrying these last ones, I replied.

I carried the last ball up and then approached my commander. It seemed like the sea was on fire. Few ships scattered around the sea were sinking slowly in red fire. Meanwhile another one also flamed on. Even without turning back, rear ships left the Strait. That was all I could see. God knows what was going on the other side of the Strait. We learnt that three of the enemy ships had sunk and the enemy had fired 723 guns that day only. We were damaged slightly. We caught so many fish later that night...

With a Turkish humbleness he said:

-That's it. Are you happy now? It is not a big deal to write about.

-Seyit, did they give you a medal?

-They called me one day and said that the German general sent me a medal.

-Did they take a photo of you that day?

-Are you kidding me, do you think that a photographer could be allowed in with us? A week later, some generals came to our redoubt with a photographer. He took it.

-Did they give you a copy?

-After a week the picture was taken, a commander called me. He said: "Look, Seyit, this is yours."

I couldn't believe my eyes, it was a small book with my picture on the cover. I didn't think that I was worthy of being on the cover. I was relieved when I saw many other soldiers inside the book but I couldn't accept it. That book was later lost.

LAND WARS

Having been decisively defeated at the Dardanelles on 18 March 1915, the Allies conceived that they could not pass through the Strait with a naval power only. Thinking that only through an amphibious warfare, where combined operations including air and land forces were carried out, would be effective, preparations were duly made for a new campaign.

The Allies' new plan was based on incapacitating the forts by deploying ground forces to the south of the Gallipoli Peninsula that would invade the commanding zones behind the forts defending the Strait and finally creating a passageway for the navy by collecting the floating mines along the way.

Turkish army command, emerged victorious on 18 March, continued preparations against a new offensive. Turkish artillery defending the Dardanelles, despite depressing moments of that day, managed to recover with the help of morale-boosting victory so that it could withstand a new campaign. Weapons and ammunition stocks were far enough for a two-day battle of similar magnitude. Moreover, the lines of mines blocking up the Strait remained untouched. Only one line of mines had been swept by the enemy and the remaining eight lines consisted of 350 mines.

The one-month truce that took effect from 22 March through 25 April as the Allied Powers set to work on gathering of the ground forces allowed the Turkish army to restock and complete preparations. Turkish forces used this unique opportunity to properly strengthen defence measures at Çanakkale Fortified Zone and Gallipoli Peninsula.

Preparations of Turkish Armed Forces and Formation of the 5th Army

18 March Victory created a great joy in İstanbul as well as throughout the country but the Turkish High-Command was expecting a renewed offensive from the British and French forces to atone for the crushing defeat and loss of prestige in the naval wars. However the expected naval attack did not take place. Upon receiving information of preparations for a combined Allied ground offensive, Turkish army decided to reinforce ground troops in the region. The most significant decision about the coming war was formation of a new field army to be tasked with the defence of the region. The Fifth Army was formed on 25 March and German General Liman von Sander, one day later, took command of the army and set up his headquarters in Gallipoli.

The Fifth Army was responsible for defending the coastal zone extending from Enez in the Gulf of Saros to Akçay in the south of Çanakkale.

Positions and responsibilities of the army units operating under the command of the Fifth Army were as follows:

Independent Cavalry Brigade: Surveillance in the coastal area from Enez to Bolayır

5th Division: Eksamil-Kavak region

3rd Army Corps: Positions of divisions under the 3rd corps in Gallipoli, were as follows:

7th Division: Defence duty in Bolayır and its environs

19th Division: Around the village of Bigalı

9th Division: Defence duty across the southern coastal zone of Gallipoli Peninsula down from Ağıldere

15th Army Corps: Positions of divisions under the 15th Army Corps in Anatolian side were as follows:

3rd Division: Kumkale-Yeniköy region

11th Division: Geyikli and its environs

Total strength of the Fifth Army was estimated to be around 80,000 men, including those serving in the six widely dispersed divisions and two army corps. With the army of 12,000 troops serving in Cevat Pasha's Fortified Zone Command added, effective strength of the Fifth Army amounted to 92,000 soldiers.

Liman Pasha devised a new plan which focused on positioning under-strength infantry along the coastal sector while disposing infantry divisions at full strength in certain sectors where they could be moved to eventual enemy landing zones as he could not predict the exact landing zones along the 150 km-coastline under his responsibility.

He identified two possible enemy landing zones. First one was Beşige Bay, where enemy troops could advance into inland forts on the Anatolian side, just opposite of Bozcaada.

Alternative landing spot, according to Liman Pasha, was Bolayır located on the shoreline that linked Gallipoli Peninsula with the Thrace. He feared that a possible enemy landing here, if successful, would cut off the Fifth Army's sea and land connection with İstanbul.

Although Liman Pasha's prediction of possible enemy landing zones was noteworthy, the two spots he identified were indeed outside the overall strategies and objectives of the Allied forces. The objective of troop landing was to ensure a safe passage in the Strait for the navy, which necessitated the seizure of forts located on both shores of the Dardanelles and sweeping mines laid in the sea. Landing units had to reach the forts using the shortest route. Landing on Bolayır would draw the Allied army away from the main target. Similarly, landing troops on the Anatolian side would not fit for purpose. The Allied forces had to seize Kilitbahir plateau which dominates the Strait as well as the forts on the Anatolian side in order to take control of the Dardanelles.

Liman Pasha's plan contradicted the views of Turkish commanders, namely the 3rd Corps Commander Esat Pasha and 9th Division Commander Captain Halil Sami Bey, who had been in the region before himself. They preferred placing strong forces on possible landing zones (*Kabatepe* and *Seddülbahir*) to prevent enemy landing and retaining some forces in reserve to counterattack against the enemy's offensive units before landing. Liman Pasha, conversely, favoured the idea of defending the shores with under-strength units and launching an offensive against the enemy forces that came ashore with troops to be deployed to the landing site.

Preparations of the Allied Powers for Landing

The unexpected defeat on 18 March of the Allied forces that set out to force the Dardanelles and seize İstanbul in a month did not discourage them from seeking alternatives. They sought ways at any cost to restore prestige and fulfil their politically and militarily primary objective of capturing İstanbul.

As it appeared that the Dardanelles would not be forced with a naval power alone, the Allied army gathered in the Harbour of Moudros, located on the Island of Lemnos, and in Egypt for a ground offensive on Gallipoli. However, landing would begin in April at the earliest as gathering and preparing the ground forces for landing was a time-drain.

The following units that had been gathering in Egypt until April, were placed under the command of British General Ian Hamilton, who was in charge of the Allied Mediterranean Expeditionary Force:

British Forces: 29th Division and Naval Division; 28,000 troops

Australian and New Zealand Army Corps: An Australian Division, An Australian-New Zealand Combined Division; 30,000 troops

French Forces: A Colonial Division; 17,000 troops

An army of 75,000 troops had gathered for landing.

As the Allied central command was working on the landing plan, it placed the greatest emphasis on the landing sites, which were supposed to have direct access to Kilitbahir Plateau, main target of the Allied ground forces. For that reason, the idea of landing troops on the Anatolian side or somewhere near Bolayır was omitted. The ultimate decision for landing was pointed at *Seddülbahir* and *Kabatepe* regions where ground forces could advance up to Kilitbahir.

The final landing plan was as follows:

Primary Landing Zone: The British 29th Division were to be landed on five different sites in *Seddülbahir*, located in the southernmost corner of the Gallipoli Peninsula. The first objective of the landing was Alçıtepe while the ultimate target was to capture Kilitbahir Plateau that dominates the forts of the Strait.

Secondary Landing Zone: Australian-New Zealand Army Corps (ANZAC) would launch a sudden attack before sunrise to the northern coast of *Kabatepe*. The troops would seize *Conkbayırı* (Chunuk Bair)-*Kocaçimen* area on the first day of landing before capturing Maltepe, situated in a commanding position over the Strait. The aim was to cut off land and sea connection of Turkish reinforcements to be deployed to the south of the Peninsula. Lastly, they would join the units who were coming from *Seddülbahir* and tasked with invading *Kilitbahir* Plateau.

Diversion Landing: A French regiment would be landed on *Kumkale* region of the Anatolian side to prevent Turkish artillery strikes on the main landing site. Moreover, two Turkish divisions in Anatolia would be denied landing on the Gallipoli Peninsula.

Cheat Landing: The Allied battleships arriving at Gulf of Saros would give a false impression of landing troops on the shores of *Bolayır*, hence delaying the deployment of two Turkish divisions in the region to the main landing site in the south. In the same vein, the Allied navy would carry out cheat landing operation on the Beşige Bay of the Anatolian side to divert the Turkish divisions here.

The Allied army arriving at Moudros Harbour on 20 April started waiting for favourable weather conditions for landing. The aim was to begin landing on 23 April but it had to be delayed two days due to bad weather.

LAND WARS START

25 APRIL 1915 LANDING OPERATION

As the Allied Powers were finalizing the plan on forcing the Strait with support from the ground forces to be landed on Gallipoli, the Ottoman Army was taking defensive measures against the expected landing operation.

Divisions under the newly formed Fifth Army were spread on the area from Saros to *Beşige* Bay on the Anatolian side. 9th Division took over the responsibility of defence of 35 km coastline between *Seddülbahir* (Helles) and *Arıburnu* (Anzac Cove) where the Allied troops waded ashore. 9th Division Command had left the defence of coastal zone around *Seddülbahir* to the 26th Regiment and *Kabatape-Arıburnu* region to the 27th Regiment. 25th Regiment of the 9th Division was kept in reserve. 31st Regiment of 3rd Division was deployed to *Kumkale* region in the Anatolian side.

Fifth Army Commander Liman Pasha expected the enemy landing at *Bolayır* and *Beşige*, although he considered *Seddülbahir* and *Arıburnu* as suitable sites for landing as well. Therefore he deployed two divisions out of six under his command to *Bolayır* and two others to *Beşige* regions. A division was to defend the main landing zone while another would be kept in reserve. Units under the Fifth Army were informed right on 25 April of the state of military vigilance against the enemy's approaching landing operation. What was unknown to the Turkish army, however, was the site or sites of enemy landing.

By the morning of 24 April, 200 large and small battleships transporting nearly fifty thousand troops involved in one of the greatest amphibious offensive that the world had ever seen set off for the Gallipoli Peninsula from the Harbour of Moudros. Fully assured of success, the Allied soldiers were bursting in advance with pride to be storming into İstanbul. Slogans like 'Turkish Delight' or 'To İstanbul and Harem' written on boards of some vessels were signs of the Allied soldiers' self-confidence.

Nonetheless, the soldiers, dreaming of İstanbul, were unaware that the great amphibious operation would result in unforeseen consequences for the Allied Powers and that it would change the length and course of WWI.

By the early morning of 25 April, reports informing the start of enemy landings on various places from *Bolayır* to *Seddülhabir* were coming to the Headquarters of the Fifth Army.

Liman Pasha hurried down to Bolayır, as he obsessively thought from the start that the enemy landing would start here. However, the reports revealed that the landings were being made on sites Liman Pasha had not expected. To misdirect the Pasha, some cheat landings planned on *Bolayır* and *Beşige*, with which Liman Pasha was more concerned, proved to be successful. The plan kept the Pasha occupied in *Bolayır* until the evening and constrained him from commanding the deadly battle in Arıburnu and *Seddülbahir* where the main landings were made. After that evening, the 5th and 7th Divisions at *Bolayır* were deployed as reinforcements to these landing sites.

The first enemy unit landed at Arıburnu before sunrise on 25 April. After the dawn, more troops under naval gunfire support landed at *Seddülbahir* and *Kumkale* on the Anatolian side.

Landings at Arıburnu (Anzac Cove)

Anzac Corps under the command of General Birdwood landed at the coast of *Arıburnu*. The acronym ANZAC stands for Australian and New Zealand Army Corps. The name came to be used for the divisions involved after the Battle of Çanakkale.

Main landing spot was the coast between *Kabatepe* and *Arıburnu*. The objective of landing was first to seize the hillside from *Kabatepe* to *Conkbayırı-Kocaçimen* and then to invade *Maltepe*, another hill with a commanding view over the Strait. So Turkish forces situated in the south of the Peninsula would lose land and sea connection in the back. In the final stage, the Allied troops advancing through *Seddülbahir* would capture *Kilitbahir* Plateau and join the British army forces.

At 03.00 am on 25 April, vessels that carried the first group of ANZAC troops dropped anchor five miles west to *Kabatepe*. Hundreds of soldiers crept to shore in twelve large whaleboats. The boats concentrated one km north of the intended landing zone. This spot, to be called ANZAC Cove from then on, lay between *Büyük* and *Küçük Arıburnu*. In fact, one km deviation from the landing point had been an advantage for the ANZAC troops because the rugged terrain in this region gave them the opportunity to take shelter from the Turkish fires and to create a front within a narrow field.

ANZAC Cove where the landing was made had been held by the 27th Regiment under the 9th Division. The Regiment Commander Colonel Şefik Bey assigned the 2nd Battalion to coastal defence and had set up headquarters with other two battalions at Zeytinlik near *Eceabat*, 8 km to *Kabatepe*.

The 2nd Battalion of the 27th Regiment set up headquarters at *Kabatepe* and the 4th Squadron was deployed to *Arıburnu* under the command of Captain Faik Bey. Captain Faik stationed himself around *Boyun* (Neck) behind ANZAC coast with a squadron and set out another squadron under the command of sub-lieutenant İbradılı Hayrettin to *Balıkçı Damları* (Fisherman's Hut) zone, a few hundred meters north of *Arıburnu*. The last squadron under the command of sub-lieutenant Muharrem was disposed to a hill, to be called *Haintepe* (Plugge's Plateau) during the war, located behind the beach.

As the boats carrying the first ANZAC corps drew up the coast at 4.30 am in the morning of 25 April, they were taken under fire by the Turkish squadron (80 troops) located at *Haintepe*. The number of troops initially landed ashore was 1,500. After half an hour, battleships covering the landing started a massive fire on the Turkish troops.

Although Captain Faik tried to drive back the enemy to the sea deploying his squadron to the beach, Australian forces, outnumbering Turkish soldiers by one to ten, succeeded in advancing inwards in a very short time, clinging to *Arıburnu* slopes.

By 05.00 am, landing was underway in the north of Arıburnu near *Balıkçı Damları* where a squadron of the 4th Division engaged in the clashes. The battle here had spread over a 2 km coastal zone across north and south of *Arıburnu*.

By 06.00 am, the number of Australian troops ashore had amounted to four thousands. Turkish troops at *Haintepe* had valiantly fought to prevent the enemy's advance and only three of the 80 soldiers from the squadron located here had survived.

By 07.00 am, most of the 4th Division's members had been martyred while the wounded and other survivors, among who was the Division's Commander Captain Faik, had withdrawn. The enemy had captured the line between *Kanlısırt* (400 Plateau) and *Yükseksırt* (Russell's Top). There remained no barrier between the Australian forces and their first target, *Conkbayırı-Kocaçimen* line.

From the sounds of artillery and gun fire at 27th Regiment Headquarters in *Eceabat*, it was apparent that the enemy troops went ashore at *Arıburnu*. Colonel Şefik Bey contacted the battalion commander at *Kabatepe* and had two battalions ready for counterattack. Yet, the commander of the 9th Division had not warranted immediate action, supposing that what was happening at *Arıburnu* could be a fake landing. Eventually, two battalions of the 27th Regiment were dispatched at 05.50 am to take part in the counterattack after Şefik Bey's repeated insistence.

Following a two-hour march, Şefik Bey deployed the two battalions for battle on the ridge at *Topçular Sırtı* –later to be called *Kemalyeri*. At 08.00 am, the 1st battalion under the command of Lieutenant İbrahim launched the counterattack at *Kanlısırt* and the 3rd battalion commanded by Major Halis started to push the enemy back at *Merkeztepe-Edirne Sırtı*. With the successful counterattack of the two battalions, the ANZACS were driven as far back as *Kanlısırt-Edirne Sırtı*. When the ANZAC troops, with reinforcements rushed to the area, began to fire back, the fighting turned to a hand to hand combat.

While the 27th Regiment of 2000 troops were suffering heavy losses, ANZAC forces were constantly being supported with reinforcementswhich raised the number of troops to 10,000 in a short time. This disproportionate balance of power had slowed and eventually stopped the 27th Regiment. When the situation began to take its toll, the 57th Regiment proceeding from *Conkbayırı* came to the rescue and relieved the 27th Regiment which was fighting in a cramped and dangerous position.

A reserve division of the 5th army, the 19th Division, commanded by Lt.Col. Mustafa Kemal, had set up headquarters in *Bigalı* village. The Division was composed of the 57th, 72nd and 77th Regiments, the last two of which arrived from Aleppo and consisted of troops from diverse ethnic backgrounds.

As soon as the news of enemy landing at *Arıburnu* arrived, Mustafa Kemal Bey ordered the 19th Division to maintain maximum vigilance. He responded to the call for reinforcement from Halil Sami Bey, commander of the 9th Division, who had requested at 06.30 am another battalion to help the troops fighting against the enemy at *Arıburnu*. Mustafa Kemal, realizing the gravity of situation based on intelligence reports suggesting that the enemy was advancing towards *Conkbayırı-Kocaçimen* line, proceeded to *Arıburnu* with the 57th Regiment under his own command. He also ordered the 72nd and 77th Regiments to move forward and draw near the fighting line.

At 10.30 am, front-line troops of the 57th Regiment arriving in the south of *Conkbayırı* began an immediate offensive and drove the ANZAC forces from *Düztepe* back to *Kılıçbayırı*. Towards noon, the enemy advance was halted by the 57th Regiment who fought on the right wing of the 27th Regiment and counter offensive began to repel the enemy. The 27th Regiment, having relieved with the arrival of the 57th Regiment, concentrated on *Kanlısırt* and cleaned up the area.

In the evening of 25 April, ANZAC forces had been shaken off by Turkish offensive and were trying to hold on the slopes of *Arıburnu* overlooking the sea. Some brigades were forced to withdraw back to the beach and requested from the Allied command for reshipping of troops. Hamilton, evaluating the request, ordered the commander of the ANZAC forces, General Birdwood, to defend and hold their ground, taking the difficulties of reshipping 15,000 troops ashore into consideration.

On the same night, Turkish side, unaware of the developments in the ANZAC area, were planning a new offensive. The 77th Regiment had followed the 27th Regiment on the battleship as reinforcement at *Kanlısırt*. However, soldiers of the 77th Regiment, unable to advance in the dark, soon dissolved. As a consequence, the troops abandoned their positions gained after great sacrifices and the 27th Regiment had to retreat back to the east of *Karayörük* Stream.

Turkish forces, amounted to 6,500 troops, bravely managed to repulse the enemy on the night of 25/26 April in the fighting at *Arıburnu* but suffered about 2,500 casualties. The number of casualties on the ANZAC side ran into 2,000. Attacks launched by the 27th and 57the Regiments shook the ANZACS and drove them back to the beach. But heavy losses and failure of the 77th Regiment prevented the Turkish side to give a conclusive blow to the enemy forces.

Landings at Seddülbahir (Helles)

On 25 April, the British troops landed at five different points near *Seddülbahir* Village in the southern part of the Peninsula. The landing points from east to west were *Morto* Bay (S Beach), *Ertuğrul* Bay (V Beach), *Tekke* Bay (W Beach), *İkiz* Bay (X Beach), and *Pınariçi* Bay (Y Beach).

The landings at the first four points followed a bombardment that began at 04.30 am on 25 April and lasted for one and a half hours. Landing at *Pınariçi* Bay (Y Beach) coincided with the start of naval gunfire on other landing zones.

Seddülbahir was being defended by the 3rd Battalion of the 26th Regiment under the 9th Division. Commander of the Battalion Major Mahmut Sabri Bey had deployed one squadron to *Ertuğrul* Bay and another one to *Tekke* Bay. Two reserve battalions were located at the headquarters set up in *Harap Kale* to the north of *Seddülbahir* Village.

As soon as naval gunfire ended at 06.00 am, the British troops began landing at *Tekke* Bay under the cover of machine guns on the ships. 12th Squadron of the 3rd Battalion, which was tasked with guarding *Tekke* Bay, stayed quiet under intense bombardment until the landing crafts carrying the British soldiers reached the shore and then began firing, which inflicted heavy losses on the British side. Survivors sheltered at two ends of the bay and recovered in a short time. Launching an offensive at 07.00 am, the British troops, greatly outnumbering Turkish forces, seized *Tekke* Bay after one hour fighting in spite of tremendous efforts of around 250Turkish troops defending the coast and proceeded to *Karacaoğlan Tepesi* and *Aytepe* behind the bay. The 12th Squadron's call for reinforcements remained unanswered as Mahmut Bey had no reserve forces.

British forces captured *Karacaoğlan Tepesi* at 11.00 am. A British battalion (1000 soldiers) landed at *İkiz* Bay (X Beach) located 1,5 kilometres north of *Tekke* Bay and took control of the area from a Turkish detachment of 9 men. Although Turkish troops deployed to *İkiz* Bay at 07.00 blocked *Seddülbahir* direction against the enemy, British forces advancing southward along the coast managed to link up with the brigade that landed at *Tekke* Bay and captured *Karacaoğlan Tepesi*.

Commander of the 26th Regiment Lt. Col. Kadri Bey sent the 7th Squadron as reinforcement to the battalion at *Seddülbahir*. But the squadron confronted and began fighting with the British troops who were dangerously advancing after landing at *İkiz* Bay.

As a state of danger emerged around *Tekke* Bay, Mahmut Sabri Bey dispatched the 9th (Reserve) Squadron, which managed to stop the British advance towards *Ertuğrul* Bay.

Landing at *Ertugrul* Bay (V Beach) located just below *Seddülbahir* Village began at 06.00 following the naval bombardment.

According to a two-stage plan, a brigade was to land at the bay, which the British chose as their main landing zone. A battalion would deploy along *Ertuğrul* Bay while two battalions on a vessel called River Clyde would disembark immediately after the vessel run ashore, which was inspired by the legend of Trojan horse. The British expected to disrupt Turkish defensive line of 240 troops and take control of *Seddülbahir* in a few hours.

As the British landing unit neared the shore, naval forces intensified bombardment on Turkish trenches. Entrapped in trenches, Turkish troops were trying to ward off bombardment while waiting for the right moment to attack as well. Soon the moment came and a heavy firing began on boats that came aboard, which disturbed the landing units. Officers and privates on the first boats had been either killed or wounded. Those who came from behind had been able to save their lives taking shelter behind a sand dune in the shoreline.

As for the River Clyde, it was stranded with two battalions (2,000 men) on board off a stony place down the *Seddülbahir* Castle. British soldiers, who got into the sea from the vessel's doors opened on both sides, with the help of ramps and stairs, were shot dead or wounded by Turkish troops' effective, accurate and rapid fire. Unloading troops from the vessel continued until 09.30 but the result was the same: All the troops leaving the vessel were shot. Thereupon, the dispatch of troops from the River Clyde stopped. Troops on board were able to get moving only after the dark.

The failure of landing on *Ertuğrul* Bay had disrupted the British plans at the outset. The British objective for the first day of landing was to capture *Alçıtepe*, located about 7 km inland.

Devoted efforts of several Turkish squadrons to keep the British away from *Seddülbahir* allowed the emplacement of Turkish defence on this front for the battle that would last 8,5 months. Notably, on the first day of landing, after all the officers in the 10th Squadron weremartyred, Sergeant Yahya of *Ezine* took command and with his fellows managed to keep numerically far superior enemy force entangled in the shore.

Morto Bay was another landing spot at *Seddülbahir* sector. A Turkish brigade of 80 troops was defending the cove against a British force of three squadrons who landed at 07.30. Once ashore, the British troops, due to their preponderance, repulsed the Turkish force and captured *Eskihisarlık Tepe* where today Monument of Martyrs stands.

A reinforcement unit from the 25th Regiment of the 9th Division tried to take the hill back but failed due to heavy fire from the British machine gun position.

The easiest landing of the British troops in the south of the Peninsula was made on *Pınariçi* Bay, which houses Monument of Nuri Yamut today, to the west of *Kirte* Village (today known as *Alçıtepe* Village). A British force of 2,200 troops raided the cove without a naval bombardment at 06.00 am. They took the hill on the steep coast without firing a single shot as there was not any Turkish defence force. Moving forward unopposed and taking *Alçıtepe* was a simple matter for the British force. But they were ordered to defend the landing position and await a joint attack to be launched from *Seddülbahir*. However, they had to wait in vain as Turkish forces obstructed landings at *Ertuğrul* and *Tekke* Coves.

26th Regiment despatched 200 troops to *Pınariçi* Bay when news of enemy landing arrived. This weak unit engaged the outnumbering British soldiers and they had to be supported by the 3rd Squadron of the 25th Regiment.

Turkish forces launched a counteroffensive and drove the British into a corner. At night, the British forces were truly troubled by persistent attacks of the Turkish side which were reinforced by two divisions. Although Turkish offensive was weakened by naval gunfire in the morning, the British understood that they would not be able to hold on the battlefield and retreated back to the ships at 11.00 on 26 April. The British unit landed at *Pınariçi* was in a position to fold the Turkish defence in *Seddülbahir*. The British consider the failure and retreat of the unit here 'a golden opportunity missed'.

Upon these developments, clashes at *Seddülbahir* intensified around *Ertuğrul* and *Aytepe* zone, where the British forces captured at dark, near *Tekke* Bay. Mahmut Sabri Bey tried to hold *Gözcübaba* Hill by hampering the British. At midnight, two reserve squadrons, which apparently were not enough, from the 25th Regiment joined Mahmut Sabri Bey's battalion, who had been fighting to stop the enemy since that morning. However, Turkish offensive attempt to take *Aytepe* back was hampered by the British machine guns.

By nightfall, the British forces made a move to capture *Ertuğrul* Bay. Troops on River Clyde came ashore, taking advantage of the nightfall and advanced forward to *Seddülbahir* Village and Castle, which witnessed bloody street battles throughout the night. Despite their extraordinary resistance, Turkish side suffered heavy casualties, leaving many officers of the battalions wounded or martyred.

In the morning of 26 April, naval gunfire and ground troop attacks left the Turkish forces defending *Seddülbahir* in the lurch. Nevertheless, Mahmud Sabri Bey was resolved to continue the defense. His request of reinforcement from the 26th Regiment remained unanswered. Lt. Col. Kadri Bey, commander of the 26th Regiment gave Mahmut Sabri the order to retreat at 10.00 in the morning. Mahmut Sabri issued the retreat command at 13.30 in the face of impossibility of holding *Seddülbahir*.

Remnants of the 3rd battalion that were pulled back arrived at *Alçıtepe*, located 3 km inland. The battalion had lost nearly half of its existing troops. Nevertheless, they had managed to hold up more than ten thousand British soldiers for about 32 hours and had devotedly fulfilled their national duty.

Landing at Kumkale

The Allied Army Command planned some cheat and diversion landings, among which the one at *Kumkale*, located opposite *Seddülbahir* on the Anatolian side, was really conducted. The landing at *Kumkale* aimed to prevent deployment of two Turkish divisions on the main landing site, *Seddülbahir*.

In the morning of 25 April, at 05.00, artillery bombardment began and French troops were confronted by a Turkish squadron of 240 men charged with the defence of *Kumkale*. Number of

French troops run ashore throughout the day reached three thousands while the Turkish troops got the support of two reinforcement units of 160 soldiers. French forces invaded the castle and the village.

Adjoining the Turkish forces were two battalions from the 39th Regiment. They launched repeated attacks all night long but failed to force the French back to sea. The following day, Turkish troops outnumbered the French side but they could not make it due to poor organization.

The French, however, fulfilled their mission to hold up Turkish divisions on the Anatolian side and despatch of Turkish forces to the main landing zone. At night, French troops embarked the ships and evacuated *Kumkale*.

Turkish casualties (martyrs, wounded, captives) at Kumkale were 1735 while the French lost 778 soldiers.

Diversion and Cheat Landings

The Allied Army Command's plan had some parts intended to deceive Turkish forces: Allied vessels were to put in *Bolayır* in the Gulf of Saros and *Beşigeler* region on the Anatolian side. They would make a show of landing troops and hold up Turkish forces there.

In the morning of 25 April, British vessels appeared off *Bolayır* and French vessels near *Beşige* Cove when the landing began at *Arıburnu* and *Seddülbahir*.

In fact, Liman von Sanders, who commanded the Turkish army, was concerned about these two regions. The Allies, as if they knew his concern, conducted diversions and attained their aim. Von Sanders became convinced of the main landing spots after the enemy forces came ashore and moved forward at *Arıburnu* and *Seddülbahir*. He then sent, in groups, the four divisions deployed at *Bolayır* and *Beşige* to the main battlefield as of 26 April.

Overview of Landings on 25 April

Despite being fewer in number and deprived of machine gun support, Turkish forces defending the coastal zone showed great resistance during the landings on 25 April which signalled the start of the Land Battles of Çanakkale. They bravely and devotedly withstood the enemy landings supported by naval bombardment.

Turkish squadron which fought against enemy troops landed at *Arıburnu* fulfilled their defence duty and sacrificed themselves. During the battles, two commanders foiled the enemy plan that aimed at capturing *Arıburnu* and *Conkbayırı-Kocaçimen* hills. Lt. Col. Şefik Bey, commander of the 27th Regiment, caught the enemy off guard with the counteroffensive he carried out with two battalions. Commander of the 19th Division, Mustafa Kemal, realizing gravity of the situation, joined the battle along with the 57th Regiment.

Tasked with defending the coast in *Seddülbahir* sector, Major Mahmut Sabri Bey, commander of the 3rd Battalion of the 26th Regiment, and his men had strived to hold their ground, taking cover in trenches, in spite of massive naval bombardment with some five thousands rounds of shell dropped. They had defended the region against a far superior enemy force for about 32 hours and prevented the enemy from capturing *Alçıtepe*, enemy's objective for the first day landing.

It appeared on 25 April that the defence plan prepared by Liman von Sanders, commander of the Fifth Army, was not working at all. According to his plan, the coastal zone would be defended with weak armed forces and reinforcements would be sent immediately to the enemy's landing sites. But he did not think that he could catch the enemy in their weakest moment while at the sea before landing. Failure of the weak forces to prevent the enemy's getting ashore enabled the back-up forces of the enemy to move inland. Soon the Turkish side understood that the enemy, supported by naval gunfire, could not be easily driven back to sea. Sanders was unable to take immediate action against enemy landings at *Arıburnu* and *Seddülbahir*. Moreover, main landing sites were not timely confirmed. The 4th Division was delayed around *Bolayır* and *Beşige* due to diversions. The 9th and 19th Divisions had to deal with all the burden of 25 April landings.

Turkish troops, devotedly resisting against *Arıburnu* and *Seddülbahir* landings, prevented the Allied forces from reaching their goal despite all the problems such as failure of the army command in management, superiority of the enemy forces in terms of number of troops and ammunitions, and lack of weapons.

Lieutenant Faik Efendi and the 'Fedai' Squadron

On 25 April, before the break of dawn, boats from British ships were being loaded with soldiers who would become the first ANZAC soldiers to land on the shore. The landing was to be made on the beach between Kabatepe and Arıburnu. However, due to the currents of the water and the dark, the ANZAC soldiers landed at the shore of Arıburnu, which was 1.5 km north of their original destination.

The coastline of Arıburnu was steep and uneven; therefore it was under the surveillance of only one squadron of the Turkish army.

While most of the 2nd Battalion of the 27th Regiment was held around Kabatepe, the 4th Squadron was sent to the ridges of Arıburnu. Only fate could have pity these 200-250 soldiers against the thousands of ANZAC troops. They had no chance of defending against this landing. The defenders concluded that their only choice was to slow down the enemy forces to gain time for the reinforcement units of the Turkish army.

On the morning of 25 April, everyone in the Squadron knew and accepted that their decision would result in martyrdom. Everyone, from the commander to the private, fulfilled the duty that was expected of them. The commander of the Squadron, Lieutenant Faik Efendi, along with his platoon commanders, sergeants and privates decided that they would only start retreating once they were wounded. Those who were not wounded deployed a controlled retreat until they depleted their entire armoury, thus significantly slowing down enemy forces. During the four hours untill the arrival of the rest of the 27th Regiment, these soldiers went beyond their call of duty.

Faik Efendi reported the enemy landing in the first hours of 25 April and their defence as such:

"That night, around 2.00, the moonlight was still there in the sky. The two reserve lookouts (Bigalı İdris and Gelibolulu Cemil) with me, reported numerous enemy ships. I stood up and looked through my binoculars. Ahead of me, I spotted ships of various sizes (not that I could differentiate). We couldn't tell if they were in motion or not. I immediately contacted battalion commander, İsmet Bey, waiting in Kabatepe by telephone and then reported our sightings. He told me that I shouldn't be worried, that if a landing was to happen, it would happen at Kabatepe. He then told me to keep watch on these ships. I went back, this time I noticed that there were more ships and that they were definitely moving towards us. As protocol demands, I contacted the division commander. The time was around 02.30 am."

Faik Efendi left to report his sightings to the division commander. Soon after that, the moon had set and the area was too dark to follow the movement of the ships. As a precaution, he appointed the reserve team as gunners. Not long after, gunshots coming from the coast were heard. They therefore became vigilant:

"After a while we heard a loud rattling noise coming from the north of Arıburnu. What I originally thought as torpedoes was actually the firing of machine guns coming from small ships. Some of the bullets firing from those guns passed over our heads. I immediately commanded our gunners to move up to the trenches in Yükseksırt. I deployed two squads under Sergeant Ahmet to the slopes of Merkez Tepe overlooking the seaside. At the same time I sent a report to the Battalion Commander that the enemy was landing at Arıburnu and that I would move with the reserve team to that direction. So we immediately moved.

As we were moving through the road we were constantly under fire by the small ships. We arrived at Yükseksırt. We held the trenches at Arıburnu. We returned fire 1300m away from the enemy.

Just ahead of us in the trenches at Haintepe, the 2nd platoon was already locked in combat from the start. Torpedoes were pulling the vessels loaded with enemy soldiers. They were going back firing as they were leaving the vessels off the shore. We managed to shoot some of the soldiers on the boats but the rest jumped into the waters, only 5-10 soldiers managed to escape our retaliation.

A while later, I heard from Korkudere that the enemy was trying to flank us from behind. Under the command of Sergeant Lapsekili Muharrem, I sent two bombardier privates. They started bombing one of the other trenches. We then came under fire from enemy soldiers about 100m to our left. That's when we continued our retaliation. In this conflict, the commander of the platoon, Sergeant Gelibolulu Süleyman was wounded along with some of our other privates. I sustained a wound in my groin and thus lost my ability to command the platoon. I left my command to Sergeant Lapsekili Muharrem and retreated. This day was just getting started.

Once I left, I learned that our platoon managed to hold out a little longer until Sergeant Muharrem was hit. At that time there were only a few privates left and once they realized that the enemy had cut them off from behind, they decided to join the 1st platoon at Balıkçı Damlar. As I was moving towards the village of Kocadere, I heard noises from Kanlısırt; 'Mehmet stop!'. They were ANZAC troops and we knew this meant that they had seized Kanlısırt."

On that fateful day, when the 4th Squadron heroically fought against the overwhelming ANZAC forces, they fulfilled their duties to their country. The commander of the Squadron, Faik Efendi, as well as the platoon commanders Sergeant Gelibolulu Süleyman, Third-Lieutenant Muharrem and Third-Lieutenant İbrahim Hayrettin sustained many injuries while the platoon commander Sergeant Lapsekili Muharrem as well as most of the 4th Squadron gave their lives protecting their country.

Arıburnu Heroes: Colonel Şefik Bey
and the 27th Regiment

On 25 April, before dawn at 04.30 in the morning, ANZAC troops began landing on the coastline between Kabatepe and Arıburnu. The region was being defended by the 2nd Battalion from the 27th Regiment. Two other battalions of the 27th Regiment had headquarters near Eceabat.

The 27th Regiment had an emergency drill under the command of Colonel Şefik that same night. The troops were awoken by the sounds of cannon balls and gunshots. Was this the beginning of the battle they had been waiting for?

Colonel Şefik immediately contacted the commander of the 2nd Battalion that was assigned to observe the coastline in Kabatepe. Yes, the enemy troops were running ashore. The soldiers were ordered to get into battle positions right away. The whole regiment was ready for the battle in no time.

While sounds of the battle were being heard from Arıburnu, Colonel Şefik Bey could not get orders from the 9th Division to take actions. The high commanders were being cautious in case the landing of troops was just a distracting scam. They were waiting for the situation to get clearer. But Colonel Şefik could not be patient. Because of the sounds of gunfire from Arıburnu and the weak defence that was fighting against the enemy, he wanted to help the soldiers as soon as possible.

He could not wait anymore so he contacted the chief of staff of the division:

- Mr. Hulusi! Our friends are under fire, are we going to wait any longer? We are waiting for your command.

Finally he got the order he was waiting for at 05.45 and he quickly moved to Arıburnu while leading two battalions. With them were the 27th Regiment's 1st and 3rd Battalions, which consisted of two thousand soldiers.

When he arrived at the second line of Arıburnu ridge –that was called Kemalyeri afterwards-, he took precautions against attacking the enemy. It was about 8 o'clock and up to this time the enemy had almost eight to ten thousand troops on land. The landed ANZAC troops were in scattered groups. Some of them were heading towards Kanlısırt and others were heading to Conkbayırı.

With the attack command of Şefik Bey, the heroic privates of the 27th Regiment went against the enemy without thinking about the fact that the enemy was four-five times stronger than themselves. In just a few hours, the ANZAC troops were repelled up to the slopes of the hills overlooking the sea. However, when the enemy got reinforcements, Turkish soldiers and the enemy troops started to fight hand to hand.

Şefik Bey explains this battle in his formal report:

"Our soldiers who were attacking to take back our artilleries located in Kanlısırt were trying to move forward bravely. They were under heavy gunfire. Our soldiers were getting closer to the artilleries. I was giving encouraging commands. The enemy was attacking with great force not only to lose artilleries but also not to leave Kanlısırt. As our soldiers moved forward, they were encountering many wounded and dead bodies of enemy troops. The battle was so heated that we could not even think about helping our wounded soldiers. This stage of the battle became so violent because we wanted to save our artilleries. Both sides were in a stubborn close combat.

Seeing the battle, it was impossible to express the desire to get involved in this heated clash. Lieutenant Emin, who is one of the commanders of squadron located on the west of Göktepe, got *a good response to his application to get involved in the fight; 'There was no any other reserve force therefore the commander wouldn't send us'.*

In spite of the negative response, Emin Efendi along with his team joined the clash near the artilleries, as he could not take it anymore while Turkish soldiers were fighting with the enemy in heated close combat, without the order from his commander who was watching the battle. Emin Efendi was martyred in the battle.

With no regard to the casualties they suffered, the enemy maintained the counterattack with bayonets. But our gallant soldiers managed to repulse the attacks forcing the enemy to withdraw and retook our artilleries.

We had retrieved the artilleries because of Allah's help. The victory that came after one hour battle near the artilleries honoured the 27th Regiment.

Şefik Bey and his brave men had successfully prevented the advance of the enemy who got ashore at Arıburnu on 25 April at the cost of their lives. They closed the doors of Çanakkale together with the lifesaver 57th Regiment defending the strategically important Conkbayırı-Kocaçimen region against the enemy. The 27th Regiment was granted gold and silver prerogative medals due to their outstanding service and gallantry they dedicated to their flag.

Commander of the Arıburnu Forces Lieutenant Colonel Mustafa Kemal and the 57th Regiment

On 19 February 1915, at the commencement of the Çanakkale Naval Wars, Mustafa Kemal and his divisional forces were on duty in apt protection of the coastal stretch and areas of Seddülbahir. 19th Division was attached to the 5th Army, which was under the command of Liman Von Sanders and was specifically established to defend the Gallipoli Peninsula against any possible attacks after the triumphant naval victory on 18 March. Mustafa Kemal and his unit was a reserve division of the 5th Army.

During the Çanakkale Land Wars which started on 23 April 1915, Mustafa Kemal's headquarters was in Bigalı Village near Eceabat. In the early hours of that fateful morning, the enemy troops began landing at Arıburnu. Due to the relative weakness of the stationed forces there, one infantry battalion force had been demanded from him by the commander of the 9th Division. However, instead of shipping a battalion, Mustafa Kemal did acknowledge the gravity of the situation and thereupon decided on his own initiative to completely dispatch the entire 57th Regiment to Arıburnu.

Mustafa Kemal, describing the incident, reported as follows: "At 9:30 am, the 9th Division's Commander Colonel Halil Sami demanded further reinforcements from me and I established immediate contacts with the 57th Regiment and artillery battery which were the nearest to the Bigalı village where my stationed headquarters was located. I instructed two unit commanders to complete their preparations and to take further action immediately.

After the 57th Division and artillery battery commanders gathered the troops in readiness to proceed, I did approach them and went to the gathering area with my aide and adjutant (Lieutenant). I turned to Kocaçimen hill myself by walking along the Bigalı stretch.

When we reached Conkbayırı, I saw a group of soldiers of the 27th Regiment which were on duty to safeguard the coast of Conkbayırı running from Hill 261 (the mount with 261m altitude) towards us. I then positioned myself in front of the soldiers and:

-Why are you running away? I said.

-Sir, the enemy! They responded.

-Where? I enquired.

-Here! They showed Hill 261.

Indeed the enemy's fighter lines approached Hill 261 and were walking and rapidly advancing forward easily.

At that time I shouted to the fleeing troops;

-You cannot escape from the enemy! I said.

-We've run out of ammunition! They said.

-If no ammunition, you have bayonets! I responded and instructed them all to fix the bayonets and lay down.

At the same time, I sent my adjutant to bring the nearest soldiers of infantry regiment and artillery battery next to me. When my soldiers fixed the bayonets and lay down, the advancing enemy forces did the same too.

This was the moment that we won!"

This was the first critical reaction of Mustafa Kemal in the Battle of Çanakkale. The enemy had landed at Arıburnu and outmanoeuvred tactically our weaker troops. They started to advance. The 27th Regiment arrived there at 8 am and immediately started clashing with the enemy. Due to the superiority of the enemy's military capacity, the casualties in time increased significantly and within a twinkling of an eye, mounted to about two thousand heroes whiles many others also ran out of power and the situation began to deteriorate. Thereupon, the 57th Regiment arrived and saved the situation in Arıburnu by joining the battle on the right flank of the 27th Regiment and putting up a strong resilience whereupon it culminated in the enemy being driven further to the coastal banks.

Thanks to the military might and successes of Mustafa Kemal at the commencement of the war, he was awarded on 30 April 1915 with "Silver Medal" for his deeds of distinction. Also, for the outstanding services and heroic actions, the 57th Regiment was rewarded with combat concession gold and silver medals.

Seddülbahir Heroes:
Major Mahmut Sabri Bey and His Battalion

On 25 April, the British troops started landing around the Village of Seddülbahir at five different points. Main landings were made at Ertuğrul Bay (V Bay) that was just below Seddülbahir and to the Tekke Bay (W Bay), which was just about two kilometres to the western stretch.

The 3rd Battalion of the 26th Regiment was set up and stationed in Seddülbahir Village to spy and defend the coastal zone against possible enemy landings. The Battalion's commander, Major Mahmut Sabri Bey, had placed the four squadrons under his command at possible landing spots. A unit from the 9th Squadron of the 3rd Battalion was to defend Morto Bay, the 10th Squadron around Ertuğrul Bay and the 12th Squadron would defend Tekke Bay while the 11th Squadron would be reserved and stationed at the Harap Kale sector located just near Seddülbahir Village.

In the early hours of the morning of 25th April, the 3rd Battalion of the 26th Regiment confronted the enemy in indomitable fortitude. Under the bombardment of enemy ships between 25 and 26 April, the 3rd Battalion's heroism against an enemy force ten times superior to that of their own was incomparable. The heroism of the two-day is mentioned in Major Mahmut Sabri's reports as follows:

"3rd Battalion of the 26th Regiment defended Seddülbahir, these forces included just 100 unarmed in 1100 rankers, sapper corps from a 200-men Division and four small 37.5 millimetres balls.

Our daytime struggle to clean and fix the ditches at the point that the enemy fire can't reach in order not to be direct target. At night, our struggle was to make an effort to complete the wire mesh with sappers and work on fixing the beach trenches. But our struggle was being foiled when the enemy torpedoes started to fire by projecting the lights. On 24 April, attacks by enemy aircrafts in broad daylight and enemy torpedoes at night were a kind of evidence of approaching landings besides disrupting our works.

On the night of 24/25 April, it was clearly moonlit nights. Due to the enemy fires on the troops dealing with the wire meshes and threatening sounds of explosions, no one was able to sleep. At dawn around 3 am, the Combat Engineer Battalion's Commander Muhittin Efendi ordered all his soldiers to stop working with the wire meshes and enter their underground shelters and tents to avoid casualties in vain.

On 25 April, around 4:30 am, hearing intense explosions, "Reserve units, arms!" he said and a whistle was heard; troops gathered with weapons. They went to the Harap Kale hill to see the coast clearly and to have an idea about the enemy's bombardment. The coast was covered with bluish and greenish smoke because most of the enemy artilleries were beating the fighter trenches. Nothing was visible because of this.

The region was incomparably small considering the amount of navy fires. Many shells had fallen side by side and shrapnel had exploded one after the other. We were entangled in the middle of fires from the south and the west. Then enemy bullets began to come from the northwest as well.

At that time, two 37,5 millimetre cannons and lots of ditches were all but destroyed. Some of the trenches that were dug to save lives became cemetery grounds. Walking wounded soldiers headed towards aid posts. Grape shots had never been seen before and nor had it been written in field manuals. They were like rounded as eggs.

While the defence force in the frontline occupied the fighter trenches waiting for the time to do their duity, the reserve units on their knees with their weapons at hand were ready to attack the enemy troops in any case. Many of the soldiers were just waiting for the time to aim their weapons at the enemy impatiently without thinking so much about the superiority of the enemy and their ammunitions, although they witnessed a great deal of their comrades die next to them while many others were lying on the ground with broken legs or chopped off heads.

Survivors were settling in the pits held by cannons and were building new trenches. Is it possible not to appreciate the soldiers of this nation who have highly passionate and strong heart. How can we not have faith in them? How can't we glorify the officers who trained these soldiers? When it was past 5 o'clock, the bombardment became rare. The ships carrying landing the troops (war and transport ships) were approaching the coast. This situation was reported to the 26th Regiment located around 5-6 kilometres away and at the southeast corner of Kirte (Alçıtepe Village).

The enemy occupied both areas of the south and southwest coast of Tekke Cape as landing areas to the Seddülbahir Pier and some of the transport ships were docked to the beach by cruisers, which supported up to 100 meters. At the time of landing, cruisers and also nordanfields, which were on the front part of the transport ships, were firing. As they were sending soldiers by boats, a huge transport ship (River Clyde with 2,000 soldiers inside) approached Ertuğrul Bay. It started resting two large pontoons within soldiers to the beach and carried troops from other transport ships to somewhere around Seddülbahir pier.

Our legendary soldiers started firing at the same time. The enemy saw our soldiers' gunfire from the cannons. Bullets were falling all over. Despite this hard situation, our soldiers were firing from the trenches without stopping. The enemy soldiers were seen as they were trying to save themselves in vain by jumping out of the boats.

In Seddülbahir pier, five enemy boats were sunk completely. Because of the heavy fire, we were not able to see Tekke Bay. The enemy fleet had to stop landings. It was 6 o'clock. Enemy navy one more time attacked the fighter trenches and everywhere was blown out. They refilled their boats and sent them to the beach but their effort failed once again. Enemy soldiers were so exhausted that they obviously didn't want to land on Ertuğrul Bay from the huge transport ship (River Clyde). Commanders and officers were directing soldiers towards the ladders by foce drawing their swords. Commanders and offices who were on sight couldn't get rid of the Turkish bullets.

The enemy was attacking incessantly and the strength of the battalion gradually began to melt. Meanwhile, the British troops, after landing with naval support, started to advance forward. When British soldiers, landing at İkiz Bay to the north of Tekke Bay, harried the Turkish force, Tekke Bay was lost and Turkish soldiers had to withdraw back to Seddülbahir.

Major Mahmut Sabri Bey could not get rescue forces. They had to fend for themselves. He then deployed the 11th Squadron located near Harap Kale Hill to the areas in need of emergency assistance. Although Tekke Bay fell, there was a stubborn defence in Seddülbahir Village and its vicinity.

"Seddülbahir and its vicinity were in need of constant reinforcements. But we did not get our strength. We had full trust in efforts and heroism of our soldiers and officers. So they certainly would not give up even if they were few in number against the enemy's superior forces. Indeed, they didn't. Half of the unit were located at the pier, while some were around the mill outside the village. Although they had lost almost half of the unit, they managed to prevent enemy landing until the evening. Hundreds of enemy soldiers and officers were killed. Our forces consisting of about 800 men who had only rifles were pushing the enemy equipped with superior weapons from all sides. More than two battalions of enemy forces were not able to proceed against our two squadrons. They couldn't take a single step forward in spite of all their endeavours."

In the afternoon of 25 April, the advancing enemy forces seized Aytepe. Although the defence in Gözcübaba Hill was strong until evening, a few soldiers of the 10th Squadron defending the area had to retreat to Harap Kale. On 25 April, enemy's landing force had been more than five battalions but they lost more than two-battalion force during the battle. The 3rd Battalion defending the coast had approximately 450 losses.

On the night of 25/26 April, it was a close combat with the enemy. The plan was to force the enemy to retreat by a bayonet charge of a battalion that arrived at night. However, the plan was abandoned as more harm rather than benefit would be done.

On 26 April, at 10 am, order to retreat was received from the garrison. The retreat began at 2.30 pm:

"Distance to the enemy was between 500 and 600 meters. At that time, a heavy fire was opened against the enemy and we got the order to withdraw to Kirte through Kanlıdere and to the second position.

We went to see the wounded soldiers at the aid post. They were told that those who can walk had better go with their comrades and those who can't should stay at the post. They were informed of the agreement, according to which the wounded shall not be maltreated. We also told them bread bags and two cans of water were reserved for them. Around 70 of them stayed there. Weapons gathered at the aid post were loaded on a donkey and sent.

It was 3 pm. Sound of gunfire died away. Our soldiers retreated into the river. The enemy infantry had not followed us. But they fired from the flanks. Naval fire was horrendous. The enemy began firing the entire field behind us. Meanwhile, we noticed that the enemy had occupied the trenches at the right side of our second line. We were not affected by enemy fire as we stayed in the water. But while we were moving through the water, no one noticed that we had passed the second line of defence. The water was up to hips in some places while up to the knees somewhere else. Those who came out of the water were becoming the target of violent enemy fire.

I moved to the right side of the creek thinking that we were close to the second line of defence. I crawled to the ridge but could not see the unit I despatched previously to protect us. There was not any officer or soldier left except for an aid man from the 11th Squadron and a drummer named Kamil. I sent the two forward to check the situation they could not move ahead and hit the dirt due to shrapnel shells. I ordered them to approach the creek and to shout the retreating troops that "Here is the second line of defence. The Major is here so come here." But they did not get any result. No one was able to get out of the water and move towards the ridges. It was understandable when you see the heavy enemy fire.

At 4 pm, there was no one else but our severely injured and martyred soldiers in the trenches on the coast of Seddülbahir. We searched for the two squadrons sent before unfortunatelly no one was found. The problems were mounting as the enemy had surrounded us from the right side and the left-rear side. We stood sentinel until 5 pm and checked available ammunition. There were soldiers who had around 20 to 50 bullets left and soldiers with no cartridges. It seemed more reasonable to retreat than to stay there at night with this unaided unit. We began moving towards Kirte at 5.30 pm. and 1,5 km away from Kirte we found the two squadrons we had sent before resting by the creek. They were ordered to come to the regiment headquarter when we arrived there.

We counted the soldiers after all of them gathered at the headquarters. Our casualties were 570, including three captains (one killed, two seriously injured) and three lieutenants (one killed, two injured). We stayed there at night as reserve unit restocking our supplies of ammunition."

On 25 and 26 April, 3rd Battalion of the 26th Regiment, relying on the help of Allah, did not refrain from showing devotion to fulfil their task of defending Seddülbahir's coastal zone although they had lost more than half of the unit against a superior enemy force.

BATTLES AT SEDDÜLBAHİR
AFTER 25 APRIL

On 26 April, Turkish forces around *Seddülbahir* sector established a defence line at 3 km south of *Alçıtepe* Village, with the efforts of the 2,000-men 20th Regiment and Gendarmerie Battalion of Bursa.

The British troops, who captured *Seddülbahir*, avoided chasing the Turkish forces and focused on fortifying their position and preparing a strong base of operation.

Halil Sami Bey, the commander of 9th Division, strengthened his unit with three more battalions on 27 April and planned a night offensive with a force of about 8,000 troops. The number of British troops at that time was around 12,000. Allied forces amounted to 17,000 troops with the addition of French forces who landed at *Seddülbahir* back from *Kumkale*.

Halil Sami's planned attack against a twice as much force did not take place on that night. Instead they resumed fortifying their position.

First Battle of Kirte (28 April 1915)

Landings on the first day gave the British a deep shock in material and nonmaterial terms. They started to act in a cautious manner after the unexpected resistance they faced. Therefore, within a couple of days, they planned an offensive to be launched on 28 April, whose ultimate target was seizing their first-day aim *Alçıtepe*.

The number of Allied troops had reached up to 17,500, twice as much as Turkish forces. More importantly, they had an enormous artillery support of 400 gun barrels situated on the Allied navy battleships.

Turkish frontline was under the command of Halil Sami Bey who defended the region with his 9th Division from the beginning. With the support of soldiers from the 7th and 5th Divisions, Turkish defence force amounted to 8,000 men.

The First Battle of Kirte started at 08.00 with the naval gunfire of the Allied battleships at close range from both flanks. Naval bombardment was quite influential as Turkish trenches were not thoroughly completed. Thus, outpost forces had to retreat.

Main battle started at 09.00. Turkish defence line split in two on *Alçıtepe-Seddülbahir* route. The western route was being held by the 20th Regiment while the eastern route was being defended by the 25th and 26th Regiments, which replaced the lagging 19th Regiment.

The British forces comprising about 10,000 troops were attacking the front defended by the 20th Regiment, which was eventually fended off. Turkish forces took control of *Kirte* route after the central enemy attack was stopped.

The real threat, however, appeared on the eastern flank of the front. The Allied forces were holding down the weakened and exhausted 26th Regiment while the naval gunfire was destroying the trenches. At last, warning signs of disintegration of the 26th Regiment emerged. Halil Sami, who commanded the Turkish side in the battle, gave the order of withdrawal as he noticed that the eastern flank had dissolved and no barrier remained in front of the enemy forces heading for *Alçıtepe.*

According to the order, all the units would retreat to the ridges 2-3 km back. The decision was rather dangerous because the battle was resuming and the 20th Regiment was successfully defending the right flank. Following an air of panic, the *Seddülbahir* front would fully get out of possession.

At this very critical moment, Major Mahmut Sabri Bey, who had not given passage to the enemy forces at *Seddülbahir* on 25 April, reappeared and completely changed the course of the battle.

With a reserve squadron under his command, Mahmut Sabri Bey came up from behind as the 26th Regiment began to retreat on the eastern side of the front. He rushed forward to the emptied positions gathering the withdrawing troops. The heaven-sent, timely and spirited move by Mahmut Sabri not only revived the Turkish forces but also befuddledly stopped the British. This move indeed changed the fate of the battles.

Now that all the enemy attacks had been stopped across the front, Turkish forces took full control of the area. The Turkish counter offensive began when two battalions of the 19th Regiment arrived at 3 pm, after which the British and French troops were driven back to *Yalçıtepe* and to the north of Morto Bay.

The clashe ended completely on 28 April at 6 pm. Result of the unsuccessful attack was heavy for the Allied powers. Their casualties had been more than 3,000 in the First Battle of Kirte. Turkish forces, on the other hand, had suffered 2,300 casualties, including both the dead and the wounded.

Army Commander Liman von Sanders realized that the main target of the enemy landing was *Seddülbahir* and they aimed at reaching *Kilitbahir* through *Alçıtepe*. After a few days, he decided to dispose some forces to the region from Saros and Anatolia.

The number of combatant units in *Seddülbahir* region amounted to 16,000 with reinforcements arrived until the evening of 30 April. Liman Pasha assigned Captain von Sodenstern, of German origin, to the general command of these unit comprised troops from different divisions.

Night Attacks on Seddülbahir Front (1/2 May – 3/4 May 1915)

Both the Supreme Military Command in İstanbul and the 5th Army Command gave orders to put the enemy's landed forces away. According to the orders, a night attack was planned with the forces gathered at *Seddülbahir*.

On the night of 1/2 May, at 10 pm, the Turkish attack began and made inroads in the British position. But the attack launched against an enemy force of 15 battalions had to stop at 1 am. A second attempt also failed in front of the British machine gunfire. On the left flank, where the French forces were located, hand to hand clashes took place but the enemy line could not be crossed and Turkish forces had to withdraw.

Unprepared, poorly coordinated and inadequately commanded night attacks had changed nothing in the frontline. But it led to the death of 6,000 Turkish troops in a night while the enemy loss was about 3,000.

The costly night attack on 1/2 May did not stop Turkish command to plan another attack for the next night. The 15th Division, arriving from İstanbul, was to join the new attack.

According to the plan, 10,000 troops would participate in the attack while 8,000 troops in the 15th Division would get through the enemy line.

At 11 pm, on the night of 3/4 May, the 9th Division launched a failed attack and no progress was made due to the naval gunfire which was supported by searchlights of battleships. The fighting continued until 2 am and two parties, suffering heavy losses, had to get back to their previous positions.

On the left flank, units attached to the 7th Division tried to move forward but were precluded by machine gunfire of the French forces consisting of 17,000 troops and naval gunfire supported by searchlights. The 15th Division arrived in groups in the front at 1 am and was sent forward under some uncertain orders and objectives. Having no adequate knowledge of the terrain and enemy position, the newcomers of the division courageously made a move forward in the dark. The offensive continued throughout the night. Just with the first peep of day, a disaster was waiting for the Turkish troops in the 15th Division, who came under heavy bombardment of the enemy battleships in the open field. Some units of the division had advanced as far as Morto Bay through the enemy line at night. Half of the unlucky division, about 4,000 soldiers were lost during this night attack.

Turkish soldiers bravely and devotedly fought here, despite the absence of plan, coordination and objectives set out with due regard to basic principles of war. Well-trained and brave troops of the division were thrown to the wolves for nothing. This division would be very beneficial in another battle but it could not get over for so long due to the heavy losses.

After these futile attempts carried out on *Seddülbahir* front, a new organisation was introduced on 4 May. The incapable and incompetent Captain von Sodenstern was replaced by the 15th Army Corps Commander in Anatolian side, German General Weber, and the front was renamed as the Southern Group.

Second Battle of Kirte (6-8 May 1915)

After inconclusive night attacks of the Turkish Army, the Allied Army Command decided to undertake a general offensive on *Seddülbahir* front to make use of this opportunity. A reinforcement unit of 5,000 men from the *Arıburnu* front joined the Anglo-French force and the Allied troops, amounted to 42,000 in total, whose aim was to capture *Alçıtepe*.

Turkish front was being defended by regiments attached to the 7th and 9th Divisions and some individual units. On paper, Turkish force consisted of 23 battalions but in reality total number of Turkish troops was around 13,000 since almost all the regiments had suffered heavy losses. The 15th Regiment was then assigned as a reserve unit.

The Second Battle of Kirte began after the naval bombardment on 6 May at 10.30 am. Turkish forces initially stopped the British attack on the right flank with machine gun and infantry fire. French troops started on the left flank and advanced up to 400 meters in the direction of *Kerevizdere*. But the attack was eventually prevented. However, the clashes went on between the outpost lines all night long.

On the morning of 7 May, the Allied attack began afresh. They made some gains with the support of naval gunfire on the right and left flanks of the Turkish defence line. Especially, on the right flank, the British had advanced 300 meters in *Zığındere* region.

Next morning at 10 am, the unprecedented offensive including bombardment from land and sea and lasting for 15 minutes devastated the Turkish line. Following this massive bombardment, the British and ANZAC troops started an attack from both flanks of *Zığındere* Valley and made inroads about 300 meters, which was stopped at last. On the left flank, the French troops carried out an ineffective offensive as well.

Before nightfall, the Allied troops carried out a bayonet charge following a massive and effective artillery fire, which was restrained by the brave Turkish soldiers. The only achievement of the attack for the Allied forces was the seizure of Hill 83 located near *Kerevizdere* by the French troops.

The Allies had been 3 km away from their first-day target, *Alçıtepe*, by the time the three-day attack they carried out with a great effort and superior forces ended. Across the entire front, their advance was between 400 and 600 meters. However, their loss was beyond comparison; the casualties they suffered were about 6,500 soldiers. The Turkish side, on the other hand, had suffered 2,000 casualties, including the dead and the wounded.

Trench wars and some local clashes continued throughout May after the Second Battle of Kirte. The French forces scored some success near *Kerevizdere* on the left flank of Turkish line, capturing some points with a series of limited objective attacks.

Naval battles resumed in May as well. On the night of 13 May, Turkish *Muavenet-i Milliye* (National Solidarity) under the command of Major Ahmet Bey had torpedoed the British battleship *Goliath* anchored in *Morto* Bay. Hit by three torpedoes, *Goliath* had sunk with its crew of 570 men. In another attack against the Allied navy, U-21 submarine of the German navy, on 25 May, torpedoed the British *Triumph* off the coast of Arıburnu. After two days, the submarine hit and sank another British battleship Majestic anchored near *Tekke* Bay in *Seddülbahir* region.

Due to three sunken battleships in 15 days and increasing movement of German submarines in the sea, the Allied command ordered the retreat of battleships back to safe ports. This decision not only helped reduce the pressure on the Turkish defence but also demoralised the enemy troops in the battlefield as they lacked naval gunfire support.

Third Battle of Kirte (4-6 June 1915)

The Allied command decided to launch a general offensive in June upon pressures from the headquarters after they failed in accomplishing their objectives and were stuck in front of the Turkish defence.

The Allied forces at that time consisted of 20,000 British and 10,000 French troops supported by an artillery unit with 108 gun barrels.

As for the Turkish defence line, the 9th Division was holding the right flank while the newly arrived 12th Division controlled the left flank. Turkish force comprised 24,000 troops in total, 18,000 of whom were combatants and 6,000 were retained as reserve.

On the morning of 4 June, at 8 am, an unprecedented and prolonged massive bombardment started. When the two and a half hour bombardment ended, the Turkish trenches appeared all devastated and unsuitable for shelter. The Allied attack began afterwards. The French launched an unsuccessful attack on the left flank where the 12th Division was located. The British attack on the central position was initially effective in front of the 36th Regiment. With the help of the 22th Regiment, the British advance was halted. The British forces turned to the west of *Alçıtepe-Seddülbahir* route and went 1 km forward, forcing the 9th Division to set back. Turkish reinforcement units helped stop the advance of the British units and force them to retreat.

Turkish counterattacks continued on 5 and 6 June to stop the British advance. The French forces were repelled by the bayonet charge carried out by the 2nd Reserve Division.

The result of the three-day battle was that the Allies had moved 500 meters forward in the central position, with no gains in the right and left flanks. The loss of the Allied forces was 7,500 troops. The damage on the Turkish side was severe as well. Especially, in the central front, 1 km advance of the British had shocked the Turkish troops at first but they managed to recover with the bayonet charge carried out with the help of reinforcement units. Casualties of the Turkish side were nearly 10,000 including 3,000 martyrs.

Battles of Kerevizdere and Zığındere (21 June-13 July 1915)

Towards the middle of June, the Allied command had been convinced that it was almost impossible, with the existing forces, to break through the Turkish defence and capture *Alçıtepe*. Turkish defence had been quite strengthened; the trenches had been benched and deepened so as not to be affected by heavy bombardments. So, the Allies turned their attention to tactically significant and limited objective attacks in certain areas instead of general offensive targeting *Alçıtepe*. To this end, they gave up forcing through the centre and planned to destroy the Turkish front from the flanks, thus aiming to take control of *Kerevizdere* and *Zığındere* sectors.

First Battle of Kerevizdere

First attack came to the left flank of the Turkish front, to the opposite of the French position. The battle, known as the First Battle of Kerevizdere, started on 21 June. This zone was being defended by the 2nd Division, which was weakened when almost half of the division had been lost during the clashes at *Arıburnu* on 19 May.

On 20 June, the Anglo-French artillery bombardment with more than 20,000 shells on *Kerevizdere* was so powerful that the Turkish trenches were almost completely destroyed and flattened.

On the morning of 21 June, the French commenced an offensive operation on the destroyed Turkish trenches. But they encountered a stubborn resistance of the Turkish 2nd Division, which they were able to overcome although the Turkish resistance was strengthened by the bayonet charge of the reinforcement units from the 71st Regiment. The French had taken control of an area with a dominating view to *Kerevizdere*. Threatening advance of the French troops compelled the Turkish side to send the 34th Regiment of the 12th Division forward. Day and night, the fighting raged on the ridges overlooking *Kerevizdere* left 3,500 French troops dead although they had gained 200 meters of ground. On the Turkish side was heavier loss. The number of martyrs and wounded amounted to 6,000. The 2nd Division, already weakened due to previous battles, had been smashed up. For this reason, it was replaced by the 12th Division.

Battle of Zığındere

The French gains in the left flank of the Turkish line encouraged the British to plan an attack on the Valley of *Zığındere*, which was held by the 33rd and 126th Regiments of the 11th Division. The 127th Regiment of the Division was in reserve position in the north of *Alçıtepe* Village (Kirte).

On 28 June, the heavy bombardment on the Turkish trenches was followed by the ground offensive. The bombardment had devastated the trenches. A 15,000-men British force commenced the attack at 11 am against the Turkish trenches defended by 8,000 soldiers in total. Moving forward through the valley, the British forces invaded the Turkish outposts, they finally lost their grip in front of the Turkish defence advancing on the open field on both flanks of the stream. However, the British held their head high and continued their attacks persistently, which proved successful. Advancing through the ridge located between *Zığındere* and the sea, they made some gains in the Turkish trench line. Their advance was halted on *Keçi Deresi* area with the resistance of the 33rd Regiment and the 16th Reserve Regiment.

The situation during the battles that continued until the morning of 30 June grew more and more fraught when the British forces passed behind the Turkish line on the seaward side of *Zığındere*. Yet more, the Southern Group Commander Weber Pasha had considered pulling the defence line back. But, with the arrival of the 1st Division under the command of Lt. Col. Cafer Tayyar Bey, Turkish defence line recovered.

The Turkish soldiers were urged to respond to the losses in *Zığındere* sector and the Army Command ordered them to counterattack to get back the trenches on the seaward side. But, it seemed almost impossible. What complicated the situation was the difficulty of ensuring success for an offensive in the open field under the threat of machine guns and artilleries. Despite everything, the decision was made. The newly arrived regiments attached to the 3rd and 5th Divisions would launch the impossible attack.

It was 5 July when the Turkish offensive commenced on both flanks of *Zığındere* Valley. At 03.45 am, Turkish force of 13,000 troops lunged forward with an incomparable passion and courage. However, they were forced back due to heavy machine gunfire from the well-fortified British trenches. Half of the Turkish force, about 6,000 troops, were either killed or wounded.

The Battle of Zığındere, lasting from 28 June to 5 July, witnessed the bloodiest clashes in Gallipoli. Turkish casualties throughout the battles had reached 16,000 in total.

Second Battle of Kerevizdere

The Turkish forces had not fully recovered when the new Anglo-French offensive began on the left flank of the Turkish defence line on 12 July. While the British were forcing the centre, the French aimed to invade *Yassıtepe* near *Kerevizdere*. Both accomplished their objectives: The former moved 500 meters forward and captured Turkish trenches along the way. The latter invaded *Yassıtepe* with a dominating position over *Kerevizdere*.

The Allies recommenced attacks on 13 July, threatening *Kerevizdere*, but their advance was halted by the Turkish resistance and specifically by the bayonet attacks of the 16th and 17th Regiments of the 6th Division which were performed at their own discretion.

At the end of the Second Battle of Kerevizdere, also known as the Battle of 12-13 July, the Turkish defence force retained their positions, though losing control of certain points. But the casualties were incomparable. The Turkish side had suffered 10,000 casualties while the Allied forces' loss was around 4,000 at the two-day battle.

It was really not a good time for the Turkish troops as they were shattered at the Battles of Kerevizdere and Zığındere. Moreover, troops, regiments and divisions were completely disorganised.

During the truce, a new arrangement was put into effect. Units of the 2nd Army commanded by Vehip Pasha were sent to the front and replaced the divisions with heavy losses while the latter began to retreat. Accordingly, Weber Pasha was discharged and replaced by Vehip Pasha.

Seddülbahir Front from August to Evacuation

Having been unsuccessful in their attempts on the *Seddülbahir* front during the battles between 21 June and 13 July, the Allied forces, well convinced of fruitlessness of a new attack in this region, decided to take their chances in another area. To this end, they decided to land new forces at Anafartalar region in the north of Gallipoli in order to widen the battle zone and encircle the Turkish army from the north.

The most important attack on Turkish positions at *Seddülbahir* coincided with the landing of Allied troops at Anafartalar on 6 August. The objective of the offensive was to contain Turkish units in the region and to prevent the transportation of reinforcements to *Anafartalar-Arıburnu* zone in the north. But the attempt proved inconclusive. The offensive was halted by the Turkish forces and Vehip Pasha disposed the 4th and 8th Divisions to the Northern Group as reinforcements.

After August, Turkish defence at *Seddülbahir* was improved. The British and French forces, on the other hand, went into the effort of retaining their position instead of forcing the Turkish defence line. Both sides were busy with bolstering their trenches. Although narrow-scoped offensives took place at times until the evacuation of the region by the Allied forces, the dominant character of the clashes at *Seddülbahir* was routine trench warfare.

How Muavenet-i Milliye (National Solidarity) Torpedo Boat Sank the British Battleship Goliath?

With the positioning of the enemy warships strategically stationed at the Morto Port, large numbers of casualties were inflicted upon the Turkish troops defending the frontline, especially to the trenches close to the Strait, under a constant fire. A dangerous mission of forcing them to leave the area by organizing a raid against the enemy ships, was assigned to Muavenet-i Milliye torpedo boat. At night the boat would secretly draw near the enemy ship to torpedo a suitable target.

At midnight, at a makeshift change, the enemy ship would be unceremoniously attacked. Senior Captain Ahmet Saffet Bey, who commanded the Muavenet-i Milliye torpedo, on the night of 12/13 May at 00:45 quietly, removed the anchor. To prevent sparks from the chimney, the speed of the boat was adjusted to 8 mile. There was fog at that night. Because of the blackout on the ship, the two enemy ships were clearly invisible by about 600-800 meters away. At 01:00, the boat reached the anterior of Eskihisar and there appeared two tremendous ships lying unprotected. There was a distance of 1,200 meters between Muavenet-i Milliye and one of these two ships, whose name was Goliath. At the front side of the torpedo boat, the rudder turning right in the open sea continued to advance confidently. Without wasting time, the hives of the torpedo that were ready to fire were converted to starboard. It continued its way through Domuz Burnu passing quietly by two British battleships. Just then due to the bullet fired by the enemy, Goliath spotted Muavenet-i Milliye and immediately asked about an identification password. The Muavenet-i Milliye crew, with the aim of buying-time and getting closer, kept answering questions with questions, sent out a lot of meaningless signs, wanting them to think that it *was indeed one of their own torpedo boats. Without causing suspicion, Muavenet, approaching 200-300 meters of its target, first fired three of its torpedoes in succession and turned back. Goliath, weighing 13,160 ton, was shot at the head, centre and stern; with the explosion of the ammunition in the stern it sank 74 meters deep with 567 men aboard.*

Tasvir-i Efkâr newspaper, on 18 May 1915, narrated this great victory achieved by Muavenet-i Milliye in an article titled "How Did Goliath Sink?"

"We received new information of the brave and heroic move by the Muavenet-i Milliye who assaulted the British Goliath armoured warships. This battleship was sunk by our torpedo.

The armoured battleship was purchased by Muavenet-i Milliye and also once served in the German fleet under the name (S- 165). This armoured battleship has gained reputation and recognition with its heroic activities. Partly, this was achieved by wise and intelligent activities undertaken by our valiant, self-sacrificing soldiers in our fast and strong battleship. This feat should never be erased from our memories.

The first dangerous assignment of the torpedo boat was to pass through the mined zone in the Strait, while heading straight for the targeted ambition on the fateful night of 12/13 May. After successfully passing this difficult stage, it had to cross the narrow way leading where the two enemy ships had anchored. After this stage, Muavenet-i Milliye would come across two possible targets and the commander would decide which British ship should be torpedoed and sank into the deep sea. In the narrow passage, however, eight British battleships were sailing two by two in every direction to prevent an attack from outside. Turkish torpedo was able to get out of sight and attention of these destroyers and draw near the battleship to be torpedoed as close as a hundred meter. That day, the Goliath battleship joined the bombardment of Seddülbahir front until 11.30. There later, the battleship and its crew retreated into silence. When one of the enemy's stationed guards on duty around the battleship asked: 'Who is it?' Our crew thought that they had been identified and that searchlights would turn on themselves within a twinkling of an eye.

But no! There was absolutely nothing ... Silence ... The torpedo easily took up position. The first torpedo hit the targeted enemy ship with a very big crash in the silence of the night. Searchlights of the enemy ships could not be pointedly directed at the torpedo. The darkness and tranquillity continued as such. A moment later, a second torpedo hit the ship's boiler room, which caused some movement inside the enemy ship. But the searchlights still remained inactive. Finally, the third throw caused a stronger smash to the rear of the ship and completely ignited red flames. The ensuing flames illuminated the Morto Port and nothing was left of it after a little while. The sea had completely swallowed everything.

Our heroes, a fortune of salvation, painstakingly became more vigilant to accomplish their task. They crisscrossed gently and slipped through the eight British torpedo ships unseen and unnoticed. The enemy torpedoes were all thumbs in their capturing us as much as they were in their discovery task. So confused and hopelessthey were. They were puzzled as to what to do. As close a distance as it could have been, a second British warship could not think of rescuing their doomed friends. The British Admiral at the time using a wireless-radio set sent a telegraph report about their humiliation and embarrassment of the British fleet in the incident. Young crew of Muavenet-i Milliye, who managed to torpedo a giant battleship with an open-sea boat for the first time, was returning back, evenly and prideful, through the mined zone of the Strait in the darkness of the night."

This resounding victory had boosted the morale of the troops fighting at Kerevizdere sector of Seddülbahir front and suffered heavy casualties due to the fire from Goliath. The victory of a small boat, weighing about 765 tons, over Goliath, weighing 13,000 tons, had become one of the incidents that led to resignation of Lord Fisher and Churchill.

Volunteers at Gallipoli

The Battle of Gallipoli, where quite a large number of volunteers participated, is seen in the eyes of the entire nation as a struggle for life and death. Besides the regular army troops, individuals or groups from every corner of the country came to join the battle against the enemy. The number of valiant volunteers willing to participate and to challenge the enemy in the combat had reached hundreds of thousands. The volunteers were not only citizens from within the affected geography, but consisted of inhabitants from Rumelia such as Turks, Albanians and also Bosnian Muslims who heeded to the battle's call against all odds and participated in the battles at Gallipoli. Unfortunately, at Gallipoli, due to the absence of a concrete or accurate form of regular registration at the time, the names of valiant volunteers, who participated and martyred in the war, are still unknown.

At Gallipoli, martyrdom was voluntarily desired by Turkish troops for the sake of religion and homeland. Captain Saip Bey mentioned the story of one of the anonymous and unsung heroes, Ünyeli Rıza (Rıza of Ünye) and his comrades, who participated in the clashes at Seddülbahir:

"It was at the end of June. On the Seddülbahir front, we found ourselves dependent on the 7th Divisional command of the Kerevizdere zone, in their trenches which continued to be a point of intense violent from the days of the fierce battles, which found tranquillity in a while. Against the possibility of raids and occasional attacks that could spark another fiery battle alone, battles were taking place at a distance of 6 metres to the enemy in the bomb trenches and both sides recorded casualties.

Distance between the trenches of the 1st Battalion, under the command of Captain Saip, of the 21st Regiment and the enemy forces ranged from 6 metres to 150 metres.

One day, the battalion adjutant brought five civilians to the 1st Squadron. These people were from among the folks of the Black Sea coast. When they received the news of on-going fierce battles at Gallipoli, they could not stand idle to watch the place come under fire, -despite being old- coupled with the Turkish blood running in their veins. They appealed for the defence of their country and wanted to be martyrs for the homeland.

Their desire was accepted and the commander of squadron was ordered to use them in reconnaissance services, trench raids, capturing enemy forces –officers in particular-, and recovering heavy machine guns from the enemy.

They bore arms and ammunition after resting for a day and then started their mission the following day in the trench of the squadron. They were later sent forward in turns for security and reconnaissance services. They made raids on enemy patrols and brought back the weapons they seized.

Within ten days, two of the volunteers had been martyred. The rest came to the commander of the squadron and said:

"Captain! We have been performing reconnaissance and surveillance for three days. We have discovered the footholds of the enemy's machine guns and cannons. After midnight tonight, three of us will attack the machine gun pit."

All the officers and recruits of the squadron had witnessed some of their friends get martyred or injured by the heavy machinery of the enemy and were very satisfied with the discovery of the enemy's weaponry location. They welcomed the planned raid with great enthusiasm. However, approaching the enemy trenches, and then going over the mighty fence and finally invading the fortification were certainly a difficult task. Success was not guaranteed but what was certain was that it would end in death.

Recruits, like the commander of the squadron, did not want to lose their new friends.

Nevertheless, they decided to wait for martyrdom; and they said, "We sacrifice our lives for the nation". Eventually, their plan was accepted. They determined from where and how they would carry out the raid. They had with them just five grenades, bayonet and wedges; by 1:30 at midnight, these three heroes came out of the trenches, diving into the terrifying darkness filled with death.

The squadron waited anxiously in the trench for the result of the raid by this small platoon. An hour passed without hearing any voice. Finally, at 2:45 am, a furious bomb sound signalled the beginning of the raid. The British troops began firing and that continued 15 minutes with all its violence. Then, things reverted to a dead silence. At that moment eyes were searching and piercing through the darkness to see whether these heroes would return or not.

Later in the darkness, they saw a creeping shadow approaching, with a machine gun; and it was Ünyeli Rıza. His comrades were not by his side:

"My captain", he said, "We infiltrated the trenches with a silent movement; however we found the enemy holding there with strength and vigilance. We jumped into the trenches with bombs. While two of my colleagues were grappling with the British with bayonet, I took my wedge and killed four British, then took their rifle. Throat by throat, my friends were martyred in this fight."

The commander of the squadron kissed Rıza's forehead and the rest of the recruits in the trenches congratulated him. Rıza's eyes were filled with sadness for leaving his friends behind in the bloody battlefield. After duly performing his duties for the country, Rıza returned to his hometown.

Battle of Zığındere and the Three on Attack

In the month of June, the Seddülbahir front was a scene of bloody battles. Until 20 June, in the Battles of Kirte, the Anglo-French Allied Army had carried out three massed attacks on the Turkish defence line but failed. They adopted a new tactic and tried to break through the Turkish defence from the sides. The French forces, on 21 June, attacked upon Kerevizdere sector on the left side of the Turkish defence line following an unprecedented bombardment; seizing a section of the trenches but without forcing a way through the front line.

On 28 June, this time the British attacked the right side of the Turkish defence line, attacking both sides of the valley on the Zığındere front. After being on the offensive with thousands of bullets, again they attacked the line with navy ships and cannons. With artillery bombardment, the enemy destroyed the trenches and left behind a mass grave for the Turkish soldiers. The British also succeeded in gaining a section of the trench line.

When the trench lines finally fell into the enemy's hands, it created a dangerous situation on the Turkish front line. This resulted in a planned attack on the enemy to get back the lost territories.

The assault set for 3 July 1915 was to be performed by the 3rd Battalions of the 70th, 71st and 124th Regiments of 1st Division under the command of Lt. Col. Cafer Tayyar Bey. Major Reşat Bey, the commander of the 3rd Battalion of the 70th Regiment, was going to lead the attack.

The 70th Regiment, in the defence of Shkoder in the Balkan Wars, provided remarkably great service. In the defence of Shkoder Castle surrounded by the Bardanyol hill against enemy forces of over three folds, they valiantly defended the passage and prevented the enemy from entry. Thus earning the nickname "the Bardanyol Regiment" as a reputation for the courage shown. This regiment would undertake an offensive with their brother regiments in the same division.

This operation was referred to as "the three on attack", as the 3rd Battalions of the Regiment would carry out a joint offensive. With this attack, they would throw back the British who had found a wedge-like entrance on the Turkish defence line, located on the ridges of Alçıtepe.

The attempted assault was very dangerous, because the trenches in the enemy hands were fortified with machine guns and supported with rearward artillery and under this condition; any operation was bound to be dissolved under fierce rifle attack. In his discretion of the magnitude of the danger, Cafer Tayyar Bey finished with the following utterances in the order of the attack:

"I supplicate to Allah to grant us success in the offensive for the survival of Ottomans and Islam and I ask for sacrifice and heroism of my colleagues. To the souls of the would-be martyrs I recite Fatiha and I kiss the eyes of the would-be wounded veterans."

A little while before sunset, Turkish batteries with their restricted munitions started to attack continuously for about 15-20 minutes. Assault troops were making headways toward the exit positions. The British weapons were sweeping across the area from the sea and the ground. The three battalions in a single row behind each other came out of a single communication trench, which measured the height of a man at the beginning, then decreased to knee-deep and finally opened completely.

In the front was the Battalion Commander Major Reşat, following him was adjutant Ensign Sadi and after him was the commander of the Squadron Captain Hüseyin Hüsnü, Ensign

Halit and the battalion's İmam Hüseyin Efendi. The rest of the troops followed them.

The soldiers quickly encountered the enemy's fire from both land and sea. The whole weaponry of the enemy was geared towards crushing these three Turkish battalions. The trench was immediately blocked. It was supposed that the soldiers were not moving forward. It was dark now. However, waiting for the night to move forward had exhausted the troops. The Commander of the 70th Regiment, Lt. Col. Vasıf Bey -who was later martyred on the Caucasian front, on the ridges of Oğnut- gave the following order to adjutant Süleyman from the 2nd Battalion:

"The fire stopped. No report or no news from our people. Go see Reşat Bey and find out the situation of the battalion and quickly get back to me with a report."

Süleyman quickly moved. Blessed corpses of heroes and fallen soldiers had filled communication trench; he encountered some of the surviving soldiers and officers, asking direction and hurrying to fulfil his mission. After a short while, the trench was over. He started to advance in the open field. A voice from the darkness shouted:

"Move quickly, that zone over there is under fire".

He jumped, passed that area and came behind the enemy's foothold. The area was bursting at the seams. He finally found Reşat Bey. The 71st Regiment's 3rd Battalion Commander, Şerif Bey was busy issuing orders with Major Reşat who was wounded in the head. Şerif Bey said:

"The situation is as you have seen, but we identified the enemy. We learned that the captains and lieutenants of the battalions, and the adjutant were martyred. The Imam of the battalion had suffered severe injuries. More than half of the battalion are lying dead or wounded."

These remaining heroes were able to get back a couple of trenches in subsequent days. However, the enemy again seized these trenches with counterattacks and the plan foiled.

Only one or two officers and also 400 out of 1,000 soldiers of the 3rd Battalion of the 70th Regiment had survived. Each battalion sent one officer to the 3rd Battalion and Süleyman took command of one of the squadrons in that battalion.

Bloody Battles at Seddülbahir

The Seddülbahir front was the place where Gallipoli's most intense and bloody battles took place. Anglo-French allied army constantly attacked to split the Seddülbahir front; the Turkish soldiers countered these attacks, thereby not leaving the enemies with any opportunity. However, given the large number of martyrs in the battles, the front had continuously been strengthened with new troops.

One of the reinforcement units that served in the front was the 10th Division. Münim Mustafa who served as a reserve officer in the 30th Regiment of the division came to Seddülbahir towards the end of July. His first observation on the Seddülbahir front was as follows:

"The second day after assuming the command of the trenches, together with the regiment commander, we went to surveillance point which was built at a place where the enemy could not figure out. From the surveillance site, I came across a traumatizing view as I surveyed the enemies' defence line. The casualties on both sides of previous battles were lying in the area between our defence line and that of the enemy! Foots in new boots, new clothes on their back, the little-used rifle with bayonet grasped with both hands... Newly arrived soldiers were lying face down. Blood flowing from the wounds on their head and chest painted their dress and the area red, approximately two kilometres of land within the territory was filled with human bodies."

The battles at Seddülbahir were not only fought on the ground, but that they continued through underground tunnels. In the Battles of Çanakkale, both sides frequently used the underground tunnels to attack, especially on Arıburnu and Seddülbahir fronts. Soldiers were digging tunnels 10-15 meters under the enemy trenches and filling with hundreds of kilograms of explosives to blow up and seize the trenches. Münim Mustafa had witnessed an explosion under his own trench by the enemy troops on 30 July 1915.

"It was half past four. To get rid of the enemy's artillery fire, we took refuge in an underground shelter. As my own eyes followed through the unlimited explosion of shrapnel shells at our bedside, I suddenly heard a moan, a movement from inside the soil as if it was being pressured. Less than a second, I was stunned by the sound of an explosion as if the earth was departing to the sky. I did not understand what happened to me. It was a shocking moment.

I was dazed by the humming sounds of painful explosions, which had not passed by my ears. I pulled my head out of the underground shelter to see what was happening. Although it was a sunny summer day, between the sun and us was like a cloud yielding a layer of soil, preventing the sky and the sun to be seen. From the atmosphere to the ground continuously rained rocks and soil, alongside fragments of people's limbs, arms, legs, bones falling from the sky. The place we found ourselves was covered with suffocating black smoke, we were unable to see anything. A suffocating smell created by dynamite did not allow us to breath. The pits, the streams had an intolerable degree of burning smell of gas. Everyone's throat was burning; some were lying in an unconscious state. Our clothes were blackened like people coming out of the chimney beyond recognition.

I hurtled. Aytepe, the enemy's first line of defence on the right flank, disappeared due to the tunnel blast underneath. There was no trace from the troops there. I was looking for Aytepe which was exposed to the enemy bomb the most but I could not see it. There was a dimple now in place of Aytepe. On 6 August, the enemy launched simultaneous attack on the Seddülbahir front to prevent Turkish reinforcements from the southern group directed against the landing at Anafartalar in the north and the attack on Conkbayırı. The enemy attack was most severely and intensively felt in the 30th Regiment of Münim Mustafa.

On the morning of 6 August began a hellish, unceasing bombardment, which lasted for hours, from land and sea on our forces in the trenches. In the afternoon the offensive followed the artillery bombardment, whereby the British troops managed to slip in to the trenches. But Turkish forces retook the trenches with the support of reinforcement units. Only a small part of the trenches had remained in the hands of the British, upon which Lieutenant Mehmet Ali organised an attack with his squadron. The trench was completely taken back but Lieutenant Mehmet Ali was killed by some bayonet wounds he sustained. Münim Mustafa, visiting the trenches upon the order of his commander to report what was going on in the trenches, mentioned the situation in his memoirs as follows:

"We had started this venture under the rain of bombs, shrapnel and mitrailleuse. We started working inside the trenches, where stacked human bodies were laid everywhere. I trembled when I saw young lieutenant Mehmet Ali, wounded with bayonets during the counteroffensive, fallen with his hand upon the wound on his chest. His eyes were semi- closed. His uniform was covered with a little soil in trenches. There was blood on it. If his uniform were cleaned, one woul think that he was not dead but sleeping.

On the other hand, Lieutenant Kemal took two dangerous wounds. While being taken to the aid post by two soldiers, one of the soldiers was, too, hit by a shrapnel.

Captain Mustafa was all covered in blood. While fighting the enemy, his squadron had perished and he had received a serious wound. Privates, corporals, sergeants, all badly wounded in the arm, leg, chest, belly and head, were being taken to the aid post. These wounds were like Victoria Cross. Some of them were wounded again on the way."

BATTLES AT ARIBURNU
AFTER 25 APRIL

NZAC troops panicked after being driven back to the coast by the joint offensive of Turkish regiments. In the morning of 25 April, the 27th and 57th Regiments successfully stood to the ANZAC landing. Towards the evening, together with the 72th Regiment from the 19th Division, they repelled the enemy advance. Due to this futile attempt, a request was sent to Allied Army Commander Hamilton to withdraw troops. Hamilton's decision was to resume hanging on, upon which ANZAC forces, digging new trenches, strengthened their position on the beachside ridges of *Arıburnu*, 1-1.5 km inland.

Not having any information about the situation on the ANZAC side, Turkish forces, with the participation of the 77th Regiment of the 19th Division, were prepared for a new attack. But the attack failed and the troops dissolved before entering the enemy line. Afterwards, the 1st Battalion of the 27th Regiment which was based at *Kanlısırt* also retreated and was placed in the east of *Karayörük* Stream. The advantage gained on 25 April had beenlost. The ANZAC forces were not able to notice the disorganisation in the Turkish units and the evacuation of *Kanlısırt*. Both sides were unaware of each other and they could not get the benefit of negative status of their enemy.

26 April was the most dangerous day for the Turkish forces at *Arıburnu*. Turkish units defending *Arıburnu* could not get any support and they also lost the 77th Regiment as they were scattered at the night assault. All the forces at hand comprised just 8,000 to 9,000 soldiers. But the ANZAC forces continued landing troops all night, number of troops reaching 20,000.

In the morning of 26 April, a heavy bombardment on the right flank of the Turkish front began and was followed by ground offensive. The 57th Regiment initially halted the offensive which was renewed throughout the day. With the support of artillery units, the ANZAC troops took control of *Kılıçbayırı*.

The *Arıburnu* front was strengthened with the newly arrived 64th and 33rd Regiments in the morning of 27 April and commander of the 19th Division Lt. Col. Mustafa Kemal decided to launch an attack. In the battles continuing till the evening, *Kılıçbayırı*, which was captured by the enemy the day before, was finally seized by Turkish forces, after changing hands several times. The clashes in the centre and south of the Arıburnu front turned into chest to chest battle, especially in *Kanlısırt-Kırmızısırt* sector. After the dusk, Turkish troops recaptured *Kanlısırt* and *Kırmızısırt*.

After the victory, Mustafa Kemal decided to keep on the offensive through the night to push the enemy back to the sea. The fighting raged all night long but the stubborn attacks by the Turkish forces had to stop after failure in hitting the targets due to the enemy bombardment with the support of searchlights. Lt. Col. Şevki Bey, commander of the 33rd Regiment, was martyred after being wounded in these battles.

On 28 April, both sides renewed their attacks to hold the control of emplacements. On 29 and 30 April, ANZAC offensives failed while, within these two days, the Turkish front was supported by new coming forces. With the arrival of the 125th Regiment of the 16th Division and 14th and 15th Regiments of the 15th Division, Turkish forces at *Arıburnu* reached up to 20,000 troops.

Turkish Offensive on 1 May

The idea of a new offensive on *Arıburnu* with the support of reinforcement was being considered by both the 5th Army Command and Mustafa Kemal. Finally, a decision was made to embark on a general offensive scheduled for 1 May.

15,500 troops including the regiments of the 19th Division, who were on the front from the first day, the regiments arrived later and the individual units were supposed to participate in the offensive. Meanwhile ANZAC forces on the opposite side had reached up to 24,000 soldiers.

Main zone for the offensive, started on 1 May at 5 am, was *Bombasırtı-Merkeztepe* line in the centre of *Arıburnu* front. The attack carried out by the units under the 14th Regiment was not able to move ahead under the machine gun fire of the enemy despite the support of all forces.

The attacks, exacerbated with the participation of new forces till the evening, was not so influential in the face of well-fortified enemy positions. Upon the order of Mustafa Kemal, Turkish forces continued attacking all night long across the whole front. However, the offensive proved unsuccessful despite heavy losses.

During the 24-hour offensive on 1 May, Turkish side lost about 6,000 troops, which was one-third of all its forces at *Arıburnu*.

The only achievement of the offensive was approximating the Turkish frontline towards the enemy positions. Distance between the trenches of the two sides was 200-500 meters before the operation and it went down to 50-200 meters after 1 May. It was closer in some places, dropping to 5-10 meters *Bombasırtı-Merkeztepe* line.

The close distance between trenches on the *Arıburnu* front forced the two sides to organise night assaults. Especially, night raids were carried out to get the control over the enemy trenches at *Bombasırtı, Kırmızısırt* and *Kanlısırt* sectors.

From the first day of landing at *Arıburnu*, Turkish forces gathered here were under the command of Lt. Col. Mustafa Kemal, commander of the 19th Division. Due to his 23-day command of the area, he came to use the title of 'Commander of Arıburnu Forces'. However, with the arrival of the 16th and 5th Divisions and the increase in the number of troops in the region, 3rd Army Corps Commander Esat Pasha took command of the Turkish forces, transferring his headquarters which was much far in the rear of the front to *Kemalyeri* sector. From 17 May on, Mustafa Kemal continued his duty as the commander of the 19th Division.

19 May Turkish Offensive on Arıburnu

On 11 May, Deputy Commander-in-Chief Enver Pasha arrived at *Arıburnu* for an on-site inspection. After observing the front and collecting information about the situation, he ordered a general offensive to smash the enemy forces. As the 5th Army Commander Liman Pasha also favoured such an attack, the pressure on Esat Pasha increased. Decision was made on the condition that a new and fresh division from İstanbul would come and join the fight. The 2nd Division was chosen to participate in the offensive which was due to take place on 19 May.

The details of the offensive were passed on to all the units on 18 May. According to the plan, the 19th Division at the right wing would attack on the northern side of the enemy; the 5th Division would move on the centre, the 16th Division at the left wing would smash into the southern wing of the enemy forces. The main attack would come from the 2nd Division which was expected to break through the enemy line at *Kanlısırt-Kırmızısırt*.

The number of Turkish troops were increased to 42,000 while the ANZAC forces consisted of 17,300 men.

Before dawn on 19 May, at about 3.30 am, all were set for the battle. The Turkish troops had prepared adequately enough to fight the enemy untill their last breath. But the ANZAC units were already poised for the battle when the Turkish offensive began. Preparations of the Turkish forces had been detected during the aerial surveillance.

When the attack began, the 19th Turkish Division on the right flank could not get things right at the beginning. The 5th Division was forced to take up position at a distance of 15-20 meters to the enemy line after suffering heavy casualties during the enemy fire at close range.

The heroic attack carried out by the 2nd Division, the striking power of the Turkish forces, fell through in the face of the enemy infantry's resistance and especially machine gun fire. The attacks were repeated along with forward march. At the end of offensive of the 2nd Division that lasted until the morning twilight, nearly half of division were either martyred or wounded between the trenches.

After the dawn, the situation seemed bleak: Turkish offensive had not been successful across the front. Turkish soldiers were lying on the ground martyred or wounded. Despite the gloomy state of affairs, a new order came to repeat the offensive. This time, the 19th Division gained some success at the beginning but could not hold their gains and had to retreat. At the centre, the 5th Division was unsuccessful in the head-to-head battle with the enemy that mainly used machine gunfire. The 2nd Division, after heavy losses, carried out an ineffective attack with weak forces. On the left flank, the 16th Division was not able to organise the attack. At 10 am, all the attacks across the frontline were stopped.

Casualties on the Turkish side after the 4-5 hour battle were about 10,000, including 3,800 martyrs.

The loss of 10,000 troops was the result of the uncoordinated and disorganised offensive of the Turkish forces in the face of well-fortified enemy positions supported with a large number of machine guns.

An 8-hour armistice was declared by General Birdwood and Esat Pasha on 24 May for mass burials of 3,000 Turkish martyrs who were lost during the 19 May offensive.

Intense fighting at close range was difficult for both sides. Hand grenades were causing about 300 deaths daily on both sides.

The close proximity of trench lines necessitated undermining or tunnel warfare, in which specialist miners dug tunnels and placed explosives beneath enemy trenches. With the detonation, the trenches would be destroyed and captured.

At *Arıburnu*, the first tunnel was dug in Bombasırtı by the 14th Regiment soldiers. Following the explosion, the attempt to seize the trench failed. Tunnel warfare, in which the ANZACs were also involved, went on until the end of the war.

Trench and tunnel warfare had been routine until 4 June when the ANZACs attacked the Turkish reserve unit, the 57th Regiment who were deployed to the south to join the Third Kirte Battle at *Seddülbahir*. Although the New Zealand troops initially captured two Turkish parapets, they had to set back after counter offensive of Turkish troops.

On 28 June, the British, in an attempt to conceal the Zığındere Battle at *Seddülbahir*, launched an assault on *Kanlısırt*. The ANZAC forces made some progress before they withdrew. Next day, Turkish troops began an offensive, at the presence of Enver Pasha, on Yükseksırt by the 18th Regiment. Due to the lack of support from the 57th Regiment, the offensive eventually failed with the loss of 800 troops.

Towards the end of July, battles both on the *Seddülbahir* and *Arıburnu* fronts had been deadlocked. Both sides concentrated on strengthening their positions and burying the dead. It appeared in the present circumstances that neither of the sides was be able to defeat the other.

This was far from the initial expectations of the Allied forces. They had to make a decision: Either to deploy new forces to break the stalemate or to evacuate Gallipoli. They chose the first option which meant the landing of Allied troops at *Anafartalar* as the last chance.

BATTLES AT ANAFARTALAR

How Did the Allies Decide to Land Troops at Anafartalar and Open a New Front?

The decision to either support the forces at Gallipoli or evacuate the region heavily depended on the situation on the western and eastern fronts. During the summer of 1915, the situation in Europe was not promising for the Allies in the face of Germany. In addition to the problems on the western front, Russian losses in the east obliged the Allies to make an attempt to win the war.

80,000 Allied troops who would be deployed to the western front in case of evacuation of Gallipoli had little prospect of changing the course of the war. On the other hand, if supported by enough reinforcements, the Allied troops would manage to invade the south of the Peninsula, to destroy the bastions along the Strait, to sweep the mines, and to open the way to İstanbul for the navy. This would ultimately leave the Ottoman Empire knocked out of the war. In this case, the Balkan states would take side with the Allies, Russia would be supported to launch joint attack on Germany-Austria and eventually the war would be won.

When viewed from this aspect, resuming the Gallipoli campaign seemed crucially important with a direct influence on the future of the Great War. A strong advocate of the campaign, Churchill, in the report he submitted to the new cabinet in June claimed that "there had remained no enough troops and ammunitions to get a result in the French front but a relatively small support to be given to Hamilton would change the things".

British War Minister Lord Kitchener, strongly opposing the idea of sending new troops to Gallipoli from the beginning, had to agree with Churchill, considering the gains to be won in case of success the only way out.

In the Council of War, convened in early July of 1915, Churchill and Kitchener persuaded the member of the council to send three new divisions to Gallipoli. These reinforcements, with the addition of two other divisions, were positioned in Limni and İmroz (Gökçeada) towards the end of July.

State of Affairs Prior to Anafartalar Landing and Arıburnu Offensive

When the Allied forces began preparations for a new offensive, the number of Turkish troops was about 250,000, including reserves.

Combat troops of the enemy forces, on the other hand, was 80,000. Total number of the enemy units would reach 150,000 with reinforcements.

Since 25 April, two divisions of the ANZAC troops under General Birdword had been stationed on the *Arıburnu* front which was one of the targets of 6 August offensive.

The Allied command had sent reinforcements to strengthen their presence at Gallipoli and to take control of *Kocaçimen-Conkbayırı-Düztepe-Kılıçbayırı* line, with the newly arrived

13th Division, a brigade of the 10th Division and the 29th Indian Brigade. With the arrival of these units comprising 25,000 men, the total number of troops under General Birdwood amounted to 37,000.

The Allied Strategy of the Arıburnu-Anafartalar Offensive and Preparations

Among the Allied powers, no consensus was reached about where to deploy the new troops. The French was insisting on landing two out of three British divisions at the Anatolian side while some favoured landing on *Bolayır*. However, the Allied Army Commander Hamilton had not given up the *Arıburnu-Anafartalar* plan, being prepared since early July.

The plan, initially drafted by the ANZAC Commander General Birdwood in June and later revised at the headquarters, seemed attractive for Hamilton, who himself had not believed that an offensive on *Seddülbahir* would provide positive outcomes.

The plan they worked on throughout July was quite complicated and detailed. The plan was kept confidential by Hamilton considering that if it was leaked to the Turkish army they would have to turn over a new leaf.

The offensive plan was formulated as follows: On the night of 6/7 August, two divisions to be landed at *Suvla* Bay would try to capture *Tekketepe* line behind *Küçük Anafarta* Village in the east of *Anafartalar* Plain and move towards *Kocaçimen Tepesi* in the south. Simultaneously, two offensive units consisting of 20,000 men would advance through *Sazlıdere, Çatlakdere, Ağıldere* valleys in the north of Arıburnu and take control of *Conkbayırı-Kocaçimen*. The two attack force would unite and encircle the Turkish forces on the *Arıburnu* front. If the Allied troops seized *Conkbayırı*, it would be impossible for the Turkish troops to hold ground in *Düztepe, Kılıçbayırı, Cesarettepe, Bombasırtı* and *Kanlısırt*. Therefore, they aimed to capture the *Arıburnu* front as soon as possible to make the Turkish forces in *Seddülbahir* sector caught between two fires.

Although the plan seemed perfect, its success depended on certain conditions like unexpected situations, structure of land, and resistance of Turkish soldiers.

Hamilton's plan was like a chain of offensive operations starting from the southernmost corner of Gallipoli Peninsula and spreading to *Anafartalar* in the northern end.

The Allied powers would deploy 70,000 new troops to the Peninsula for their last chance, increasing the total number of Allied soldiers to 150,000.

Defensive Measures taken by the Turkish Army Command against the Allied Offensive

Turkish Army Command was aware of the fact that the war had been going on despite they had managed to stop the enemy advance after 25 April landing. In August, they received the news about deployment of new troops to the enemy line. But the question was 'where would these troops land?'

The possible enemy landing zones encompassed within the area from *Enez* in the Gulf of *Saros* to southwards including *Bolayır, Suvla* Bay, south of *Kabatepe* or somewhere in the Anatolian side.

Taking this into account, 5th Army Commander Liman von Sanders had three divisions positioned in both *Saros* and the Anatolian side. These divisions would be able to move wherever the need arises. In addition, against the possibility of enemy advance to *Kocaçimentepe*, 'Anafarta Platoon' comprising five battalions supported by an artillery unit would be defending the area from Ece Harbour to Anafartalar.

At *Kumptepe,* located between the *Seddülbahir* and *Arıburnu* fronts, the 9th Reserve Division took up position against a possible enemy landing.

Both sides had completed the preparations by 6 August. The Allied offensive began on 6 August at 2.30 pm at *Seddülbahir.* The clashes that spread northward within that day were just the beginning of a five-day battle across the Peninsula.

Battles at Arıburnu-Anafartalar-Conkbayırı (6-10 August 1915)

Five-day battles that took place at *Seddülbahir, Arıburnu, Anafartalar* and *Conkbayırı* between 6 and 10 August were all complementary parts of a general plan carried out in different zones for the same goal.

Seddülbahir Region

The British army launched an offensive on *Seddülbahir* with an aim to cover landing at *Anafartalar* and to limit the time available to the Turkish side to deploy the reserves to main landing zone.

The operation began with the bombardment, at 2.30 pm, of Turkish positions on the right wing of the road from *Alçıtepe* to *Seddülbahir.* One-hour bombardment was followed by the British infantry's attack on the Turkish trenches defended by the 30th Regiment of the 10th Division. Initially, the British brigade made some gains, breaking through the first line of Turkish trenches but Turkish troops supported by reinforcements took the trenches back and inflicted heavy casualties on the

British side. During the offensive, the 88th British Brigade lost 2,000 out of 3,000 troops.

The main purpose of the Anglo-French offensive on *Seddülbahir* was to obstruct Turkish forces to deploy reinforcement from south to north. But the Turkish Army Command, realizing the main threat at *Arıburnu* and *Anafartalar*, gave orders, on 6 August at 7.20 pm, to the Southern Group that 'the 4th Division with its two regiments to be sent to the rear of the *Arıburnu* front'. Lt. Col. Cemil Bey immediately set off to the north on that night. Southern Group Commander Vehip Pasha sent, on his own initiative, the 12th Regiment to the north on the morning of 7 August in view of the threat emerged.

The British 42nd Division had not given up the offensive plan set for 7 August although the offensive by the 29th Division the day before had hit the wall. The offensive, if successful, would prevent the Turks at *Seddülbahir* from shifting troops to *Arıburnu* by keeping them under pressure.

The offensive on 7 August followed the same pattern: A heavy bombardment and flank attack. The British forces broke through the Turkish trenches in the east of *Alçıtepe-Seddülbahir* road but was not able to hold the ground. Suffering losses of some 1,500 men, they were repelled by the evening.

24-hour clashes between 6 and 7 August had left 3,500 casualties on the British side. Southern Group Commander Vehip Pasha responded his brother Northern Group Commander Esat Pasha's request for help by sending the 4th and 8th Divisions and the 28th and 41st Regiments and prevented the invasion of *Conkbayırı*.

After 8 August, *Seddülbahir* did not witness a large-scale movement, which was due to the fact that the Allied operations at *Anafartalar* and *Arıburnu* had come out. The British, instead of launching a new offensive on *Seddülbahir*, preferred to wait for the result of the operation in the north.

Arıburnu Region

As of 6 August, Turkish defensive line was positioned in two rows; the 19th Division running from *Sazlıdere* to southward and, to the left, the 16th Division from north to south.

Two regiments of the 5th Reserve Division were located in the north of *Kocadere* village. If needed, the 9th Division, defending the southern coast of *Kabatepe*, would also be deployed to the Northern Group.

Prior to the Allied offensive, the number of Turkish soldiers at *Arıburnu* had decreased to 20,000 due to the casualties. The Turkish command in the region noticed the landing of new Allied troops, which increased the possibility of an offensive.

In contrast, the number of ANZAC troops, as of 6 August, had been increased significantly. The total number was about 37,000 troops, including the 1st Australian Division and the 2nd ANZAC Division, both of whom had been at *Arıburnu* from the beginning, the 13th British division, 29th Irish Brigade and the 29th Indian Brigade.

The plan was to carry out an attack, on the night of 6/7 August, on *Conkbayırı* with the ANZAC 2nd Division and reinforcement units from *Arıburnu*. Before starting this offensive, two operations were to be performed in order to identify the Turkish units at *Arıburnu* and to prevent their deployment to the northern battlefield.

The first one to be launched in the afternoon on 6 August targeted the Turkish trenches at *Kanlısırt* while the second operation aimed to support the offensive forces supposed to arrive at *Conkbayırı* on the morning of 7 August by attacking the trenches at *Cesarettepe* (Nek).

Kanlısırt Offensive

Offensive on *Kanlısırt* began on 6 August at 3 pm with a preliminary bombardment of Turkish positions in an increasingly violent manner. All the naval and field artillery units were participating in the unprecedented offensive, whose main target was the trenches of the 47th Regiment.

Turkish trenches were covered with timber to get protection from balls and shrapnel shells   Fire was delivered from the loopholes inside the trenches. The bombardment, however, had led to the collapse of the timbers and the closure of the loopholes and trenches. Most of the soldiers inside the trenches had died or had been wounded. Survivors had been stunned by the release of gas from the shells.

At 5.30 pm, the artillery fire shifted to the ridges in the rear and four Australian battalions from the 1st Brigade launched attack in four waves on Turkish trenches at *Kanlısırt*. Turkish troops of the 47th Regiment were not able to open defence fire as most of them had been dead or wounded. Nor did they manage to resist the enemy with their bayonets. Few survivors tried to withstand the Australian troops fighting inside the trenches but could not stop the enemy from capturing the trenches at *Kanlısırt*.

The Northern Group Commander Esat Pasha immediately sent the 13th Reserve Regiment of the 5th Division and then the 1st Battalion of the 57th Regiment to *Kanlısırt*. Turkish forces began a counterattack at 7 pm but it failed.

Esat Pasha dispatched the 15th Regiment of the 5th Division, the last remaining reserve unit, to the frontline and ordered the 9th Division positioned at *Kayaltepe* under the command of German Colonel Kannengiesser to be sent to *Kanlısırt*.

With no reserve unit left under his command, Esat Pasha requested reinforcements from the 5th Army Command, drawing attention to the danger at *Arıburnu*. Liman von Sanders immediately transferred the 4th Division, a reserve unit in the Southern Group, to fight in the Northern Group.

The Northern Group Command attached great importance to taking back the trenches captured by the enemy at *Kanlısırt*. Therefore, all the Turkish units in the region, including the 15th Regiment, began an all-out-attack at 11 pm. The Turkish offensive that lasted until the morning ended inconclusive. Turkish troops were fighting to the death courageously. During the battle, Major Tevfik Bey, Commander of the 47th Regiment, and Lt. Col. İbrahim Şükrü Bey, Commander of the 15th Regiment, was martyred. Despite heavy casualties, Turkish forces failed in taking the trenches back.

Cesarettepe (Nek) Offensive

The second British offensive on the *Arıburnu* front was to start from *Yükseksırt* and spread towards *Kılıçbayırı* and *Cesarettepe*, where Sergeant Mehmet's Memorial lies today. General Birdwood had planned this attack to be carried out jointly with the offensive to be launched from the right wing on *Düztepe* after capturing *Conkbayırı* on 7 August. Undeterred by the delay in the deployment of new troops to *Conkbayırı* and few chances of success in the offensive, he insisted on the attack on *Cesarettepe*.

Two regiments of the 19th Division were defending the Turkish frontline here; the 18th Regiment at *Cesarettepe* and the 27th Regiment at *Kılıçbayırı*.

It was only at 4.30 am on the morning of 7 August, following half an hour bombardment, that the offensive commenced. The Australian units, comprising a total of four waves of 600 men, were fallen flat on their face in a jiffy in front of effective fire from the Turkish trenches (This attack was depicted in the final scene of 'Gallipoli', a movie produced in 1981 about the Battle of Gallipoli).

As the offensive on *Cesarettepe* turned out to be a failure for the British side and the area came under the Turkish control, more and more attention was devoted to the trenches at *Kanlısırt* once again. Esat Pasha was insisting upon retaking the trenches captured by the enemy troops despite a futile attempt that costed heavy casualties on the night of 6/7 August. In the order passed on to the Commander of the 16th Division Rüştü Bey, he said *"I certainly expect to hear from you that the trenches were taken back promptly at all costs"*. However, the shattered 16th Division went away empty-handed despite all attempts.

Esat Pasha assigned the 12th Regiment from the Southern Group to the command of the 16th Division on 8 August. They performed an offensive from two sides on *Kanlısırt* at 5 am. Some part of the second line of defence was taken back from the enemy, however, desperate attempts to recapture the first line failed.

The four-day battle at *Kanlısırt* had caused heavy damage on the 16th Division. Therefore, Turkish forces gave up the idea of launching a new attack after 10 August and strengthened the defence line. But the artillery bombardments persisted for days.

The offensive, first designed as diversion to cover the operation on *Conkbayırı-Kocaçimen*, turned out to be more than that; it was an immediate and serious danger for the

Turkish army at the *Arıburnu* front, because of which all the reserve units under the Northern Group had been deployed here. Turkish side had suffered heavy casualties during the offensives they carried out to regain lost ground without fail. Regiment commanders had bravely fought along with their soldiers to encourage them. Commander of the 47th Regiment Tevfik Bey had been martyred by a shell during the clashes.

The clashes at *Kanlısırt* between 6 and 9 August caused many losses on the Turkish side. Total number of Turkish casualties was 7,100, including martyrs, wounded and missing soldiers while the Australians lost 1,700 men.

Anafartalar Region

Commander of the British forces to be landed at *Suvla* Bay on the evening of 6 August was General Frederick Stopford, who had been to *Seddülbahir* previously in the middle of July and commanded the British Army Corps here. He was informed of the 6 August plan for the first time on 22 July. The British had already known that Turkish forces at *Anafartalar* comprised only three battalions. According to the plan and strict order given by the command, 11th Division of the British Army would quickly move and seize two strategically important points on the *Anafartalar* Plain, namely *Tekketepe* and *İsmailoğlutepe*, until the morning.

However, Stopford, though saying he would put in his utmost effort, seemed oblivious to the rigor of the plan. General Hamilton, without insisting on this point, had left Stopford at his own discretion in determining the next move on the ground after landing. Yet, this meant a big deviation from the proposed plan from the start and brought about the loss of precious moments for the British.

As for the Turkish side, the coast of *Anafartalar* was being defended by the Anafartalar Platoon made up of three battalions under the command of Lt. Col. Wilmer. The three battalions, totalling 3,000 troops, were Gallipoli Gendermarie Battalion situated at *Ece* Harbour in the east of *Kireçtepe*, Bursa Gendermarie Battalion located around *Küçük* and *Büyük Kemikli* Cape, and finally the 2nd Battalion of the 31st Regiment at *İsmailoğlutepe* and *Mestantepe*.

In the hands of the Turkish Army, the only units that could be sent to the region against *Suvla* landing were the 7th and 12th Divisions, also known as the Saros Group, on the Gallipoli-Bolayır zone. Distance of these units from *Anafartalar* was estimated to be approximately 30-40 km, which takes about a day to arrive at the landing spot. Therefore Anafartalar Platoon's mission was to keep the enemy busy at any cost until the arrival of reinforcements from *Saros*. Considering that the number of enemy troops to go ashore on the night of 6 August was about 25,000, it was apparently a difficult task.

General Hamilton was aware of the critical situation of the Turkish side and wanted the landing British troops to swiftly seize hills line on 7 August. But neither Stopford nor the 11th Division Commander Hammersley had recognized the vital importance of rapid action. Even, in the order given by Stopford to the brigade commanders, the only mention of advancing forward was to "seize the hills if possible".

First Battle of Anafartalar

In *Gökçeada*, the British 11th Division boarded the landing crafts on the night of 6 August and landed four battalions around *Küçük Kemikli* in the south of *Suvla* Bay at 10 pm without having any confrontation. A Turkish surveillance squad here withdrew after shooting rounds of fire on the enemy until they ran out of bullets. The British troops chased the Turkish force and was met by Turkish despatch rider unit near *Lalebaba*. However, this small force was forced to retreat further back and thus *Lalebaba* was captured by the British.

Turkish soldiers opened fire on the British brigade which came ashore at *Büyük Kemikli* Cape in the north of *Suvla* Bay. Hardly ashore, the British brigade began an offensive against *Softatepe*. Bursa Gendarmerie Battalion defending the region resisted the British forces until 3 am. The Battalion both inflicted heavy casualties on the British troops and kept them busy for a while.

On that night, the 11th Division was able to disembark troops at *Suvla* Bay but stalled in the face of stubborn resistance of Bursa Gendarmerie Battalion and did not find the opportunity to move forward.

In the morning, the Irish 10th Division also landed in the north of *Suvla* Bay. Now the British had two divisions of about 25,000 troops at the bay. There remained only the Anafartalar Platoon between the British troops and the hill line surrounding the *Anafartalar* Plain which was the main target of *Suvla* landing.

On the morning of 7 August, the Turkish troops at *Softatepe* were repelled by the British brigade, who then advanced to *Karakoldağı*.

Seeing that they were threatened by the enemy from both sides, Bursa Gendarmerie Battalion set to retreat to *Sülecik* and its north in *Küçük Anafarta* direction. Here, they fired the British back, forcing them to withdraw.

The advancing British brigade to seize *Mestantepe* in the south of *Suvla* Bay was met by the 2nd Battalion of the 31st Regiment. Occupying the British troops until sunset, the battalion retreated to the eastern *İsmailoğlutepe* at dusk.

The task of the detachments monitoring the coast on the *Anafartalar* Plain was to prevent the enemy landing as much as possible. In addition, without entering into serious clash with the enemy, they were supposed to set back to the main defence line in the rear, taking the risk of being encircled into consideration. Because, for the British army corps of 25,000 troops, seizing *Küçük Anafarta-Tekketepe* line, driving the Turkish detachments of 3,000 troops eastward, was not difficult at all.

Devotedly fulfilling their duties, Turkish battalions in the area prevented the British advance and inflicted casualties on the enemy soldiers by using convenient hiding places as possible. So, the British troops ashore abstained from moving forward. This gave the Turkish forces the opportunity to bring up reinforcements.

The 5th Army Commander Liman von Sanders ordered the deployment of the 7th and 12th Divisions as quickly as possible to Anafartalar since reinforcements after the enemy landing at *Suvla* Bay, upon which the 7th Division on the morning of 7 August and the 12th Division at noon headed for *Anafartalar*.

Meanwhile, the two newly deployed divisions, the Anafartalar Platoon and the units already situated around *Kocaçimen-Conkbayırı* were all united under the command of Ahmet Fevzi Bey as Anafatalar Group. The order was issued at 10 pm by the Army Command.

The newly established Anafartalar Group's Commander Fevzi Ahmet Bey quickly arrived in the region and received reports. Accordingly, the situation was as follows as of 7 August:

British soldiers landed on the north and south of *Suvla* Bay seized *Mestantepe*. The opposing Turkish forces on this flank were Bursa Gendarmerie Battalion at *İsmailoğlutepe* and the 2nd Battalion of the 31st Regiment.

British forces aimed to advance in *Kireçtepe* direction after capturing *Karakoldağı*. *Kireçtepe* was under Gallipoli Gendarmerie Battalion's control while no movement was seen on the *Anafartalar* Plain.

On the night of 7 August, at 10 pm, the 7th Division had reached the *Sivli* village behind the *Anafartalar* front. A regiment of the 12th Division was also there but the other two regiments were yet to arrive. Liman von Sanders gave the order, without losing any time, to attack the British army on the morning of 8 August.

The offensive which was planned to begin on the morning of 8 August ordered by the Army Commander fell through because some units of the 12th Division had not reached yet. Then, Liman von Sanders updated the time of the offensive as the evening of the same day. According to the plan, the 12th Division would aim at *Mestantepe* through *Küçük Anafarta* while the 7th Division would attack the Australian units that threatened *Kocaçimen*.

Colonel Ahmed Fevzi Bey wanted to get the views of the division commanders on the offensive in a meeting. Both commanders stated that the troops had been very tired and sleepy after a 30-40 km walk under the scorching hot sun. Drawing attention to the possible dangers of the attack at dusk in an unknown area, they came out in favour of the attack being carried out next morning at dawn.

As no British advance had been detected on the *Anafartalar* Plain, Fevzi Bey agreed with the commanders who saw no need for urgent action. So, taking all the responsibility, he delayed the offensive to the next morning, which would have serious consequences for himself.

It happened just that way. Liman von Sanders burst with anger over the postponement of the offensive. Fevzi Bey was removed from the Anafartalar Group Command and, on 8 August, he was replaced by Mustafa Kemal, commander of the 19th Division, who was given the order to launch the delayed attack on the morning of 9 August.

Meanwhile, the British army, interestingly enough, was experiencing a similar kind of crisis. General Hamilton's order to take hold of *Tekketepe* after landing at *Anafartalar* was not fulfilled due to General Stopford's negligence and recklessness.

Angry with this situation, Hamilton sent one of his staff officers, Aspinall, to *Suvla* to get the latest news from Stopford. Aspinall, arriving at *Suvla* on 8 August before the noon, thought that the targeted hills had been taken since everything was calm at the harbour and the beach was full of soldiers bathing in the sea. Aspinall noticed that Stopford was on board and had never come ashore. Aspinall delivered what had been expected of Stophord and hurried him to move without losing time. Stopford, however, mentioned that they could move the next day due to the overall fatigue and heavy casualties suffered.

Getting the news about Stopford's approach, Hamilton paid a personal visit to *Suvla*. He sternly warned Stopford for acting slowly, pointing out that Turkish reserve units had been on their way to *Suvla*. He was thinking that the following morning Turkish forces would take over the *Anafartalar* hills; therefore, warned that immediate action was needed. Upon his insistence and warning, a British brigade of the 11th Division was given the duty of seizing *Tekketepe* before the dawn.

And so now began a desperate race against time for both sides. On the night of 8 August, Turkish forces were making preparations for the offensive on *Anafartalar* while the British side was starting to move to capture *Tekketepe*.

Mustafa Kemal took over the command of the Anafartalar Group on 9 August, the day after he met with the 5th Army Chief Kazım Bey, shared his concerns over the approaching British attack on *Conkbayırı-Kocaçimen* and even finally stated that there remained no other way but putting all the units in the region under his own command.

On the morning of 9 August, at 4 am, Mustafa Kemal issued an order to all the troops under his command to follow the same plan prepared and instructed by Ahmet Fevzi Bey.

On the night of 8/9 August, two Turkish divisions, arriving from *Saros* region, completed preparations for the offensive while British corps simultaneously started to move upon the order given by Hamilton after two-day delay.

The 12th Division, taking up position near *Tekketepe-Kavaktepe*, began the offensive in the morning against the British forces located at *Sülecik-Mestantepe*. The 35th Regiment of the 12th Division confronted the British 11th Division, while descending into the plain from *Tekketepe*, and forced them to retreat after a sudden attack.

The British units advancing towards *İsmailoğlutepe* was met by the 34th Regiment, which halted the British advance and strengthened the position there.

Two squadrons attached to the Gallipoli Gendermarie Battalion slowed down the British troops moving forward through the ridges of *Kireçtepe*. But the squadrons were forced to back off in the face of superior enemy forces. With the support of three new squadrons, Turkish soldiers were able to stop the enemy in *Arslantepe* sector.

The objective of the 7th Division, ordered to attack on *Damakçılık Bayırı*, was to repel the Australian forces advancing towards *Kocaçimen*. Thus, the right flank of the Turkish units in *Kocaçimen-Conkbayırı* line would be secured. In addition, this would prevent the enemy forces from combining with the newly landing British units and creating a continuous front line with the ANZAC troops in the north of *Arıburnu*.

The Turkish forces suffered massive losses during the offensive on *Damakçılık Bayırı* in the face of well-fortified Australian positions supported by numerous machine guns. When two regiments of the 7th Division lost their commanders, one dead and one wounded, the offensive had to be stopped.

When the First Battle of Anafartalar ended by 9 August, the hills surrounding the Anafartalar Plain was under the Turkish control. Wasting time on the coast when they first landed, the defeated British corps, consisting of 25,000 troops, had missed a 'golden opportunity', as referred by the British.

Turkish units, 13 battalions in total, had won a tremendous victory against the 22 British battalions. After the fruitless operation of the British, which they aimed to extend from *Suvla* towards *Kocaçimen, Kireçtepe*, the ridges of *Anafartalar* and *İsmailoğlutepe* remained in the hands of Turkish forces.

Conkbayırı Region

The crucial point of the Arıburnu-Anafartalar Operation, also called 'Anzac Plan' by the British, was the outflanking manoeuvre into *Conkbayırı-Kocaçimen* direction from *Arıburnu*.

While all the attention of the Turkish command was concentrated on the offensive carried out on *Kanlısırt* on 6 August, the Allied Army Commander Hamilton put his main plan into practice.

According to the plan, 20,000 troops under the command of General Goodley, passing through the valley in the north of *Arıburnu*, would seize *Kocaçimen-Conkbayırı-Düztepe* line before sunrise, which would presumably bring about the collapse of Turkish defensive line on the Arıburnu front. They would then reach the Dardanelles and all the roads leading to the south of the Peninsula would be brought under control.

In fact, debates on enemy intentions to move towards *Kocaçimen-Conkbayırı* line after an offensive on Ağıldere sector, relatively weak in the north of Turkish front at *Arıburnu*, had been a matter of discussion between Mustafa Kemal and Esat Pasha two months ago in June. Mustafa Kemal had anticipated the 6 August offensive, laying emphasis on the importance of *Ağıldere*, and requested a clarification on chain of command and order in the region.

On the night of 6/7 August, an enemy unit, setting out from *Arıburnu*, as exactly predicted by Mustafa Kemal, turned to *Conkbayırı* through *Halid Rıza Tepesi-Pilavtepe-Keskintepe-Şahinsırt* direction.

Turkish positions were located along an outpost line defended by the 2nd Battalion of the 14th Regiment. It was almost impossible for the Turkish units scattered over a very wide area to stop an enemy force of 20,000 troops.

British offensive forces began the attack on 6 August at 10 pm. First attacks were launched on Turkish outposts at *Halid Rıza Tepesi, Keskintepe, Pilavtepe* and *Yaylatepe.*

The British plan was based on raids and quick attacks; therefore, they resorted to some tricks of war. One of these tricks was prepared to seize the strongly-held *Halid Rıza Tepesi.*

Danger posed by the enemy offensive was not initially grasped by the Turkish side. Esat Pasha was directing all the reserve units to *Kanlısırt.* Yet, the British had attacked the 2nd Battalion in Ağıldere and cleared the way for Kocaçimen-Conkbayırı. It was Mustafa Kemal who first realized the danger at Conkbayırı after receiving information on the British offensive on *Ağıldere.*

The 19th Division, defending the area from today's 57th Infantry Regiment's Cemetery to Sergeant Mehmet's Memorial, came under heavy fire on the evening of 6 August. However, a greater threat for the 19th Division had emerged somewhere else. Enemy forces advancing from Ağıldere had targeted *Conkbayırı* via *Şahinsırt.* In case of the fall of *Conkbayırı,* the right flank and back of the 19th Division would face an extremely dangerous threat and the Arıburnu front would completely collapse.

In the face of this dangerous situation, Mustafa Kemal immediately deployed two squadrons under his command and the 1st Battalion of the 14th Regiment, sent by Esat Pasha as reinforcements, to *Conkbayırı.*

The commander of the 1st Battalion of the 14th Regiment was ordered to confront the enemy at *Conkbayırı.* Two squadrons from 1st Battalion of the 72nd Regiment were tasked with closing the road from *Şahinsırt* and *Sazlıdere* to *Conkbayırı.* These units managed to stop the enemy forces at *Şahinsırt* and

Conkbayırı until the arrival of the 9th Division dispatched by Esat Pasha.

The 9th Division, defending *Kumtepe* sector in the south of *Kabatepe*, was sent to *Kanlısırt* due to the Australian capture of Turkish trenches in the region. When a threat emerged in *Kocaçimen-Conkbayırı* line, the 9th Division was directed to *Conkbayırı* by Esat Pasha because of its vital importance.

The German Colonel Kannengiesser, commander of the 9th Division, paid a visit to *Conkbayırı* on the morning of 7 August and saw the situation up close. *Conkbayırı* was in the hands of the Turkish troops that included the 1st Battalions of the 14th and 72nd Regiments. Towards afternoon, the 25th and 64th Regiments also reached the region, which formed a solid front line for the Turkish forces.

Meanwhile, the left flank of the British forces redirected their action towards *Ağıldere* in the northern side of *Kocaçimen*. Turkish troops from the 2nd Battalion of the 14th Regiment and the 1st Battalion of the 32nd Regiment were trying to stop their advance.

The German Colonel Kannengiesser, taking the command in *Conkbayırı* region, dispatched the 64th Regiment of the 9th Division to support the 14th Regiment fighting with the enemy in *Asmadere*. The 25th Regiment was also ordered to join the attack in *Conkbayırı*.

At 8 am, two regiments of the 9th Division formed a strong line so as to block the New Zealand troops from expanding their control at *Şahinsırt*. Just then Colonel Kannengiesser got wounded and had to be replaced by Lt. Col. Cemil Bey, commander of the 4th Division previously dispatched to *Arıburnu* from *Seddülbahir*. The Turkish force at *Conkbayırı* was further strengthened with the arrival of the 11th Regiment on 7 August and the 33rd Regiment on 8 August.

On the morning of 8 August, at 3.30 am, the New Zealand troops launched an attack on *Conkbayırı*. They were unexpectedly successful to take control of the area from the western slopes of *Conkbayırı* -beachside of the Hill 261- to the fountain located by the road in the south of *Conkbayırı*.

Easy capture of the trenches by the New Zealand units resulted from the withdrawal of Turkish troops from the outposts which were left only with watchmen and a machine gun. Lack of attention by these watchmen created an opportunity for the enemy to capture the trenches.

On 8 August, the 64th Regiment under the command of Lt. Col. Servet Bey struggled to take back the trenches from the enemy that posed great danger at *Conkbayırı* but failed to clean up the region, though inflicting heavy casualties on the New Zealand side.

As of the noon of 8 August, the situation at *Conkbayırı* seemed that of a face to face battle, the distance between the two sides being as close as 25-30 meters.

On the very same day, all the units at *Kocaçimen-Conkbayırı* had been banded together in the Anafartalar Group under the command of Colonel Ahmet Fevzi Bey. Also, Lt. Col. Cemil Bey, who commanded the unit at *Conkbayırı*, was replaced by the German Lt. Col. Pötrih, who succeeded Kanengiesser as the commander of the 9th Division.

The 8th Division commanded by Colonel Ali Rıza Bey, a reserve unit in the Southern Group, was deployed to *Conkbayırı* as well. Immediately after the arrival at the region, they launched an offensive on the enemy forces but was not able to pull them back.

Before dawn on 9 August, the British troops launched a massive attack on *Conkbayırı-Besimtepe-Kocaçimentepe*. This attack was quite effective on Besimtepe which came under the control of the Gurka units of Nepals attached to the Indian Brigade. Meanwhile Turkish forces positioned at *Abdurrahman Bayırı* inflicted casualties on the Gurka forces with a heavy and effective bombardment from well-aimed artilleries. Finally Turkish infantry units began a counter offensive and took *Conkbayırı* back from the enemy.

As of the evening, the zone had been under the control of Turkish forces. The only area that the British would be effective were the trenches on the beachside of *Conkbayırı*.

Conkbayırı Bayonet Charge on 10 August 1915

On the night of 9/10 August, the situation in *Conkbayırı* was as follows:

The 23rd and 24th Regiments of the 8th Division were located 20-30 meters opposite of the enemy forces in *Conkbayırı-Şahinsırt* line. To the left, the 10th Regiment was holding *Düztepe* all the way from the Hill 261. To the far-left was the 19th Division's front. The 25th and 26th Regiments of the 9th Division and two battalions of the 33rd Regiments were located between *Conkbayırı* and *Kocaçimen*.

Southern ridges of *Asmaderesi* and *Abdurrahman Bayırı* were being defended by two battalions from both the 14th and 11th Regiments and one battalion from 32nd Regiment. To the right of this line was the front of the 7th Division, which had participated in the Battle of Anafartalar on 9 August.

Conkbayırı-Kocaçimen defense line was under the control of ten regiments from five different divisions, intermingled in some places. Only the 23rd and 24th Regiments of the 8th Division were in regular position.

Commander of Anafartalar Group, Mustafa Kemal had planned an attack, at sunrise on the morning of 10 August, to be launched by the 28th and 41st Reserve Regiments, who were about to arrive from the Southern Group to *Conkbayırı*.

At 10 pm, the 28th Regiment was reported to be close but no news was heard about the 41st Regiment.

Mustafa Kemal expressed the details of the plan, to be implemented next morning, to the commanders at the headquarters of the 8th Division, whose commander Captain Ali Rıza Bey and chief of staff Galip Bey opposed the operation. They voiced their concerns by reminding of the non-stop but unsuccessful offensive carried out for the last two days in *Conkbayırı*, which resulted in heavy casualties. They further stated that these exhausted forces would not be used for a new offensive. Moreover, it was not certain that the two incoming regiments would necessarily accomplish the task that had not been fulfilled so far. At the end of the day, it would not be reasonable to perform the offensive with only one regiment as the other one had not arrived yet.

Objections of the commanders to the timing of the operation on *Anafartalar* were based on valid grounds. First of all, moving from *Saros*, the soldiers had walked in a day a distance of 30-40 km under the sun; carrying bags weighing approximately 20 kg, they were tired and sleepless for the last 24 hours. Halil Bey, commander of the 7th Division, intimately knew the hazards of the overnight attack in a large and unknown field, as ordered by Liman von Sanders, because, in early May, he had participated in such attacks carried out in *Seddülbahir* and resulted in heavy casualties. On the other hand, although the British troops landed at *Suvla* had advanced a bit, the *Anafartalar* Plain was empty. Therefore, there seemed no need to care about the urgency of a night attack. Time difference between the Army Commander's order of offensive and Ahmet Fevzi Bey's offer was only 7-8 hours. Indeed, after Ahmet Fevzi Bey was removed from his post and replaced by Mustafa Kemal, his plan was implemented without ever changing at the very time he had determined.

In contrast, the situation was different at *Conkbayırı*. British Army Command had changed the tired ANZAC forces, which had suffered heavy losses, with the newly arrived brigades attached to the 13th Division. They also increased the Allied forces in and around *Conkbayırı*. In other words, the enemy was also preparing for a new offensive.

In *Conkbayırı*, both sides were positioned at a distance of 30-40 meters from each other. Behind the positions were steep slopes, and in some places, cliffs. Seizure of *Conkbayırı* Hill was possible for both sides. But it was a matter of who would take the action first. Having realized that, Mustafa Kemal considered a bayonet attack necessary with the existing forces despite all the objections and unfavourable conditions.

The decision was made. The offensive would be carried out. The 41st Reserve Regiment was not a part of the plan. On the front line, the 24th Regiment and some individual units would be located 20-30 meters away from the enemy line. Behind these units, the 23rd Regiment was to be deployed at a position overlooking *Conkbayırı* while the new comer 28th Regiment would hold the position overlooking *Şahinsırt*. Quiet and well-organised, they would be positioned 20-30 steps behind the front line combatants.

Soldiers would only use their bayonets. Guns and artilleries would not be allowed. It was planned as a truly sneak attack. At a pre-determined time, offensive blocks would lunge at the enemy and front line fighters would join them.

The 41st Regiment had been absent by the time the offensive began. Therefore, the 23rd and the 28th Regiments moved immediately into attack formation, the former towards *Conkbayırı* and the latter towards *Şahinsırt*.

All the preparations were completed on 10 August in the morning at 04.30. And lastly, Mustafa Kemal addressed the soldiers before the offensive:

"Soldiers! There is no doubt that we will defeat the enemy. But do not rush. First, I go forward. You lunge at the enemy altogether when I mark my whip."

Everyone was ready for the attack: Officers at the forefront were holding their guns and swords. Troops were holding their bayonets with their eyes peeled. As soon as they heard 'the time has come' command, they all rushed forward, shouting 'Allah, Allah'.

The attack was so sudden that the enemy could not find the opportunity to use their weapons. The enemy forces were defeated with a bayonet charge in the British trenches after a bitter struggle.

Devoted Turkish soldiers were fired up, jumping over the enemy trenches and proceeding ahead. Even those who witnessed the scene described that the Turkish soldiers were chasing the enemy as if they flew over the hillside.

The 23rd and 24th Regiments had completely wiped out the enemy from *Conkbayırı*. The 23rd Regiment run after the fleeing enemy troops. They engaged in close combat with the

British brigade under the command of General Baldwin near *Ağıl* (called Farm by the British), just below *Conkbayırı*. Hours-long bayonet fighting was the fiercest and the most terrifying one ever witnessed in Gallipoli. The British took heavy casualties here, including General Baldwin and chief of staff.

Meanwhile, the 28th Regiment advanced in *Şahinsırt* direction, but could not go further after heavy losses due to machine gunfire and land-sea bombardment.

Following the successful bayonet attack in *Conkbayırı*, the 9th Turkish Division, located on the ridges of *Kocaçimen-Abdurrahman Bayırı* region in the north, wiped out the Australian and Indian brigades from the hillside and captured the ridges of *Çamçık Pınarı*.

Turkish forces eliminated the British threat across *Kocaçimen-Conkbayırı* region. *Şahinsırt* was the only vital position left under the British control. But it was not easy to attack on these well-fortified positions under the land and sea bombardment. Therefore, Turkish forces were ordered to stop advancing and strengthen their positions.

Mustafa Kemal had personally commanded the bayonet charge just behind the firing line. He had never left this dangerous zone throughout the battles. A cannon fired from the British battleship exploded very close to Mustafa Kemal. A shrapnel coming from the shell hits Mustafa Kemal's right chest. The shrapnel was stopped by the chain watch in his pocket. As a memory for the victory, Mustafa Kemal gave the shattered watch to the Commander of the Fifth Army, Liman von Sanders, as a gift. In return, Liman gave his own watch to Mustafa Kemal as a gift.

On 10 August, Turkish troops who participated in *Conkbayırı* offensive moved forward without intimidation despite intensive and effective artillery fire and advanced beyond the enemy lines. At 1 pm, when the battle ended, the commanding heights within an area of 2 km from the Hill 261 to *Conkbayırı* and from *Besimtepe* to *Kocaçimentepe*, including the ridges -with a depth of 500-600 meters- descending seaward, had all came under Turkish control, except for the western slopes of *Şahinsırt*.

The British launched a new offensive on 13 August at *Kavaktepe-Tekketepe* zone after their successive defeats at the First Battle of Anafartalar on 9 August and at *Conkbayırı* on 10 August. Their advance was halted by the 35th and 36th Regiments, leaving 700 casualties at the British side.

Battle of Kireçtepe (15-16 August 1915)

The British, who had been unable to pass through the centre at *Anafartalar*, decided to advance on the ridges of *Kireçtepe*, to the far right of the Turkish defence line. Capturing the ridges, their next aim was to wind around *Tekketepe* and encircle the 12th Division at the *Anafartalar* Plain.

On 15 August 1915, the British forces supported by naval gunfire were encountered by the Gallipoli Gendarmerie Battalion under the command of Captain Kadri, who had been defending the ridges since the landing. The Battalion had to set back despite the reinforcements from the 19th and 39th Regiments, thus leaving two hills at *Kireçtepe* to the British control.

Turkish soldiers launched a counter attack and took *Aslantepe* back. Battles at *Kireçtepe* had continued on 16 August, specifically escalated at *Aslantepe*. While both sides fought hand to hand with bayonets, the hill had changed hands, finally falling under the control of the Turkish side. The retreating British forces took up position at *Sivritepe*. British casualties consisted of 2,000 soldiers while the Turkish losses were around 1,700.

Captain Kadri, who bravely commanded his battalion during the battles, had been martyred, too.

Second Battle of Anafartalar (21 August 1915)

Having been defeated in all offensive operations at *Anafartalar*, the British worked on a last-ditch effort to break through the Turkish defence. They amassed a force of some 30,000 troops with reinforcements from *Seddülbahir* region. Although the offensive would flare across all *Anafartalar* front, the initial targets were *İsmailoğlutepe* and *Bombatepe*. Thus, the link with the ANZAC troops at the left flank of *Arıburnu* front would be established.

On the Turkish side, however, Anafartalar Group Commander Mustafa Kemal, being aware of the preparations for an offensive on the British side, pulled the reserve units under his command towards the frontline. Turkish force here comprised four combat divisions and two reserve divisions.

As usual, the battle started under heavy artillery bombardment on 21 August at 2.30 pm. First target of the British troops was *Yusufçuktepe*; however, their advance was stopped by Turkish flanking fire.

The British offensive on the trenches of the 7th Division near *Kayacıkağılı* was relatively successful. The enemy had captured some positions in the nightlong clashes. As of 22 August, the British made minor gains at *Yusufçuktepe* and *Kayacıkağılı* region but could get no further forward.

At the end of the Second Battle of Anafartalar, the result was bleak for the British. They suffered the highest number of casualties in an offensive they launched with the highest number of troops on the broadest front. Their casualties were almost 8,000 while the Turkish side lost nearly 3,000 troops.

Battle of Bombatepe (27 August 1915)

The last major British offensive at *Anafartalar* region was performed on 27 August on *Bombatepe* which was strategically important as a link between *Anafartalar* and ANZAC fronts. The offensive followed a heavy bombardment on 27 August in the mid-afternoon. Southern slopes of *Bombatepe* were seized by the enemy forces, who maintained the offensive all night long until the morning. Turkish troops managed to stop the attack which left heavy casualties for both sides. The British loss amounted to 1,100 and the Turkish casualties were about 700.

Battle of Bombatepe was the last large-scale British offensive at *Anafartalar-Arıburnu* region, after which the battles here turned into trench wars. Bloody battles that sealed Gallipoli's fate were fought around *Anafartalar-Arıburnu* between 6 and 28 August. Turkish soldiers, despite suffering great losses, were able to shatter enemy's hopes by throwing a monkey wrench into their plans. Turkish forces demonstrated great courage and devotion in the battles where thousands of soldiers were martyred alongside nine regiment commanders.

Evaluating the Arıburnu-Anafartalar Front

During the battles on the *Arıburnu* front, Turkish side was more on the offensive until June. With the ANZAC troops stranded on the coastal zone, Turkish command dominating the central zone headed for the offensive. Persistent attacks on 1 and 19 May yield nothing but countless martyrs and wounded soldiers. Until August, battles at *Arıburnu* were more like trench wars, including artillery attacks.

During the landings at *Anafartalar* in August, the *Arıburnu* front played a tactically significant role for the Allied forces, who undertook a coordinated offensive operation in the two fronts. In response, Turkish army formed a new command centre, Anafartalar Group, for the defence of the region.

The Allied offensive on *Arıburnu-Anafartalar* region began with the landings at *Anafartalar* and ended with Turkish bayonet attack on 10 August. During the five-day battle, the British side had lost 12,000 out of 37,000 troops. The remaining British force would only be able to hold the existing positions, and there remained no possibility of undertaking an offensive. Thus, the 'ANZAC Plan', developed by General Birdwood to seize *Sarıbayır* zone had failed before it started.

The plan to control *Conkbayırı-Kocaçimen* line looked perfect on paper, yet what was more important was how to implement it. From the very beginning, unforeseen circumstances had influenced the course of the offensive. These included rugged terrain in *Ağıldere* region, the guide's wrong choices on the directions, stubborn resistance of Turkish soldiers, and inability of the commanders in making right decisions and putting the required effort.

On the other hand, Turkish command had opened some doors for the British by paying greater attention to the enemy operation on *Kanlısırt* and leaving *Conkbayırı-Kocaçimen* zone unprotected. But timely intervention of Turkish commanders (Esat Pasha and Mustafa Kemal) helped the Turkish forces ride out the storm.

The most salient phase of the British offensive on *Arıburnu-Anafartalar* was the seizure of *Kocaçimen-Conkbayırı* zone, which would facilitate further gains in the south, especially *Düztepe-Kılıçbayırı* line. The British considered that Turkish troops would be forced to retreat if encircled in *Arıburnu*. The fall of *Arıburnu* front would lead to the British advance up to the Strait and closing of access roads used by Turkish troops in the south of the Peninsula.

The offensive operation that would bring enormous advantages for the British army and would ultimately break the Gallipoli deadlock had been repulsed by the bravery and devotion of Turkish soldiers. Anafartalar victory on 9 August and Conkbayırı Bayonet Charge on 10 August wrecked the enemy's hopes. The offensive launched after long preparations had been smashed by Turkish bayonet.

The days between 6 and 10 August had been historic moments for the Turkish army. All the battlefields across Gallipoli had witnessed heroic defence of Turkish troops, who had duly performed their duties and sacrificed their lives.

An obvious example of this struggle is Conkbayırı Bayonet Charge. During the fighting at *Conkbayırı*, Turkish troops had rushed forward to attack the enemy as if they were jumping off a cliff, thus adding a new page on the glorious book of Turkish history.

Harmony and coordination of efforts among Turkish commanders positively affected the general atmosphere in the army. This was clearly seen in the defence of *Kocaçimen-Conkbayırı* zone, where the Northern Group Commander asked help from the Southern Group, whose commander Vehip Pasha had not declined the request despite the Anglo-French offensive at *Seddülbahir* in the south of the Peninsula. He initially sent the 4th and 8th Reserve Divisions to the north. On 9 August, upon the request by the Northern Group Commander Esat Pasha, he deployed the last remaining regiments, namely the 28th and 41st, under his control to support the defence in *Conkbayırı* which had been under serious threat of enemy forces (Vehip Pasha and Esat Pasha were brothers).

The seizure of *Conbayırı* by New Zealanders is a controversial issue even today. The New Zealand Memorial located on top of *Conkbayırı* signified that the point had been seized. However, the Turks claim that the hilltop had never been captured by the enemy, which is, according to the claim, demonstrated by Mustafa Kemal Atatürk Monument nearby.

To elaborate, the New Zealand troops captured, on 8 August, the zone between Conkbayırı and Hill 261, where today Mehmetçik Epitaph stands. This zone was not the hilltop but the beachside slope of the hill, on 20 meters west to the hilltop. Right across, on the eastern side of the hill top, Turkish positions were located 30-40 meters away. Consequently, the 200-meter long hilltop was the buffer zone between the two sides.

Uninterrupted bloody battles at *Arıburnu-Anafartalar-Conkbayırı* regions between 6 and 10 August had left countless casualties for both sides.

Turkish casualties within five days were around 20,000 in total; 6,000 at *Kanlısırt*, 9,200 at *Conkbayırı*, 3,000 at *Anafartalar* and 1,800 at *Cesarettepe-Kılıçbayırı* sector.

As for the British, the number of casualties was higher: 2,000 at *Kanlısırt*, 12,000 at *Conkbayırı*, 8,400 at *Anafartalar* and 2,600 at *Cesarettepe-Kılıçbayırı*, thus amounting to 25,000 in total.

Glorious victory of 'Turkish bayonet' at Gallipoli belonged to all of the members of the Turkish army, from the privates to the highest-ranking commanders. Likewise, at *Conkbayırı*, all the regiments deserved great credit for the victory they won. The victory also brought Colonel Mustafa Kemal into prominence. Especially, his successive victories at *Anafartalar* and *Conkbayırı* on 9-10 August had added new heroic pages to his career. In a short time, he became famous as the 'hero of Anafartalar and Conkbayırı' across the country. Doubtless, his deserved fame after the victory at Gallipoli played great role in his acceptance by the nation as a trusted leader in the Turkish War of Independence.

Sergeant Mehmed at Cesarettepe-Arıburnu

The most common name of the soldiers reputed for their courage in the Battle of Gallipoli was Mehmed. During the naval battles before the start of the land wars, Sergeant Mehmed had participated in the defence of Seddülbahir against the 200-men enemy landing aimed at destroying Turkish artilleries on 4 March 1915. Mehmed, serving with the 3rd Battalion of the 27th Regiment, had attacked the enemy with stones after his gun broke down. Wounded in the head, Sergeant Mehmed was granted a medal upon Mustafa Kemal's offer of award.

Another Sergeant Mehmed, renowned for his bravery in Gallipoli, was fighting at the right flank of Arıburnu front. He defended the trench with his comrades for days.Originally from Mecidiye district of Kırşehir, Sergeant Mehmed had fought in the Balkan Wars and got wounded. Upon mobilisation order, the experienced sergeant was recruited again during the Battle of Gallipoli.

New arrivals began to strengthen the defence in Arıburnu where the enemy troops landed on 25 April. The 64th Reserve Regiment had arrived on 27 April. The 3rd Battalion of this regiment was assigned to defend the right flank of the front.

Sergeant Mehmed, the platoon commander in the battalion, was defending a hill with his unit on 27 April. The hill was a direct target of the enemy offensive. Sergeant Mehmed, who was in aged soldiers battalion, ordered the team to move forward without receiving orders from his commanders as he recognized the strategic importance of the hill. He captured the hill with a heroic attack on the enemy. While Mehmed and his comrades were taking up position, the clashes escalated. After a while Sergeant Mehmed, who had completely lost touch with the regiment behind, was suddenly left alone with his friends in the middle of the enemy trenches. At that time, the sergeant and his team of up to 60 men had fought against a superior enemy force for about a week. There was no hope of any help and assistance. Alone they had to prevent the advance of the enemy in their own strength and sacrifice so that they would protect the right flank by holding the hill. They clashed day and night continuously for seven days. Eventually, they ran out of ammunition and food as well. This time, one or two bouncers from the team came to offer them some refreshments. With the darkness, they successfully came passing closer to the enemy lines, crawling on the ground and bringing ammunition, food and beverages from the units fighting in the left side.

The same situation repeated itself within a week. With determination and enthusiasm, they fought with the enemy persistently. All the soldiers in the team were wounded and Mehmed was shot three times. The enemy troops did not know exactly what to do when these brave soldiers came up unexpectedly. The enemy was only mowing down their position. Nevertheless, it was a futile attempt as Sergeant Mehmed and his team were rooted to the spot.

There came a moment when Sergeant Mehmed considered staying always on the defensive inappropriate. He launched a massive attack on the patrol team and routed them. This latest incident demoralised the enemy and the attacks on the hill were eased off. On the other hand, the regiment left behind had repelled the enemy. At last, Sergeant Mehmed and his team reunited with their comrades at dawn. They immediately fortified the hill; thus in this way, it became very difficult and impossible for the enemy to progress beyond that sector of Arıburnu. It was Sergeant Mehmed, who led this accomplishment of a 60 man-force.

After this extraordinary incident, the hill that witnessed the bloody clashes was named 'Cesarettepesi' and the trench, where the brave Turkish troops repelled the enemy forces of about 1,000 men, after a weeklong fighting, was named 'Sergeant Mehmed Trench'.

Afterwards Sergeant Mehmed, when wounded, was evacuated and he was transferred to İstanbul for treatment, his campaign over. His extraordinary heroism spread around quickly. The Supreme Military Command promoted him to the rank of lieutenant and awarded all his comrades separately.

Sergeant Mehmed while receiving treatment at the hospital in İstanbul offered his own views to a reporter on the experienced event as follows:

"When the hill was attacked by the enemy, I gave the order to my troops to 'attach the bayonet' and later on, I said 'move forward!'. I immediately began to climb the hill. The enemy attacked the hill with machine guns and artillery, burning and blasting there. But we did not care; we proceeded by taking refuge in Allah....

We held onto the hills by nightfall. We remained in the trenches for three days and three nights without anyone having any information of our whereabouts. Probably everyone thought we were dead. We lingered where we were by maintaining fire against the enemy. On the night of the third, some members of my team dug a passage big enough for a man to pass by crawling. In this way, I managed to report the situation to my brigade and I received ammunition and food...

The enemy on the other hand was badgering us to death and attacking us at least three times a day. I sensed out that it would not end this way, so I ordered my team to prepare for an attack. After all, if you want to gladden soldiers in this war, just say "we will attack!". Out of the joy, they all said "Inshaallah (Allah willing)". Whatsoever, I, together with my comrades, mounted the attack and repelled the enemy. The enemy did not dare come to attack us again. After a day or two we reunited with the rest of the soldiers".

Fedais (Bouncers) at Arıburnu

The 16th Division was sent to Gallipoli upon the commencement of the war on that front at the end of May. The 125th regiment were holding one of the most dangerous trenches on the Arıburnu front, Kırmızısırt (Johnston's Jolly). The 125th regiment, formed out of the soldiers from the Adana and Mersin region, defended the position till the enemy was discharged around 20 December 1915. The 125th Regiment, also called 'offensive regiment', was renowned with toughness and heroism of its soldiers.

The situation of the Turkish trenches on Kanlısırt (Lone Pine) - Kırmızısırt (Johnston's Jolly) lines were not quite strong. This section, which had changed hands several times, appeared very narrow with the rest of the land completely flattened. Here again, there was an ANZAC foothold equipped with machine guns, which kept on firing at our trenches. It became necessary to capture Şehitler Tepesi (Martyrs' Hill) in order to ameliorate this weak position and at the same time to gain a strategic position against the enemy. With every passing day, the enemies' fortification was gaining strength on the hill. Without wasting much time, it became vital to take action. With this intention, a detachment platoon made up of 140 men was formed. A volunteer officer, first lieutenant Saffet, commander of the 3rd Battalion's 10th Squadron, was to lead the unit.

The mission was extremely dangerous as it was since there was no possibility of coming back. The incursion would take place on the night of 7/8 May.

The unit that would capture the enemy's foothold on Şehitler Tepesi moved at night around 10 pm. The enemy was yet to make a move. The infantry felt a sporadic fire, the exposed ships appeared to be standstill, and adroitly the platoon was approaching the enemy's foothold in the trenches. According to the plan, they would suppress the enemy instantaneously without arousing them. If the planned raid was successful, there would be the need to get an infantry squadron that would invade and defend the hill. The squadron moved, completed its troop basis and was prepared to move at Kanlısırt.

They quietly approached towards the enemy trenches. However, the enemy soldiers, noticing the attack, opened a robust fire with grenades on them. They aimed at the noise made by the wounded Turkish soldiers and opened fire on them from all around, thereby suppressing the volunteer group's attack.

They fell into a whole pit of fire, without the possibility of progressing forward, giving rise to a high number of casualties. The movement lost its raiding fibre. Despite all these, the forces did not want to turn back. The mission was repeatedly renewed. All the soldiers who wanted to hop into the enemy trenches were martyred. More than half the troops in the platoon were wiped away. First lieutenant Saffet was also wounded. The available detachment was decreased to about 60-70 men. Although the armies left behind had initiated a fresh attack, there had been no positive result.

When first lieutenant Saffet was wounded, the squadron met with disaster, as command and control were lost. While going back wounded, lieutenant Saffet sent a report to the Commander of the Front, Mustafa Kemal, revealing how all the soldiers at Gallipoli carried out their defence. This document expressed the secrets of this mission:

"Sir;

On your orders, we attacked the enemy trenches. Half of my soldiers were on top of the trenches; other section together with me went round behind the trenches to throw bombs at them. The enemy began to flee the trenches straight towards the sea. We had 10 soldiers killed and 6 wounded. But I was hit from my left shoulder and the bullet came from behind me. My soldiers were in front of the trenches and were about to go back. They brought me back to the aid post. While coming back, I gave information to the other volunteer officers. The soldiers did not break up. I said "reinforce the offensive ahead while you attack continuously".

Oh Sir! They should continue ahead with the military operation. I feel sad that I did not die in the trenches. The wound I got was due to the second bullet.

First lieutenant Saffet
Commander of the 10th Squadron
Commander from the 125th Regiment

Saffet Efendi, together with the 125th Regiment, fought till the end of the battle at Kanlısırt location of Arıburnu front and got wounded four times. The consequence of the sacrifices and heroism he demonstrated, he became one of the veterans of the victories earned at Gallipoli.

Truce at Arıburnu (24 May 1915)

At Arıburnu, lionhearted and devoted Turkish force lost almost 3,000 of their men in the unsuccessful offensive they waged on 19 May 1915.

Two days after this incident, the British raised a white flag of truce on their trenches. In response, Turkish troops inquired about their intention. The British side indicated that they would like the Turkish side to send a representative for a temporary ceasefire agreement in order to pave way for the rescue of the many injured soldiers, who are lying and groaning at the point between the two battle lines. On 22 May 1915, Liman von Sanders, Commander of the 5th Army, assigned Major Kemal Bey of Ohrid, who was serving in the staff operations, to negotiate with the British.

Lt. Col. Fahrettin Altay, who was chief of staff for the 3rd Army Corps, narrated the negotiations as follows:

"Kemal discussed the principles of a possible protocol of ceasefire that aimed at rescuing the wounded between the trenches; the two parties agreed to send delegates in the morning to meet in Kabatepe at a seaside location between the two battle lines. The case was reported to the Commander of the Army. He also accepted this and sent me out."

The next morning, I went to our trenches located opposite to the meeting point unarmed with a translator, an officer and two privates. They also took up their position. There was a distance of 100 metres between us. At a given time, the two sides came out of the trenches, both lifting a white flag, and we walked to the meeting point. That moment the clashes stopped. When we met with representatives of the enemy forces, we shook hands and greeted each other. Their chief of staff, Lt. Col. Sikkin's first comment was as follows:

'We are four here, but you are five...'

Following this concern, I immediately asked one of the soldiers with me to leave. In the course of the negotiation, when some challenges appeared to prolong matters, Sikkin told:

-Let's not forget that any delay in our work now could endanger the lives of the wounded we are trying to save.

The British commander was trying to whip up our compassion using these humane words. However, as I will explain below, there are wheels within wheels. At the end of the negotiation, the summary of the protocol I prepared was like this as far as I remember:

"From 8.00 in the morning to 4.00 in the evening both parties will observe a ceasefire on the land, sea and the air. To ensure that the ceasefire is actually in effect, each side shall constitute a ceasefire application commission to start working in this regard. The commission shall form a boundary of unarmed soldiers between the lines of the two sides. In a distance of 15 meters, the commission was to line up one Turkish soldier and one British soldier over this boundary. Thus, an intermediary line shall be present for medical teams of the two sides, which would take on the task of recovering bodies of the wounded on their side. Those belonging to other parties shall be brought to the middle line for recovery by their comrades. The weapons, with their mechanisms taken away, shall be delivered in the same way. Nobody shall be allowed to carry gun, revolver or binoculars. A telephone centre shall be established to facilitate communication between the commissions and their respective commanders. The ceasefire implementation commission shall consistently be moving around to resolve any difficulties that would be observed. The Protocol would be examined tonight by the commissions of the two sides and tomorrow morning those with the authority to sign would join-up at the same point."

We departed amicably with greetings. Immediately we returned to our front line, the ceasefire ended and the fighting resumed. The environment returned into a mess."

The Commander of the 3rd Army Corps mentioned the ceasefire negotiations and its implementation on his memories:

"In order to have a discussion with the British on how to convey the dead and the injured, I sent Major Kemal, a person who had a good understanding of French and English, to Kabatepe.

Kemal Bey met with a delegation from the British side at Kabatepe's beach. The delegate from the British side told him that it would be better for them to go to the headquarters. Kemal then accepted this. Although we never demanded for bid, a British staff officer was left with us as a hostage.

Kemal Bey's eyes were blindfolded and his hands were held to help in him move. Because his eyes were blindfolded, he could not see the path they were following. However, he could understand that it was a land route. After a considerable walk to the headquarters of the British commander, they placed him inside a ward in a blind spot and then untied his eyes. The Commander of the ANZAC forces at Arıburnu, General Birdwood, had welcomed Kemal Bey and requested that they prepare an agreement, which would outline how the dead soldiers could be buried. The British had been looking forward to having a discussion like this. Because most part of Gallipoli's wind blows from the north to the south, where the British headquarters were located. As a result, the bad smell of the rotten dead bodies was blown directly to their end. General, while the delegates were preparing the agreement, was busy with the letter, in French, he was going to send me. General Birdwood later became a marshal and attended Atatürk's funeral as the King's representative.

In the evening, Kemal Bey returned to our headquarters with the agreement he prepared and signed with the British delegation *and the letter written by General Birdwood. After his arrival, we delivered the hostage soldier back to them.*

The Army Commander signed the delegates' agreement. It was written in French with two copies. Kemal Bey was given the authority to sign documents on my behalf.

On Monday at 07.30, on 24 May, both sides ceased fire to pave way for the dead to be picked by a staff officer, a doctor and privates from both sides. The Australians stood up from the trenches but did nothing against the signed agreement. Our soldiers continued to obey their commands and therefore remained in the trenches. I was watching the events from surveillance spot with my binoculars. Everything proceeded according to the agreement. Surprisingly between the two trenches, the Australian soldiers were seen having friendly talks with signs with our soldiers. When an impending war was staring everyone, the Australians were busily collecting dress buttons as reminder of war in return for chocolate.

In the evening, when burying the dead and carrying the wounded on both sides was completed, both sides resumed their fire exchanges. We had buried 2,981 martyrs and collected the rifles, 2,688 in good condition while 1,493 with some missing parts."

War Memoir of Ensign Süleyman in Conkbayırı Bayonet Attack

The 3rd Battalion of the 70th Regiment attached the 1st Division, which participated in the Battle of Zığındere that took place in early July on the Seddülbahir front, had had heavy casualties in this battle. Only one or two officers in the battalion and 400 out of the 1000 soldiers available before the battle survived. Other battalions had each given an officer to this battalion. Ensign Süleyman was among these officers and he had been given the command of a squadron under the battalion.

At the start of violent wars in Conkbayırı in early August, before the 3rd Battalion of the 70th Regiment could replace their fallen soldiers on the Seddülbahir front, it served as the 3rd Battalion of the 28th Regiment and received command to march to Conkbayırı. In the morning of 10 August, the 28th Regiment was going to join the upcoming bayonet attack in Conkbayırı.

On the night of 9/10 August when darkness fell, the battalion came to the mouth of a stream in the south of Conkbayırı. This place was going to be the 28th Regiment's vigilance. Because of daylong march, the battalion fell into a deep rest, avoiding the land and air surveillance of the enemy forces.

They heard the command '28th Regiment 3rd Battalion up!' and all of a sudden the battalion grabbed their guns and ascended the Conkbayırı hill.

It was almost morning. Attacking forces gathered in groups and officers were uttering encouraging words to boost morale of the soldiers. The battalion was given a place among troops in the front line. Offensive front was narrow. The battalion and recruits were put in a combat mode, however, putting one-step forward they waited for a sign of combat. The battalion officers had one concern: they had just received the command of the battalion. The battalion had not yet replenished the casualties sustained after the 'battle of three' which took place on the Seddülbahir front in Zığındere. They didn't know about the spirit of the soldiers either.

At this point, they noticed a reckless group from the back, on the left. In the front was the Anafartalar Commander Mustafa

Kemal, beside him were 24th Regiment Commander Nuri Conker, 23rd Regiment Commander Recai and Command Officers Saim and Zeki. Mustafa Kemal, on the morning of 10 August, examined the preparations for bayonet attack on-site. He stood in front of the battalion. The recruits lying so close to the enemy felt the Turkish blood in their veins to the hilt and began to swell with feelings of perseverance and rigour when they saw the brave mission command who marched on in front of the battalion without any regards to the on-going enemy fire. Mustafa Kemal approached:

'Hello soldiers' he said. 'You, with the beard! Can you throw a British to the ground in one move?' (To another) 'You, can you throw a couple of British to the ground in one move?' 'By looking into your eyes, I see that you can do it' he said. Mustafa Kemal got what he wanted; all the recruits answered in the positive with high spirits.

Later he asked those around him; 'Are we ready?' All of them at once answered; 'we are ready'. . Mustafa Kemal, given way to a recruit he said, 'Come on son! Allah, Allah! At this point, he has also given a sign of battle. Running Turkish bayonets like a novaflowed to the British trenches like lightning and these heroes found themselves in an instant in British second line of trenches. Here, from throat to throat, bayonet to bayonet, a stubborn war began. In every minute, officers were bringing messages to Ensign Süleyman, who had been fighting up front, saying that 'five buried ten under the ground.' In Şahinsırt, casualties also increased due to the enemy's machine guns. Fighting with great courage, Sergeant Kazım of Aydın was among those martyred by the bullets of the machine guns.

By the time the offensive stopped and the battalion was withdrawn, they saw that they had lost half of 400 officers. However, the success was greater. The battalion has lost its most precious parts during the unsuccessful war on the Seddülbahir front and had had 600 casualties. Now it had saved Conkbayırı with 200 casualties and Turkey had scored a historic victory.

Survivors of the battalion including Ensign Süleyman in the lead were awarded after this battle. Although they were small in number, they continued to fight in the Battle of Çanakkale in a very high spirit.

Lieutenant Hasan Cevdet Bey's Diary of Conkbayırı

Lieutenant Hasan Cevdet was the commander of the squadron in the 1st Battalion of the 14th Regiment, which was the first to defend the vacant Conkbayırı during the British offensive on the night of 6/7 August. He depicted the battle in his diary as follows:

"Friday, 6 August: The battalion moved to get under the charge of the 17th Division at 7 pm. We arrived at Kemalyeri around 11 pm. Through the 18th Regiment's trenches, we went behind the 72nd Regiment as reserve. We were exhausted by the night.

Saturday, 7 August: Until dawn, the enemy had been bombarding around us. Howitzers were surrounding us like hell. The enemy had occupied the central position and begun attacking from the right side, eventually seizing the trenches there. Initially, we fought at Düztepe. Then we were sent to the right side. We settled in an emplacement, to the north of Conkbayırı, where there were no trenches. Throughout the day, the battle continued vigorously. The night was quiet.

Sunday, 8 August: In the morning, after a severe bombardment, the enemy proceeded to Conkbayırı and occupied the ridge, breaking the lock to İstanbul. Yet, thanks to our artillerymen and infantry, we took the hill back. (The nation owes a debt of gratitude to two battalions of the 64th Regiment and the 1st Battalion of the 14th Regiment, who recaptured the hill). The war continues with its severity. It is like an ensample of the hell.

Monday, 9 August: The battle resumes. Howitzers are bursting and crashing around us.

Tuesday, 10 August: In the morning, our infantry on the Conkbayırı hill attacked and took the trenches back from the enemy. As the battle continues with all its vigour, the enemy's inner resources seemed to be broken.

Around 7 pm, an attack from Conkbayırı started and ended successfully. We pillaged four machine guns from the enemy and they suffered many casualties. The number of prisoners is equal to the sum of those taken captive so far (800).

We suffered many casualties.

We will launch another attack from this front. May Allah let us succeed.

The number of troops in my squadron was decreased, though not certainly, from 224 to 60 in four days and three officers were also injured.

Junior Lieutenant Urfi Efendi: "We are attacking the enemy at Conkbayırı"

Junior Lieutenant Urfi, the commander of the 2nd Squadron of the 1st Battalion in the 28th Regiment, narrated "Conkbayırı bayonet charge' that took place on 10 August 1915:

"Marching through Seddülbahir all night, we arrived at Conkbayırı's back zone. According to the orders given, the 1st and 2nd squadrons of every battalion is supposed to occupy a frontline while the 3rd and 4th squadrons were to hold another line behind. I was in the 2nd squadron and therefore my unit took up position in the frontline.

We settled down on the left side of Conkbayırı, just behind the summit. We crouched, as we did not want to be seen by our enemy. The offensive would start when our regiment's flag was to lean forward three times and point our waypoint.

Before any attack order was given, the enemy had started an artillery strike. Enemy shells made arms and legs fly in all directions. The incident had a very massive effect on us so we immediately wanted to attack.

We did not wait long as our regiment's flag pointed our way for three times. We started walking in front of our team with swords in our hands. After walking for 30-40 meters, we found ourselves on the top of the ridge. Here was a fighter line of us. Both the dead and alive were lying on the front line. We could not detect which one was alive or dead. After a few more steps, we arrived at the other side of the hill and came across the British. That was a scene I could never forget.

We did neither stop nor cared about the trenches and the British we left behind. Downslope, we were attacking with all force. We noticed that people around us had died and so we could not keep advancing under the heavy machine gunfire coming from the flanks and front. When we looked back, we saw that we left Conbayırı far behind.

That was when our disaster started. We were being fired at from all sides and felt that the enemy navy was making a hell around us. Despite all of these, the enemy could not move an inch."

Mustafa Kemal's shattered watch

Anafartalar Commander Colonel Mustafa Kemal had commanded bayonet charge in Conkbayırı on 10 August 1915. During the artillery strikes of the enemy, one of the artillery exploded very close to Mustafa Kemal. A shrapnel coming from the shell hits Mustafa Kemal's chest but with an extraordinary luck the shrapnel was stopped by the chain watch in his pocket. As a memory for this day, Mustafa Kemal gave the shattered watch to the Commander of the Army, Liman von Sanders, as a gift. In return, Liman also gave his watch to Mustafa Kemal as a gift.

Anafartalar Platoon Commander Mayor Haydar Mehmet Alganer was one of the people who witnessed the incident and he narrated as such:

"During the Battle of Gallipoli, the enemy's second landing on the beaches of Arıburnu and Suvla was successful.

We were at Tekketepe, which housed the headquarters in Anafartalar. The commander of this sector was German Cavalry Lieutenant Colonel Wilmer and I was the supreme commander.

We understood that the enemy was preparing to attack southwards from Conkbayırı on the left side of our region, which was separated by the Bulgarderesi (Bulgar River).

Anafatalar Group Commander Mustafa Kemal took the command of Conkbayırı regiment to counter the possible enemy attack.

It was one of the hot days of August.

We were following the Conkbayırı offensive with a telephone from our headquarters in Tekketepe. We could see the on-going artillery and infantry strikes on Mestantepe Hill. However, the enemy was not able to advance from there so the other enemy squads tried to defend their left flank.

The 5th Army Commander, Liman von Sanders, was following the operation from our headquarters. The news stating Mustafa Kemal's counter attack had been successful made us very happy.

In the evening, Mustafa Kemal and chief of staff came to the headquarters to tell Liman von Sanders details of the operation carried out under his own command. He was explaining the things in French. We were all listening with a great curiosity and excitement. Mustafa Kemal said:

"In all trenches our infantry operated using bayonets with my order to stop the enemy trying to climb the Conkbayırı Hill. Our troops drove the enemy back to the sea. Meanwhile, a shrapnel hit me right in the chest. My watch saved my life. I wish to give this watch to you as a memory of today's victory." So he gave the shattered watch to Liman von Sanders.

We were all standing and it was almost impossible to express our tears of happiness. I saw Sanders shaking with excitement and filled with tears. While congratulating him, Sanders took the watch and gave his golden watch in return to Mustafa Kemal saying:

"I also want to give you my watch as a symbol of gratitude and my admiration and a memory of your great victory"

EVACUATION

Gallipoli Campaign, launched by the Allied Powers with high hopes and with the aim of changing the course of the Great War, was doomed to failure in the face of Turkish defence in spite of all the attempts by naval forces and ground troops respectively. Allied Powers considered the Ottoman Empire, which was busy binding up the wounds following the loss of Rumelia and heavy defeat it had suffered in the Balkan Wars, an easy meat. It was a daring attempt, in defiance of Turkish military competence, of the Allied Powers to attack on the Dardanelles. Yet Turkish soldiers, whom the British had hoped that they would lay down weapons and flee their ground seeing the British battleships at the entrance of the Dardanelles, sacrificed themselves against the naval bombardment. They withstood the Anglo-French Allied Army, landed on the Gallipoli Peninsula with the best weapons of the time, in a way no one had anticipated, fighting heroically and losing their lives.

Allied attacks on *Seddülbahir* and *Arıburnu* between 25 April 1915 and August 1915 were beaten off by Turkish defence forces. When plans to extend the Allied position and encircle the Turkish army with the arrival of fresh soldiers at

Anafartalar on 6 August failed, there remained two ways for the Allies: either to continue forcing passage through seaway to İstanbul or to evacuate Gallipoli, finally admitting failure in Çanakkale Campaign.

As of September, trench wars had begun on all fronts across the Peninsula. Turkish forces had fortified their positions at *Seddülbahir, Arıburnu* and *Anafartalar* and the number of troops had been raised to 300,000 with new arrivals.

The number of Allied troops at Gallipoli had increased, with the opening of a new front at Anafartalar, to 150,000. However, the course of the war provoked considerable opposition in Britain after September 1915. Anti-war opposition had begun to question the campaign which killed so many Allied soldiers and eventually proved to be a bloody blind alley. Under tremendous pressure, British War Secretary Kitchener asked Hamilton, Commander of the Allied Army, for an estimate of the casualties expected in case of evacuation from Gallipoli. Hamilton reported that a proposed evacuation would cost up to 50 percent casualties. Hamilton was still hopeful of success in breaking the Turkish defence and requested for more men. He was promptly sacked after being discredited due to the failure at Gallipoli combined with overall air of gloom in Britain. On 15 October 1915, Hamilton was replaced by General Charles Monro.

General Monro was convinced that WWI would be decided on in the French front rather than anywhere else and took a dim view of the Gallipoli operation from the start. After he was despatched to the Gallipoli peninsula to replace Hamilton, he paid a personal visit to Gallipoli on 30 October and swiftly got around three fronts. He realized that Turkish defence would not be broken with the existing military capacity of the Allied forces and that it would be quite hard to hold on as the winter was quickly approaching. Soon Monro issued his recommendation to British authorities: to evacuate Gallipoli.

British government feared that a complete withdrawal from Gallipoli would damage British prestige, both politically and militarily. The British Cabinet confirmed the decision to evacuate *Anafartalar* and *Arıburnu* fronts in December while holding their ground in *Seddülbahir.*

Evacuation began in early December from *Anafartalar* and *Arıburnu* with 92,000 troops withdrawn within weeks. Without arousing the suspicion of the Turkish side, troops and equipments were boarded and were taken off after dark. To disguise the departure, some units carried empty boxes and crates into the trenches in the daytime. The remaining troops were sent to the frontline and they kept up trench battles.

The final evacuation stage took place on 20-21 December night. By the morning, all the Allied troops had abandoned *Anafartalar* and *Arıburnu.* Evacuation was complete and well-executed, with no casualties being reported. However, a great deal of stuff was left behind to distract the Turkish forces. Although some of the stuff was destroyed by naval bombardment, a considerable amount of booty had been captured by the Turkish army.

On the Turkish side, the evacuation of the enemy troops had not been noticed. The last thing the Allies needed was a possible Turkish offensive on the last day at Anafartalar-Arıburnu fronts before all the troops had been evacuated – considering that there were 30,000 Allied troops left behind. Consequently, well-hidden and well-organised evacuation operation slipped past the notice of Turkish troops at these fronts.

With the evacuation finished without incident, the battles at this region came to an end. The only region on the Gallipoli Peninsula with the Allied presence was *Seddülbahir*.

The British government initially wanted to keep its bridgehead in *Seddülbahir* but realizing the difficulty of holding to the region, it later decided to evacuate *Seddülbahir* as well. However, the evacuation of *Seddülbahir* would not be as easy as that of other fronts in the face of vigilant and cautious Turkish soldiers.

The same previous plan was pursued in *Seddülbahir*. On one hand, people and equipments were being taken to the ships at nights. On the other hand, they pretended as if they were running troops and equipments ashore during the day. The French troops were the first to be evacuated. As of 1 January 1916, no French troops had remained on the Peninsula. The trenches were being guarded by approximately 20,000 British troops.

Suspicious of evacuation of the enemy forces, the Turkish command wanted to find out the situation and planned a reconnaissance operation. On 7 January, units of the 12th Division were dispatched to *Zığındere*. But the operation was halted by the response of the British forces defending the parapets with all their strength.

On the night of 8/9 January, the last remaining British forces, about 17,000 troops, left *Seddülbahir*, thus ending the British presence on the Peninsula. The greatest success of the Allied forces who were unable to breach the Turkish defence in Çanakkale, was evacuation of 120,000 Allied troops on three fronts, without any casualties.

In return, evacuation of the Allied forces from *Seddülbahir* with no casualties was a major weakness of the Turkish command considering that it had been an expected move after the evacuation of *Arıburnu-Anafartalar* fronts and that the *Seddülbahir* front was easy to observe from both *Alçıtepe* and the Anatolian side.

CONCLUSION

Battle of Gallipoli was a defining moment not only in Turkish history but also in world history. Apparently, the battle symbolises the great resistance of the Ottoman Empire in a period of break-up against the most powerful armies of the world. Europe's imperialist states which strived to wipe Turks out of the Balkans and Anatolia suffered a devastating defeat at Gallipoli.

Few nations in the world's history have the strength and potential to engage in wars like Gallipoli. The power and courage to resist the world's two major countries, Britain and France, indicate the greatness of Turkish nation. Although Turkey was invaded following the defeat at WWI, the nation maintained the spirit of heroism displayed at Gallipoli in the War of Independence as well managing to eject the invaders from the country.

The victory at Gallipoli has strengthened the dignity of the nation and the state which was damaged at home and abroad after the Balkan Wars. The Allied Powers, looking at the result of the Balkan Wars, had assumed that the Turkish army had lost its war capability. Throwing caution to the winds and underestimating the strength of Turkish army, they found themselves at Gallipoli. They even thought that Turkish soldiers would take away their weapons and flee.

However, things did not happen that way. Contrary to the enemy's expectations, Turkish soldiers saw Gallipoli a real opportunity to remove the disgrace and stain in the Balkan Wars and fought to the death. Indeed, plenty of examples exist. For instance, Mustafa Kemal Atatürk revealed this emotional state as he delivered a speech to his commanders before the offensive operation on the Arıburnu front on 1 May 1915: *"I rule out the possibility of presence of anyone, among us and among our troops, who would not prefer dying to witnessing a second phase of the disgrace at Balkans. If you know anyone like this, let's execute them by shooting.*

As is seen, the defeat in the Balkan Wars had traumatised the Turkish soldiers. This trauma had to be overcome. In a similar vein, a wounded reserve officer, as quoted by Hamdullah Suphi while visiting a hospital in Çanakkale, was saying to the aid man that: "Let it be shed! Only this blood can remove the Balkan stain". Thus, the victory at Gallipoli had removed the trauma and frustration of the Balkan Wars no longer than two years.

Moral strength of the Turkish soldiers who fought at Gallipoli has to be acknowledged. They were well aware that they had been fighting for protecting the state and the caliphate. Moreover, they knew that survival of the Ottoman Empire and defence of the holy lands, Mecca and Medina, depended on their effort. Morality that was based on the considerations above set ground for the triumphant defence of their homeland; they fearlessly lunged at the enemy troops to become martyrs. Mustafa Kemal Atatürk narrated another example of heroism of Turkish soldiers: *"We are not interested in individual heroic incidents. But, I cannot help telling you what had happened at Bombasırtı. Distance between trenches was eight meters, death is certain, certain... All the troops in the frontline trenches are wholly shot down, others in the support trenches are replacing them, but if you could only know how calm and faithful they were! They see their comrades dying, know they would die in three minutes but do not fall into a state of languor. No shaking! Those who know how to read Quran are waiting to enter Jannah. Those who do not know are advancing, repeating the confession of faith. This is an astonishing example of inner strength of Turkish soldiers that must be congratulated. That's for sure this is the spirit that brought the victory at the Battle of Gallipoli."*

Bayonet attack at *Conkbayırı* on 10 August 1915 provides another example of morality of the Turkish soldiers. They attacked the enemy as if they were jumping off a cliff, thus adding a new heroic story to the glorious book of Turkish history. Mustafa Kemal, then Anafartalar Group Commander, had addressed the soldiers before the attack:

"Soldiers! There is no doubt that we will defeat the enemy. But do not hurry. Let me move forward first. Wait for my signal with the whip to attack!"

Then the attack began. Again, Mustafa Kemal narrated how they attacked the enemy and the victory came:

"I also ordered the commanders and officers to draw attention of soldiers to my signal. Then I moved to a point in front of the attacking line and I raised my whip and ordered to attack.

All the soldiers and officers had forgotten anything else and directed their attention with their eyes and hearts to the signal. Soldiers were waiting with their bayonets and one foot in front of the other. In the front are officers with their pistols and swords in their hands. All bravely rushed forward like a single iron block as my whip down. After a second, nothing but a heavenly shout was heard from the enemy trenches: 'Allah, Allah, Allah!...' The enemy could not find time even to use their weapons. After a heroic fighting, we had destroyed all the enemy units in the forefront."

As far as the psychology of the two sides is concerned, Turkish soldiers had far higher morale than the enemy troops. Diary of an Australian soldier reveals the dispiritedness that the Allied soldiers had during the war:

"26 April 1915; what a terrible night it was. As Turks slowly came nearer and nearer as close as twenty steps, we began spraying bullets at them. But the warlike Turks never dreaded and kept attacking us. Their machine guns were real killer. They badgered us to death. Today was a long day.

This place is hell on earth. The enemy attacked us through the whole night. We struggled to pull them back. When would we get supplies and reinforcements to launch a counterattack? Somehow the day passed. We have to defend our position until ammunition arrives. We excessively consumed ammo at night."

Obviously, their distress grew more and more as the war prolonged. Many soldiers readily wished to escape the battle scotched.

A British soldier was making a confession in the letter, dated 8 September 1915, he sent to the European newspapers:

"Here, fighting in these trenches, it is really difficult to occupy İstanbul. We are convinced of that."

Seemingly, not only did the enemy soldiers have a low morality but also they did not have faith in their goal of seizing İstanbul.

The British, also using psychological war techniques, failed in demoralising Turkish soldiers. They aimed to influence Turkish soldiers with leaflets dropped from their aircrafts:

"Ottoman soldiers!

As you know great numbers of British and French soldiers came ashore but they never feel enmity towards you. On the contrary, they are utterly upset with being forced to fight against you.

The British government was forced to declare war in order to save you from the yoke of Germans, whom your politicians gave you in to. As long as you go on resisting the Allied forces, they will have to continue, with reinforcements, the occupation of your country. Your officers and comrades who were taken captive in the last clashes appreciate the fair treatment they are shown every day. Wounded Turkish soldiers get treatment in the same way that the British soldiers get. The world knows your heroism and bravery. Why do you prolong the war waged just for the interest of Germany? If you give up fighting and take away your weapons you will be gathered to your homes and kids. We will return to our homeland too.

"The Ottomans! How long would you listen to the German plans? They take your food and leave your kids in hunger. They send guns and cartridges and call on you to fight. Their aim is to easily invade your country after all your youth die. Germans always lie. But their lies increased because they got so many defeats recently."

The rest of the leaflet covered the defeats suffered by the Germans to convince Turkish soldiers to lay down arms. But it did not work at all. Turkish soldiers, well aware of the fact that defending Gallipoli meant defending İstanbul and homeland, were not influenced by the British propaganda. On the contrary, they resisted more bravely.

Political and military prestige of the British and French was heavily damaged in their colonies due to the Battle of Gallipoli. It gave birth to movements of independence across the world. Gallipoli has become a part of Australia's and New Zealand's national identities.

On the other hand, the mastermind and advocate of the war, Winston Churchill had to resign after defeat and take a break from politics for a while.

Gallipoli demonstrated that Turkey and Turkish nation still retained the power and dynamism it owned. The Battle was the precursor of the Turkish War of Independence. Many commanders, with the experience and confidence they had in Gallipoli, successfully fought for the independence. These commanders included notably Mustafa Kemal Atatürk, Fevzi Çakmak, Kazım Karabekir, Cafer Tayyar, Fahreddin Altay, Selahaddin Adil, İzzettin Çalışlar and Şükrü Naili Gökberk. Also, services and roles of other officers and privates including Cevat Pasha, Esat Pasha, Vehip Pasha, Lt. Col. Şefik Bey, Major Mahmut Sabri Bey, Sergeant Mehmet of Biga, Corporal Seyit, Sergeant Yahya of Ezine must always be remembered. The list includes some German officers as well. And finally, Sultan Mehmed Reşad as the Head of State and Enver Pasha as the Minister of War and Deputy Commander-in-Chief considerably contributed to the victory.

Due to the Battle of Gallipoli, WWI continued for another three years. The heaviest blow to the Allied prestige during WWI was the defeat at Gallipoli. Russia tasted disappointment too as his dream to control the Straits collapsed. Internal struggle hit the Tsarist Russia and the Bolshevik Revolution came in 1917. Soviet Union replaced Russia and this was to change the world history.

This was the battle of junior officers; their heroic efforts inspired and affected Turkish soldiers. Thus they triumphed over the enemy. Many well-educated young people were lost during the war, whose adverse effects were heavily felt in the War of Independence and in the republican era.

During the 8.5-month battle, both sides had fought with a force of 500,000 troops. Official number of casualties, according to the Ottoman General Staff, of the Turkish side was 251,359 in total, including 55,177 martyrs, 100,177 wounded, 10,067 missing, 21,498 death due to diseases, and 64,440 sick leave.

When those who died while getting treatment due to injuries or diseases are included, the number of martyrs in the Turkish army reaches 101 thousand.

The British casualties in the Battle of Çanakkale were about 30,000 dead and nearly 80,000 wounded; the French casualties included 14,500 dead and 17,000 wounded.

As for the ANZAC troops, the battle left 9,000 Australians dead and 20,000 wounded; while the New Zealanders suffered nearly 3,000 dead and 5,000 wounded.

During the war, about 90,000 Allied troops were evacuated from Gallipoli due to diseases; including these, total number of casualties of the Allied forces was almost 270,000.

The Turkish army had fought against various nations in the war; on the front line these comprised the British, Irish, Scottish, Canadians, Australians, New Zealanders, Maori people, Sikhs from India, Hindus, Gorkhas from Nepal and Jews under the British flag. The French, Senegalese, Gambians, Tunisians and Algerians participated in the war under the French flag.

The Greeks, Egyptians and Russians were other actors of the war behind the front.

From time to time, the Battle of Gallipoli is called as "gentlemen's war". Although there were some examples of gentlemanliness throughout the long war, it is hard to see the entire war as such. In fact, such acts came more from the Turkish soldiers. Most of the Allied actions were not gentlemanly at all. Wars have their own rules and fundamentally armies fight against enemy soldiers. If civilians are attacked in a war, then no one can mention gentlemanship. In fact such incidents took place in Gallipoli. The Allied forces hit civilian targets. Even beyond that, it is known that the Allied aircrafts deliberately bombed hospitals and killed a large number of civilians and soldiers. A plenty of examples exist. Such behaviours cannot be considered as gentlemanlike.

Turkish side, on the contrary, paid strict attention to behave in a more high-minded way. In that regard, it is useful to browse through some of the statements of Allied soldiers and officers reflected in European newspapers of the period:

According to the Ottoman archives; an article, titled "Turkish Gentlemanship" was published in Gazette de Hollande on 16 December 1915 against the bombing of hospitals by the British. In the article, a British officer, making reference to how Turks were fighting gentlemanly, said: "Any British officer and soldier who knows something about Gallipoli and the Battle of Çanakkale has observed this".

Near East correspondent of United Press, Shepherd, wrote that a British officer told him:

"One day we placed one of our batteries very close to a hospital. It was first noticed by Turks and gave us this signal

with heliography: *'If you do not take your batteries from there, we have to open fire'.*"

What a British prisoner told is also noteworthy: *"Turks initially cheated us. Although we had many casualties, we thought that we had made some progress. But, after we seized the first trench, our attempt to advance further was responded by a storm of fire and our battalion was completely shot down. When we saw this, we realized that our progress at the outset had not been a success but a trap designed by Turks. When Turkish soldiers returned to their previously occupied trenches they took us prisoner and found the rest of the battalion dead. I can assure you that not even four or five soldiers survived from our battalion. Turkish aid men dressed our wounds and looked after us. Now we prefer being prisoners to fighting."*

Another prisoner told: *"The battle annoys us all. In fact, as we were volunteers we would have been serving in places where we approved with our signature. But they led us here. A few soldiers remained in Britain. Ever after, no one wants to be a soldier. We are very pleased that we are prisoners."*

On 4 May 1915, the ANZAC offensive on *Kabatepe* encountered heavy fire. Thereupon Captain Ray Leane, realizing that they would not go any further, requested lifeboats to evacuate the wounded. Leane explains what had happened: *"Turks ceased fired as soon as they saw discharging soldiers carrying the wounded to the lifeboats, thus showing a great example of magnanimity. They did not fire a single shot until all the wounded were taken to the boats. This behaviour is an indication of how gentleman the Muslim fighters are. "*

Countless soldiers had been martyred in Gallipoli and this left deep wounds in the hearts of people. In order to help heal the wounds, martyrs commemorations started before the end of the war. First Gallipoli commemoration was held on 27 June 1915 in *Mekteb-i Sultanî* (Galatasaray High School). As is known, among the soldiers and martyrs who voluntarily fought in the Dardanelles were students of the school as well.

In the ceremony, fathers of martyrs, Müşir Fuat Pasha, Ata Bey and Hüsnü Bey, many graduates, the school's administrators, teachers, civil servants, students and more than three hundred veterans were present. First the noon prayer was performed in the school's mosque and mawlid was recited. Then Ata Bey, whose son was martyred in Gallipoli, delivered an emotional speech and ended his words by saying: *"Long live the nation, long live the homeland, long live the soldiers, and long live our Caliph and Sultan"*. Then Faik Bey introduced Fuat Pasha, whose three children were martyred in the war, to the crowd. With eyes swimming with tears, he gave a speech and said: *"My three children lost their lives in the battlefield for the sake of religion and homeland. Our lives do not matter at all. I am very upset with not having the honour of the rank of my sons for the sake of religion and nation. I envy their position"*. Upon this speech, all in the commemoration burst into tears. At the end, candy and cigar were offered to the crowd. The guests left the old and distinguished schools, appreciating the treatment in the ceremony.

The Gallipoli Victory's greatest gift to the Turkish nation is no doubt Mustafa Kemal Atatürk. He proved himself as a distinguished organiser and leader by winning a victory with a newly established division over a modern corps. The ability to grasp a situation, to make quick, smart decisions and to implement these decisions with determination are all indication of the strong will, knowledge and self-confidence he possessed.

The effects of the Gallipoli Victory continued during the Republican Era too.

Atatürk came to Gallipoli in 1928, toured the battlefield and visited all the places once they saved one by one. He took four-hour tour on foot around the areas where the battles took place and depicted the historic victory.

In 1934, on the occasion of 18 March Naval Victory Commemoration, Atatürk prepared a message for the ANZAC soldiers who died in the Battle of Gallipoli and their families. This text was read at the ceremony by Interior Minister Şükrü Kaya:

"Those heroes that shed their blood and lost their lives!

You are now lying in the soil of a friendly country. Therefore rest in peace. There is no difference between the Johnnies and the Mehmets to us where they lie side by side in this country of ours. You, the mothers, who sent their sons from far away countries, wipe away your tears. Your sons are now lying in our bosom and are in peace. After having lost their lives on this land they have become our sons as well."

This expression of friendship by Atatürk is very precious as it addresses the enemy soldiers who invaded his country. He had shown a great example of magnanimity, seeing enemy soldiers as his own son, in a way that no leader in the world can show. This perspective also constitutes an evidence to the manliness and the magnanimity of Turkish nation.

Again in 1934, during the opening ceremony of the Sergeant Mehmed Monument, Atatürk ordered Hafiz Yaşar Okur to recite mawlid for the martyrs. In the war, morale of Turkish soldiers was always at the top level. They attacked the enemy without any fear and hesitation, believing that they would go to Jannah. Atatürk, who commanded these troops in Gallipoli, had mawlid recited for their souls, thus offering well wishes.

It seems appropriate to quote Sami Pashazade Sezai's comments on the Battle of Gallipoli as the final words: *"Such spectacular events speak for themselves. Words and thoughts to define them fall while rising, wanes while shining. However, how possible may it be to say nothing? Today, if Turks can speak, this is thanks to the defence at Gallipoli. Today, it is the defense at Gallipoli that gave the Turks the authority to say 'I am' among the major nations... Gallipoli is the battle of 'three miracles'. It saved the day. It brought back the 'heroism and greatness' of the past. It turned our country to an 'eternal homeland'.*

BIBLIOGRAPHY

Adil, Selahaddin, Çanakkale Cephesi'nden Mektuplar-Hatıralar, Yeditepe Publishing House, İstanbul 2007.

Albayrak, Muzaffer, *10 Ağustos 1915 Conkbayırı* Süngü Hücumu, Directorate of Gallipoli Historic Site Publication, Çanakkale 2015.

Albayrak, Muzaffer-Yılmazer Tuncay, *Sorularla Çanakkale Muharebeleri I*, Yeditepe Publishing House, İstanbul 2007.

Alganer, Haydar Mehmet, Çanakkale Kara Savaşları Günlüğü, Deniz Printing House, İstanbul 2009.

Aspinall-Oglander, C. F., *Büyük Harbin Tarihi Gelibolu Askeri Harekâtı, Cilt I-II*, General Staff History of War Publication, İstanbul 1939.

Atatürk, Mustafa Kemal, *Anafartalar Muharebatı'na Ait Tarihçe*, Turkish Historical Society Publication, Ankara 1990.

Atatürk, Mustafa Kemal, *Arıburnu Muharebeleri Raporu*, Turkish Historical Society Publication, Ankara 1990.

Barlett, Ellis Asmead, Çanakkale Gerçeği, Haz. Muzaffer Albayrak, Yeditepe Publishing House, İstanbul 2005.

Belen, Fahri, Çanakkale Savaşı'ndan Alınan Dersler, Yeditepe Publishing House, İstanbul 2009.

Bilgin, Mustafa Sıtkı, İngiltere'nin Çanakkale Savaşlarında Takip Ettiği Siyaset ve Bunun İngiltere'ye Etkisi, *Yeni Türkiye Çanakkale Özel Sayısı*, pp.628-635.

Birinci Dünya Savaşı'nda Çanakkale Cephesi, V. Cilt, I-II-III. Kitap, Genelkurmay Başkanlığı ATASE Yayınları, Ankara 2012.

Conk, Cemil, Çanakkale *Conkbayırı Savaşları*, E. U. Printing House, Ankara 1959.

Engin, Vahdettin, *Mekteb-i Sultani*, İstanbul 2003.

Eraslan, Cezmi, *II. Abdülhamid'in Çanakkale Savunması*, İstanbul 2014.

Esat Paşa, Çanakkale Savaşı Hatıraları, Örgün Publishing House, İstanbul 2003.

Esenkaya Ahmet, Çanakkale Savaşı'nda Türk-Alman Birlikteliği, Çanakkale Araştırmaları Türk Yıllığı (Spring-Fall 2008, pp.15-42).

Fahrettin Altay Paşa'nın Çanakkale Hatıraları, Çanakkale Hatıraları, c. II, Arma Publications, İstanbul 2002.

Göncü, Gürsel–Aldoğan, Şahin, Çanakkale Savaşı; Siperin Ardı Vatan, MB Publishing House, İstanbul 2006.

Görgülü, İsmet, *On Yıllık Harbin Kadrosu*, Turkish Historical Society Publication, Ankara 1993.

Hamilton, Ian, *Gelibolu Günlüğü*, Hürriyet Publications, İstanbul 1972.

Hasan Cevdet, *Kıyamet Koptuğunda; Hasan Cevdet Bey'in Çanakkale ve Doğu Cephesi Günlüğü*, Yeditepe Publishing House, İstanbul 2015.

İslam Ansiklopedisi, Entry: Çanakkale.

Moorehead, Alan, *Gelibolu*, Doğan Books, İstanbul 2000.

Münim Mustafa, *Cepheden Cepheye*, Arma Publications, İstanbul 1998.

Osmanlı Belgelerinde Çanakkale Muharebeleri Cilt; I-II, General Directorate of State Archives Publication, Ankara 2005.

Özçelik, Mücahit, *Birinci Dünya Savaşı'nda Türkiye'deki Esirler*, Ankara 2013.

Perk, Kadri, Çanakkale Savaşları Tarihi, Military Journal History Section, Issue: 55, Military Printing House, İstanbul 1939.

Pomiankowski, Joseph, *Osmanlı İmparatorluğu'nun Çöküşü 1914-1918 I. Dünya Savaşı*, Translated by Kemal Turan, İstanbul 2003.

Ruşen, Eşref, *Anafartalar Kumandanı Mustafa Kemal İle Mülakat*, İstanbul 1930.

Tezer, Şükrü, *Atatürk'ün Hatıra Defteri*, Turkish Historical Society Publication, Ankara 2008.

Yılmazer, Tuncay, *Alçıtepe'den Anafartalar'a Kara Muharebeleri Çanakkale*, İstanbul 2005.

APPENDICES

MAPS AND PHOTOGRAPHS

MAPS

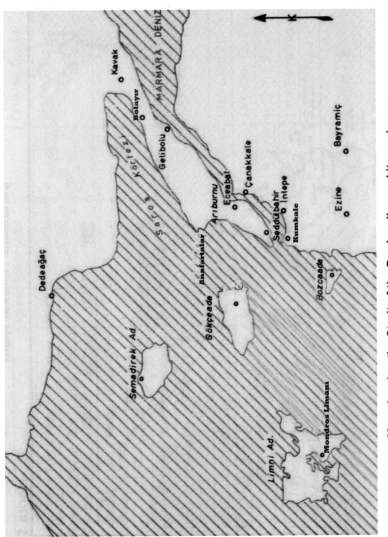

Map showing the Strait of the Dardanelles and its environs

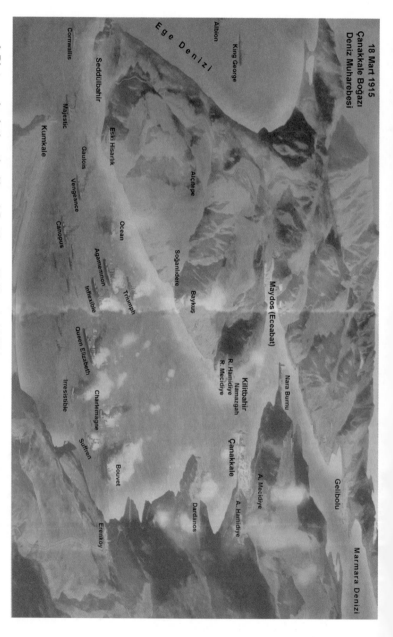

18 Mart 1915
Çanakkale Boğazı
Deniz Muharebesi

A Picture depicting the Naval Battle on 18 March 1915 between the enemy fleet and Turkish forts

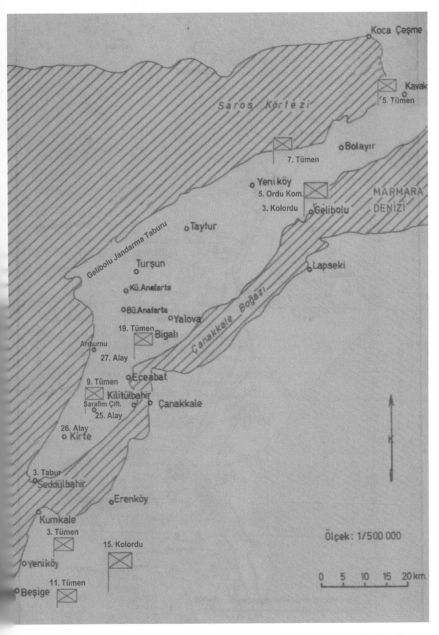

Position of units under the 5th Army before the landings on 25 April

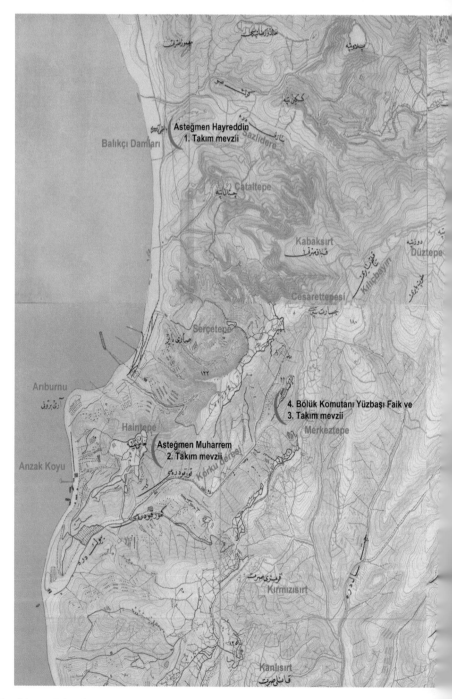

Position of the 4th Squadron of the 2nd Battalion attached to the 27th Regiment confronted the enemy landing on the coast of Arıburnu on 25 April 1915

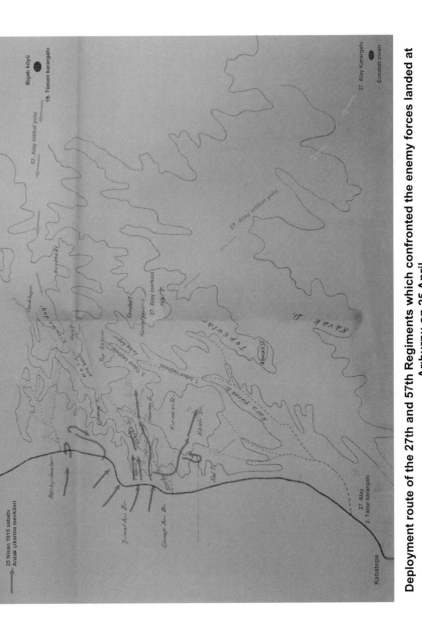

Deployment route of the 27th and 57th Regiments which confronted the enemy forces landed at Arıburnu on 25 April

Landing zones of the British forces on 25 April and the position of the 3rd Battalion of the 26th Regiment

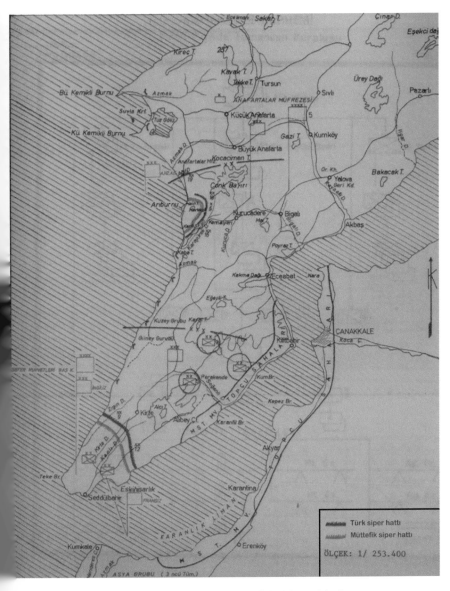

Positions of the two sides at Seddülbahir and Arıburnu
at the end of May 1915

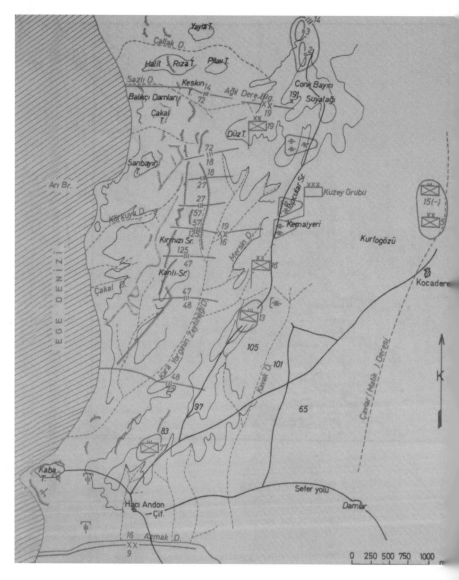

Defensive formation of Turkish forces at Arıburnu at the beginning of Augus

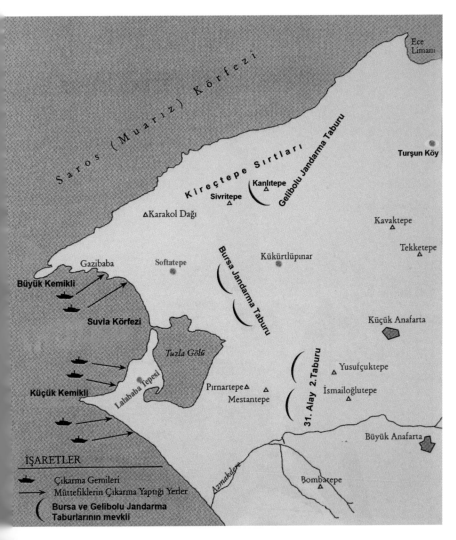

nding zones of the British forces on the coast of Anafartalar on 6/7 August 1915 and the position of Turkish defence forces

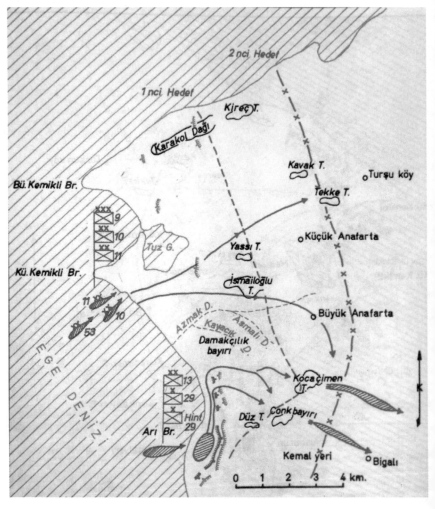

Military targets of the Allied forces during the landing at Anafartalar on 6 Augus

A modern-day photograph of Conkbayırı Hill where the Bayonet Attack on 10 August 1915 took place

—— Turkish trenches   **——** British trenches

PHOTOGRAPHS

A photograph showing Cevat Pasha with the medals awarded for his achievements in the battles

Çanakkale Fortified Zone Commander Cevat (Çobanlı) Pasha (see X) at the headquarters of the Fortified Zone with the officers

Captain Mehmet Hilmi, commander of Mecidiye Fort which sank the French battleship
Bouvet during the naval war of 18 March, and Lieutenant Fahri Bey

Crew preparing for fire of cannon, 24 cm in diameter, in one of the forts defending the
Strait. The lift of the cannon is visible in the picture. The lift that Corporal Seyit told to k
broken was used for carrying the ball into the cannon.

A photograph showing Corporal Seyit carrying a cannon ball weighing 215 kg, 1915

Nusret Mine Layer, carrying mines for its mission in the Dardanelles

British battleship Irresistible sinking, the Strait of the Dardanelles, 6 pm, 18 March 19

Headquarters on Arıburnu front

1. 3rd Army Corps Commander Esat Pasha
2. 19th Division Commander Mustafa Kemal

156

Lt. Col. Mehmet Şefik (Aker), the 27th Regiment Commander, who stopped the ANZAC troops landing at Arıburnu on 25 April 1915

Wounded commanders of the 4th Squadron of the 2nd Battalion attached to the 27th Regiment, who confronted the ANZAC troops landed at Arıburnu on 25 April, in hospital:
1. 4th Squadron Commander Captain Faik
2. 1st Platoon Commander Third-Lieutenant İbradılı İbrahim Hayrettin
d Platoon Commander Third-Lieutenant Muharrem who fired the first shot at the enemy at Haintepe
4. 3rd Platoon Commander Staff Sergeant Gelibolulu Süleyman at Yükseksırt
(Serdar Ataksor's Archive)

Medals of Privilege Awarding Ceremony to the flag of the 27th Regiment for the bravery shown at Arıburnu in the presence of Enver Pasha, Minister of War.

Landing pier of enemy on the coast of Seddülbahir Village, Ertuğrul Bay. British landing here in the morning of 25 April was confronted by Sergeant Yahya and his platoon positioned in the trenches on the slope overlooking the coast.

Esat Pasha, Commander of the 3rd Army Corps and the Arıburnu Front

3rd Army Corps Commander Esat Pasha and the officers at the headquarters

Colonel Mustafa Kemal, Commander of the 19th Division, surveilling the enemy forces from the Arıburnu trenches, June 1915

Anafartalar Group Commander Mustafa Kemal, in front of the monument made of unexploded shells in memory of Gallipoli Gendarmerie Martyrs in a valley behind Kireçtepe while the battle continues.

A trench in Zığındere sector on the right flank of the Seddülbahir Front

15-cm howitzer battery and privates in Çanakkale

Martyrs who died during the 19 May offensive at Arıburnu were buried after the ceasefire on 24 May

Turkish officers watching the enemy troops fleeing after the evacuation of Arıburnu Front

2012
SUN SIGN
BOOK

Forecasts by
Kris Brandt Riske

Book Editing: Sharon Leah
Cover Design: Kevin R. Brown
Bursts & Sunflowers: iStockphoto.com/Tony Link Design
Interior Zodiac Icons: iStockphoto.com/Trillingstudio

Copyright 2011 Llewellyn Publications
ISBN: 978-0-7387-1209-3
A Division of Llewellyn Worldwide Ltd.
Llewellyn is a registered trademark of Llewellyn Worldwide Ltd.
2143 Wooddale Drive, Woodbury, MN 55125
Printed in the USA

Table of Contents

2012 Sun Sign Book Articles

Meet Kris Brandt Riske

Kris Brandt Riske is the executive director and a professional member of the American Federation of Astrologers (AFA), the oldest U.S. astrological organization, founded in 1938; and a member of National Council for Geocosmic Research (NCGR). She has a master's degree in journalism and a certificate of achievement in weather forecasting from Penn State.

Kris is the author of several books, including: *Llewellyn's Complete Book of Astrology: The Easy Way to Learn Astrology*; *Mapping Your Money*; *Mapping Your Future*; and coauthor of *Mapping Your Travels and Relocation*; and *Astrometeorology: Planetary Powers in Weather Forecasting*. She also writes for astrology publications and does the annual weather forecast for *Llewellyn's Moon Sign Book*. In addition to astrometeorology, she specializes in predictive astrology. Her new book, *Llewellyn's Complete Book of Predictive Astrology*, will be available in October 2011.

Kris is an avid NASCAR fan, although she'd rather be a driver than a spectator. However, in 2011, she fulfilled her wish when she drove a stock car for twelve fast laps. She posts a weather forecast for each of the thirty-six race weekends (qualifying and race day) for NASCAR drivers and fans. Visit her website at www.pitstop -forecasting.com. Kris also enjoys gardening, reading, jazz, and her three cats.

New Concepts for Zodiac Signs

The signs of the zodiac represent characteristics and traits that indicate how energy operates within our lives. The signs tell the story of human evolution and development, and all are necessary to form the continuum of whole-life experience. In fact, all twelve signs are represented within your astrological chart.

Although the traditional metaphors for the twelve signs (such as Aries, the Ram) are always functional, these alternative concepts for each of the twelve signs also describe the gradual unfolding of the human spirit.

Aries: The Initiator is the first sign of the zodiac and encompasses the primary concept of getting things started. This fiery ignition and bright beginning can prove to be the thrust necessary for new life, but the Initiator also can appear before a situation is ready for change and create disruption.

Taurus: The Maintainer sustains what Aries has begun and brings stability and focus into the picture, yet there also can be a tendency to try to maintain something in its current state without allowing for new growth.

Gemini: The Questioner seeks to determine whether alternatives are possible and offers diversity to the processes Taurus has brought into stability. Yet questioning can also lead to distraction, subsequently scattering energy and diffusing focus.

Cancer: The Nurturer provides the qualities necessary for growth and security, and encourages a deepening awareness of emotional needs. Yet this same nurturing can stifle individuation if it becomes too smothering.

Leo: The Loyalist directs and centralizes the experiences Cancer feeds. This quality is powerfully targeted toward self-awareness, but can be shortsighted. Hence, the Loyalist can hold steadfastly to viewpoints or feelings that inhibit new experiences.

Virgo: The Modifier analyzes the situations Leo brings to light and determines possibilities for change. Even though this change may be in the name of improvement, it can lead to dissatisfaction with the self if not directed in harmony with higher needs.

Libra: The Judge is constantly comparing everything to be sure that a certain level of rightness and perfection is presented. However, the Judge can also present possibilities that are harsh and seem to be cold or without feeling.

Scorpio: The Catalyst steps into the play of life to provide the quality of alchemical transformation. The Catalyst can stir the brew just enough to create a healing potion, or may get things going to such a powerful extent that they boil out of control.

Sagittarius: The Adventurer moves away from Scorpio's dimension to seek what lies beyond the horizon. The Adventurer continually looks for possibilities that answer the ultimate questions, but may forget the pathway back home.

Capricorn: The Pragmatist attempts to put everything into its rightful place and find ways to make life work out right. The Pragmatist can teach lessons of practicality and determination, but can become highly self-righteous when shortsighted.

Aquarius: The Reformer looks for ways to take what Capricorn has built and bring it up to date. Yet there is also a tendency to scrap the original in favor of a new plan that may not have the stable foundation necessary to operate effectively.

Pisces: The Visionary brings mysticism and imagination, and challenges the soul to move beyond the physical plane, into the realm of what might be. The Visionary can pierce the veil, returning enlightened to the physical world. The challenge is to avoid getting lost within the illusion of an alternate reality.

Astrology Basics

Astrology is an ancient and continually evolving system used to clarify your identity and your needs. An astrological chart—which is calculated using the date, time, and place of birth—contains many factors that symbolically represent the needs, expressions, and experiences that make up the whole person. A professional astrologer interprets this symbolic picture, offering you an accurate portrait of your personality.

The chart itself—the horoscope—is a portrait of an individual. Generally, a natal (or birth) horoscope is drawn on a circular wheel. The wheel is divided into twelve segments, called houses. Each of the twelve houses represents a different aspect of the individual, much like the facets of a brilliantly cut stone. The houses depict different environments, such as home, school, and work. The houses also represent roles and relationships: parents, friends, lovers, children, partners. In each environment, individuals show a different side of their personality. At home, you may represent yourself quite differently than you do on the job. Additionally, in each relationship you will project a different image of yourself. Your parents rarely see the side you show to intimate friends.

Symbols for the planets, the Sun, and the Moon are drawn inside the houses. Each planet represents a separate kind of energy. You experience and express that energy in specific ways. (For a complete list, refer to the table on the next page.) The way you use each of these energies is up to you. The planets in your chart do not make you do anything!

The twelve signs of the zodiac indicate characteristics and traits that further define your personality. Each sign can be expressed in positive and negative ways. (The basic meaning of each of the signs is explained in the corresponding sections ahead.) What's more, you have all twelve signs somewhere in your chart. Signs that are strongly emphasized by the planets have greater force. The Sun, Moon, and planets are placed on the chart according to their position at the time of birth. The qualities of a sign, combined with the energy of a planet, indicate how you might be most likely to use that energy and the best ways to develop that energy. The signs add color, emphasis, and dimension to the personality.

Signs of the Zodiac

Aries	♈	The Initiator
Taurus	♉	The Maintainer
Gemini	♊	The Questioner
Cancer	♋	The Nurturer
Leo	♌	The Loyalist
Virgo	♍	The Modifier
Libra	♎	The Judge
Scorpio	♏	The Catalyst
Sagittarius	♐	The Adventurer
Capricorn	♑	The Pragmatist
Aquarius	♒	The Reformer
Pisces	♓	The Visionary

Signs are also placed at the cusps, or dividing lines, of each of the houses. The influence of the signs on the houses is much the same as their influence on the Sun, Moon, and planets. Each house is shaped by the sign on its cusp.

When you view a horoscope, you will notice that there appear to be four distinctive angles dividing the wheel of the chart. The line that divides the chart into a top and bottom half represents the horizon. In most cases, the left side of the horizon is called the Ascendant. The zodiac sign on the Ascendant is your rising sign. The Ascendant indicates the way others are likely to view you.

The Sun, Moon, or a planet can be compared to an actor in a play. The sign shows how the energy works, like the role the actor plays in a drama. The house indicates where the energy operates, like the setting of a play. On a psychological level, the Sun represents who you think you are. The Ascendant describes who others think you are, and the Moon reflects your emotional self.

Astrologers also study the geometric relationships between the Sun, Moon, and planets. These geometric angles are called aspects. Aspects further define the strengths, weaknesses, and challenges within your physical, mental, emotional, and spiritual self. Sometimes, patterns also appear in an astrological chart. These patterns have meaning.

To understand cycles for any given point in time, astrologers study several factors. Many use transits, which refer to the movement and positions of the planets. When astrologers compare those positions to the birth horoscope, the transits indicate activity in particular areas of the chart. The *Sun Sign Book* uses transits.

As you can see, your Sun sign is just one of many factors that describe who you are—but it is a powerful one! As the symbol of the ego, the Sun in your chart reflects your drive to be noticed. Most people can easily relate to the concepts associated with their Sun sign, since it is tied to their sense of personal identity.

The Planets

Sun	☉	The ego, self, willpower
Moon	☽	The subconscious self, habits
Mercury	☿	Communication, the intellect
Venus	♀	Emotional expression, love, appreciation, artistry
Mars	♂	Physical drive, assertiveness, anger
Jupiter	♃	Philosophy, ethics, generosity
Saturn	♄	Discipline, focus, responsibility
Uranus	♅	Individuality, rebelliousness
Neptune	♆	Imagination, sensitivity, compassion
Pluto	♇	Transformation, healing, regeneration

Meanings of the Planets

The Sun

The Sun indicates the psychological bias that will dominate your actions. What you see, and why, is told in the reading for your Sun. The Sun also shows the basic energy patterns of your body and psyche. In many ways, the Sun is the dominant force in your horoscope and your life. Other influences, especially that of the Moon, may modify the Sun's influence, but nothing will cause you to depart very far from the basic solar pattern. Always keep in mind the basic influence of the Sun and remember all other influences must be interpreted in terms of it, especially insofar as they play a visible role in your life. You may think, dream, imagine, and hope a thousand things, according to your Moon and your other planets, but the Sun is what you are. To be your best self in terms of your Sun is to cause your energies to work along the path in which they will have maximum help from planetary vibrations.

The Moon
The Moon tells the desire of your life. When you know what you mean but can't verbalize it, it is your Moon that knows it and your Sun that can't say it. The wordless ecstasy, the mute sorrow, the secret dream, the esoteric picture of yourself that you can't get across to the world, or that the world doesn't comprehend or value—these are the products of the Moon. When you are misunderstood, it is your Moon nature, expressed imperfectly through the Sun sign, that feels betrayed. Things you know without thought—intuitions, hunches, instincts—are the products of the Moon. Modes of expression that you feel truly reflect your deepest self belong to the Moon: art, letters, creative work of any kind; sometimes love; sometimes business. Whatever you feel to be most deeply yourself is the product of your Moon and of the sign your Moon occupies at birth.

Mercury
Mercury is the sensory antenna of your horoscope. Its position by sign indicates your reactions to sights, sounds, odors, tastes, and touch impressions, affording a key to the attitude you have toward the physical world around you. Mercury is the messenger through which your physical body and brain (ruled by the Sun) and your inner nature (ruled by the Moon) are kept in contact with the outer world, which will appear to you according to the index of Mercury's position by sign in the horoscope. Mercury rules your rational mind.

Venus
Venus is the emotional antenna of your horoscope. Through Venus, impressions come to you from the outer world. The position of Venus by sign at the time of your birth determines your attitude toward these experiences. As Mercury is the messenger linking sense impressions (sight, smell, etc.) to the basic nature of your Sun and Moon, so Venus is the messenger linking emotional impressions. If Venus is found in the same sign as the Sun, emotions gain importance in your life, and have a direct bearing on your actions. If Venus is in the same sign as the Moon, emotions bear directly on

your inner nature, add self-confidence, make you sensitive to emotional impressions, and frequently indicate that you have more love in your heart than you are able to express. If Venus is in the same sign as Mercury, emotional impressions and sense impressions work together; you tend to idealize the world of the senses and sensualize the world of the emotions to interpret what you see and hear.

Mars

Mars is the energy principle in the horoscope. Its position indicates the channels into which energy will most easily be directed. It is the planet through which the activities of the Sun and the desires of the Moon express themselves in action. In the same sign as the Sun, Mars gives abundant energy, sometimes misdirected in temper, temperament, and quarrels. In the same sign as the Moon, it gives a great capacity to make use of the innermost aims, and to make the inner desires articulate and practical. In the same sign as Venus, it quickens emotional reactions and causes you to act on them, makes for ardor and passion in love, and fosters an earthly awareness of emotional realities.

Jupiter

Jupiter is the feeler for opportunity that you have out in the world. It passes along chances of a lifetime for consideration according to the basic nature of your Sun and Moon. Jupiter's sign position indicates the places where you will look for opportunity, the uses to which you wish to put it, and the capacity you have to react and profit by it. Jupiter is ordinarily and erroneously called the planet of luck. It is "luck" insofar as it is the index of opportunity, but your luck depends less on what comes to you than on what you do with what comes to you. In the same sign as the Sun or Moon, Jupiter gives a direct and generally effective response to opportunity and is likely to show forth at its "luckiest." If Jupiter is in the same sign as Mercury, sense impressions are interpreted opportunistically. If Jupiter is in the same sign as Venus, you interpret emotions in such a way as to turn them to your advantage; your feelings work harmoniously with the chances for progress that the world has to offer. If Jupiter is in the same sign as Mars, you follow opportunity with energy, dash, enthusiasm, and courage; take long chances; and play your cards wide open.

Saturn

Saturn indicates the direction that will be taken in life by the self-preserving principle that, in its highest manifestation, ceases to be purely defensive and becomes ambitious and aspiring. Your defense or attack against the world is shown by the sign position of Saturn in the horoscope of birth. If Saturn is in the same sign as the Sun or Moon, defense predominates, and there is danger of introversion. The farther Saturn is from the Sun, Moon, and Ascendant, the better for objectivity and extroversion. If Saturn is in the same sign as Mercury, there is a profound and serious reaction to sensory impressions; this position generally accompanies a deep and efficient mind. If Saturn is in the same sign as Venus, a defensive attitude toward emotional experience makes for apparent coolness in love and difficulty with the emotions and human relations. If Saturn is in the same sign as Mars, confusion between defensive and aggressive urges can make a person indecisive. On the other hand, if the Sun and Moon are strong and the total personality well developed, a balanced, peaceful, and calm individual of sober judgment and moderate actions may be indicated. If Saturn is in the same sign as Jupiter, the reaction to opportunity is sober and balanced.

Uranus

Uranus in a general way relates to creativity, originality, or individuality, and its position by sign in the horoscope tells the direction in which you will seek to express yourself. In the same sign as Mercury or the Moon, Uranus suggests acute awareness, a quick reaction to sense impressions and experiences, or a hair-trigger mind. In the same sign as the Sun, it points to great nervous activity, a high-strung nature, and an original, creative, or eccentric personality. In the same sign as Mars, Uranus indicates high-speed activity, love of swift motion, and perhaps love of danger. In the same sign as Venus, it suggests an unusual reaction to emotional experience, idealism, sensuality, and original ideas about love and human relations. In the same sign as Saturn, Uranus points to good sense; this can be a practical, creative position, but more often than not it sets up a destructive conflict between practicality and originality that can result in a stalemate. In the same sign as Jupiter, Uranus makes opportunity, creates wealth and the means of getting it, and is conducive to the inventive, executive, and daring.

Neptune

Neptune relates to the deep subconscious, inherited mentality, and spirituality, indicating what you take for granted in life. Neptune in the same sign as the Sun or Moon indicates that intuitions and hunches—or delusions—dominate; there is a need for rigidly holding to reality. In the same sign as Mercury, Neptune indicates sharp sensory perceptions, a sensitive and perhaps creative mind, and a quivering intensity of reaction to sensory experience. In the same sign as Venus, it reveals idealistic and romantic (or sentimental) reactions to emotional experience, as well as the danger of sensationalism and a love of strange pleasures. In the same sign as Mars, Neptune indicates energy and intuition that work together to make mastery of life—one of the signs of having angels (or devils) on your side. When in the same sign as Jupiter, Neptune describes an intuitive response to opportunity along practical and money-making lines. In the same sign as Saturn, Neptune indicates intuitive defense and attack on the world, which is generally successful unless Saturn is polarized on the negative side; then there is danger of unhappiness.

Pluto

Pluto is a planet of extremes—from the lowest criminal and violent level of our society to the heights people can attain when they realize their significance in the collectivity of humanity. Pluto also rules three important mysteries of life—sex, death, and rebirth—and links them to each other. One level of death symbolized by Pluto is the physical death of an individual, which occurs so that a person can be reborn into another body to further his or her spiritual development. On another level, individuals can experience a "death" of their old self when they realize the deeper significance of life; thus they become one of the "second born." In a natal horoscope, Pluto signifies our perspective on the world, our conscious and subconscious. Since so many of Pluto's qualities are centered on the deeper mysteries of life, the house position of Pluto, and aspects to it, can show you how to attain a deeper understanding of the importance of the spiritual in your life.

Astrological Glossary

Air: One of the four basic elements. The air signs are Gemini, Libra, and Aquarius.

Angles: The four points of the chart that divide it into quadrants. The angles are sensitive areas that lend emphasis to planets located near them. These points are located on the cusps of the First, Fourth, Seventh, and Tenth Houses in a chart.

Ascendant: Rising sign. The degree of the zodiac on the eastern horizon at the time and place for which the horoscope is calculated. It can indicate the image or physical appearance you project to the world. The cusp of the First House.

Aspect: The angular relationship between planets, sensitive points, or house cusps in a horoscope. Lines drawn between the two points and the center of the chart, representing the Earth, form the angle of the aspect. Astrological aspects include conjunction (two points that are 0 degrees apart), opposition (two points, 180 degrees apart), square (two points, 90 degrees apart), sextile (two points, 60 degrees apart), and trine (two points, 120 degrees apart). Aspects can indicate harmony or challenge.

Cardinal Sign: One of the three qualities, or categories, that describe how a sign expresses itself. Aries, Cancer, Libra, and Capricorn are the cardinal signs, believed to initiate activity.

Chiron: Chiron is a comet traveling in orbit between Saturn and Uranus. Although research on its effect on natal charts is not yet complete, it is believed to represent a key or doorway, healing, ecology, and a bridge between traditional and modern methods.

Conjunction: An aspect or angle between two points in a chart where the two points are close enough so that the energies join. Can be considered either harmonious or challenging, depending on the planets involved and their placement.

Cusp: A dividing line between signs or houses in a chart.

Degree: Degree of arc. One of 360 divisions of a circle. The circle of the zodiac is divided into twelve astrological signs of 30 degrees each. Each degree is made up of 60 minutes, and each minute is made up of 60 seconds of zodiacal longitude.

Earth: One of the four basic elements. The earth signs are Taurus, Virgo, and Capricorn.

Eclipse: A solar eclipse is the full or partial covering of the Sun by the Moon (as viewed from Earth), and a lunar eclipse is the full or partial covering of the Moon by the Earth's own shadow.

Ecliptic: The Sun's apparent path around the Earth, which is actually the plane of the Earth's orbit extended out into space. The ecliptic forms the center of the zodiac.

Electional Astrology: A branch of astrology concerned with choosing the best time to initiate an activity.

Elements: The signs of the zodiac are divided into four groups of three zodiacal signs, each symbolized by one of the four elements of the ancients: fire, earth, air, and water. The element of a sign is said to express its essential nature.

Ephemeris: A listing of the Sun, Moon, and planets' positions and related information for astrological purposes.

Equinox: Equal night. The point in the Earth's orbit around the Sun at which the day and night are equal in length.

Feminine Signs: Each zodiac sign is either "masculine" or "feminine." Earth signs (Taurus, Virgo, and Capricorn) and water signs (Cancer, Scorpio, and Pisces) are feminine.

Fire: One of the four basic elements. The fire signs are Aries, Leo, and Sagittarius.

Fixed Signs: Fixed is one of the three qualities, or categories, that describe how a sign expresses itself. The fixed signs are Taurus, Leo, Scorpio, and Aquarius. Fixed signs are said to be predisposed to existing patterns and somewhat resistant to change.

Hard Aspects: Hard aspects are those aspects in a chart that astrologers believe to represent difficulty or challenges. Among the hard aspects are the square, the opposition, and the conjunction (depending on which planets are conjunct).

Horizon: The word "horizon" is used in astrology in a manner similar to its common usage, except that only the eastern and western horizons are considered useful. The eastern horizon at the point of birth is the Ascendant, or First House cusp, of a natal chart, and the western horizon at the point of birth is the Descendant, or Seventh House cusp.

Houses: Division of the horoscope into twelve segments, beginning with the Ascendant. The dividing line between the houses are called house cusps. Each house corresponds to certain aspects of daily living, and is ruled by the astrological sign that governs the cusp, or dividing line between the house and the one previous.

Ingress: The point of entry of a planet into a sign.

Lagna: A term used in Hindu or Vedic astrology for Ascendant, the degree of the zodiac on the eastern horizon at the time of birth.

Masculine Signs: Each of the twelve signs of the zodiac is either "masculine" or "feminine." The fire signs (Aries, Leo, and Sagittarius) and the air signs (Gemini, Libra, and Aquarius) are masculine.

Midheaven: The highest point on the ecliptic, where it intersects the meridian that passes directly above the place for which the horoscope is cast; the southern point of the horoscope.

Midpoint: A point equally distant to two planets or house cusps. Midpoints are considered by some astrologers to be sensitive points in a person's chart.

Mundane Astrology: Mundane astrology is the branch of astrology generally concerned with political and economic events, and the nations involved in these events.

Mutable Signs: Mutable is one of the three qualities, or categories, that describe how a sign expresses itself. Mutable signs are Gemini, Virgo, Sagittarius, and Pisces. Mutable signs are said to be very adaptable and sometimes changeable.

Natal Chart: A person's birth chart. A natal chart is essentially a "snapshot" showing the placement of each of the planets at the exact time of a person's birth.

Node: The point where the planets cross the ecliptic, or the Earth's apparent path around the Sun. The North Node is the point where a planet moves northward, from the Earth's perspective, as it crosses the ecliptic; the South Node is where it moves south.

Opposition: Two points in a chart that are 180 degrees apart.

Orb: A small degree of margin used when calculating aspects in a chart. For example, although 180 degrees form an exact opposition, an astrologer might consider an aspect within 3 or 4 degrees on either side of 180 degrees to be an opposition, as the impact of the aspect can still be felt within this range. The less orb on an aspect, the stronger the aspect. Astrologers' opinions vary on how many degrees of orb to allow for each aspect.

Outer Planet: Uranus, Neptune, and Pluto are known as the outer planets. Because of their distance from the Sun, they take a long time to complete a single rotation. Everyone born within a few years on either side of a given date will have similar placements of these planets.

Planet: The planets used in astrology are Mercury, Venus, Mars, Jupiter, Saturn, Uranus, Neptune, and Pluto. For astrological purposes, the Sun and Moon are also considered planets. A natal or birth chart lists planetary placement at the moment of birth.

Planetary Rulership: The sign in which a planet is most harmoniously placed. Examples are the Sun in Leo, Jupiter in Sagittarius, and the Moon in Cancer.

Precession of Equinoxes: The gradual movement of the point of the Spring Equinox, located at 0 degrees Aries. This point marks the beginning of the tropical zodiac. The point moves slowly backward through the constellations of the zodiac, so that about every 2,000 years the equinox begins in an earlier constellation.

Qualities: In addition to categorizing the signs by element, astrologers place the twelve signs of the zodiac into three additional categories, or qualities: cardinal, mutable, or fixed. Each sign is considered to be a combination of its element and quality. Where the element of a sign describes its basic nature, the quality describes its mode of expression.

Retrograde Motion: Apparent backward motion of a planet. This is an illusion caused by the relative motion of the Earth and other planets in their elliptical orbits.

Sextile: Two points in a chart that are 60 degrees apart.

Sidereal Zodiac: Generally used by Hindu or Vedic astrologers. The sidereal zodiac is located where the constellations are actually positioned in the sky.

Soft Aspects: Soft aspects indicate good fortune or an easy relationship in the chart. Among the soft aspects are the trine, the sextile, and the conjunction (depending on which planets are conjunct each other).

Square: Two points in a chart that are 90 degrees apart.

Sun Sign: The sign of the zodiac in which the Sun is located at any given time.

Synodic Cycle: The time between conjunctions of two planets.

Trine: Two points in a chart that are 120 degrees apart.

Tropical Zodiac: The tropical zodiac begins at 0 degrees Aries, where the Sun is located during the Spring Equinox. This system is used by most Western astrologers and throughout this book.

Void-of-Course: A planet is void-of-course after it has made its last aspect within a sign, but before it has entered a new sign.

Water: One of the four basic elements. The water signs are Cancer, Scorpio, and Pisces.

Ascendant Table

Your Sun Sign	Your Time of Birth					
	6–8 am	8–10 am	10 am–Noon	Noon–2 pm	2–4 pm	4–6 pm
Aries	Taurus	Gemini	Cancer	Leo	Virgo	Libra
Taurus	Gemini	Cancer	Leo	Virgo	Libra	Scorpio
Gemini	Cancer	Leo	Virgo	Libra	Scorpio	Sagittarius
Cancer	Leo	Virgo	Libra	Scorpio	Sagittarius	Capricorn
Leo	Virgo	Libra	Scorpio	Sagittarius	Capricorn	Aquarius
Virgo	Libra	Scorpio	Sagittarius	Capricorn	Aquarius	Pisces
Libra	Scorpio	Sagittarius	Capricorn	Aquarius	Pisces	Aries
Scorpio	Sagittarius	Capricorn	Aquarius	Pisces	Aries	Taurus
Sagittarius	Capricorn	Aquarius	Pisces	Aries	Taurus	Gemini
Capricorn	Aquarius	Pisces	Aries	Taurus	Gemini	Cancer
Aquarius	Pisces	Aries	Taurus	Gemini	Cancer	Leo
Pisces	Aries	Taurus	Gemini	Cancer	Leo	Virgo

Your Time of Birth

Your Sun Sign	6–8 pm	8–10 pm	10 pm–Midnight	Midnight–2 am	2–4 am	4–6 am
Aries	Scorpio	Sagittarius	Capricorn	Aquarius	Pisces	Aries
Taurus	Sagittarius	Capricorn	Aquarius	Pisces	Aries	Taurus
Gemini	Capricorn	Aquarius	Pisces	Aries	Taurus	Gemini
Cancer	Aquarius	Pisces	Aries	Taurus	Gemini	Cancer
Leo	Pisces	Aries	Taurus	Gemini	Cancer	Leo
Virgo	Aries	Taurus	Gemini	Cancer	Leo	Virgo
Libra	Taurus	Gemini	Cancer	Leo	Virgo	Libra
Scorpio	Gemini	Cancer	Leo	Virgo	Libra	Scorpio
Sagittarius	Cancer	Leo	Virgo	Libra	Scorpio	Sagittarius
Capricorn	Leo	Virgo	Libra	Scorpio	Sagittarius	Capricorn
Aquarius	Virgo	Libra	Scorpio	Sagittarius	Capricorn	Aquarius
Pisces	Libra	Scorpio	Sagittarius	Capricorn	Aquarius	Pisces

How to use this table: 1. Find your Sun sign in the left column.
2. Find your approximate birth time in a vertical column.
3. Line up your Sun sign and birth time to find your Ascendant.

This table will give you an approximation of your Ascendant. If you feel that the sign listed as your Ascendant is incorrect, try the one either before or after the listed sign. It is difficult to determine your exact Ascendant without a complete natal chart.

Using This Book

This book contains what is called "Sun sign astrology," that is, astrology based on the sign that your Sun was in at the time of your birth. The technique has its foundation in ancient Greek astrology, in which the Sun was one of five points in the chart that were used as focal points for delineation.

The most effective way to use astrology, however, is through one-on-one work with a professional astrologer, who can integrate the eight or so other astrological bodies into the interpretation to provide you with guidance. There are factors related to the year and time of day you were born that are highly significant in the way you approach life and vital to making wise choices. In addition, there are ways of using astrology that aren't addressed here, such as compatibility between two specific individuals, discovering family patterns, or picking a day for a wedding or grand opening.

To best use the information in the monthly forecasts, you'll want to determine your Ascendant, or rising sign. If you don't know your Ascendant, the tables following this description will help you determine your rising sign. They are most accurate for those born in the continental United States. They're only an approximation, but they can be used as a good rule of thumb. Your exact Ascendant may vary from the tables according to your time and place of birth. Once you've approximated your ascending sign using the tables or determined your Ascendant by having your chart calculated, you'll know two significant factors in your chart. Read the monthly forecast sections for both your Sun and Ascendant to gain the most useful information. In addition, you can read the section about the sign your Moon is in. The Sun is the true, inner you; the Ascendant is your shell or appearance and the person you are becoming; the Moon is the person you were—or still are based on habits and memories.

I've also included information about the planets' retrogrades this year. Most people have heard of "Mercury retrograde." In fact, all the planets except the Sun and Moon appear to travel backward (retrograde) in their path periodically. This only appears to happen because we on the Earth are not seeing the other planets from the middle of the solar system. Rather, we are watching them from our own moving object. We are like a train that moves past cars on the freeway that are going at a slower speed. To us on the train, the cars look like they're going backward. Mercury turns retrograde about every four months for three weeks; Venus every eighteen months for six weeks; Mars every two years for two to three months. The rest of the planets each retrograde once a year for four to five months. During each retrograde, we have the opportunity to try something new, something we conceived of at the beginning of the planet's yearly cycle. The times when the planets change direction are significant, as are the beginning and midpoint (peak or culmination) of each cycle. These are noted in your forecast each month.

Your "Rewarding Days" and "Challenging Days" sections indicate times when you'll feel either more centered or more out of balance. The rewarding days are not the only times you can perform well, but the times you're likely to feel better integrated! During challenging days, take extra time to center yourself by meditating or using other techniques that help you feel more objective.

The Action Table found at the end of each sign's section offers general guidelines for the best time to take a particular action. Please note, however, that your whole chart will provide more accurate guidelines for the best time to do something. Therefore, use this table with a grain of salt, and never let it stop you from taking an action you feel compelled to take.

You can use this information for an objective awareness about the way the current cycles are affecting you. Realize that the power of astrology is even more useful when you have a complete chart and professional guidance.

2012 at a Glance

The aftermath of the economic crisis has created a new normal both for individuals and global society as a whole. And just as we're beginning to adapt and adjust to this new normal, 2012 will bring different and also related challenges that will further define this new normal. The first signs of this were apparent in the winter and spring of 2011, with deficits at all levels of government and revolutions in the Middle East and similar upheavals in several American states. We will see more of this in 2012, and government leaders continue to grapple with the new economic conditions and citizens rebel against cutbacks.

All of this is the influence of Uranus in Aries and Pluto in Capricorn. Although they will form an exact alignment in June and September, the effects of these planets will be apparent much of the year. Uranus is the planet of change and sudden, unexpected events. Pluto is associated with global events and money; and in Capricorn, with government, rules, and structure. When these two clash, we can thus expect change on many levels—change that is all a part of the process of creating a new foundation and a new reality.

Jupiter, Saturn, and Neptune will bring their own version of change this year when they shift signs. Jupiter spends the first half of the year in Taurus, the sign of stability and money, where it should continue to help strengthen the economy. But food prices will continue to rise until Jupiter changes signs June 11, moving on to Gemini, the sign it will occupy for about the next year. In Gemini, Jupiter will emphasize learning and education, neighborhood activities, and all forms of communication, in addition to the lighter side of life.

Saturn changes signs October 5, moving from Libra to Scorpio. Relationships are the main focus of Saturn in Libra, reinforcing the value and importance of people we love rather than the things we want. Scorpio is a money sign, so Saturn's two-and-a-half year transit of this sign will bring a financial restructuring on personal and governmental levels, whether out of necessity or desire, as well as an emphasis on core values and saving money.

Neptune concludes its transit of Aquarius when it shifts into Pisces on February 3. During its long transit of this sign—until

2025—it will emphasize health and welfare, the environment, and the oceans, along with more interest in charitable causes and neighbors helping neighbors. The oceans may provide a new source of fuel, and will certainly be explored as never before.

But 2012 is not only a year of change. It's also a year of opportunity for anyone who relies on the knowledge and experience of the past and looks to the future with enthusiastic optimism. Embrace life, have faith in yourself, and recreate your world the way you want it to be!

2012 SUN SIGN BOOK

Forecasts
By Kris Brandt Riske

ARIES

The Ram
March 20 to April 19

♈

Element: Fire

Quality: Cardinal

Polarity: Yang/Masculine

Planetary Ruler: Mars

Meditation: I build upon my strengths

Gemstone: Diamond

Power Stones: Bloodstone, carnelian, ruby

Key Phrase: I am

Glyph: Ram's head

Anatomy: Head, face, throat

Color: Red, white

Animal: Ram

Myths/Legends: Artemis, Jason and the Golden Fleece

House: First

Opposite Sign: Libra

Flower: Geranium

Key Word: Initiative

Your Strengths and Challenges

You're the epitome of action, energy, and initiative, and all these traits can contribute to your success. But you also can be impulsive and impatient, dashing through life with little consideration of consequences. If you use your best qualities to advantage, however, they can help you snap up opportunities while the competition is still debating the pros and cons.

Born under the first sign of the zodiac, you're a natural leader; almost always the first in line; and the one who jumps in, takes charge, and makes decisions. This infectious enthusiasm, fueled by fiery Mars, your ruling planet, is the spark that gets things moving. With it, however, comes a challenge: follow-through. You have a passion for new endeavors, but when the newness wears off, your interest begins to wane. Try to develop some staying power; you'll go further in life.

Noted for your quick mind, you can size up a situation in an instant, easily grasping most of the important points and players. Yet there are times when you jump to conclusions and make snap decisions you later regret. Learn from these experiences and teach yourself to think before you act; careful thought truly is sometimes the wisest option. Adopt a similar approach when driving and in physical activities, where being a daredevil is foolish.

Confident and outgoing, you greet each day with optimism and the freshness of your springtime sign, ready for life's latest adventure. This pioneering attitude sets you apart as someone who truly knows how to live each day to the fullest with all the zesty enthusiasm that can lead to great achievements.

Your Relationships

Although you delight in the company of others, only those who know you well realize the high value you place on relationships. Some see you as a mover-and-shaker who flies solo, interested only in your own agenda. That's true at times, but overall you want and need human companionship and have a knack for connecting with people. Just be sure to greet differing opinions with an open mind. Chances are, you'll learn something and might even change your views.

You're a fabulous friend to those few in your inner circle, and also popular with your many acquaintances. Networking is your specialty, one of your keys to success, and you excel at teamwork when you feel it's in your best interest to join the crowd. Group activities, including clubs and organizations, bring out your best and maximize your leadership skills.

Your natural flair for romance will impress a date, or your partner. You know how to keep love alive, and partnership is very important to you because you feel incomplete until you link hearts with a soul mate—someone who can not only share your dreams but teach you the art of compromise. Libra, your opposite sign, could be your best match, and you might be compatible with a Leo or Sagittarius, the other fire signs. Airy Gemini and Aquarius would stimulate your thinking, but conflict could be more the norm than the exception with a Cancer or Capricorn.

Domestic life is equally important to you, and most Aries people are actively involved in the lives of their children and extended family—parents, siblings, cousins, aunts, and uncles. These strong ties are a part of your emotional well-being and bring out your softer, nurturing side. Your children are a source of pride, although you can overindulge them. Remember: sometimes it's better to let children learn life lessons the hard way rather than try to insulate them from reality.

Your Career and Money
You have wealth potential and a better chance of achieving it if you resist impulsive purchases. Think long-term, let your practical side emerge, and live within a budget. You also have a knack for finding bargains if you take your time. Some people with an Aries Sun receive a sizable inheritance from a family member, and you also could do well in real estate. If you enjoy do-it-yourself projects, you might profit from remodeling houses or owning rental property.

Your ambitions are centered on your career, where you have the potential to rise above the rest. Be aware, though, that it may take you longer than your peers to find your niche. Once you do, there's little that can deter you from your goal because you meet challenges head-on, knowing that with determination and effort you can succeed. So once you're on the right career path don't let impatience prompt you to move on, unless of course a new position can advance your aims.

You're good with details in your everyday work, although you also need the freedom to set your own pace. A hard worker, you expect coworkers to do the same and have little tolerance for those who don't perform up to their abilities or fulfill their responsibilities. Try to remember that not everyone has your drive.

Your Lighter Side

As an Aries, you have an insider's view of the zodiac. This unique perspective comes from your position as the first in line. You have a sixth sense about the other eleven, and the ability to use the energy of each in its purest form. It's your gift from the universe and one that can keep you a step ahead in life, relationships, family, finances, communication, and learning.

Affirmation for the Year

I value relationships and security as much
as I value independence.

The Year Ahead for Aries

People and places are emphasized this year, as are your career and money. Travel is likely, whether you take a few getaway weekends or opt for a longer trip anywhere in the world. The strong focus on people includes a partner (business or personal), friends, neighbors, and relatives, especially siblings.

Expansive Jupiter will spend the first half of the year in Taurus, your solar Second House of income and spending. Keep these two descriptive words in mind, because you may see your income rise, and you're likely to spend more. Unexpected bills could arise, primarily later in the year, so it's wise to save while Jupiter transits Taurus through June 10. You'll also have a better eye for bargains, but just because it's a good deal doesn't mean you have to buy, which you'll be in the mood to do.

Your Solar Second House is also about possessions. Take a look around you. If you see clutter or long-unused items and clothing, now is the time to restore order. You also can profit from what you no longer need. Organize a neighborhood yard sale and take clothing to a consignment shop. Chances are, you'll be pleasantly surprised by how much extra cash you can generate from recycling your discards. March is an especially good month to do this.

Jupiter's focus shifts to Gemini, your solar Third House, June 11. During the following twelve months, you'll have more contact with neighbors, siblings, and relatives, and might even take a weekend trip with some of them. Overall, relationships with these people will be upbeat. You might also have a sudden desire to get involved (or more involved) in your community or a neighborhood project. Be a little cautious, though, if such an activity requires more than a minimal personal financial commitment.

Jupiter in Gemini will also stimulate your interest in learning. You might decide to return to school or simply become a voracious reader. Or take a class for the fun of it to learn more about a subject that has always interested you. This transit, however, can also make it tough to keep up with what will be a more hectic daily pace. Meetings, calls, texts, e-mail, and social media sites could eat up an incredible amount of time if you're not careful.

Saturn transits Libra, your solar Seventh House, through October 4, and then moves on to Scorpio. During its time in Libra, Saturn will focus on the relationships in your life, especially a partner and those closest to you. Although Saturn here can indicate strained relationships, it doesn't always manifest this way. Solid ties are usually strengthened, while you may choose to distance yourself from those you've outgrown.

Saturn is the planet of lessons and karma, so be alert for people who might fit in either of these categories. Learn from them, and if you realize you dislike something about the other person, it's likely to be a lesson about your own view of relationships. You'll also want to take care not to prematurely break ties, lest you have to repeat the lesson in the future. Overall, this transit can be a blessing in that you will learn much about yourself from observing and interacting with others.

Saturn's emphasis shifts to your solar Eighth House of joint resources when it moves on to Scorpio October 5. Here you will have the opportunity to better learn the value of budgeting and financial management, including investments and preparing for retirement (however many years away it is). If you have created sizeable consumer debt, this is an excellent transit for paying off what you owe during the next two and a half years, and for building up savings through regular deposits. However, if debt is not an issue, you'll be even more financially conservative, spending less and saving more.

Joint resources include your partner's income, which could be reduced, as well as insurance, inheritance, loans, and your credit score. Be sure to check the latter as errors related to the past can pop up now. Insurance premiums can increase during this transit, or coverage could be less comprehensive, so be sure to read any policy changes and to double-check that property is adequately covered.

Uranus continues to advance in your sign this year, where it will be until 2018. This independence-loving planet can motivate you to flip your life upside down, especially during the year it contacts your Sun. During the other years, you'll periodically feel its presence when an unusually strong spontaneous urge takes hold. The unexpected may become more the norm than the exception in your life.

However, Uranus's main influence as it moves through your Sun sign is to encourage you to embrace personal change. This could be your outward appearance, or you might sense an increasing desire to aim your life in a new direction with a fresh set of goals that will help you to maximize your skills and talents. You'll also welcome new experiences, things that never interested you in the past. The best way to fulfill your new-found need for freedom is to change self-limiting behaviors rather than let the energy emerge as a rebellious streak. Use this influence in a positive way and by 2018 you will view and approach the world differently and for the better.

Neptune, which entered Aquarius in 1998, concludes its transit of your Solar Eleventh House February 2. Friendship and groups are the main focus of Neptune here, and during these many years you've undoubtedly seen the best and the worst of both. You've been inspired and disappointed, and wondered how you could have been so wrong about some people. Others, however, have helped to fulfill your life by serving as mentors or simply by being there when you needed them. And you have done the same for many, becoming wiser in the process.

Now Neptune begins its next fourteen-year transit, this time in Pisces, your solar Twelfth House. Neptune is very comfortable here, transiting its home sign. In the coming years you might at some point become involved in a good cause as a volunteer, or take on the role of care-giver for a relative. But Neptune's main influence is to encourage you to look inward, to retreat from your hectic life at times in order to get in touch with your inner voice and the inner you. Meditation can be beneficial and also help to nurture your sixth sense, which will be more active during this transit.

This sector also relates to all things hidden and behind the scenes, so take care not to become involved in any activities, even unwittingly, that could in some way damage your reputation. Honesty and integrity are of utmost importance now as anything else is liable to catch up with you sooner rather than later. At the same time, find your spiritual connection and use it to build a strong faith in yourself and your abilities. Be true to yourself and your word.

Transformative Pluto continues in Capricorn, your solar Tenth House of career and status. This transit can spark your ambitions, elevate you to stardom, or result in a complete reversal of career fortunes. In many respects, a Pluto transit is less about the individual and more about societal trends. It often indicates massive changes on a national or global scale that affect the individual. But Pluto also has its personal element, initiating needed change that ultimately results in a far better and transformed life.

Pluto's transit will be more apparent during the year it contacts your Sun. At other times you might see career-related changes such as restructuring, the departure of coworkers and supervisors and the arrival of new ones, and disruptive power plays or even dictatorial attitudes. Rise above them and try not to get caught in the middle as you cultivate your ambitions.

What This Year's Eclipses Mean for You

There are four eclipses this year, two lunar and two solar, with two in Gemini, one in Sagittarius, and the fourth in Scorpio. The influence of each is in effect for six to twelve months.

May 21 is the date of the first solar eclipse in Gemini, your solar Third House of communication and quick trips. Two weeks later (June 4), a lunar eclipse in Sagittarius will light up your solar Ninth House of travel and education. November 28 will bring the year's second lunar eclipse, this time in Gemini.

This emphasis in Gemini and Sagittarius (your solar Third-Ninth House axis) has many possibilities, and even more so because lucky Jupiter arrives in Gemini on June 11. Chances are, you'll travel for business, pleasure, or both; possibly to visit relatives or attend a reunion or conference. You'll also be in contact with many people, perpetually on the go, and juggling many commitments. These eclipses may be just the motivation you need to begin a course of study that will benefit your career. If so, investigate online learning programs that offer a flexible schedule. Just be sure not to fall into the Jupiter trap of taking on too much. You'll also come in contact with other cultures through travel, reading, or meeting people whose roots differ from yours. This could lead to an interest in learning another language.

The second 2012 solar eclipse is November 13 in Scorpio, the same sign Saturn enters October 5. Like Saturn, this eclipse will focus your attention on debt, savings, long-term investments, insurance, and inheritance. Whatever your age, you should devote some time to thinking about and planning for your financial future. If you're part of a couple, get your partner involved and make joint decisions of mutual benefit. You could also use this eclipse to learn about financial planning and how to better manage your resources. It's possible that you or your partner will need to handle a relative's financial affairs.

Saturn

If your birthday is between April 10 and 19, Saturn will contact your Sun from Libra, your solar Seventh House of relationships, before October 5. Every planetary contact to your Sun serves a particular purpose, and with Saturn here, your challenge is to deepen your understanding of people and relationships. Saturn doesn't always make this an easy task, but what you learn now will serve you well for the next twenty-eight years, when Saturn will again return to this position. It's possible that someone from the past could re-enter your life now.

Low vitality is also common during this transit so rest and sleep should be priorities. This can be compounded if you try to do it all, taking on responsibilities that aren't rightly your own. Strained relations with some people, especially workplace supervisors (or a business partner) can make you feel as though you're backpedaling rather than narrowing the gap between you and your goals. But this too is a Saturn lesson, and you may connect with someone who can be a mentor or in some way help you succeed about five years from now.

If you were born between March 20 and 29, Saturn will contact your Sun after it enters Scorpio, your Solar Eighth House of joint resources, October 5. Because it will make this solar connection again during the first nine months of 2013, you should think of this year's contact as a first step. For example, if you have credit card debt, commit to a pay-off plan and you could be debt-free by the end of next year. Do the same with a savings goal, getting a head start as Jupiter completes its transit through Taurus during the first half of 2012. But if you're need of a loan or mortgage, be prepared for delays and a possible negative response. If this occurs, ask the lender what you can do to qualify next year. You might also find an error in your credit report or a long-forgotten, unpaid debt.

Your financial attitudes will gradually evolve during this transit, which is one of Saturn's missions here. Another is to assess what you value and whether, for example, owning the latest status symbol is more important to you than financial security. Saturn will promote the latter as it contacts your Sun and encourages you to think long-term rather than just about tomorrow. If you're part of a couple, you and your mate could disagree about financial matters, but this too is part of Saturn's role: learn to compromise.

Uranus

If you were born between March 20 and 28, Uranus in Aries will join forces with your Sun, so plan on a year that features change and the unexpected. You'll discover (or rediscover) the meaning of your life, what is most important to you and what you need in order to achieve success and happiness. This process will free you, in a sense, to grow into yourself and become the real you as you shed accumulated baggage. While this is positive, it also can be detrimental to those around you, especially your relationship with a partner. Cutting ties just to achieve freedom, for example, is not the best use of this Sun-Uranus contact. Although changing the outward circumstances of your life might be momentarily invigorating, this transit is directed most strongly toward the inner you, and major life changes made now will be irreversible.

Used at its best, your Uranus year can be one of the most exciting and stimulating of your life. This energizing contact can turn every day into an adventure, and you'll feel more and more in touch with yourself as you truly discover what makes you a unique individual. But you might want to ask a close friend to apply the reins when your impulsive side emerges. Despite how things may look on the surface, not every opportunity is worth pursuing.

Neptune

If you were born April 17, 18, or 19, Neptune will contact your Sun from Aquarius, your solar Eleventh House, just as it did last year. Friendship is a main focus here. Some of these relationships could fade away before Neptune enters Pisces February 3, and you could meet someone who touches your heart. Take time to finalize the wish list of goals that began to emerge last year, and then inspire yourself to put plans in motion. Journaling can serve as a helpful reminder because you can go back and read words written during this inspirational period.

Neptune will contact your Sun from Pisces after February 2 **if your birthday is between March 20 and 23.** With the energy coming from your solar Twelfth House, your dreams could be significant, and you'll be more aware of your sixth sense. Listen to hunches and record your dreams so you can refer to them as events occur and unfold. This will help you nurture your inner voice as it releases subconscious thoughts and images. In turn, you'll benefit from the inspiration that comes from having faith in yourself.

You're likely to hear many secrets and other confidential information as Neptune connects with your Sun. Keep it all to yourself even though it will be tempting to spread the news. Similarly, this is not the time to share your deepest secrets with others; sooner or later they will be revealed. You should also be alert for people who appear to be supporters but in reality have a hidden agenda that could be detrimental to you.

Pluto

If your birthday is March 27, 28, or 29, Pluto will contact your Sun from Capricorn, your solar Tenth House. Stay alert and in touch with what's happening in your job and career field. Significant changes, including downsizing, are possible this summer or fall when Uranus in your sign squares off with Pluto in your career sector. In any case, a major career change is possible. It could be the result of you being caught in a power play or a clash with a supervisor. You also could make a sudden decision to move on because of a difficult situation and an overwhelming desire to pursue your own dreams. This isn't the best year to make such a move, however, because planetary alignments caution against self-employment or finding a new position.

Although this Pluto-Sun contact can be very challenging, you'll appreciate its value in a year or so when your life and career begin to reap the benefits of this influence. Both will ultimately be the better because of this transformational period. Patience and tolerance are part of Pluto's message, as is the need to adapt and go with the flow in order to become the best that you can be.

Aries | January

Planetary Lightspots

The domestic scene attracts your interest as the January 9 Full Moon in Cancer shines brightly in your solar Fourth House. This lunar energy is especially favorable for entertaining friends, enjoying time with family, and using your creativity to update decor on a budget. You'll also enjoy cozy, relaxing evenings at home watching videos and celebrating love and romance.

Relationships

Social events and time with friends delight you with January's emphasis on your solar Eleventh House. The energy continues to flow with the Sun, Venus, and Mercury in Aquarius part of the month, along with the New Moon on the 23rd. If you're single, a friend could introduce you to a potential romantic interest mid-month.

Money and Success

Visibility is your best career asset January 8–26 as Mercury transits Capricorn, your solar Tenth House. Speak up. Share your ideas. An opportunity could come your way during the first two weeks of the month. But be prepared for a setback in plans the third week of January when management could block progress.

Planetary Hotspots

Try to do as much as possible at work before January 23, when Mars turns retrograde in Virgo, your solar Sixth House. Do the same with personal endeavors. Progress will be slow in the following three months, and you can expect reversed and delayed decisions and more than a little frustration at times. Keep your cool and go with the flow rather than try to force things.

Rewarding Days

3, 4, 5, 6, 7, 10, 11, 15, 18, 19, 23, 27, 29

Challenging Days

8, 9, 12, 13, 14, 16, 20, 22, 28

Aries | February

Planetary Lightspots

Venus arrives in your sign February 8, which is a real plus for your powers of attraction. So focus on what you want and then release the energy with positive thoughts and every expectation that it can be yours. Venus here will also boost your charisma, and you could meet someone exciting around February 9.

Relationships

This is another great month to socialize, especially near the February 7 Full Moon in Leo, your solar Fifth House. And with Mercury in Aquarius, your solar Eleventh House of friendship, through the 12th and the Sun in the same sign through the 18th, you can widen your circle of acquaintances and possibly meet a new romantic interest. Mid-January could bring a reunion with a friend you haven't seen for a long time.

Money and Success

Retrograde Mars in Virgo continues to slow the pace of work, but try not to let the frustration get to you. Think calm thoughts in mid-February, when difficult planetary alignments could trigger a clash with a coworker or supervisor. Also do your best steer clear of controlling people, and be wary of anyone who wants to form a behind-the-scenes alliance. Ultimately, you could end up being blamed for something that is in no way your fault.

Planetary Hotspots

Treat yourself well this month to help prevent a cold or flu, which could be triggered by the February 21 New Moon in Pisces, your solar Twelfth House. Also do your best to minimize workplace stress. Emphasize sleep, rest, and healthy food.

Rewarding Days

2, 6, 11, 14, 16, 19, 20, 25

Challenging Days

3, 4, 15, 17, 22, 24

Aries | March

Planetary Lightspots

The March 22 New Moon in Aries puts you in the spotlight, ready to dash into your new solar year. Before you do that, though, pause and think about what you want to achieve in the next twelve months and how you plan to get there. Then you'll be ready to put all your energy into the future when Mars, your ruling planet, turns direct next month.

Relationships

Relationships are prone to mix-ups and misunderstandings after Mercury turns retrograde in your sign March 12. Confirm dates and places, think before you speak, and clarify your thoughts. You can also use retrograde Mercury to your advantage after it retreats into Pisces, your solar Twelfth House on the 23rd. Listen to your intuition, which can help you sense how best to handle workplace issues.

Money and Success

Your bank account could benefit from Venus in Taurus, your solar Second House, after March 4. Even better, it joins forces with several planets, including lucky Jupiter, mid-month. You could hear news of a nice raise, bonus or additional company benefits, and receive a long-hoped-for gift. Be cautious, though, if you're offered a promotion or new position as you may not have all the facts.

Planetary Hotspots

Although slow progress continues to prevail in the workplace, you could make moderate strides near the March 8 Full Moon in Virgo, your solar Sixth House. Finesse will be of utmost importance, however, if you hope to impress decision-makers. Resist the urge to push coworkers even if they do frustrate you. Instead, let your natural leadership skills emerge. Make a point to avoid difficult people at month's end.

Rewarding Days

1, 5, 6, 13, 14, 18, 23, 26

Challenging Days

2, 3, 4, 9, 15, 20, 27, 30

Aries | April

Planetary Lightspots

Look forward to April 13. That's the date that Mars, your ruling planet, turns direct in Virgo, your solar Sixth House. Just don't expect an instant turnaround in job matters put on hold. Momentum will gradually build in the following weeks, and soon your life will be back on track.

Relationships

Two planetary influences favor relationships and communication this month: Venus enters Gemini, your solar Third House, April 3, and Mercury resumes direct motion on the 13th and enters your sign three days later. Use all this positive energy to meet new people, get acquainted with neighbors, and straighten out any mix-ups that occurred while Mercury was retrograde. End a conversation the first week of the month if you sense conflict, especially with a relative.

Money and Success

Money could flow your way again this month, thanks to the April 21 New Moon in Taurus, your solar Second House. If you didn't receive a raise last month, it could come through now. But be alert for a tendency to buy on impulse the last week of April. Take your time and think thrifty. Then a sale could net some work clothes at a great price.

Planetary Hotspots

Workplace relationships could be challenging around the April 6 Full Moon in Libra, your solar Seventh House. A power play could be part of the scenario as the lunar energy triggers difficult planetary alignments. It will be tough to for others to see things from your point of view. Be sure to document important talks and meetings, and to get instructions in writing.

Rewarding Days

1, 2, 10, 12, 14, 18, 19, 25, 28, 29

Challenging Days

3, 5, 9, 11, 15, 16, 20, 26

Aries | May

Planetary Lightspots

Pack a weekend bag and head for a nearby location near the May 20 New Moon (solar eclipse) in Gemini, your solar Third House of quick trips. If you can't spare the time, make it a day trip instead, or treat yourself and your mate or the family to a night at a local luxury hotel or resort. This New Moon is also good for a holiday get-together with neighbors. Among them could be someone who becomes a good friend or networking contact.

Relationships

Relationships are mostly easygoing this month despite the potential pitfalls of Venus retrograde, which can trigger misunderstandings. Mercury, the communication planet, visits three signs—Aries, Taurus, and Gemini—and in each it will put you in contact with many people. Personal relationships are featured early in the month, followed by career connections, and finally, siblings and neighbors. Promising career news could come your way mid-month.

Money and Success

The May 5 Full Moon in Scorpio, your solar Eighth House, has much potential to trigger financial gain for you or your mate. Save for a summer vacation or expenses that could arise later this year, rather than spend just for an ego boost. Take a chance on the lottery around the Full Moon.

Planetary Hotspots

Your social life could suffer a setback as Venus in Gemini travels retrograde from May 15 to June 26. Placed in your solar Third House, its retrograde status can also affect communication, especially with a partner. If you're wavering about a commitment, postpone the decision until after Venus turns direct. Weddings and major purchases are also inadvisable during this period.

Rewarding Days

7, 8 11, 17, 20, 22, 26, 27, 31

Challenging Days

3, 4, 9, 13, 16, 23, 30

Aries | June

Planetary Lightspots

This month's Full Moon (lunar eclipse) on June 4 in Sagittarius, and the New Moon in Gemini on the 19th activate your solar Ninth and Third Houses of quick trips, travel, and learning. The New Moon is a better influence if you want a change of scenery again this month, especially because lucky Jupiter enters Gemini on the 11th. Take a best seller along and relax. Or take a class for the fun of it to learn more about a subject that interests you.

Relationships

You can easily resolve any recent disagreements or misunderstandings after Venus turns direct on the 27th. And if you've been considering taking a relationship to the next level, your thoughts and feelings will become clear at month's end or in early July.

Money and Success

In addition to your career sector being this month's hotspot, you'll have some job challenges in early June when planets clash with Mars in Virgo, your solar Sixth House. This is all the more reason to keep thoughts and comments to yourself, and to be careful about sharing confidences with coworkers.

Planetary Hotspots

June 24 is the date of this year's first Uranus/Pluto alignment (the second is September 19) in Aries and Capricorn, your solar First and Tenth Houses. You'll need to hold yourself back and keep your impulsiveness in check. Anything else could have a detrimental effect on your career. This influence could also affect domestic life, with a possibility for disruptive relocation or weather damage to your home. And, this is not the time to ask anyone to join your household.

Rewarding Days

3, 7, 8, 13, 17, 22, 23, 26, 27

Challenging Days

5, 10, 11, 12, 20, 21, 24, 29

Aries | July

Planetary Lightspots

Home is your favorite location as the July 19 New Moon in Cancer accents your solar Fourth House. A summer vacation at home might be more appealing than travel this year, especially because you'll be in the mood to tackle your domestic to-do list. Just don't invest a lot of money in new furnishings or decor while Mercury is retrograde.

Relationships

Mars enters Libra, your solar Seventh House, on the 3rd. It will add passion to a partnership, but can also spark disagreements, which you'll be all too aware of in mid-July. Challenges with a coworker or supervisor are possible at that time, and in turn you could take your frustrations home. Think calm thoughts and say little.

Money and Success

Last month's difficult planetary energy will be triggered by the July 3 Full Moon in Capricorn, your solar Tenth House. Career matters, particularly relations with superiors, will continue to need careful handling. Try not to let your frustration get the best of you. This influence will pass in time. In the meantime, think of it as an exercise in patience.

Planetary Hotspots

Mercury reverses motion, turning retrograde in Leo July 14. This can lead to mix-ups in dates, times, and places for social events and your children's activities, so be sure to confirm plans before you head out the door. Avoid investment decisions, no matter what someone urges you to do, because you won't have all the facts. However, you can use the retrograde period to fine-tune hobby projects.

Rewarding Days

1, 5, 6, 10, 14, 15, 20, 28

Challenging Days

3, 9, 17, 18, 19, 24, 30

Aries | August

Planetary Lightspots

Once past mid-month, Venus in Cancer, your solar Fourth House, adds a beneficial influence to family ties and domestic projects. Ignite your creative spirit and update a room with paint or wall-covering and artwork. Do it all with your budget in mind and without using credit. The results will add fresh energy to your home.

Relationships

Relationships are in high focus this month, thanks to the August 1 Full Moon in Aquarius, your solar Eleventh House, and the New Moon in Leo, your solar Fifth House, on the 17th. They're an ideal match to energize your social life. See friends, get involved in a community organization, and cheer your children in their activities. Along the way you're likely to meet some fascinating people, and if you're single, a new romance could be in the forecast.

Money and Success

Mars zips into Scorpio, your solar Eighth House, August 23. This can be a positive financial influence, but you'll need to curb the urge to snap up easy credit, which will be very tempting. Concentrate instead on increasing income.

Planetary Hotspots

You'll find August to be far more easygoing than July, with mostly favorable planetary alignments. However, don't be hasty about family and domestic decisions mid-month. Change for the sake of change is seldom the best idea. Also take care to get plenty of sleep in the two weeks following the August 31 Full Moon in Pisces, your solar Twelfth House. It will help your immune system fend off a cold.

Rewarding Days

2, 5, 9, 10, 11, 25, 29

Challenging Days

6, 7, 12, 13, 20, 21, 26

Aries | September

Planetary Lightspots

Your social life continues to be active this month, thanks to Venus in Leo, your solar Fifth House, after September 5. See friends, spend quality time with your kids, and set aside a few evenings for romance. Venus here also accents creativity. Express your unique self through a hobby project. But be cautious with investments because you could end up with a net loss.

Relationships

Despite the difficulties surrounding some relationships this month, most are upbeat as several planets connect with Jupiter in Gemini, your communication sector. Touch base with siblings and get better acquainted with neighbors. Seek the opinions of others and brainstorm ideas around the 7th.

Money and Success

Your job and daily work are generally satisfying this month with Mercury in Virgo, your solar Sixth House, through the 15th, the date of the New Moon in the same sign. Aim for high productivity with attention to detail, but be cautious about sharing personal information and negative thoughts about your workplace. Either of these could have repercussions.

Planetary Hotspots

September 19 brings the year's second Uranus/Pluto alignment in Aries and Capricorn, your solar First and Tenth Houses. Relationships will be the target at month's end when the Full Moon in Aries on the 29th also activates your solar Seventh House. The lunar energy also could trigger conflict with a supervisor or your partner. Again, focus on calm images and say little. Impulsive, self-indulgent actions could have undesirable results.

Rewarding Days

3, 7, 12, 13, 17, 21, 25, 30

Challenging Days

2, 10, 11, 16, 20, 23, 24, 29

Aries | October

Planetary Lightspots

Travel could be in the forecast this month or next with Mars beginning its seven-week transit of Sagittarius, your solar Ninth House, on the 6th. You also can use this influence to take a quick class to learn a specific skill, or to attend a company training class in anticipation of possible career advancement before year's end. Go for it, especially if a decision-maker encourages you to make the effort.

Relationships

Relationships are at their best under the October 15 New Moon in Libra, your solar Seventh House. If you're part of a couple, use the first few days of October, before Saturn leaves Libra, to reflect on all you've learned about yourself, those closest to you, and relationships in general during the past few years. When you think about it, you'll discover your attitudes have changed as much as your knowledge of human nature.

Money and Success

Venus transits Virgo, your solar Sixth House, October 3–27, making this an ideal time to strengthen coworker relationships both on and off the job. But steer clear of a workplace romance, which won't sit well with your company. And people will know, despite what you might think.

Planetary Hotspots

Saturn enters Scorpio, your solar Eighth House, October 5, a two-and-a-half year influence that advises financial caution as well as debt reduction and the possibility of reduced income. This month, however, the Full Moon in Taurus, your solar Second House, on the 29th, will be quick to point out where you need to conserve and what steps you need to take to achieve financial security.

Rewarding Days
5, 10, 13, 18, 19, 22, 28, 31

Challenging Days
1, 4, 7, 11, 14, 20, 27

Aries | November

Planetary Lightspots

The daily pace picks up under the November 28 Full Moon (lunar eclipse) in Gemini, your solar Third House, which will also bring increased contact with siblings and neighbors. Look for holiday social invitations, and also consider hosting a party of your own in December.

Relationships

People close to you will be full of surprises in early December as Venus, which advances in Libra through the 20th, connects you with many people this month. This influence is especially favorable for couples, and quality time with loved ones and your best friend. But choose your words with care or say nothing at all at month's end when challenging days could trigger conflict.

Money and Success

Mars enters Capricorn, your solar Tenth House of career and status, on the 16th. Although it will give you extra incentive for hard work, be sure to first clarify instructions and assignments. This is not the time to let your initiative run wild, or to implement your ideas before first clearing them with a supervisor.

Planetary Hotspots

November 6 marks the start of another Mercury retrograde period, this time in Sagittarius, your solar Ninth House. Travel will thus be prone to delays and cancellations, especially the third and fourth weeks of the month. On the 14th, Mercury slips back into Scorpio, your solar Eighth House, the sign of the November 13 New Moon (solar eclipse). Although you could see income rise, the check may be slow in arriving. But you could find some bargains around the time Mercury turns direct on the 26th.

Rewarding Days

2, 6, 7, 11, 14, 15, 24, 29

Challenging Days

3, 10, 12, 16, 23, 25, 30

Aries | December

Planetary Lightspots

The urge to get away from it all will be strong under the December 13 New Moon in Sagittarius. Make travel plans for the new year or try to squeeze in a long weekend now, time permitting. The lunar energy could also awaken your spirituality as well as your sixth sense. Listen to the messages released by your subconscious and your dreams, both of which can open your mind to new perceptions of your place in the world.

Relationships

Family ties become more important as the December 28 Full Moon in Cancer accents your solar Fourth House. But you'll also be pulled by career responsibilities. The goal here is to find a balance without neglecting either one. This can be tough to achieve in late December, but becomes more manageable in January. Mars will help things along after it enters Aquarius, your solar Eleventh House, on the 28th, to emphasize friendship and socializing.

Money and Success

You could be rewarded with a modest year-end bonus in late December. Remember that Saturn's message as it transits your solar Eighth House: save, pay off debt, and invest for the long term.

Planetary Hotspots

Continue to take precautions this month regarding work procedures and contact with supervisors, especially during the last week of December, when tension can also be an issue. Hard work and long hours, combined with less personal and family time, can push your limits and trigger impulsive actions. Find a stress reliever to help yourself unwind, and be sure to thank your family for their support.

Rewarding Days

3, 12, 16, 17, 21, 26, 31

Challenging Days

1, 7, 8, 14, 20, 28

Aries Action Table

These dates reflect the best—but not the only—times for success and ease in these activities, according to your Sun sign.

	JAN	FEB	MAR	APR	MAY	JUN	JUL	AUG	SEP	OCT	NOV	DEC
Move										7, 8		2
Start a class				24, 25	21, 22, 26, 30, 31	17, 18						
Join a club	28–31	1–11										
Ask for a raise									5			
Look for work									15, 15			5, 6
Get pro advice									25			
Get a loan										16		10
See a doctor									5			
Start a diet									12	5, 6		
End relationship												
Buy clothes				29								31
Get a makeover				18, 19			9					20, 21
New romance								17				
Vacation									20–22			12–31

TAURUS

The Bull
April 19 to May 20

♉

Element: Earth

Quality: Fixed

Polarity: Yin/Feminine

Planetary Ruler: Venus

Meditation: I trust myself and others

Gemstone: Emerald

Power Stones: Diamond, blue lace agate, rose quartz

Key Phrase: I have

Glyph: Bull's head

Anatomy: Throat, neck

Color: Green

Animal: Cattle

Myths/Legends: Isis and Osiris, Cerridwen, Bull of Minos

House: Second

Opposite Sign: Scorpio

Flower: Violet

Key Word: Conservation

Your Strengths and Challenges

Dependable, thorough, and practical, you also have exceptional follow-through and finish what you begin. Rarely are you sidetracked once you focus on a task, so people rely on you to deliver. But there are times when stubbornness emerges. You can benefit, too, if you practice the art of give-and-take as well as letting the wishes of others prevail. You enjoy comfort, cherish your established routine, and dislike being rushed. You do nothing half way and always move at your own pace, with patience and care. Motivated by a high need for security and stability, you dislike change. But this also means you can get stuck in a rut, which can diminish your life success. Change is inevitable, so accept it and occasionally initiate it. You might discover it's easier than you think. You're especially attuned to the sense of touch and unconsciously feel clothes and objects when shopping; a hug renews your spirit. Your voice may be distinctive, and you could be a talented amateur or professional singer or speaker. Venus, your ruling planet, gives you an eye for beauty and many people with a Taurus Sun surround themselves with artwork and collectibles. The homes of some, however, are cluttered from basement to attic, with every closet stuffed to the max. If this describes your space, ask yourself why it's so tough to let go.

Your Relationships

Your earthy sign is the most sensual of the zodiac, and you cherish passionate moments. You also take matters of the heart seriously. Although lifetime commitment is your goal, it can be a challenge because you're highly selective about whom you date. That's admirable, but remember that first impressions aren't always accurate. Take a chance and you could meet the soul mate you desire. Possessive by nature, your partnership lesson is to develop trust and confidence in love. Face your fears rather than let jealousy become a relationship issue. You could make a sizzling match with Scorpio, your polar opposite, and you have much in common with earth signs Virgo and Capricorn. Cancer and Pisces complement your solar energy, but life with Leo or Aquarius could have you feeling insecure.

You take great pride in your home, and are loyal and devoted to those you love. They're a source of confidence for you, as you are for them. Your home is also an expression of your ego and you strive to make it a reflection of yourself and your worldly achievements.

Taurus parents expect a lot from their children, often to the point of perfection. Even though you have their best interests at heart, this can undermine their self-esteem. So rather than be critical, aim for constructive, supportive encouragement. Praise their efforts as you grant them the freedom to explore their own interests, which may or may not be your own.

You're a caring, compassionate friend who goes out of your way for those in your inner circle. Most are worthy of your generosity, but there will always be those few who take advantage of your kind heart. Be selective and trust only those people you know well, who also benefit from your talent for inspiring others to do and be their best.

Your Career and Money

Your financial instincts are among the best, and you have a knack for making money. Value is of utmost importance, and no matter the price, you rarely spend unless you get your money's worth. You have a sixth sense about where to shop and when. Many people with a Taurus Sun gain through a family inheritance or careful, long-term investments, as well as high earnings. Budgeting, however, is also important, because you can be overly optimistic and spend on a whim.

You'd prefer a life-long career with stability that makes you feel safe and secure. But this area of your life is prone to sudden changes. In today's world it's important to be aware of trends so you can take action before it becomes a necessity. And by doing this, you can make your own luck and seize the best opportunities. Day to day, you're happiest in an upscale environment with congenial coworkers; conflict and controversy are not for you.

Your Lighter Side

You love your leisure time, and nothing compares with an evening in a comfy chair. But you also get great satisfaction from the results of practical hobbies such as gardening, woodworking, refinishing furniture, and home improvements. All of these are popular free-time activities for many born under your sign. It's even possible you could turn a weekend interest into a profitable second income.

Affirmation for the Year

Change inspires me to broaden my horizons.

The Year Ahead for Taurus

Money is a featured theme this year, and with careful planning, saving, and thrifty shopping, you can greet 2013 with a bigger bank account. Much of this will come your way the second half of the year, which is just as well because you should postpone investment decisions and loan applications until after April. People are another 2012 emphasis—both friends and your partner. If you're in a serious relationship, you could make a lifetime commitment this year.

Optimism accompanies Jupiter's transit of your sign through June 10. This influence, which only occurs every twelve years, boosts enthusiasm and has the potential to bring you many blessings. With Jupiter's luck on your side, more often than not you'll be in the right place at the right time to snap up opportunities that come your way. But like every planet, Jupiter also has a downside. Overconfidence can encourage you to take on more than you can accomplish. So tame your high hopes with your natural common sense and try not to overdo it. Jupiter in your sign can also lead to weight gain simply because you'll tend to overindulge at times.

Chances are, you'll cash in as Jupiter transits Gemini, your solar Second House of personal resources. Set your financial priorities before this expansive planet begins its year-long transit of Gemini on June 11. Your income could definitely rise, but so could expenses, primarily because you'll be in the mood to spend and your thrifty eye will find much to purchase. So set a budget when your income gets a boost, and commit to a regular savings program.

Saturn spends much of the year in Libra, your solar Sixth house, moving on to Scorpio October 5. Since November 2009, when Saturn entered this sector, work has been a major theme in your life. This transit is in a very real sense all about working hard and proving your ability. But recognition is often missing. Be patient. Recognition will begin to come after Saturn enters Scorpio later this year, and it will reach a peak in about seven years when Saturn enters your solar Tenth House of career. Aim high and set your sights on your desired career pinnacle. In the meantime, follow procedures to the letter, learn all you can, and find satisfaction in a job well done.

The Sixth House is also a wellness sector, so get a check-up if you haven't had one recently and listen to your body's rhythm. If you could benefit from improvements in this area, make this one of your goals for 2012. Walking or moderate exercise can also help to relieve work-related stress.

Saturn concludes the year in Scorpio, entering this sign October 5 to focus on your relationship sector. Although this transit can be viewed as a negative, it isn't necessarily so. Deep bonds can form with Saturn in your solar Seventh House, and people who commit to a partnership under this influence often remain together for a lifetime. But you may also purposely distance yourself from some people, and others will be drawn into your life for a specific purpose, usually because of something important you can learn from them.

Saturn in Scorpio also encourages you to learn more about relationships, human nature, and how you interact with other people. Everyone has room for improvement in this area, and there is nothing Saturn likes more than being the teacher. Be observant, listen to your own responses, and recognize your challenges as you celebrate your strengths in this area. Then share the information with those closest to you, and don't be surprised when they confirm all you say.

Uranus focuses on your solar Twelfth House this year as it continues its transit through Aries, the sign it will occupy until 2018. Placed here, in your self-renewal sector, Uranus encourages you to look within for insights into your life and lifestyle. Because this is a health sector, you can use Uranus as the spark of change to alter your diet or begin an exercise program.

At times, you'll get flashes of insight—hunches activated by Uranus and your subconscious. Listen to them, especially concerning friends and your career. You might also be drawn to a good cause that would benefit from your time and effort. But be cautious about sharing your deepest secrets, even with your closest friends. All could be revealed in the least expected moment.

Neptune wraps up its time in Aquarius on February 2. During its long transit of your solar Tenth House of career and status, you've undoubtedly experienced every facet of this mysterious planet. Neptune is known for confusion and illusion, but also inspiration, creativity, and glamor. Set aside time during the first month of 2012 to reflect on all the Neptune-related events that have occurred in the past fourteen years. Then take these lessons with you as Neptune moves on to Pisces, your solar Eleventh House.

You'll connect with many people through 2025 as Neptune transits Pisces. Some friends will trigger the inspiration you need to pursue and achieve your goals, while others will disappoint you and leave you wondering why you ever trusted them. Be a little cautious about inviting new people into your life, because first impressions can be deceiving. One of the best uses of this transit is to get involved in a group activity at work or on your own that will benefit others. You also can be a motivational force by using Neptune to sense what others need.

Pluto in Capricorn, your solar Ninth House, emphasizes knowledge, wisdom, and education. Explore the idea of returning to school even if it's unrealistic to do so this year. At some point during Pluto's long transit of Capricorn (until 2025), you'll feel compelled to take this journey. This sector also governs spirituality (and religion), legal affairs, and long-distance journeys, as well as gaining an appreciation for other cultures and customs. However, travel to other countries isn't the best idea this year because of difficult planetary alignments this summer and fall. Expand your horizons instead through books, the Internet, and travel programs.

However, the main thrust of Pluto's transit is transformation—a profound change in thinking or life direction. Don't be surprised if you find yourself questioning long-standing beliefs and principles, some of which are closely tied to your childhood. Self-help books could be especially valuable as you work through this process.

What This Year's Eclipses Mean for You

Four eclipses highlight two of your favorite areas of life: money and relationships. The influence of each, which lasts six to twelve months, will be reinforced by Jupiter and Saturn later in the year.

The first of two solar eclipses is in Gemini, your solar Second House of personal resources, May 21. Two weeks later, the first lunar eclipse (June 4 in Sagittarius) will shine its rays in your solar Eighth House of joint resources, followed by another lunar eclipse on November 28 in Gemini. All of this is very promising for income, including the possibility of a significant windfall. But the planetary alignments can also trigger extra expenses, so maintain your usual thrifty attitude, saving first and spending later.

This year's second solar eclipse is in Scorpio, your solar Seventh House of relationships, November 13. By this time, Saturn will be in the same sign, prompting some with a Taurus Sun to commit to lifetime togetherness. If you're involved in a long-term relationship, Saturn can renew your love and commitment. Be a bit cautious, though, if you're considering a business partnership. The outcome could be a very expensive lesson.

Saturn

If you were born between May 12 and 20, Saturn will contact your Sun from Libra before it leaves this sign October 5. Saturn's influence will be focused in June and July **if your birthday is May 11, 12, or 13**. If you were born on any of the other dates, Saturn will contact your Sun twice, once between January and May, and again in August or September.

With this planet in your solar Sixth House, your work life will feel unsettled and you'll have an indefinable sense of dissatisfaction. Your thoughts are likely to drift toward changing jobs, although it will be tough to zero in on exactly what you seek and the position that would make you happy. This is only the universe at work, encouraging you to consider various options and which path to pursue. Aim for the one that can lead to maximum results in about eight years. In the short term, you'll be better prepared to find your niche in 2013.

You'll also want to listen to your body because the Sixth House is associated with health and wellness. Get a check-up in addition to doing a self-assessment. If you could benefit from a healthier lifestyle, educate yourself on the advantages of exercise and healthy eating, and then use your determination to implement the change. You could even go a step further and take several cooking classes to learn how to make tasty, low-fat meals. All of this will have the added benefit of easing work-related stress.

You'll be among the first to have Saturn in Scorpio contact your Sun **if you were born between April 19 and 29**. With this emphasis on your solar Seventh House from October 5 to year's end, you'll experience both the upside and downside of relationships. Some will be amazingly positive, while others will incline toward conflict. There is something to be learned from each of these connections—about you, the people in your life, and how you react in various situations. Chances are, you'll see more than a little of yourself in the responses you receive from others.

Someone from the past may reappear, giving you an opening to resolve any lingering issues. You might also have more contact with elderly people, and form new business or professional alliances. If you've been contemplating a romantic commitment, this transit will push the decision, either by you or your potential mate.

Uranus

If you were born between April 19 and 28, Uranus will contact your Sun from Aries, your solar Twelfth House. Because this is the sector of hidden matters, you'll hear secrets and confidential information this year. This could involve an employer, your boss, or your future with the company. Be cautious. It's possible someone could try to make you a scapegoat. But Uranus can also reveal surprising information that could give you access to decision-makers. Above all, take no risks with your reputation.

On another level, this Uranus transit is about your subconscious mind. Memories of past events may suddenly emerge and you could, for example, remember an incident from your teenage years that impacted your self-esteem. Overall, though, the purpose here is to identify patterns of negative self-talk and issues that hold you back. View them from a more enlightened perspective and fill your mind with upbeat thoughts. In the process you may sense that your intuition is coming alive or growing stronger. This can help you in many everyday situations and trigger new insights into yourself and the people that surround you.

Neptune

If your birthday is May 18, 19, or 20, Neptune will contact your Sun between January 1 and February 2, as it completes it transit of Aquarius, your solar Tenth House. On both a personal and career level, this transit can have you feeling somewhat lost at sea and questioning exactly what it is you want from life. But this isn't the best time to make major life decisions, because it's tough to see any issue with clarity or even to define the source of your dissatisfaction. The best course is to do nothing. Once this transit passes in early February, answers will begin to emerge. Neptune also has an upside: you can easily adapt to any situation, presenting the image that will yield the greatest gain.

If your birthday is between April 19 and 23, Neptune will contact your Sun after it enters Pisces, your solar Eleventh House, February 3. This favorable connection will bring many enjoyable and inspirational moments with friends and in group endeavors. You could meet someone who will become a mentor or serve as a valuable networking contact, and you might do the same for others through a charitable organization. At its best, Neptune is the planet of compassion, so by helping others to help themselves you will receive intangible gifts from the universe.

However, try not to put too much faith in anyone other than yourself. Not everyone shares your good intentions. Be cautious and skeptical when people make promises you sense are too good to be true. You also could become disillusioned with a friend or organization, wondering how you could have been so wrong. Overall, though, you will gain much from interacting with longtime friends as well as new ones.

Also listen to your sixth sense, which is active this year, and take note of your dreams. Both provide clues about current life events.

Pluto

Pluto will favorably contact your Sun from Capricorn this year **if your birthday is between April 26 and 29.** This emphasis on your solar Ninth House can involve legal matters, higher education, travel, in-laws, or a spiritual awakening. Give serious thought to returning to school to begin or complete a degree or certification program.

Even if you don't directly experience the events associated with Pluto's transit, at least some of them will be active in your life or the lives of those around you. It's important to remember that Pluto triggers needed—not unnecessary—change as a means of removing the old to make way for the new. And when you combine this planet's considerable willpower with your own, you can accomplish amazing things. Stay focused on your mission and refuse to be deterred.

Because of its friendly contact with your Sun, Pluto's transformational process would normally be an easier one. But this year, Uranus in Aries, your solar Twelfth House, will align itself with Pluto in June and September. The clash of these two planets can trigger unexpected events related to your solar Ninth and Twelfth

Houses. You could be involved in the care of a relative, particularly an in-law, who is confined or otherwise institutionalized. Take every precaution to avoid potential legal entanglements, including always using a designated driver. If possible, avoid overseas travel this year, as well as unknown or desolate areas of your own country.

For all the potential negatives of the Uranus/Pluto configuration, however, you'll also experience the positive power of change. This is primarily an internal process, and one that can ultimately better your life as you look toward the future.

Taurus | January

Planetary Lightspots

Need an excuse to take a day trip or to dash off for the weekend? Tap into the energy of the January 9 Full Moon in Cancer, your solar Third House of quick trips. With Mercury in Capricorn, your travel sector, from the 8th to the 26th, fresh scenery can provide needed stress relief. Business travel could also be on your agenda. If so, try to work in an extra day for fun.

Relationships

Your social life gets a boost from Venus in Pisces, your solar Eleventh House, from January 14 on. Line up get-togethers with friends where you can meet other people. But try to avoid dates around the 14th and 20th, when you and a friend or someone you meet could clash on philosophical differences. Also try to avoid in-laws on those dates.

Money and Success

Success and high visibility are yours under the January 23 New Moon in Aquarius, your solar Tenth House. Make the most of the following two weeks, which could bring surprising news and support from someone behind the scenes. Be cautious, though, because this person could have other motives that are yet to be revealed.

Planetary Hotspots

A dating relationship could cool as Mars turns retrograde in Virgo, your solar Fifth House. Consider the retrograde period (January 23– April 12) a gift of time to think about your feelings and whether you want to continue on a path toward commitment. If you're a parent, your children may need extra attention during this time. The time is right for completing unfinished hobby projects, as well. Be very cautious, however, with investments.

Rewarding Days

3, 4, 9, 12, 13, 17, 25, 30, 31

Challenging Days

2, 7, 14, 16, 19, 20, 22, 28

Taurus | February

Planetary Lightspots

Home life is satisfying in the two weeks following the February 7 Full Moon in Leo, your solar Fourth House, because these will also be busy career weeks. Talks with loved ones can be uplifting, and the 18th is a good choice if you want to entertain friends or coworkers. Set aside some time, because it's not too early to think about or begin planning any summer redecorating or home improvement projects.

Relationships

Friendship takes on added importance under the February 21 New Moon in Pisces, your solar Eleventh House. Schedule evenings out and weekend activities, and encourage your friends to bring their friends along. It's a good way to expand your circle as long as you're a little wary. First impressions can be deceiving. With Mars still retrograde in Virgo, your solar Fifth House, you're unlikely to click with a potential romantic interest this month.

Money and Success

You benefit from the visibility promoted by the Sun and Mercury in Aquarius, your solar Tenth House of career and status, during the first part of February. Maintain the momentum by building on January's achievements, and take advantage of favorable planetary alignments around the 7th and again mid-month. This timing is great for presentations and impressing decision-makers.

Planetary Hotspots

The stress and strain of daily life could catch up with you as Venus, your ruling planet, transits Aries, your solar Twelfth House, from February 8 on. View this as a signal to take time off or to spend some evenings and weekends with a favorite activity. Time alone or in meditation can also help ease job stress or a difficult situation with a relative or in-law.

Rewarding Days
5, 8, 9, 13, 18, 21, 26, 27

Challenging Days
3, 4, 10, 15, 22, 24

Taurus | March

Planetary Lightspots

This is a special time of year because Venus, your ruling planet, will be in your sign after March 4. In addition to increasing your powers of attraction, you'll have an extra level of charm and charisma that can bring positive people and events your way. This is also a great time to treat yourself to a spa day, get a massage, or update your look with a makeover or new hairstyle.

Relationships

The timing is perfect, because with Venus in your sign and the March 8 Full Moon in Virgo, your solar Fifth House, you'll want to get out and socialize. Join friends mid-month at a favorite dinner or night spot, and catch up on all the latest news and activities. In early and late March, however, try to avoid talking with relatives.

Money and Success

Put this month's favorable planetary alignments to work for you. Take the initiative to expand your investment and money management knowledge. Choose trusted websites with objective information rather than those sponsored by various companies. This way you can learn and form your own opinions about how best to maximize your resources.

Planetary Hotspots

Life will proceed at a slower pace this month. Not that this is a bad thing. But you'll need to counteract the frustration that can accompany Mercury's switch to retrograde motion on March 12. Placed in Aries, the same sign as the March 22 New Moon in your solar Twelfth House, you can still your mind through meditation or during quiet moments. This will help to activate your sixth sense, leading to fresh insights about life and yourself.

Rewarding Days

3, 7, 11, 12, 16, 18, 21, 25, 26

Challenging Days

1, 5, 9, 13, 15, 22, 27, 30

Taurus | April

Planetary Lightspots

April 21, the date of the New Moon in your sign, marks the symbolic beginning of your new solar year. With it comes the inspiration of Neptune and the energy of Mars, which turns direct April 13. Both these planets are favorably aligned with the New Moon, so tap into them and use their influence to help achieve your goals.

Relationships

Mercury turns direct in Pisces, your solar Eleventh House, on the same date as Mars turns direct in Virgo, your solar Fifth House. Connect with friends in the next few weeks, and if you're single, ask them to introduce you to anyone they know who might be a good match. You could also connect with new people by getting involved in your children's sporting activities where you can meet other parents.

Money and Success

The April 6 Full Moon in Libra, your solar Sixth House, spotlights your work life. Although you'll have the incentive for high productivity, try not to push yourself too hard. Otherwise you could wear down your immune system and end up with a cold or flu. Make wellness just as much of a priority as work output, including getting plenty of sleep. Avoid difficult coworkers the week of the 15th.

Planetary Hotspots

Finances require caution the first week of March, when difficult planetary alignments signal confusion in money matters. This is not the time for financial decisions or investments. And don't hesitate to say no if a friend or relative asks for a loan. It's doubtful you will be repaid. Apply the same caution to purchases and anyone who guarantees a return on an investment.

Rewarding Days

4, 8, 12, 17, 19, 21, 22, 27

Challenging Days

5, 7, 11, 13, 15, 23, 26

Taurus I May

Planetary Lightspots

Mercury transits your sign May 9–23, giving you a charming way with words. Favorable planetary alignments add an enthusiastic optimism that will help put you in touch with many, from friends to family to colleagues. You could receive encouraging news near the 13th, when quality time with your children can give you a new appreciation for their individuality.

Relationships

The May 5 Full Moon in Scorpio, your solar Seventh House of relationships, works in tandem with Mercury in your sign to also help you connect with people. It's especially positive for couples and business partners because you'll be on the same wavelength. Take advantage of this opportunity to share your hopes and wishes as well as your frustrations and challenges with each other in a supportive environment. Then share your advice.

Money and Success

Although retrograde, Venus in Gemini can delay the arrival of an anticipated check, although the May 20 New Moon in the same sign makes this a promising financial phase. The exception is investments. Don't ignore your usual financial sense no matter what anyone tells you. Also be prepared for your children to launch a campaign for you to buy the latest must-have items.

Planetary Hotspots

Progress on plans will slow somewhat as Venus, your ruling planet, turns retrograde May 15. Use the following six weeks to evaluate personal plans and directions; revise as necessary. On the plus side, your thrifty mindset can lead you to great values during this time. Two cautions apply, however: be sure all items can be returned if you change your mind, and avoid major purchases.

Rewarding Days

1, 2, 6, 12, 13, 14, 18, 19, 24

Challenging Days

3, 4, 7. 8, 9, 17, 23, 28, 29, 30

Taurus | June

Planetary Lightspots

Mars continues to advance in Virgo, your solar Fifth House, where it energizes your social life as well as your creativity. Hobbies and sports can provide excellent stress relief this month, and you'll also enjoy time with your kids and their activities.

Relationships

Home life is at its best after Mercury enters Leo, your solar Fourth House, on the 25th. A talk with a family member can be uplifting at month's end, when you might also receive good news. Work relationships will also be generally upbeat, but you'll want to avoid meetings and important talks the third week of June.

Money and Success

You may have challenges in other areas of your life, but finances are not among them. Three planetary events signal potential for a bigger bank account by month's end: Jupiter moving into Gemini, your solar Second House, June 11, along with the New Moon in the same sign on the 19th, and the June 4 Full Moon (lunar eclipse) in your solar Eighth House. Remember to save before you spend as money flows your way.

Planetary Hotspots

Uranus in Aries and Pluto in Capricorn make the first of their two alignments this year. (The second is in September.) With these two planets in your solar Twelfth and Ninth Houses, and this month's trigger coming from your solar Third House, you should avoid long-distance travel as well as trips to nearby locations. Be especially cautious on your daily commute, where accidents can happen in a flash through no fault of your own. The influence will be particularly active around the 11th, 12th, and 29th.

Rewarding Days

1, 2, 9, 14, 15, 16, 19, 25, 28

Challenging Days

5, 10, 11, 12, 20, 21, 24, 27, 29

Taurus | July

Planetary Lightspots

Luck is with you as Venus and Jupiter in Gemini, your solar Second House, make favorable connections this month. You could stumble upon a lucky find around the 21st. Browse consignment and thrift shops and look around your home for childhood favorites or collectibles that might have gained in value over the years.

Relationships

Mercury's retrograde period from July 14 to August 7 can disrupt family life with mix-ups and misunderstandings. Double-check schedules, and also take the time to clarify your thoughts and words. The effect is likely to spill over into your work life where confusion could cause difficulties with a supervisor or coworker. But this is a good time to revisit previously made family and domestic plans to be sure everyone is still in agreement.

Money and Success

Mars dashes into Libra, your solar Sixth House, on the 3rd. With it comes a faster pace at work, which could cause you to overlook details. Check all work for errors. Be especially cautious on the 17th and 18th, when you could find yourself caught in the middle of a power play and pushed to take sides. Remain neutral and let others resolve their own problems.

Planetary Hotspots

Travel continues to be inadvisable as the July 3 Full Moon in Capricorn, your solar Ninth House, activates difficult planetary alignments. The same is true of the New Moon in Cancer, your solar Third House, on the 19th, which can trigger delays and cancellations. The New Moon could also bring the need for a vehicle repair. Don't ignore a suspected problem as it will only become worse.

Rewarding Days
7, 8, 11, 12, 21, 26, 27

Challenging Days
9, 17, 18, 24, 28, 30

Taurus | August

Planetary Lightspots

Domestic life is upbeat, especially after Mercury in Leo turns direct in your solar Fourth House on the 8th. That's followed by the New Moon in the same sign on the 17th. You can use all this positive energy to improve your home or redecorate a room. Even better, your thrifty mind-set and planetary alignments will help you maximize your budget.

Relationships

There are two Full Moons this month, with the second, on the 31st, highlighting your solar Eleventh House. Lunch, outings, and social events with friends are a great way to wrap up your summer as you head into September. Be choosy, though, about which friends you see, as some will take advantage of your generosity, expecting you to pick up the tab.

Money and Success

August begins with a Full Moon on the 1st with potential to make you an attention-getter. Placed in Aquarius, your solar Tenth House, and aligned with Jupiter, the lunar energy could trigger a nice raise and recognition. You'll also realize that several years of extra hard work are beginning to pay off and that your efforts truly are valued. Enjoy the boost in self-esteem as you celebrate with loved ones.

Planetary Hotspots

Relationship challenges and mechanical problems could pop up again this month after Venus enters Cancer August 7. Be alert for these mid-month, when travel disruptions are also possible. The same time frame could bring increased stress and frustration at work. Ease it with a lunchtime walk so you can get a fresh perspective.

Rewarding Days

3, 4, 8, 9, 14, 18, 19, 22, 27

Challenging Days

6, 7, 13, 15, 20, 21, 26, 28

Taurus | September

Planetary Lightspots

Kick back and relax a little with your favorite people at home after Venus enters Leo, your solar Fourth House, on the 6th. Continue with a decorating project you began last month or choose to enjoy the final days of summer with lazy weekend hours outdoors in the company of a good book.

Relationships

As much as you'll delight in lazy hours at home, the September 15 New Moon in Virgo, your solar Fifth House, will trigger the urge to socialize. Line up outings with friends and other families, spend time with a hobby, and also put romance high on your priority list. Some singles will launch a new dating relationship with much potential, while couples celebrate love. But be wary if a friend makes lofty promises or tries too hard to persuade you to embrace another opinion.

Money and Success

Finances follow the status quo most of this month as Jupiter continues to advance in Gemini, your solar Second House. But you'll be tempted at times to forget your thrifty attitude in favor of spend, spend, spend. Be kind to your budget and your savings account. An investment could pay off nicely this month.

Planetary Hotspots

The Uranus/Pluto alignment returns September 19, but you feel its strongest effects at month's end. Most of the challenges will be job-related and occur around the time of the Full Moon in Aries on the 29th. Someone may try to convince you to forget your ethics. Be your strong and determined self. If a supervisor is involved, be sure to document conversations and other communication. It's also possible you could be called for jury duty or be involved in a legal matter.

Rewarding Days

1, 5, 6, 8, 9, 14, 27, 28, 30

Challenging Days

2, 10, 11, 16, 19, 20, 23, 26, 29

Taurus | October

Planetary Lightspots

Your social life continues to be active this month, thanks to Venus, which enters Virgo, your solar Fifth House, on the 3rd. So you can look forward to more fun with friends, and possibly even a day trip or weekend away. Venus here is an even better creative influence than last month's New Moon. Take advantage of it. Get a head start on crafting small holiday gifts for coworkers and friends.

Relationships

Your solar Seventh House is the site of a major relationship influence this month: Saturn enters Scorpio on the 5th, where it will be for the next two and a half years. If you're part of a couple, this serious planet can reinforce your partnership. For others, it will bring commitment. With Mercury transiting this sector October 5-28, you and those closest to you will be on the same wavelength, so use this time for long, leisurely talks that can strengthen ties.

Money and Success

Your job is in focus this month as the October 15 New Moon in Libra highlights your solar Sixth House. Work will be busy but you can easily keep up with it all. Finances could benefit from Mars in Sagittarius, your solar Eighth House, from October 6 and on. Try not to spend as fast as you earn.

Planetary Hotspots

Perceptions can steer you in the wrong direction this month, especially with money matters. This is not the time to take out a loan, even a short-term one without interest; or to hire a financial advisor or stock broker. But if a loan is an absolute must, read all the fine print rather than take someone's word for it. Chances are, you'll find a hidden clause that could cost you money.

Rewarding Days
2, 3, 8, 12, 16, 21, 24, 26, 30

Challenging Days
1, 7, 9, 11, 14, 20, 31

Taurus | November

Planetary Lightspots
You'll find inspiration in the words of others, and they'll appreciate the same from you. Just as easily you can motivate others, especially coworkers and friends, with your enthusiastic optimism. You also can be a steadying influence in the midst of everyday chaos as Venus transits Scorpio from the 21st on.

Relationships
Despite retrograde Mercury, relationships will be a high point this month as the November 13 New Moon (solar eclipse) in Scorpio energizes your solar Seventh House. This could trigger an engagement for some couples. You'll also create fond memories with friends, and people in general are responsive and helpful. But there could be challenges with someone at a distance, possibly an in-law. Be patient and think calm thoughts.

Money and Success
The November 28 Full Moon (lunar eclipse) in Gemini, your solar Second House could bring you a raise or holiday bonus within the following two weeks. But the urge to splurge will return because of Jupiter's influence. Spend it if you have it and when you get it. But first add a percentage to savings.

Planetary Hotspots
You could get frustrated when Mercury turns retrograde on the 6th in Sagittarius, your solar Eighth House, before it retreats into Scorpio (your solar Seventh House). This makes money matters and relationships prone to mix-ups and misunderstandings. Check bills for errors when they arrive, and be sure payments are actually received. Like last month, this is not the time to apply for a loan or to sign a contract. Clarify your thoughts and words. Don't assume the other person knows what you mean.

Rewarding Days
4, 8, 20, 21, 22, 27

Challenging Days
3, 5, 10, 16, 18, 23

Taurus | December

Planetary Lightspots

Try innovation and creativity when your holiday budget reaches its limits. Make ornaments, get the family involved in baking, and keep a sharp eye out for deep discount sales. With what you find on sale, you can create and innovate cheery baskets for your closest friends. Include a photo of the two of you together. Favorable alignments with Uranus will help spark even more ideas.

Relationships

December is all about love and togetherness as Mercury transits Scorpio, your solar Seventh House, through the 9th, and Venus is in the same sign through the 14th. These planets, in addition to favorable alignments with Neptune in Pisces, your solar Eleventh House of friendship, will enhance your social life and bring opportunities to get together with those closest to you.

Money and Success

With Mars entering Aquarius, your solar Tenth House of career on the 25th, the last week of the year could be a busy one. But it will only be the start because Mars will transit this sector until early February. You and your mate could receive some nice gifts and even some cash, thanks to the December 13 New Moon in Sagittarius, your solar Eighth House.

Planetary Hotspots

If you plan to travel this month, avoid the last week of the year. The December 28 Full Moon in Cancer, your solar Third House, will activate difficult planetary alignments that could trigger delays and cancellations, possibly because of weather. It's also possible your vehicle could have mechanical problems if you plan to drive out of town. Be safe. Stay home or travel earlier or later.

Rewarding Days
1, 2, 5, 6, 9, 10, 23, 24, 29

Challenging Days
3, 4, 14, 16, 20, 30

Taurus Action Table

These dates reflect the best—but not the only—times for success and ease in these activities, according to your Sun sign.

	JAN	FEB	MAR	APR	MAY	JUN	JUL	AUG	SEP	OCT	NOV	DEC
Move								16–21				
Start a class						20–25			10			1
Join a club	25, 26	22–29										
Ask for a raise				24								
Look for work	28–31	1–13							17–30			
Get pro advice										16, 24–26		12, 17, 20, 31
Get a loan									20, 21			
See a doctor				18, 19								
Start a diet												
End relationship	17											10
Buy clothes								18	14, 15	12		
Get a makeover									4, 5			
New romance									14, 15	12, 13		
Vacation	12–22											21–25

GEMINI

The Twins
May 20 to June 20

Ⅱ

Element: Air

Quality: Mutable

Polarity: Yang/Masculine

Planetary Ruler: Mercury

Meditation: I explore my inner worlds

Gemstone: Tourmaline

Power Stones: Ametrine, citrine, emerald, spectrolite, agate

Key Phrase: I think

Glyph: Pillars of duality, the Twins

Anatomy: Shoulders, arms, hands, lungs, nervous system

Color: Bright colors, orange, yellow, magenta

Animal: Monkeys, talking birds, flying insects

Myths/Legends: Peter Pan, Castor and Pollux

House: Third

Opposite Sign: Sagittarius

Flower: Lily of the valley

Key Word: Versatility

Your Strengths and Challenges

You're always on the go, and people wonder how you manage to do all that you do—and seemingly all at the same time. That's because you have the mental agility to quickly switch topics, thought patterns, and activities in a flash. You can even think about two things at once. That's the nature of your mutable air sign, which also excels at multitasking. In fact, the more things you can juggle at once the happier you are. But this also makes it easy to spread yourself too thin and difficult to focus on demanding tasks.

Lively, witty, and fun-loving, you have a youthful spirit, whatever your age. Your notable curiosity is part of your charm, and you know a little about a lot of things—just enough so people perceive you as an expert in many subjects. Depth, however, is not your strength because your interests are wide and varied.

Mercury-ruled Gemini is the sign of communication. A master at gathering information, you enjoy learning and sharing what you know. But some Geminis forget to listen, and thus dominate conversations. And this can frustrate other people more than you can imagine. If you're among the Gemini talkers, you'll get further if you say less and give others your full attention. You'll also gain a lot of information you can use to advantage.

You're restless and easily bored, yet agreeable and adaptable—an ideal combination for circulating on the social scene, where you're well liked. In other areas of life, however, such as your career, follow-through is essential to success. Try to complete important projects before beginning new ones, which will ultimately reduce your stress level.

Your Relationships

Gemini is the consummate flirt of the Zodiac, which makes you popular on the social scene, and in touch with many potential mates during your dating years. But as much as you enjoy playing the field, you prefer a single dating relationship at a time—even if this means only one or two dates before moving on to the next person who catches your eye. It's togetherness you crave—that special feeling of one-on-one that prompts some Geminis to mistake infatuation for true love.

Your soul mate is likely to be someone at least as carefree as you are and even more adventuresome. In fact, the two of you should set aside designated togetherness time every week. Otherwise you could find yourselves passing in the night as you each dash off to the next adventure. A match with another air sign—Libra or Aquarius—would fulfill your need for intellectual stimulation, but the relationship might be too easygoing and lack passion. An Aries or Leo would keep things lively, but earthy Virgo or watery Pisces probably isn't your style. Your best match might be enthusiastic Sagittarius, your opposite sign.

Family communication is a high priority for most Geminis, and you encourage your children to share their thoughts and lives with you, even when they're adults. Your home probably has bookcases, games, and the latest technology and is either messy or neat—nothing in between—but still organized, even if you're the only one who can find everything! Geminis usually have a friendly if somewhat distant relationship with in-laws, but some develop a solid friendship with them.

Your friends are few, your acquaintances many, and people move in and out of your ever-evolving circle. That's just the way you like it; new people stimulate your active mind and you especially enjoy getting to know people. In a best friend you want a strong mental rapport as well as someone who's as active and spontaneous as you are.

Your Career and Money

Many Geminis seek a career in the communications field or one that requires strong communication skills. Creative expression is a must for career success, whether it takes the form of ideas, design or artistic talent, or finding the right approach in sales or promotional activities. But be patient with yourself if it takes you longer than most to find your ideal career niche. Because so many things interest you, it can be tough to settle on a single endeavor. This is why some Geminis have dual careers—one to pay the bills and another to satisfy their emotional needs. In your day-to-day work environment you're happiest when in charge. So look for positions that allow you the freedom to structure your daily work. You also like privacy in the workplace and prefer to keep your work and home lives separate.

Although you have a periodic spending streak, overall you're more conservative about money than you are about a lot of things. You also understand the value of thinking long-term, especially with savings and investments. Some Geminis, however, shop when they're feeling low and end up with a closet full of unworn clothing. If this describes you, find an alternative to boost your spirits, such as exercise or a creative hobby. Your bank account will benefit from it. You're also likely to see your net worth increase more rapidly later in life, and could receive an inheritance from a male relative.

Your Lighter Side

People find you fascinating, albeit a bit of a puzzle. You can blend in or stand out, speak on almost any topic, out-charm the best of them, and adapt to fit into almost any situation and group. It's rare that you're exactly the same two days in a row, or sometimes from one hour to the next. This keeps people guessing and wondering as they try to identify the many facets of the real you.

Affirmation for the Year

My life is an opportunity!

The Year Ahead for Gemini

You're in the spotlight this year, thanks to Jupiter and two eclipses in your sign. And although you'll have plenty of opportunities for fun, friends, and close relationships, your job and career will come into focus later in 2012 to set a pattern for the next several years.

Jupiter begins 2012 in Taurus, the sign it transits through June 10. Placed in your solar Twelfth House, Jupiter accents special times with your favorite people, including your partner. You might also get involved in a charitable cause, possibly with a group of coworkers, to in some way benefit others. Chances are, you'll gain far more from this activity than you ever imagined possible.

By far, though, the best influence of Jupiter here is that it functions like a guardian angel. It won't always save the day, but it will come to your rescue more often than not, and in March it could bring a minor windfall or a beneficial financial decision. Just don't get too carried away because you may need any extra funds this summer or fall.

Look forward to June 11. That's the date Jupiter begins its year-long transit of your sign. You'll attract luck, people, and opportunities, all of which may lead to a career or leadership position this summer. Part of the reason for this is that you'll have an abundance of enthusiastic optimism, so much in fact that it will be easy to take on far more than you can reasonably accomplish. Be selective, and find a way to stay organized because it will be tough at times to keep up with your life. Also plan ahead to eat healthy foods. With so much going on, it will be all too easy to resort to calorie-laden fast food.

Saturn will be in Libra, your solar Fifth House, for about the first nine months of the year, and then move on to Scorpio. During its time in Libra, the sign it has occupied since late 2009, Saturn will focus its energy on children, creativity, leisure-time activities, such as sports and hobbies, investments, and romance. Although Saturn can put a damper on whatever it touches, it's also a planet that delivers rewards earned in the past or over the long term.

You should thus invest with no thought of an immediate return. In matters of the heart, a former romantic interest could reappear, or you might decide to either end of take a long-term dating relationship to the next level. Your children and their activities could generate extra expenses, and if they're young, Saturn encourages you to begin a college fund and then make monthly contributions. This is not the year, however, to make a significant investment in a hobby you think could generate a second income.

Your focus will shift to the workplace when Saturn enters Scorpio, your solar Sixth House, October 5. Prepare yourself for several years of extra job responsibilities and the feeling that you're underappreciated. What you do now will eventually pay off, so don't be tempted to cut corners. At the same time, resist pressure from coworkers to handle tasks that aren't yours to do.

Saturn in your solar Sixth House also emphasizes service and wellness. This means a healthy diet, moderate exercise, and a volunteer activity could be the ideal antidotes for job stress. Do something nice for yourself: get a check-up early in this transit period. An elderly pet could require more of your time and attention now.

Uranus continues its seven-year transit of Aries, your solar Eleventh House, where it will be until 2018. Its influence here is friendship, groups, and organizations, so you'll be involved with all of these during these years. New people will suddenly appear, and some will just as quickly disappear, having served their purpose in your life. With only a little effort you can expand your business and personal network with a wide variety of acquaintances.

Uranus in your solar Eleventh House will also work on a more internal level, urging you to assess and realign your goals in terms of your overall life philosophy, what is most important to you, and where you want to invest the best of your time and effort. Your thinking is likely to focus on job satisfaction, career direction, and income. Listen to your sixth sense in July when a flash of insight and understanding could unexpectedly reveal answers, possibly through a friend. Seize the opportunity to take charge of your life!

Neptune also changes signs this year, spending about the first month of 2012 in Aquarius. During its long transit through your solar Ninth House, this mystical planet has emphasized spirituality and knowledge, and encouraged you to look beyond the material world. Rewind your mind to 1998, when Neptune entered Aquarius, and review all the years in between. You'll discover you've gained a greater sense of who you are, greater faith in yourself, and knowledge that you can use in your career as Neptune moves on to your solar Tenth House.

After a brief visit in Pisces in 2011, Neptune makes its permanent shift into this sign February 3, where it will be until 2025. Neptune here has both a positive side and a challenging one. You can mix with many people you meet through your career, but you'll be more susceptible to false promises. Misunderstandings and confusion can occur, and you will question your role in life and whether your career has true value at times. A mentoring relationship can be helpful, although you should put more faith in yourself and your abilities than rely on someone else to come through for you. Remember: Neptune provides the inspiration, you provide the motivation.

Pluto continues its long trip through Capricorn. Its influence here, in your solar Eighth House, is joint resources, including your partner's income, insurance, inheritance, and loans and lenders. As the planet of transformation, Pluto pushes for change wherever it's located and will not take no for an answer. It's therefore easier to do what Pluto asks of you rather than try to resist the inevitable.

In this sector, Pluto urges you to establish a path toward financial security. Pay off debt, spend less, save, and create a retirement plan even if it's years away. Also take the time to update insurance coverage and compare premiums. But don't do all this alone. Get your partner involved in financial planning and decision-making. If you're planning a major purchase such as a home, take your time, look for the best mortgage rate, and bargain hard. Don't put funds at risk, however, because Pluto can trigger a major loss.

What This Year's Eclipses Mean for You

There are four eclipses this year, two of which put you in the spotlight. The third highlights your relationship sector, and the fourth accents your work life. Each is in effect for six to twelve months.

The May 21 solar eclipse in your sign is all about you and the empowerment to achieve your goals. With Jupiter entering your sign about three weeks after the eclipse, you'll have an extra edge here, along with optimism and good fortune to make things happen. Not all you touch will turn to gold, but with a clear direction you can turn the odds in your favor. Measure your progress at the November 28 lunar eclipse in your sign, adjust as necessary, and continue on your path into 2013.

Other people will be an integral part of your success the second half of the year because the June 4 lunar eclipse will be in Sagittarius, your solar Seventh House of relationships. You can use this influence to connect with people, network, and expand your list of contacts. But its main significance is in close relationships—your partner and dearest friends. This eclipse could trigger a marriage or commitment if you're involved in a serious relationship.

November 13 will bring a solar eclipse in Scorpio, your solar Sixth House. With Saturn also in Scorpio by then, you can expect your work life to be a main focus well into 2013. Although Saturn here will add to your responsibilities, the solar eclipse will give you an opportunity to shine. Stretch your leadership skills and aim high, while remembering that decision-makers will be watching. This eclipse will also give you the willpower to adopt a healthier lifestyle

Saturn

If you were born between June 11 and 21, Saturn will contact your Sun from Libra before October 5. This easy connection is a steadying influence that will give you additional stamina and strengthen your ability to focus on the task at hand. With the energy coming from your solar Fifth House, you can deepen your relationship with your children of any age while teaching them responsibility and other life skills. If you're the parent of a teen, you may need to adjust when your child heads off to college, including helping with expenses.

Investments can be profitable if you think long term, because there are no quick returns where Saturn is involved. Be cautious and conservative. Another good use of this contact is to add or perfect a hobby or creative skills, learn a sport, or travel where you can experience another culture. Do all you can to acknowledge your talents, strengths (and challenges), and the knowledge you've gained from life experience. With this ego boost firmly planted in your mind, you'll be ready for the next Saturn stage in your life.

If your birthday is between May 20 and 30, Saturn in Scorpio, your solar Sixth House, will connect with your Sun during the last three months of 2012, and again next year. Get ready to experience a new dynamic in your job, one that will have you feeling unsettled at times and elated at others. Whether you're in a new position, a longtime one, or returning or entering the work force, be prepared to be adaptable even though this can be a challenge. Also make a point not to share too much information with coworkers about your personal career goals.

Because this is a wellness sector, you should organize your life to include time for you, moderate exercise, leisure time, and activities that can help ease tension. By making a balanced lifestyle a priority you'll be more effective at work, where you'll feel overloaded at times and as though you're the only one who's working hard. All of this is perfectly normal with this Saturn connection. Take note of what occurs regarding your job late this year and put this knowledge to work for you in 2013.

Uranus

If you were born between May 20 and 30, Uranus will contact your Sun from Aries, your solar Eleventh House. With the spotlight on friendship and group activities, this is an opportunity to widen your circle of acquaintances. Any group endeavor, from an organization to teamwork in the workplace, can further your aims, and you could be tapped for a leadership position. Some of the people you connect with will enlighten you and others will spark fresh ideas for future achievements. On another level, this Uranus-Sun connection in tandem with Jupiter in your sign the second half of the year, encourages you to look beyond today and toward the future. Opportunities will come your way, but the cues may be subtle so you'll need to be aware in order to take full advantage of them. Intuition and networking can spark possibilities, but the best will come through being in the right place at the right time. Be aware, especially in July. Make your own luck.

Neptune

Neptune will contact your Sun from Aquarius during the first month of 2012 **if you were born between June 17 and 21.** You experienced this favorable connection last year, and now Neptune encourages you to take action on the dreams and aspirations that began to take hold in 2011. Use the time before February 3, when Neptune moves on to Pisces, to record your thoughts and reflections in a journal so you can refer to them as your journey progresses. This way you'll be able to recharge yourself with inspiration when you need it.

If you were born between May 20 and 24, Neptune will contact your Sun after it enters Pisces February 3. Known as the planet of illusion, Neptune in your solar Tenth House of career and status has the potential to bring fame (or infamy), or simply make you wish for a starring role in life. Take a more realistic view and you can benefit from the almost magical aura of popularity this mystical planet can bestow. On the flip side, however, is a tendency to believe that rules can be broken and that you can get away with just about anything—without consequences. This influence also makes it easy to be lulled into a false sense of security and complacency, which could result in you ending up as the scapegoat. Find a trusted friend or mentor who can confirm or challenge your career decisions. Even though you believe your thinking is on track, it may not be.

At times you may feel somewhat adrift, questioning whether you and your career are on track. Resist the urge to jump into something new that seems like the ideal. This too is unrealistic because Neptune will still be active in any new endeavor. Instead, have faith in yourself, who you are, what you know, and your many talents, skills, and abilities.

Pluto

If you were born between May 27 and 30, Pluto will contact your Sun from Capricorn, your solar Eighth House of joint resources. Because this transit indicates a certain level of stress and strain involving finances, you should spend less rather than more and make savings and debt reduction your priorities. Be very cautious with investments and avoid loans if at all possible. It's also possible you or your partner may see a decrease in income or benefits. This is not the year to invest in a business of your own despite enthusiasm for the idea.

Financial challenges may arise when Pluto clashes with Uranus in Aries in June and September. The source could be a friend who asks for a loan or wants you to cosign for one, or one who pressures you to get involved in a business enterprise. Say no even if it damages the friendship. You're unlikely to ever again see your money. These same periods could bring difficulties with an insurance settlement, legal matter, inheritance, or in-laws. And if you're involved in an organization or group activity, be alert for a power struggle.

Gemini | January

Planetary Lightspots

Learning and teaching are strong themes this month with the January 23 New Moon in Aquarius, your solar Ninth House. You could travel on business to attend a conference, or be asked to teach a class in your workplace. This influence also favors taking a class for fun. Make a point to connect with out-of-town friends, but be cautious if someone from the distant past reappears in your life.

Relationships

Personal relationships, especially with a partner, benefit from Mercury in Sagittarius, your solar Seventh House through January 7. Set aside a weekend or weeknight evening for dinner and talk, as it's a perfect opportunity to catch up on each other's lives. Or get together with a close friend. A dating relationship could reach a turning point around the 7th. However, be wary if a coworker tries to enlist your support around the 14th or 20th.

Money and Success

The January 9 Full Moon in Cancer, your solar Second House, could trigger a surprising raise or bonus that may be more or less than you expect. Either way, be gracious, and also keep the information to yourself rather than share it with coworkers. Extra expenses could pop up at month's end.

Planetary Hotspots

Home life could be a bit rocky the next few months as Mars in Virgo travels retrograde from January 23 to April 13. With this influence in your solar Fourth House, the wise choice is to avoid home improvement projects as well as inviting anyone to share your space as a roommate. Mechanical problems with appliances are also possible, and family conflict could arise at times.

Rewarding Days

2, 5, 6, 10, 11, 15, 18, 23, 24, 27

Challenging Days

1, 12, 13, 14, 16, 20, 22, 26

Gemini | February

Planetary Lightspots

The February 7 Full Moon in Leo triggers your curiosity and renews your interest in reading, games, and puzzles. Visit the library or download a novel to your e-reader, and challenge your kids to a card or board game. The lunar energy is also a plus for getting better acquainted with neighbors, so consider hosting a get-together near the 20th.

Relationships

Friendships benefit from Venus, which enters Aries, your solar Eleventh House, February 8. This is great influence for long talks with your best friends as well as for widening your circle of acquaintances. Someone exciting could enter your life around the 9th, and if you're single, you could feel an instant attraction to a potential romantic interest. You might also hear surprising news from a close friend.

Money and Success

February 21 will bring the New Moon in Pisces, your solar Tenth House of career. Make the most of this lunar energy by snapping up every opportunity to showcase your skills and talents. This could elevate your status in the eyes of decision-makers. If your goal is a promotion, your desire could be fulfilled mid-month.

Planetary Hotspots

Although February is mostly easygoing, difficult planetary alignments can trigger conflict around the 15th and 24th with a friend, family member, or coworker. The trigger could be as simple as an ego clash or as challenging as money matters. Do your best to keep things in perspective and to avoid getting emotionally involved. Don't let anyone pressure you into parting with your money unless you truly believe it's the right thing to do. If someone asks for a loan, view it as a request for a gift.

Rewarding Days

1, 2, 5, 6, 11, 12, 19, 20, 25

Challenging Days

3, 4, 15, 17, 18, 22, 24

Gemini | March

Planetary Lightspots

Indulge the urge the spend more time at home when the March 8 Full Moon in Virgo activates your solar Fourth House. Spend time with family, entertain friends, and simply enjoy time to kick back and curl up in your favorite chair with a best seller. If you feel motivated, begin making a list of domestic projects you'd like to accomplish after Mars, also in Virgo, turns direct next month.

Relationships

Friends delight you under the March 22 New Moon in Aries, your solar Eleventh House. Make plans to get together with your favorite pals, but be sure to confirm details. Groups are also emphasized here, and you could be part of a job-related teamwork project or get involved in a community or professional organization. Don't agree to a leadership role just yet, though, as conditions could change in April or May.

Money and Success

Double-check details at work, and then do it again, especially after retrograde Mercury retreats into Pisces, your solar Tenth House of career, on the 23rd. And don't be surprised if projects are put on hold or seem to be in a constant state of flux. Choose family time over socializing with coworkers the first few days of the month.

Planetary Hotspots

Mercury, your ruling planet, turns retrograde March 12, as it does three or four times each year. So you can expect the usual mix-ups and misunderstandings during its retrograde period, which lasts for about a month. Also expect some frustration in personal plans, and challenges with achieving your immediate goals. Laughter is a good antidote. Use it often!

Rewarding Days
1, 5, 6, 14, 18, 19, 23, 28

Challenging Days
3, 4, 7, 9, 13, 20, 27, 30

Gemini | April

Planetary Lightspots

The universe grants you a gift this month: the April 21 New Moon in Taurus, your solar Twelfth House. Take advantage of the following two weeks to kick back a little and spend time with your favorite activities. You can also use the lunar energy to clean closets and storage spaces in preparation for a spring yard sale with neighbors. Or cash in by taking the best to a consignment shop.

Relationships

A dating relationship could reach a turning point under the April 6 Full Moon in Libra, your solar Fifth House. Don't hesitate to move on if it isn't living up to your expectations, and especially if finances are a stumbling block. The same influence could trigger the need to reinforce family rules with your children. As tough as that can be, remind yourself that it is in their best interests.

Money and Success

Breathe a sigh of relief April 13. That's the date Mercury turns direct in Pisces, your solar Tenth House. Career matters will gradually resume momentum, although you can expect previous decisions to be reserved and errors to come to light. At least you'll feel as though your career and life overall are getting back on track because Mars turns direct the same day.

Planetary Hotspots

Be prepared for challenging days in early April when difficult planetary alignments could trigger domestic, financial, or family difficulties. Keep your cool and your patience. It may take until month's end to sort it out, with a few rough spots along the way, but things will improve by May.

Rewarding Days

1, 2, 10, 14, 17, 19, 22, 25, 28

Challenging Days

3, 5, 7, 9, 11, 15, 16, 26

Gemini | May

Planetary Lightspots

Despite Venus's retrograde motion, you'll be a shining star after the May 20 New Moon (solar eclipse) energizes your sign. Use it to renew your inspiration for career achievements as well as personal ones, and launch yourself in a new direction. Just be sure to set realistic goals rather than set yourself up for disappointment.

Relationships

See friends on the 4th or 8th, as Mercury transits Aries, your solar Eleventh House, through the 8th. But avoid the 5th, when you and a pal, or romantic interest, could disagree. Enjoy time with your partner and away from the social scene while Mercury is in Taurus, your solar Twelfth House, May 9–23. Then you'll be refreshed and ready to engage your mind when Mercury enters your sign four days after the New Moon.

Money and Success

This month's Full Moon in Scorpio, your solar Sixth House, will step up the pace at work. Even better, it will boost your overall luck, steering you to the right place at the right time. A lucky break is possible, and you could hear good news if you're in search of a new job. Just be sure you consider the potential downside in addition to the many positives.

Planetary Hotspots

Venus turns retrograde in your sign on the 15th, and will stay that way until June 26. It will be tougher, although not necessarily impossible, during this six-week period to connect with people and especially to convince them to support your plans. Less likely to grant favors, they will at least listen, so you can use this time to lay the groundwork for future help. This is not the time, however, to take a relationship to the commitment level.

Rewarding Days

4, 8, 11, 12, 17, 20, 22, 26, 31

Challenging Days

3, 7, 9, 13, 16, 21, 24, 28, 30

Gemini | June

Planetary Lightspots

Jupiter enters your sign on the 11th to begin a year-long lucky influence. So get ready to dash into a future with high personal expectations and enthusiasm. You'll get another burst of incentive from the second 2012 New Moon in your sign on the 19th. Consider this a bonus from the universe and use it well rather than indulge Jupiter's tendency to take it easy.

Relationships

The June 4 Full Moon (lunar eclipse) in Sagittarius could initially bring a rocky few days with someone close to you as it aligns with retrograde Venus in your sign and Mars in Virgo, your solar Fourth House. Reflect on words spoken and actions taken and use them as learning experiences in the importance of compromise. You'll be able to see relationships with maximum clarity after Venus turns direct on the 27th.

Money and Success

Finances will be up and down with Mercury in Cancer, your solar Second House, June 7–24, and the Sun in the same sign from the 20th on as these planets contact Uranus and Pluto. Be proactive rather than dwell on these matters, and don't let frustration take hold when resolution is delayed.

Planetary Hotspots

Money matters will be in high focus as Uranus in Aries clashes with Pluto in Capricorn June 24. However, it will be the last few days of June when you'll experience the most impact from this alignment, with the first clues appearing around the 11th and 20th. You could lose a valuable, a friend could ask for a loan (say no unless you can designate it as a gift), or you could have an unexpected expense. Check your credit reports for errors.

Rewarding Days

7, 8, 9, 13, 17, 18, 22, 23, 27

Challenging Days

5, 6, 10, 11, 12, 20, 21, 24, 29

Gemini | July

Planetary Lightspots

Good fortune is on your side this month, with the two most beneficial planets, Venus and Jupiter, in your sign. They won't solve everything, but they will bring you much-needed help when you need it. The 5th, 6th, and/or 20th could bring opportunities through a friend or group as well as valuable advice. Listen and think.

Relationships

Mars energizes your solar Fifth House after it enters Libra on the 3rd. This is great for your social life and leisure-time interests, but possibly not a romantic relationship or friendship, either of which could end when values or money become an issue. One of your children could display a strong independent streak that results in a battle of the wills. But you'll also have the love and support of many to help you weather the challenges.

Money and Success

Last month's financial difficulties continue as the July 3 Full Moon in Capricorn and the New Moon in Cancer on the 19th activate Uranus and Pluto. And even though it may not feel like it at the time, you will make progress toward resolving these issues.

Planetary Hotspots

Just when it seems like your life might be getting back on track, Mercury turns retrograde July 14 in Leo, your solar Third House of communication. This will interfere with your quest for information and also trigger mix-ups in dates, times, and places. Laughter can help as much as the knowledge that this phase won't last forever (until August 8). You'll also need patience.

Rewarding Days

1, 5, 6, 10, 14, 15, 20

Challenging Days

2, 9, 17, 19, 4, 26, 30

Gemini | August

Planetary Lightspots

If you can manage a few days away, plan a long weekend near the August 1 Full Moon in Aquarius, your solar Ninth House. It's a better choice than the New Moon in Leo, your solar Third House, on the 17th, when the trip could be pricey. If time is at a premium, explore new horizons by taking a community class to enhance hobby or financial skills, or to learn more about something that's always been of interest.

Relationships

Relationships benefit from Mercury after it turns direct in Leo, your solar Third House, August 8. Easy planetary alignments enhance the effect, although the potential for challenges with a friend still exists. Touch base with siblings and relatives later this month, and also set aside a day for a fun outing with your kids. They'll appreciate the extra attention.

Money and Success

The 31st brings this month's second Full Moon, this time in Pisces, your solar Tenth House. This will favor career matters into September, as will Mars, which advances into Scorpio, your solar Sixth House of daily work on the 23rd. You could earn a small raise near month's end, but praise is more likely.

Planetary Hotspots

The recent financial pattern continues as Venus in Cancer, your solar Second House, clashes with Uranus and Pluto mid-month. But again you'll see progress, and Venus could bring you additional income. It will also guide you to bargains, and you could profit from a yard sale or items taken to consignment shops.

Rewarding Days
1, 11, 16, 25, 28, 30

Challenging Days
7, 13, 20, 21, 24, 26, 27

Gemini | September

Planetary Lightspots

This month's New Moon in Virgo on the 15th aligns beautifully with Mercury in your solar Fourth House. In addition to encouraging family communication, you'll enjoy spending as many hours as possible at home. Earlier in September, planetary influences favor cleaning and cleaning out closets, cabinets, and storage spaces. You'll be in the mood to toss a lot, so be careful not to overdo it.

Relationships

Despite the relationship difficulties indicated by Uranus and Pluto this month, you'll also have many upbeat moments, primarily with those closest to you. Venus in Leo, your solar Third House, makes this another good month to connect with neighbors and siblings. You also could make a valuable networking contact near the 13th, possibly through a community activity.

Money and Success

Work continues to be fast-paced this month as Mars advances in Scorpio, your solar Sixth House. But slow the pace a little rather than race through projects. Otherwise you could miss important details, which will come to light at month's end.

Planetary Hotspots

The Uranus/Pluto alignment makes a return engagement on the 19th, to re-activate this summer's financial challenges. This time, extra expenses could arise regarding your children or another family member. Also in focus could be a friendship or dating relationship that might have been rocky in recent months. If so, you could finally end the relationship when the Full Moon in Aries on the 29th aligns with Uranus and Pluto.

Rewarding Days

3, 7, 8, 13, 16, 17, 25, 30

Challenging Days

2, 4, 10, 11, 23, 24, 29

Gemini | October

Planetary Lightspots

Home life and all things domestic get the best of Venus in Virgo, your solar Fourth House, October 3–28. Household projects will catch your interest, but you could take on far more than you can do yourself or accomplish in your free time. Scale back and tackle one room at a time. Creativity will help you stretch your budget.

Relationships

The October 15 New Moon in Libra, your solar Fifth House, accents your social life and quality time with your children. Plan a day trip with your kids to a museum or local attraction, and also be their loudest cheerleader at sporting events and other activities.

Money and Success

Investments could be profitable this month, but you'll still want to be cautious about anything other than those for the long term. A better use of the energy might be to learn more about specific investments and financial planning in general. Listen for praise at work in early October, but take care at month's end not to make assumptions.

Planetary Hotspots

Saturn enters Scorpio, your solar Sixth House, October 5. This transit signifies hard work with limited recognition. Think carefully if a promotion comes your way. It may or may not be a true step up. Instead, you could actually put in more hours, thereby reducing your hourly rate. You'll begin to grasp the meaning of this transit in your life near the October 29 Full Moon in Taurus, which also advises you to balance work with time for yourself and family.

Rewarding Days

5, 6, 10, 18, 22, 27, 28

Challenging Days

4, 7, 9, 11, 14, 20, 25

Gemini | November

Planetary Lightspots

The November 28 Full Moon (lunar eclipse) shines brightly in your sign, bringing you to the attention of many. It's best influence, however, is in relationships with those closest to you, including your partner. Treat your mate to a special evening out, and take the time to tell your favorite people how important they are to you.

Relationships

Your social life continues to be active this month, thanks to Venus in Libra, your solar Fifth House, through the 20th. But be sure to estimate the price before you go. If it's too high for your budget, be ready to suggest an alternative. But avoid the 3rd, which is equally unfavorable for dates. Also take care to avoid misunderstandings at work near the 12th and 23rd.

Money and Success

The November 13 New Moon (solar eclipse) in Scorpio energizes your work life with potential that extends into 2013. Plan now how you can make the most of this influence as you move forward into the new year. Mars transitions into Capricorn, your solar Eighth House, on the 16th to remind you to budget carefully for holiday spending. Remember coworkers with something small, an ornament or a tin of homemade cookies.

Planetary Hotspots

Mercury, your ruling planet, begins retrograde travel November 6 in Sagittarius, your solar Seventh House. It then slips back into Scorpio, your solar Sixth House, on the 14th, before turning direct on the 26th. Work and personal relationships are thus prone to mix-ups and misunderstandings, and you'll need to give careful attention to detail. Confirm times, dates, and places for meetings and social events, and be sure to clarify your thoughts before you speak.

Rewarding Days
2, 6, 7, 9, 11, 14, 15, 24, 29

Challenging Days
3, 10 12, 16, 18, 19 23, 30

Gemini | December

Planetary Lightspots

Mars dashes into Aquarius, your solar Ninth House, on the 25th. Plan a vacation trip for February rather than now, as planetary alignments caution against travel. Or invite out-of-town friends to visit you during the holidays. This influence will also trigger your curiosity and desire for knowledge. Take it a step further and enroll in a short-term class in January that can benefit your career.

Relationships

Memorable moments with your partner and those closest to you are in the forecast as the New Moon in Sagittarius spotlights your solar Seventh House on the 13th. Two days later, Venus, the universal planet of love, will enter the same sign, and Mercury promotes communication with its transit of Sagittarius December 10–30. The combined influence will prompt some Geminis to take a relationship to the next level, and others will celebrate an engagement.

Money and Success

Although money will be tight in the two weeks following the December 28 Full Moon in Cancer, your solar Second House, you could earn a small year-end bonus that will help to balance your budget. You could also earn more this month, possibly through a temporary job. Take care, though, not to push yourself too hard.

Planetary Hotspots

Be choosy when you plan your December social schedule. There's no need to see friends you'd rather avoid. Remember that living within your budget is more important than stretching it in order to give expensive gifts to everyone on your list. Scale back and focus on thrift. And don't give in if a friend or coworker pressures you to support a favorite cause. Put you and yours first.

Rewarding Days
12, 15, 16, 17, 21, 26, 31

Challenging Days
7, 11, 18, 20, 28, 30

Gemini Action Table

These dates reflect the best—but not the only—times for success and ease in these activities, according to your Sun sign.

	JAN	FEB	MAR	APR	MAY	JUN	JUL	AUG	SEP	OCT	NOV	DEC
Move	12, 13								14, 15	12, 13		
Start a class								11–21				
Join a club		24, 25, 29	1–4	17–21				6, 7				
Ask for a raise								13, 14				
Look for work								31	1	23–26	26–30	1–11
Get pro advice										29–31		12–20
Get a loan	12, 13 17, 18											14
See a doctor	17									16, 17		10
Start a diet					18							10
End relationship	19					29						
Buy clothes						3			16, 17			
Get a makeover				24								
New romance				5						15		
Vacation	28, 31	1–12				7–9						

CANCER

The Crab
June 20 to July 22

Element: Water

Quality: Cardinal

Polarity: Yin/Feminine

Planetary Ruler: The Moon

Meditation: I have faith in the promptings of my heart

Gemstone: Pearl

Power Stones: Moonstone, chrysocolla

Key Phrase: I feel

Glyph: Crab's claws

Anatomy: Stomach, breasts

Color: Silver, pearl white

Animal: Crustaceans, cows, chickens

Myths/Legends: Hercules and the Crab, Asherah, Hecate

House: Fourth

Opposite Sign: Capricorn

Flower: Larkspur

Key Word: Receptivity

Your Strengths and Challenges

You're sensitive, caring, and sympathetic, and when you get close to people you want to fulfill their every need and desire. It's this nurturing quality that draws others into the warmth of your aura. You're also intuitive and easily sense how others feel, but you need to be cautious about becoming too emotionally involved in their lives and problems.

Because you're so responsive to others, some people underestimate your inner strength, believing you're a pushover. Not so! Cancer is a cardinal water sign, which gives you two major assets—dynamic action and the ability to win people's loyalty. And when someone pushes you too far, you're more than capable of holding your own.

Your Moon-ruled sign is very sensitive to the environment. When entering a room you pick up the vibrations, both positive and negative. It's partly your sixth sense and partly your receptive nature. This can be a real plus when you need to know how to present your ideas, for example. But it's also wise to mentally surround yourself with a protective shield rather than take the chance of absorbing unwanted energy.

You're happiest when life is predictable, safe, and secure. But with the Moon as your ruling planet, your life and your emotions are in a continual state of flux. That gives you a reputation for moodiness and others find it difficult to understand why you're up one minute and down the next. This is especially true when someone hurts your feelings, whether this is reality or only your perception.

Traditional and patriotic to the core, you value the past, might collect or refinish antiques, and probably have a large collection of family photos and memorabilia. Most Cancers are excellent cooks and enjoy entertaining friends and family in their tastefully decorated homes.

Your Relationships

Because Cancer is the universal sign of family, most people with the Sun in this sign have strong ties to loved ones—parents, grandparents, children, siblings, cousins, aunts and uncles. Most also want children to cherish and nurture. But as a parent you can be overly protective and try to shield your children from the hurts and realities that are good learning experiences. Give them room to grow and to explore their own personalities and talents while they have the safety and security of a supportive, loving home life. They'll thank you later when they become adults.

As a friend you're one of the best—loyal and supportive. Your circle, whether large or small, is filled with people around whom you can be yourself, and you most enjoy time with them one-on-one or in small groups. Generous with your time and resources, you treasure your friendships and have many lifelong associations. Some of these people become members of your extended family.

In love, your feelings run deep and at times you can be possessive and even jealous, hanging on to a dating relationship when you know in your heart it's time to move on. You also experience the ultimate in passionate, romantic moments when you're with the right person. Although it might take you longer than your peers to find a soul mate, when you find your ideal match, he or she is likely to share your desire for financial security and a stable family life. You could find happiness with one of the earth signs, Taurus, Virgo, and especially Capricorn, your polar opposite. The other water signs, Scorpio and Pisces, are in tune with your energy, but it could be difficult to satisfy your emotional needs with an Aries or Libra.

In all relationships, Cancers have a tendency to sacrifice their needs for others. Although compromise is necessary when two people come together, being too accommodating is unhealthy for both parties. Strive for a fifty-fifty average, sometimes giving more, sometimes less, in order to satisfy both your and your mate's needs, hopes, and wishes.

Your Career and Money

You have excellent financial instincts and a talent for making money. That's a plus to fulfill your security needs. But some Cancers take things too far and never achieve this goal because enough never seems to be enough—even when assets run into the millions. And this can encourage a fearful mind-set as well as a miserly one. Learn to keep finances in perspective and be thrifty and wise, investing for the long term and saving to cover the inevitable unexpected expenses that are a normal part of life. Periodically reward yourself and loved ones with the luxury items you desire.

Your cardinal-sign initiative is especially evident in your career life where you invest maximum energy to achieve your goals. A career with growth potential is a must, as is one where you can use your leadership skills. But therein lies a possible challenge. If promotions don't come as fast as you wish, your thoughts soon turn elsewhere. This can lead to job-hopping, which could slow your progress even more. Patience can pay off handsomely. In your daily work you need an upbeat, enthusiastic environment with a high level of activity and freedom, or at least limited supervision. For this reason many Cancers avoid desk jobs. You also need a job in which you can learn or teach others, formally or informally, along with open-minded coworkers and a free exchange of ideas.

Your Lighter Side

It's a well-kept secret that Cancer is one of the most observant signs of the zodiac. Little escapes your notice, thanks to intuition and your excellent eye for detail. This and your tenacity make you an outstanding researcher. You persist until you find the answers. It's also difficult, if not impossible, for your children and others close to you to get away with much of anything as you're nearly always a step ahead of them.

Affirmation for the Year

People are my foundation, but strength comes from within.

The Year Ahead for Cancer

This year you can achieve an ideal balance of socializing and retreat. Although the two are completely different, you'll be able to enjoy people when you're in the mood and enjoy the comforts of home when you're not. Some relationships will be rocky and others will bring you joy. This is also a great year for travel and widening your horizons. Do that earlier in 2012 if you can because the second half of the year will bring an increased focus on work.

Fun, friendship, and socializing are highlighted through June 10 as Jupiter transits Taurus, your solar Eleventh House. This sector also governs groups and organizations, so you could find yourself in a leadership position or involved in a job-related teamwork project. Any of these can bring you luck during this transit, but because Jupiter is also the planet of expansion, take care not to become overcommitted. Social events with friends and coworkers will bring new networking opportunities, and you could form a strong personal or professional alliance with someone you meet in March. This transit also encourages you to assess and redefine your career goals, especially as they relate to your daily job activities.

Jupiter spends the second half of the year in Gemini, your solar Twelfth House of self-renewal. Time for yourself will become more of a priority, and this influence is one of the best for meditation and looking within in order to learn more about yourself, what motivates you, and what holds you back. People will confide in you, sharing their secrets, and a behind-the-scenes supporter could help to advance your career or status in July. Jupiter in this sector can also function like a guardian angel, providing just the help you need, often at the eleventh hour.

Saturn changes signs late this year after spending the first nine months in Libra, your solar Fourth House. Transiting here, Saturn emphasizes home and family as well as your roots and everything domestic. Saturn has been in Libra since November 2009, so you may have already relocated; if not, this could be the year you decide to find a new home. This influence can also trigger a desire for a major remodeling project, or a change in your household with someone moving in or out. You might research your family history, or resolve any family-related issues.

Give some thought to where you'd like to be career-wise in about twelve years when Saturn moves into your Solar Tenth House. Although this might seem like a long time, what you do between now and then can contribute greatly to your success. And it's tough to know where you're going without a map to get there.

Saturn enters Scorpio, your solar Fifth House, October 5. Here, Saturn will influence children, creativity, romance, investments, and leisure-time activities. All of these will in some way have a role in your life in the next few years, and most will have the more serious overtone of Saturn, which is also the planet of responsibility. So this can be a time when you develop a stronger relationship with your children, see them grow into young adults, or become more involved with their lives, whatever their age. A dating relationship could evolve into one that is comfortable but without the passion and motivation to take it a step further.

A new hobby could capture your attention, including learning all you can to perfect your creative skills. At some point it could become a source of extra income or even evolve into a career in the more distant future. Investments should be handled with a long-term view as Saturn here can limit immediate gains. A conservative approach is the best choice now. You could also use Saturn strength to begin or enhance an athletic skill, or to simply devote some of your evening or weekend hours to walking or working out at the gym.

Uranus continues its multiyear trip through Aries. This planet of the unexpected will bring change to your career life at some point, even if not this year. Or it's possible you experienced this in the past two years. Although an unexpected change is disruptive at best, Uranus here encourages you to look beyond the immediate and well into the future. By reinventing your career and the self-identity you associate with it, you will ultimately become closer to achieving financial security.

This year a sudden career opportunity could pop up in May or July. Consider both the upside and the downside before making a change because optimism can get the best of you. A better use of this might be networking and aligning yourself with the most advantageous decision-makers. The result could be job protection or gain through a small advancement.

Neptune concludes its transit of Aquarius, your solar Eighth House, on February 2, and then moves on to Pisces. During its time in Aquarius, you've experienced its effect on joint finances. Use the first month of 2012 to handle any financial matters left unresolved from last year, especially loans, insurance, and communication with lenders. Also check your credit report.

Neptune moves on to Pisces, your solar Ninth House, February 3, where it will be until 2025. This is an excellent influence if you have yet to complete your education or want to get an advanced degree or training. If not this year, you may begin a course of study when Neptune contacts your Sun. But even then you might have to push yourself to commit the time and effort, despite the knowledge that it would be in your best interest. Neptune is great for dreaming but less than effective for action. Wherever you are in life, make it a point to learn. Read, take a class for fun, study something you've always been curious about, or learn another language. Neptune is also likely to pique your interest in other cultures, and you might develop a desire to see many other countries around the world. If you plan a trip this year, schedule your departure for mid-April or later, or even better, in mid-October, when Neptune will favorably align with Saturn in Scorpio. It's wise to avoid legal matters while Neptune is in Pisces as it will be more difficult to resolve them.

Pluto continues to advance in Capricorn, your solar Seventh House of relationships. It will bring many relationship changes as people enter and depart your life. Some of these people will be positive and uplifting, encouraging you on a personal level. Others, however, will be decidedly negative and controlling. Both types of people will teach you more about relationships and your role in them. As a result you may purposely make a healthy choice to distance yourself from some. In this sense, Pluto in your relationship sector is more about you than about others. The best part of this transit is self-awareness and the courage to do what's right for you.

What This Year's Eclipses Mean for You

There are four eclipses this year, two solar and two lunar. Three of them bracket your solar Sixth/Twelfth House axis, and the fourth is in your solar Fifth House. Each is in effect for six to twelve months.

The year's first solar eclipse is in Gemini, your solar Twelfth House, May 21. Two weeks later (June 4) a lunar eclipse in Sagittarius will highlight your solar Sixth House. November 28 will bring a lunar eclipse in Gemini. The emphasis on these solar sectors will focus your attention on wellness, work, and service, and it will be amplified by Jupiter in Gemini the second half of the year. Tune in to yourself, assess your lifestyle and your health, and use this time to focus on what's best for you. With eclipses in these opposite signs, the goal is to strive for a balance between work and play, and to make wellness a priority through diet and exercise. You also could use your nurturing spirit to help others who are less fortunate.

November 13 is the date of the year's second solar eclipse. Placed in Scorpio, your solar Fifth House, this eclipse emphasizes socializing, leisure-time activities, children, and romance. By the time this eclipse occurs, Saturn will be in Scorpio, so you can use the combined energy to strengthen the close relationships in your life. Most of all, though, this can reinforce self-reliance and faith in yourself, creating a much greater sense of security than you can gain from other people.

Saturn

If you were born between July 13 and 22, Saturn will contact your Sun from Libra, your solar Fourth House before October 4. You'll experience the full effect of Saturn in June or July **if your birthday is July 13, 14, or 15.** Cancers born on the other dates will be under Saturn's influence twice, once between January and May, and again in August or September.

This Saturn-Sun contact can have you feeling low and as though your life is not progressing as you wish. It also can lower your vitality, so adequate sleep is a must. This is all perfectly normal with this planetary alignment, which is designed to encourage you to assess both your accomplishments and challenges in the past seven years. Then use this knowledge to set your path for the next seven and fourteen years.

On another level, you can expect home and family to be more of a priority, and to bring increased responsibilities. Elderly relatives or a parent may need your time and attention, and you also could see an adult child or another relative move in or out of your household. It's also possible your home may need significant repairs or that you could relocate.

Be cautious, though, if you're considering a property purchase or a new roommate. Both are likely to bring more difficulties than rewards. If you do buy a home, be sure to make the sale conditional on the results of an expert property inspection. However, if you've been trying to sell a home, Saturn could make this a reality. Also double-check that your insurance coverage (renter's or homeowners) is adequate for any eventuality.

Uranus

If you were born between June 21 and 29, Uranus will contact your Sun from Aries, your solar Tenth House of career and status. Uranus could trigger a sudden career change—a step up, a new job, or unfortunately, the loss of one. But Jupiter in Gemini, especially during July and August, puts the odds in your favor for a positive outcome. Keep in mind, though, that Jupiter promises a lot but sometimes fails to deliver.

On a personal level, Uranus can trigger an unrelenting desire for freedom, independence, and change. This can be positive if you initiate change for all the right reasons, including reinventing yourself in order to be more effective in the world and your overall life. The danger lies in change for the sake of change because actions taken under this transit are rarely reversed.

Uranus can also trigger sudden changes initiated by others or events in your environment. This is often ultimately positive because Uranus is simply fulfilling its mission to bring needed change into your life. Upon reflection, you will know this is true even though the process and adapting to new conditions will challenge you.

Neptune

Neptune will be in Aquarius, your solar Eighth House, through February 2, where it will contact your Sun **if you were born between July 19 and 22.** You also experienced this transit in 2011, when it may have triggered financial worries, mix-ups, and misunderstandings. Overall, Neptune adds confusion to money matters, making it difficult to take action or to successfully resolve financial issues. Now is the time, however, to make one more attempt. Chances are, you will be able to accomplish your goal.

If you were born between June 21 and 24, Neptune will contact your Sun from Pisces, your solar Ninth House, after it enters this sign February 3. This favorable alignment is ideal for creative projects, education, and travel. It also will boost your sixth sense and initiate a spiritual journey. You will view your world through a different lens during this transit, which is also one of idealism rather than practicality. Be cautious. It will be much easier now to accept people on faith, believing that everyone shares your high ideals. Unfortunately, this may not be the reality. Be skeptical. Some people you encounter will not have your best interests in mind.

Pluto

Pluto will contact your Sun from Capricorn, your solar Seventh House, **if you were born between June 27 and 30**. Although this is a difficult transit that occurs only once in a lifetime, it also has its upside. Pluto transforms whatever it touches. This means you and someone close to you will undergo irreversible change in the coming year: the relationship could deepen or end as Pluto does nothing half way. What Pluto challenges you to do is to examine not only the relationships in your life but your perspective of them, and then to make the necessary changes. This process probably won't be an easy one, but you'll emerge stronger and wiser, which is Pluto's ultimate aim. And nearly everyone who undergoes a Pluto transit is a better, more confident person for the experience. You can also use Pluto to revamp yourself through diet, exercise, and healthy eating and living.

The toughest part of this transit, however, may be Pluto's clash with Uranus in Aries, your solar Tenth House, in June and September. This could trigger a career-related change such as company restructuring, power politics, or a clash with a controlling supervisor. Do all you can to avoid people or situations that could put your job in jeopardy. Also keep your options open to new opportunities. Unfortunately, you could encounter the same difficult people and environment if you accept a new position. This is also not the year to form a business partnership, even with someone you know well.

Cancer | January

Planetary Lightspots

You attract energy and people during the two weeks following the January 9 Full Moon in Cancer. Take advantage of the time to connect with neighbors. Be on the lookout for a possible career contact, someone who might open a door for you later this year. A sibling could share surprising information mid-month.

Relationships

Relationships are mostly positive this month as Mercury transits Capricorn, your solar Seventh House, January 8–26. But you can expect a few challenges along the way. You could be at odds with a coworker, supervisor, or family member around the 8th, 14th, or 18th. Change will be the issue, and although you should be true to your values, life will be easier if you keep an open mind. Time with friends is uplifting in early January and at mid-month.

Money and Success

Money matters get a boost from this month's New Moon in Aquarius (January 23), your solar Eighth House, and Venus in the same sign through the 13th. Be prepared, though, to remember your budget when socializing with friends. A generous mood could encourage you to pick up the tab, expecting others to do the same in the future. They may not.

Planetary Hotspots

Mechanical problems with a vehicle or appliance may pop up late in the month as Mars in Virgo travels retrograde from January 23 to April 12. Check problems out sooner rather than later. This retrograde period will also affect communication. Be especially cautious about job-related e-mail—what you say and when you click the send button. Postpone the purchase of electronics, phones, and computers unless absolutely necessary. Consider an extended warranty.

Rewarding Days
3, 4, 13, 16, 17, 25, 31

Challenging Days
1, 6, 7, 8, 12, 14, 18

Cancer | February

Planetary Lightspots

If you can manage the time, let the February 21 New Moon in Pisces, your solar Ninth House, motivate you to take a winter vacation or even a long weekend away. Either one will be just the change of scenery you need to refresh your mind and spirit. Ask friends to join you, or choose sweet days of romance with your partner.

Relationships

You could hear positive news from an out-of-town friend or relative around February 13, and again near the 25th. But avoid contact with relatives and neighbors on the 22nd and 24th, when you should take extra care on the road. Overall, you'll have a tough time reaching people this month as Mars continues to retrograde through your solar Third House. Don't push others for decisions, especially on the job. Be patient.

Money and Success

Cross your fingers for extra income and favorable financial news as the February 7 Full Moon in Leo spotlights your solar Second House of personal resources. You could be approved for a loan, or receive an anticipated check or gift from a family member. The lunar energy is also beneficial for budgeting and organizing tax information. If you file now, you could get a nice refund.

Planetary Hotspots

You'll be an attention-getter as Venus transits Aries, your solar Tenth House of career, from February 8 on. That's all to the good. Unfortunately, difficult planetary alignments around the 10th and 15th could trigger workplace conflict. Do your best to remain on the sidelines rather than get involved, and take care not to challenge the boss. Jealousy on the part of a coworker is possible.

Rewarding Days

5, 9, 12, 13, 21, 23, 26, 27

Challenging Days

3, 4, 10, 15, 16, 17, 22, 24

Cancer | March

Planetary Lightspots

Although Mars is still retrograde in Virgo, the March 8 Full Moon in the same sign favors communication and socializing with friends and neighbors. Someone you connect with mid-month could bring you luck, and possibly help you network your way to career gains.

Relationships

Venus in Taurus, your solar Eleventh House, benefits your social life after March 4. Join a group of friends for an evening out on the 12th or 14th, or ask another couple to meet you and your mate for dinner and a movie. If you're single, March could bring a romantic opportunity, but it's unlikely to be long-lasting. Nevertheless, enjoy the brief connection, which can widen your circle of acquaintances.

Money and Success

Career-related changes could be in the forecast as the March 22 New Moon in Aries, your solar Tenth House, merges its energy with Uranus and retrograde Mercury. This may or may not affect you directly, and is likely to remain unfinished business until later in April. If you have your sights set on a promotion or a new job, submit your resume before March 8.

Planetary Hotspots

Mercury turns retrograde March 12, and stays that way until April 13. Take precautions during this time to minimize mix-ups and misunderstandings. Confirm dates, times, and places, and double-check details even if you're sure everything is correct. But you can also use this period to advantage by reviewing, revising, and improving previous projects. Beware of computer viruses, and re-read important e-mail before you click the send button.

Rewarding Days

7, 11, 12, 16, 18, 21, 25, 26

Challenging Days

2, 4, 9, 13, 15, 20, 30

Cancer | April

Planetary Lightspots

The April 6 Full Moon in Libra highlights your solar Fourth House of domestic activities. Although you'll have little time that week for household projects, the crunch will ease later in April, when you can make up for lost time. Plant flowers, give your place a spring cleaning, and host a get-together around the 21st or 28th. Take care, though, not to toss out anything that belongs to your mate or your children.

Relationships

Friendship gets the spotlight under the April 21 New Moon in Taurus, your solar Eleventh House. Connect with friends you haven't seen a while, and also get a group of coworkers together for an evening out. Ask them to bring their friends and then take advantage of this networking opportunity. Think carefully, though, if you're asked to take on a leadership role at work or in an organization. There could be personality challenges.

Money and Success

After resuming direct motion, Mercury returns to Aries, your solar Tenth House, on the 16th, where it will be the rest of the month. Previous work will probably need revisions, but you'll also be well placed to catch the attention of decision-makers. Share your ideas.

Planetary Hotspots

Although Mars and Mercury turn direct April 13, planetary alignments caution against travel. You could experience anything from car trouble to lost luggage and weather-related cancellations or delays. Find a good substitute to satisfy curiosity, such as visiting a local museum or historic spot. Also avoid difficult relatives and in-laws this month if you can. There will be no way to please them.

Rewarding Days

4, 8, 12, 17, 21, 22, 27, 28

Challenging Days

3, 5, 7, 11, 13, 15, 23, 26

Cancer | May

Planetary Lightspots

Like Venus in Gemini, this month's New Moon in the same sign on the 20th encourages you to slow the pace a little. Treat yourself well, sleep, relax, and eat healthy foods. All of this will help to boost your immune system and prevent a cold. Set aside at least thirty minutes a day just for you. Read, meditate, go for a walk, or do something else you enjoy.

Relationships

The May 5 Full Moon in Scorpio, your solar Fifth House, aligns with Jupiter in Taurus, your solar Eleventh House of friendship. Make time for your closest friends, who can be an inspiration as they spark laughter and optimism. One of them could connect you with someone who will be a valuable networking contact in the future.

Money and Success

Mercury spends the first eight days of May in Aries, your solar Tenth House of career and status. Although the first few days of the month will be challenging ones, you and your efforts will be recognized and you'll have an opportunity to learn from someone whose wisdom can guide you in the coming months. Expect finances to be status quo, but an extra expense at month's end could be related to a vehicle repair.

Planetary Hotspots

Your social life will take a back seat to other areas of life while Venus travels retrograde in Gemini, your solar Twelfth House, May 15–June 26. Not that this is a bad thing. Used to advantage, this is a great period to spend quality time with your favorite people in a relaxed setting. It's also possible you'll need to help care for an elderly family member, which will limit the hours available for all else in your life.

Rewarding Days

1, 6, 13, 14, 18, 19, 24

Challenging Days

3, 4, 7, 9, 16, 17, 30

Cancer | June

Planetary Lightspots

Lucky Jupiter enters Gemini, your solar Twelfth House, on the 11th. Transiting here, as it will be for the next twelve months, Jupiter functions much like a guardian angel. Lean on it when you need it, but don't assume it will come to your rescue all of the time.

Relationships

Your social life will get back on track after Venus turns direct on the 27th, and before then you'll enjoy the last days of Jupiter in Taurus, your solar Eleventh House of friendship. Although the Uranus-Pluto alignment will affect career-related relationships, it can also impact personal and family ties. Try not to take your frustrations out on those you love. Instead, look to them for support and return the favor.

Money and Success

You'll be pushed to the max under the June 4 Full Moon (lunar eclipse) in Sagittarius, your solar Sixth House. This will contribute to the tension that builds as the month progresses because the lunar energy will activate difficult planetary alignments. This is not the time for a workplace romance, but if you're already involved in one, that could trigger this month's challenges.

Planetary Hotspots

June 24 is the date of this year's first Uranus/Pluto alignment. (The second is September 19.) This difficult planetary alignment will focus on your career and business, and on personal relationships. The outcome this month depends in part on how you handle challenging situations, but some events will be out of your control. Think before you speak and act, say little, and try not to challenge supervisors. If you push things too far, your job could be in jeopardy. Events will center around the 11th and 29th.

Rewarding Days

1, 2, 14, 15, 16, 19, 21, 25, 28

Challenging Days

5, 6, 10, 11, 12, 20, 24, 27, 29

Cancer | July

Planetary Lightspots

The July 19 New Moon in your sign marks the symbolic beginning of your new solar year. Use it to set an ambitious agenda for the next twelve months, with a focus on home life. You could relocate before the end of 2012, or embark on a journey to learn more about your ancestors and to discover your genealogical roots.

Relationships

Last month's relationship challenges will again be apparent when the July 3 Full Moon in Capricorn, your solar Seventh House, aligns with Uranus and Pluto. This time, though, you'll have a better change to resolve the pertinent issues, or you will if you and the other person listen with open minds and search for a compromise. Set ground rules before you talk.

Money and Success

Finances require close attention this month after Mercury turns retrograde on the 14th in Leo, you solar Second House. Bills can go astray, even if you use online payments, and you could find errors on statements. Take extra precautions to safeguard your wallet or purse when out and about, especially when in crowds. But you also could find something you lost in June or early July.

Planetary Hotspots

Mars enters Libra, your solar Fourth House, July 3. Although this is a positive influence for household projects, you'll want to hold off on them until after the 10th. Before then, Mars could spark everything from a domestic accident to family conflict. Be especially careful with electricity, tools, and sharp objects, and in the kitchen.

Rewarding Days

7, 8, 11, 12, 16, 22, 23, 27

Challenging Days

2, 3, 9, 10, 17, 18, 24, 30

Cancer I August

Planetary Lightspots

The 31st is the date of this month's second Full Moon. Take advantage of this Full Moon in Pisces, your solar Ninth House, to plan or depart on a vacation. The change of scenery will refresh your spirit and your faith in yourself in addition to providing some much-needed stress relief. Or if that's not realistic, opt for a long weekend at a nearby destination where you can relax and get away for a few days.

Relationships

Mars moves on to Scorpio, your solar Fifth House, August 23, just in time to enjoy the last weeks of outdoor summer activities. Plan a family day trip to an amusement park or sporting event that your kids would enjoy. Reserve some time for yourself, too. Take a daily walk or visit the gym, enjoy a hobby, and socialize with friends. The goal is fun!

Money and Success

Money matters benefit from the August 1 Full Moon in Aquarius, your solar Eighth House, and the New Moon in Leo, your solar Second House, on the 17th. Also a plus is Mercury, which resumes direct motion in Leo on the 8th. You could gain through a raise or bonus, or even a small windfall. Shop for clothing before Mercury turns direct, when you could find some sensational bargains. Just be sure the store allows returns.

Planetary Hotspots

Venus enters your sign August 7, but you may not experience its beneficial influence until after the 16th. Before then, you'll need to deal with more relationship issues as Venus clashes with Uranus and Pluto. The 8th and 9th, however, could bring helpful information, and your sixth sense will be active on the same dates.

Rewarding Days

3, 4, 8, 9, 14, 19, 22, 23

Challenging Days

6, 7, 13, 16, 20, 21, 26, 28

Cancer | September

Planetary Lightspots

Neighbors, siblings, and a fast-paced daily life are all featured this month as the September 15 New Moon in Virgo accents your solar Third House. Take advantage of this time to get acquainted with neighbors, possibly through involvement in a community project. This sector is also associated with learning, so consider taking a quick class for fun. And be sure to set limits for calls, e-mail, and more as these can quickly eat up time.

Relationships

Seeing friends and spending time with your kids continue to be priorities this month as Mars advances in Scorpio, your solar Fifth House. But you could have issues with a dating relationship in early or late September. Don't be hasty, but don't postpone ending things if it's the best choice for you.

Money and Success

Money matters continue on the upswing this month, thanks to Venus in Leo, your solar Second House, from the 6th on. You could make a lucky find and see a raise earned last month appear in your pay check. Mostly, though, you'll have the funds you need when you need them. Be prepared, however, for some extra expenses related to your children.

Planetary Hotspots

September 19 brings this year's second Uranus/Pluto alignment, but you'll experience it most strongly around the 29th when the Full Moon in Aries triggers these two planets. Events will involve your career, relationships and home life, with changes in all or some of these sectors. This is not the time to invite someone to join your household, whether roommate, relative, or romantic interest.

Rewarding Days

1, 3, 5, 6, 9, 13, 27, 28, 30

Challenging Days

2, 10, 11, 16, 19, 20, 23, 24, 29

Cancer | October

Planetary Lightspots

Home life is upbeat this month with various planets and the October 15 New Moon in Libra, your solar Fourth House. This is a great time to winterize your home, redo a room, or simply enjoy being cozy and comfortable in your own space. If you want to entertain friends, the 12th is a good choice.

Relationships

Saturn changes signs this month, entering Scorpio, your solar Fifth House, October 5. Soon after, you could be traveling on a family or business trip. During the next several years, Saturn will help you strengthen some relationships, and you'll be more involved in your children's lives, whatever their age. This month the October 29 Full Moon in Taurus, your solar Eleventh House, could trigger contact from someone from the past. If it's a romantic interest, remember why you're no longer together.

Money and Success

The work pace will pick up after Mars enters Sagittarius, your solar Sixth House, on the 6th. It will stay that way until mid-November, so be sure to plan ahead and carefully budget your time. An exciting opportunity could come your way this month. Think before you leap and don't take on more than you can realistically do.

Planetary Hotspots

Life will be more easygoing this month, but you'll need to listen to your sixth sense in the month. Someone could appear to be a supporter who has your best interests in mind. This may or may not be true. Be wary if this person pushes too hard, tells you what you want to hear, or makes guarantees. If promises sound too good to be true, they probably are.

Rewarding Days

2, 3, 8, 12, 16, 21, 24, 30

Challenging Days

1, 4, 7, 14, 20

Cancer | November

Planetary Lightspots

Despite retrograde Mercury, your social life will move into high gear under the November 13 Full Moon (solar eclipse) in Scorpio. Fill your calendar through the holidays with social events and outings, but reserve time to romance your partner. Fun-filled hours with your kids are also in the forecast, and you'll be a proud parent at their after-school events.

Relationships

Mars enters Capricorn, your solar Seventh House, November 16. This transit has its pluses and minuses for relationships. As much as it can spark passionate moments, there will also be tense and difficult times reminiscent of last summer. Be alert around the 23rd and 30th. Go slowly if a potential romantic interest enters your life this month as your interest may quickly wane.

Money and Success

You could hear confidential information at work around the November 28 Full Moon (lunar eclipse) in Gemini, your solar Twelfth House, when the Sun will be in Sagittarius, your solar Sixth House. The news could offer a hint of what might come your way in December or early next year, but don't bank on it.

Planetary Hotspots

When Mercury turns retrograde November 6, it will influence two sectors rather than one before it resumes direct motion on the 26th. While in Sagittarius, your solar Sixth House, you'll need to pay close attention to details and double-check all work for errors. Even then, some will be missed and come to light in December. Mercury will retreat into Scorpio, your solar Fifth House, on the 14th, where it can trigger mix-ups with dates, places, and times for social events and your children's activities. Confirm plans before you go.

Rewarding Days

4, 8, 9, 11, 12, 20, 27

Challenging Days

3, 10, 16, 18, 23, 30

Cancer | December

Planetary Lightspots

Mercury transits your solar Fifth House through the 10th, and Venus does the same through the 15th. Both continue to enhance your social life. They also provide just the creative spark you need to decorate your home for the holidays and to craft gifts or bake cookies for coworkers and friends. Get your children involved in these projects so they too can explore their creativity.

Relationships

Some of the best and most uplifting relationships this month will be those with coworkers. Plan an after-work get-together or step up and offer to organize a holiday party. You'll also connect with several out-of-town relatives and friends, and could get acquainted with some new faces while participating in a volunteer effort for a good cause.

Money and Success

You could receive a year-end bonus or nice gift from your employer during the two weeks following the December 13 New Moon in Sagittarius, your solar Sixth House. If you're job-hunting, take advantage of the lunar energy to submit your résumé on the 15th. Shop for gifts on the 1st, when you can find bargains, but avoid the 16th when it will be tough to find what you want.

Planetary Hotspots

December's Full Moon in your sign on the 28th could trigger yet more relationship challenges as it activates several planets. Don't hesitate to walk away from controlling people rather than reinforce their behavior by entering into a battle of the wills. And remember, you have the strength of Saturn in Scorpio on your side. Tap into it.

Rewarding Days

1, 2, 6, 9, 15, 19, 23, 24, 29

Challenging Days

5, 7, 8, 14, 20, 28, 30

Cancer Action Table

These dates reflect the best—but not the only—times for success and ease in these activities, according to your Sun sign.

	JAN	FEB	MAR	APR	MAY	JUN	JUL	AUG	SEP	OCT	NOV	DEC
Move									16, 17 25–29			
Start a class	12, 13					25			14, 15	12		
Join a club												
Ask for a raise												
Look for work				18, 19	7		9, 10	6				12–31
Get pro advice												14
Get a loan												
See a doctor				24								12, 13
Start a diet					7	3						
End relationship	21											
Buy clothes										16	30	1, 10
Get a makeover												1
New romance	16											1, 9
Vacation					9–14							

LEO

The Lion
July 22 to August 22

♌

Element: Fire

Quality: Fixed

Polarity: Yang/Masculine

Planetary Ruler: The Sun

Meditation: I trust in the strength of my soul

Gemstone: Ruby

Power Stones: Topaz, sardonyx

Key Phrase: I will

Glyph: Lion's tail

Anatomy: Heart, upper back

Color: Gold, scarlet

Animal: Lions, large cats

Myths/Legends: Apollo, Isis, Helios

House: Fifth

Opposite Sign: Aquarius

Flower: Marigold, sunflower

Key Word: Magnetic

Your Strengths and Challenges

You're generous, lovable, and outgoing, and almost always the center of attention. People can't help but notice you because they're drawn to your sunny smile, your warmth, and your upbeat attitude. A true extrovert, you're also a leader who instinctively knows how to bring out the best in people.

Your ruler, the Sun, is also the planet associated with ego, so it's only natural that you're confident in your skills, talents, and abilities. Nevertheless, your pride is easily wounded, and you're far more sensitive to slights than most people imagine. The solar energy also gives you a flair for the dramatic. But some Leos let ego interfere with worldly success, because they find it difficult to share the spotlight and expect constant royal treatment.

Leo is the fixed-fire sign of the zodiac, which gives you the determination to go after what you want and achieve it. When the spark ignites, nothing holds you back, and you have the follow-through to complete what you begin. Used positively, these qualities can fulfill your ambitions and set you apart from the crowd. But there's a fine line between determination and stubbornness, so learn to give in and adapt when necessary; flexibility will get you further in life. The same applies to your thinking. Generally broad-minded, you're nevertheless sometimes unwilling to compromise your strong beliefs and opinions. Be the leader you are and listen to others. They just might have a better idea that will reflect positively on you if you join the team.

Your playful spirit endears you to many, and your creative energy is exceptional. Whether you express it through the arts, ideas, your job, or hobbies, you add a distinctive zest to just about everything you do.

Your Relationships

People enjoy your company and your lively, outgoing personality so it's no surprise that you have many acquaintances. An excellent networker, you're a favorite on the social scene and excel at circulating a room and charming everyone you meet. You definitely have a way with words and a talent for making people feel they're the center of your universe. Close friends, although few in number, stimulate your thinking and help keep you on track toward your goals. Long talks with them are among your fondest memories.

You have a sixth sense for romance, and know exactly how to impress a date with the dramatic flair that wins hearts, whether that's a picnic in the park or a candlelight dinner. Playing the field is just your style, and it gives you plenty of opportunities to meet a potential mate. He or she is likely to be tough to catch, however, because you're attracted to independent souls. That's the influence of Aquarius, your partnership sign. In fact, you could make a beautiful match with someone whose Sun is in that sign. You have much in common with the other fire signs, Aries and Sagittarius, but it could be tough to share center stage with another Leo. Gemini and Libra are intellectually on your wavelength, but a Taurus or Scorpio could be too possessive.

You're an enthusiastic parent who enjoys participating in your children's activities, especially sports. You also promote learning and encourage them to expand their experiences and knowledge. But you can be a soft touch, giving in when taking a stand would be more beneficial. Go ahead and spoil them once in a while. You have deep feelings about family, and at least one relative probably had a profound influence on your childhood. Overall, you prefer to keep family matters private and enjoy having a space within your home reserved just for you, even if it's only a comfy chair. Many Leos enjoy home remodeling and renovations and profit from real estate.

Your Career and Money

You're an ambitious hard worker who will stick with a career field, company, or job as long as your skills and talents are recognized. Opportunities for the future are a must, and you can excel in supervisory positions. Just remember that it takes a while to move up the ladder; patience is required. You prefer a structured, task-oriented daily work environment with measurable goals, and one where your knowledge and experience are valued. Coworker relationships, although congenial, are usually limited to business. You instead invest your energy in developing contacts that can advance your career.

You expect to be well paid for what you do, and you should be because you're worth it. Most Leos are meticulous about personal financial records, but you're prone to worry, often unnecessarily, and can put too much emphasis on small change rather than the big picture. Think long term and aim for steady growth in savings and investments, which you should closely monitor. Otherwise, you could find yourself poorer but wiser; the same applies to promises of guaranteed gains. If in doubt, don't. Do, however, use your sixth sense and negotiate for better terms, benefits, and compensation.

Your Lighter Side

Whatever your age, you have the fun-loving spirit of a kid who's fearless and competitive, adventuresome and spontaneous. And there's no reason not to act like one during your leisure-time hours, which many Leos fill with sports, travel, creative endeavors, and learning for the fun of it—in addition to socializing and romance, of course.

Affirmation for the Year

Knowledge enhances success.

The Year Ahead for Leo

Your job and career will be in the spotlight this year. Take advantage of the first half of 2012 if you're aiming for more, because your work life could be rocky the last six months of the year. Relocation or extensive business travel is possible. Home and family will capture more of your interest as 2012 winds to a close, and will bring bonus opportunities for socializing and romance.

Your popularity rises through June 10 as lucky Jupiter transits your solar Tenth House. This could also give you a career boost; a promotion or new position that advances your status. But there's also a potential downside: planetary alignments during the remainder of the year urge caution in job and career matters. What seems to be a great opportunity this spring may be much less than you hoped for, or you could be faced with relationship and communication challenges. So weigh your options carefully, considering the risk versus the reward, because these hurdles will occur wherever you are.

Jupiter advances into Gemini, your solar Eleventh House, June 11, where it will remain throughout the year. Placed here, Jupiter emphasizes friendship, groups, and setting and achieving goals. Luck can come through friends and organizations, emphasizing the importance and value of networking. Consider getting involved in a club or organization that can help to advance your aims, and make an effort to widen your circle of acquaintances. Jupiter in Gemini could also bring relationship challenges, however, if you're involved in a job-related team effort. All will not go as smoothly as you'd like, and it will be difficult to reach consensus at times. And, someone may tell you what you want to hear, omitting pertinent facts. So cover your bases if you're asked to take on a new responsibility in June or July. Difficulties will reach a peak at year's end.

Saturn transits two signs this year, completing its time in Libra transit and entering Scorpio October 5. This planet of responsibility entered Libra, your solar Third House, in November 2009, and during the past few years has emphasized communication, siblings, extended family relatives, short trips, and learning. Saturn here also tends toward serious thinking, especially regrets. But rather than dwell on the past, look toward the future with Jupiter's help and take action to deal with lingering issues that limit success.

Complete a course of study you began when Saturn entered your solar Third House or embark on one that can benefit your career. It's also a great time to learn or perfect do-it-yourself skills, get involved in a neighborhood improvement project, and even to take on a leadership position in the community. Strive to resolve past difficulties with siblings or other relatives, or at least to understand where they're coming from. This will free your mind to focus on where you're going rather than where you've been. On a practical level, be sure to schedule routine maintenance on your vehicle. Neglect this and you'll compound or create a problem.

The emphasis shifts to your solar Fourth House when Saturn begins its two-and-a-half year transit of Scorpio. During this time you may relocate or undertake a major home improvement project. Be cautious, though, about purchasing property, especially if you have no legal relationship with the other person.

This Saturn transit is excellent for discovering your roots, researching your family tree, and organizing a family reunion. You can also successfully come full circle on your childhood years, recognizing the events and experiences that benefit you today as well as the challenging lessons that give you strength and resilience. It's also possible you may become more involved with the care of an elderly relative or parent.

Uranus continues its seven-year trip through Aries, your solar Ninth House of travel, knowledge, legal matters, life philosophy, and spirituality. You may experience all of these or only some of them at various times between now and 2018, when Uranus will shift its focus to your career sector. And each will have an element of the unexpected, which is what Uranus is noted for. Uranus can also bring amazing flashes of insight and sudden clarity.

Rather than focus solely on today, however, look to the future, whether in days, months, or years, because you'll be especially prone to spontaneous, and possibly premature, actions and decisions. Think before you act, and keep Uranus' future transit of your career sector in mind. What you do between now and 2018 can be to your benefit or detriment when Uranus moves on to your solar Tenth House. Consider returning to school, read self-help books to discover what you really want out of life, and learn about other cultures through reading or travel. All of this and more will help prepare you for a bigger role in the wider world.

Neptune also travels in two signs this year, spending its last weeks in Aquarius before moving on to Pisces, your solar Eighth House, February 3. As this planet of illusion and inspiration concludes its long transit through your solar Seventh House, reflect on what you've learned about relationships since it entered Aquarius in 1998. This, like all planetary influences, has a purpose and what you learn from it can be invaluable in the years ahead. Chances are you've experienced both disappointment and inspiration as you connected with people, and may have had the same effect in the lives of others.

Neptune will transit Pisces, its own sign and your solar Eighth House, until 2025. Although it won't be active at all times, there will be periods when Neptune can affect your finances, both positively and negatively, especially the years when it contacts your Sun. Nevertheless, the wise choice is to be cautious with money matters that involve other people and financial institutions: loans, mortgages, investments, insurance, and all related documents. Take time to read the fine print and check references, and avoid the trap of betting on a "sure thing." Chances are, it will be anything but.

Pluto, the slowest moving planet, continues to creep ahead this year in Capricorn, your solar Sixth House of daily work, health, service, and pets. This transformative planet does nothing half way, and it's often associated with events on a global scale that then influence life on a personal level. Change is Pluto's mission, and it offers you maximum willpower in order to achieve the transformation.

You can use Pluto, for example, to embrace a healthier lifestyle that includes exercise and a more nutritious diet. Effort expended as a volunteer for a good cause can be especially rewarding under this transit. But there's also potential for job difficulties, particularly during the years when Pluto contacts your Sun. These challenges can come as a result of personality conflicts, your employer's financial situation, or possibly because of your family situation.

What This Year's Eclipses Mean for You

There are four eclipses this year, two lunar and two solar. Three spotlight your solar Fifth and Eleventh Houses, and the fourth occurs in your solar Fourth House. Together they make 2012 a year with added focus on home and family, and contact with many people. Each eclipse is in effect for six to twelve months.

May 21 brings the first solar eclipse of the year. Placed in Gemini, your solar Eleventh House, it emphasizes friendship, networking, groups, organizations, and goals. It mixes well with expansive Jupiter, which enters this sector June 11, to provide added emphasis and good fortune through others. The influence continues into 2013, because the November 28 lunar eclipse will be in the same sign. Make a point to expand your world this year by getting involved in an organization or another group where you can connect with many people, possibly worldwide. Some of these people, especially a Gemini, may become lifelong friends, while others will be your link to potential opportunities.

Sagittarius, your solar Fifth House, is the sign of the June 4 lunar eclipse in Sagittarius. This is perfect for summer fun and romance. If you're a parent, plan to spend extra time with your children and get involved in their activities, which is another way to meet new people. This eclipse also emphasizes leisure-time activities, such as sports and hobbies, as well as socializing with friends. Romance is in the forecast for singles and couples alike.

The November 13 solar eclipse in Scorpio, your solar Fourth House, emphasizes family life. This eclipse could trigger relocation or major home improvements. But the solar energy also invites you to strengthen your connection with family members, and to assess your life progress, especially in career matters. Set long-term goals with an eye to where you want to be in fourteen years.

Saturn

If you were born between August 13 and 22, Saturn in Libra will contact your Sun between January 1 and October 4 as it completes its transit of your solar Third House. Leos with **August 13, 14, or 15 birthdays** will experience Saturn's influence in June or July, while Saturn will contact the Sun of other Leos twice, once between January and May, and again in August or September.

The emphasis here is on communication, primarily as it relates to your job and career. You'll want to be especially tactful in May, when job conditions will feel unsettled, leading to worry and tension. The same timing could bring a health concern; if so, consult a physician rather than let this trigger added stress.

Saturn in this sector also encourages deep thinking and learning, both of which can ease and benefit your path now and for many years to come. Formal learning is one option to boost your skills, either in a classroom or online. Or you could also take a class for fun, explore yourself and your life through journaling, or stretch your brain by reading books on a variety of subjects.

Neighbors and your community will also influence you during this Saturn transit, and although all these experiences may not be what you wish for, you will learn and benefit from them. You could be a positive force in changing conditions in your community, such as a project or policy related to libraries, schools, parks, or pets.

If you're a Leo born between August 22 and 31, Saturn will clash with your Sun after it enters Scorpio October 5. This transit through your solar Fourth House can affect both your career and your domestic and family lives. Relocation for employment is possible, and there could be challenges with family members and your home. Make a point to handle all household repairs when they arise, and be cautious if you plan to purchase property. Purchase less rather than more in order to minimize payments. Take a similar path if you rent. A new roommate is inadvisable now.

Also be prepared for increased family demands, or concern about a relative who may need your assistance. But you can also use this time to resolve lingering childhood issues and to deepen family relationships. Sleep will be especially important now as this transit can lower your vitality. Plan ahead so you can spend more time at home to rest and relax.

Uranus

If you were born between July 22 and 31, Uranus will favorably contact your Sun from Aries, your solar Ninth House. July will be a memorable month **if your birthday is July 29, 30, or 31**, and **Leos born July 25, 26, or 27** will benefit most from this transit in December.

Travel is associated with this sector, and 2012 may be the year you take your dream vacation, possibly to another country. Business trips could also be on your agenda. Another way to respond to this Uranus transit is to return to school for advanced training or to earn a degree in order to advance your career. This may come about because you realize further advancement is remote at best without more education. If so, your employer might help fund the endeavor. However you choose to do it, motivation will be strong to experience and increase your knowledge of the wider world.

This influence could also prompt you to examine long-held philosophical, spiritual, or religious beliefs. Reaffirm them or pursue what is more appropriate to the person you have become. The same is true of your basic values and those of people closest to you. Be true to yourself regardless of how others try to influence or persuade you to see things their way.

Neptune

If you were born between August 20 and 22, Neptune will contact your Sun from Aquarius, your solar Seventh House of relationships. This transit, which is in effect through February 2, is a terrific influence for romance, especially for couples secure in their love. Unfortunately, there is a downside to this transit. It's all too easy to hear what you want to hear and see what you want to see, and this of course makes you highly susceptible to people who only want to deceive you.

Be as cautious in professional relationships as in matters of the heart. Double-check references before hiring an attorney, realtor, or accountant, for example, and postpone a new business alliance. Do the same if you're considering marriage, which could also fail to meet your expectations.

Pluto

If your birthday is between July 29 and August 1, Pluto will contact your Sun from Capricorn, your solar Sixth House. With this influence in your job sector, you can expect increased tension at times. Your best course of action is to maintain a professional distance with coworkers and supervisors, and to avoid being drawn into power plays and the manipulative behavior of others. Because Uranus in your solar Ninth House will square off with Pluto in June and September, it's important to take every precaution to avoid becoming entangled in a legal matter, especially one that could jeopardize your job.

Family conflict involving in-laws is also possible with the Uranus-Pluto alignment, including debate over whether to relocate to be near them or pressure for them to join the household. Relocation might also be associated with your or your partner's job, or you could return to school or accept a position that requires extensive travel.

Leo | January

Planetary Lightspots

The universe brings you a gift this month: the January 9 Full Moon in Cancer, your solar Twelfth House of self-renewal. Listen when your mind and body encourage you to balance hectic work days with time alone and restful evening hours in the company of your favorite people. Stock up on books or videos, put on your PJs and be lazy. This and sleep will also help you avoid a cold or flu.

Relationships

Personal relationships benefit from the January 23 New Moon in Aquarius, your solar Seventh House, and Venus in the same sign through the 13th. This influence is especially positive for couples, who will be on the same wavelength. Plan a romantic evening for the 13th, when Venus meets Neptune in Aquarius. Some Leos take a romantic relationship to the next level this month, and others announce an engagement.

Money and Success

Make budgeting and saving your priorities as Mars travels in Virgo, your solar Second House, from January 23 to April 12. Double-check that all bills are paid on time, open statements when they arrive and look for errors, and try to avoid major purchases, new loans, and financial decisions. Also take care to protect valuables when you're out and about.

Planetary Hotspots

Your work life will be hectic and tense at times this month. And, difficult planetary alignments involving the Sun and Mercury in Capricorn, your solar Sixth House, have the potential to trigger conflict and controversy. Be alert for controlling people, and expect changing conditions and delayed decisions. Avoid meetings and important talks the third week of the January.

Rewarding Days

2, 3, 5, 10, 13, 15, 23, 28

Challenging Days

8, 11, 12, 14, 20, 21

Leo | February

Planetary Lightspots

The spotlight is on you under this month's Full Moon in your sign (February 7). Give yourself a mid-year checkup by reviewing all you've accomplished since your birthday last summer. Then use the lunar energy as motivation to achieve much more in the next six months. Ask someone close to you for objective feedback.

Relationships

Long talks can strengthen personal ties as the Sun and Mercury in Aquarius, your solar Seventh House, align favorably with Saturn in Libra, your communication sector. You'll also gain quite a bit of useful information if you do the same—listen as you socialize with coworkers on the 6th, 12th, or 19th. These dates are also good choices for meetings or appointments.

Money and Success

The February 21 New Moon in Pisces, your solar Eighth House, focuses your attention on joint resources. With Neptune arriving in the same sign February 3, and merging its energy with the New Moon, you'll want to be cautious about money matters and financial decisions. If you apply for a loan, deal only with the most reputable financial institution and read all the fine print even if you're told the paperwork is in order. Also check your credit report and take action to correct errors, which could take several months to clear up.

Planetary Hotspots

Job conflict could be an issue mid-month as Venus clashes with Pluto in Capricorn, your solar Sixth House of daily work. Be alert the preceding week when you may see initial signs of what might be on the horizon. Above all, do your best to avoid controlling people again this month, and don't get mixed up in a workplace romance. You'll regret it if you do.

Rewarding Days

2, 6, 11, 12, 16, 19, 20, 25

Challenging Days

3, 4, 5, 15, 17, 22, 24

Leo | March

Planetary Lightspots

The March 22 New Moon in Aries spotlights your solar Ninth House. The urge to travel may be strong, but postpone it if you can. With Mercury turning retrograde here, travel and travel planning are prone to mix-ups, changes, and delays. Opt for the next best thing if you need a change of scenery: explore your city or spend the weekend at a nearby resort.

Relationships

Relationships experience the usual ups and downs this month. Communication with relatives (including in-laws) and neighbors could be challenging, but you'll find work-related communication to be generally positive. Unexpected news is possible in early March.

Money and Success

Despite this month's potential financial difficulties, you could earn a raise after Venus enters Taurus, your solar Tenth House, March 5. The second full week of March is the most likely timing, but there could be a delay before you see it in your paycheck. Major purchases are inadvisable this month with Mars still retrograde in Virgo, your solar Second House.

Planetary Hotspots

Money matters are in focus again this month, which can be challenging and require close attention. Financial actions begun under last month's New Moon will continue to slowly evolve, with delays in pending matters. The primary reason for that is Mercury, which turns retrograde in Aries March 12, and then retreats into Pisces, your solar Eighth House, on the 23rd. Guard your valuables and be careful where you use credit and debit cards. Also be sure bills are paid on time, and hold off until late April or May if you want to apply for a loan. Check your credit reports for errors early in March.

Rewarding Days

1, 5, 6, 14, 18, 19, 21, 23, 25, 26, 28

Challenging Days

3, 4, 9, 13, 15, 20, 24, 27, 30

Leo | April

Planetary Lightspots

Both Mars and Mercury turn direct April 13 in your solar Second and Eighth Houses of money. This is positive, and recent financial challenges will gradually begin to improve in the following weeks. The April 6 Full Moon in Libra ramps up the daily pace as it highlights your solar Third House. It's also good for a weekend getaway or day trip, but avoid the 15th. Meetings and important calls will be more productive around the 17th, after Mercury enters Aries, your solar Ninth House, on the 16th.

Relationships

The first few days after April 3, the date Venus enters Gemini, your solar Eleventh House, could bring difficulties with a friend. After that, however, your social life will get a boost from this beneficial planet in your friendship sector. Fill your calendar with lunch and dinner dates, especially where you can meet other people. If there's enough interest, organize an after-work event with colleagues.

Money and Success

This month's New Moon in Taurus on the 21st could bring positive career developments, including a raise or step up in status. Be cautious the next week, however, about what you say and to whom. A power struggle with a coworker could develop, possibly because of jealousy over your success. Say little.

Planetary Hotspots

Up until Mars and Mercury turn direct April 13 in your solar Second and Eighth Houses of money, you'll have some additional hurdles to jump, so carefully monitor expenses and your budget. Postpone an evening out the first week of the month. It could be far more expensive than you anticipated.

Rewarding Days

1, 2, 10, 14, 17, 19, 22, 25, 28, 29

Challenging Days

3, 5, 7, 9, 11, 13, 15, 26

Leo | May

Planetary Lightspots

Expect to be pulled in two directions—career and family—as the May 5 Full Moon in Scorpio highlights your solar Fourth House. With the Sun and Jupiter merging in Taurus, your solar Tenth House at that time, you'll want to be in both places at once. Balance your time so you can get the best of both, which will be a high point this month.

Relationships

The May 20 New Moon (solar eclipse) in Gemini has great potential to energize your social life. It may not be as active as you like because of retrograde Venus, but you'll still have ample opportunities to see friends and attend social events. Team projects at work and your involvement in an organization also benefit from this New Moon. If you're asked, accept a leadership position, or volunteer for one.

Money and Success

As Mercury advances in Taurus May 9–23, you'll have many chances to showcase your talents for decision-makers. Watch for them and take advantage of each one. Also be the first to volunteer if you have an opportunity to make a presentation or to organize a teamwork project. Aiming for a promotion? Go for it! The odds are in your favor.

Planetary Hotspots

With Venus retrograde in Gemini, your solar Eleventh House, you should take precautions to protect valuables while out socializing. Also be sure to confirm places, dates, and times so you don't miss out on the fun. Someone you meet during the retrograde period, May 15–June 26, will make another appearance in July. Keep this in mind if you think you've missed an opportunity to connect with a potential romantic interest or networking contact.

Rewarding Days

4, 8, 11, 12, 17, 20, 22, 26, 31

Challenging Days

3, 7, 9, 13, 16, 21, 23, 30

Leo I June

Planetary Lightspots

The universe brings you a nice stress reliever in the June 4 Full Moon (lunar eclipse) in Sagittarius, your solar Fifth House of creativity, leisure, and fun. Plan family activities, see a sporting event, take your kids to an amusement park, or spend the day at a nearby recreation spot. Reserve some time for you and your interests, as well as romantic moments with your mate.

Relationships

Jupiter enters Gemini, your solar Eleventh House, June 11, marking the start of a year-long emphasis on friendships, groups, and organizations. It gets a jump-start this month from the New Moon in the same sign on the 19th. Plan ahead for an active social life, seeing friends and attending events. You can widen your circle through a community or professional organization, where you could be chosen for a leadership position.

Money and Success

Mars continues to advance in Virgo, your solar Second House of income and spending. Remember your budget around the 5th, when you'll be tempted to splurge, and take time near the 21st to organize and file important financial information. Shred what you no longer need.

Planetary Hotspots

Uranus in Aries and Pluto in Capricorn square off this month, indicating stress in your solar Ninth and Sixth Houses. Avoid travel if possible this month, and ride with a designated driver when you're out socializing. This alignment also could trigger challenges with a coworker or a supervisor near the 11th. Be cautious about what you say and do. Don't put your job at risk. You could be called for jury duty. However, personal legal action is unlikely to be successful.

Rewarding Days

1, 2, 9, 14, 15, 16, 19, 25

Challenging Days

5, 10, 11, 12, 18, 20, 27, 29

Leo | July

Planetary Lightspots

The July 19 New Moon in Cancer, your solar Twelfth House, complements the energy of retrograde Mercury. It encourages you to slow the pace a little so you can listen to your inner voice. You'll especially appreciate the time to relax and catch up on sleep after busy days earlier in July.

Relationships

Mars enters Libra, your solar Third House of communication and quick trips, on the 3rd. Try to avoid important talks and meetings on the 17th and 18th, when Mars will clash with Uranus and Pluto. These days could also trigger a power struggle or conflict with a coworker. Do your best to stay out of it. People will not be in the mood to listen or compromise, so don't waste your time. Also be especially cautious on your daily commute.

Money and Success

Expect a couple of stressful weeks at work following the July 3 Full Moon in Capricorn, your solar Sixth House. You'll be pushed to do more in less time, and there could be news of major changes in your workplace that will directly or indirectly affect you. With Mercury turning retrograde, though, it could be several months before you know all the details.

Planetary Hotspots

Be prepared for periodic frustration after Mercury turns retrograde in your sign mid-month. Personal plans and goals are prone to delays and confusion, and it will be easy to mix up dates, times, and places. But this is also something of a gift from the universe. Use the retrograde period, which lasts through August 7, to think about and identify what you want to accomplish in the twelve months following the August New Moon in your sign.

Rewarding Days

1, 5, 6, 14, 15, 16, 20, 23, 28, 29

Challenging Days

9, 13, 17, 18, 24, 25, 26, 30

Leo | August

Planetary Lightspots

August is all about you. Bask in the limelight of the August 17 New Moon in your sign, which will direct plenty of attention your way. You'll have plenty of opportunities to socialize and see friends, thanks to beneficial planetary alignments throughout much of the August.

Relationships

Relationships shine brightly under this month's first Full Moon, August 1 in Aquarius, your solar Seventh House. Even better, this is a lucky influence that could link you to a valuable networking contact or a new romantic interest. Either one could come through a mutual friend within days of the Full Moon, so plan ahead to socialize with friends the first weekend of the month. You'll also want to reserve a few evenings for your partner. Spoil your love a little.

Money and Success

Money matters get a boost from the August 31 Full Moon in Pisces, your solar Eighth House, and you or your mate could see a bigger paycheck in the following two weeks. But a loan might also be necessary. If so, take your time, do some research, and shop around for the best rate and the best deal on a major purchase. A friend could be helpful with this, but be wary of lofty promises that could fall flat.

Planetary Hotspots

Life is more easygoing this month than it has been recently. Take advantage of this lull to enjoy some summer fun. If you have vacation time scheduled, consider staying home. Planetary alignments continue to caution against travel, which is prone to delays during the first two weeks of August, and your vehicle or an appliance may need repairs this month as well. If you need a replacement, try to wait until after Mercury turns direct on the 8th.

Rewarding Days

2, 11, 15, 16, 17, 25, 29

Challenging Days

6, 7, 13, 20, 21, 26, 28

Leo | September

Planetary Lightspots

Your charm and charisma are at their best from September 6 on, when Venus is in your sign. This influence also boosts your powers of attraction, so focus on what you want and then ask the universe to deliver. You'll have luck on your side.

Relationships

Mercury in Libra, your solar Third House, from September 16 on can trigger harsh words with a coworker or supervisor, primarily because of stressful events. Fill your mind with calm thoughts and try to stay emotionally removed. Tempers won't change personalities or situations. But you'll also have an uplifting talk with a friend in the midst of turmoil that will inspire you to look to the future with optimism.

Money and Success

The September 15 New Moon in Virgo could enhance your bank account with a welcome deposit. Save some, spend some, but don't let your generous nature get carried away, especially with friends. Reserve that for yourself and your family. Treat those you love to a special night out.

Planetary Hotspots

Uranus and Pluto clash again this month, just as they did in June. Although you'll feel the effects of this alignment earlier in September, it will be most apparent when the September 29 Full Moon in Aries activates both planets. As in June, avoid travel all month if possible—especially the last two weeks. Also be very cautious and aware when driving. Expect further developments regarding any job matters that arose in June, and try not schedule meetings and talks for the 20th or at month's end. Any legal matters that began in June could be resolved now as well, but probably not to your liking.

Rewarding Days

3, 6, 7, 13, 17, 21, 25, 30

Challenging Days

2, 10, 11, 16, 20, 23, 24, 29

Leo | October

Planetary Lightspots

Although conditions aren't the best for long-distance travel, consider a weekend away near the October 15 New Moon in Libra, your solar Third House. In addition to being a nice change of pace, a nearby destination will provide fresh scenery to refresh your spirit. Take the family, or opt for a romantic few days designed for two.

Relationships

Fill your leisure time hours with fun, socializing and seeing friends, hobbies, and more as Mars transits Sagittarius, your solar Fifth House, October 6–November 15. Be prepared, though, for a few surprises from your kids in addition to their pleas for a new toy or gadget. Spoil them a little, but not a lot. Maintain a balanced budget. Mars could also motivate you to join a gym, but take it easy at first.

Money and Success

Finances continue in positive territory, thanks to Venus in Virgo, your solar Second House, October 3–27. Skip shopping the first few days of the month, however, because you'll have a tough time finding what you want. Your career is also in focus this month, and the October 29 Full Moon in Taurus, your solar Tenth House will carry the influence into November. But you'll have a tendency to overwork. Strive for balance.

Planetary Hotspots

Saturn enters Scorpio October 5, the sign it will transit for the next two and a half years. As it advances through your solar Fourth House, you may relocate or embark on a major home improvement project. Set aside thoughts of a home-based business, however, as conditions won't favor that for at least several years. You also could find it necessary to manage an elderly relative's affairs or to be more involved in your parents' lives.

Rewarding Days

5, 6, 10, 13, 18, 22, 28

Challenging Days

1, 4, 7, 9, 14, 20, 25

Leo | November

Planetary Lightspots

Despite retrograde Mercury, family life will be upbeat in the weeks following the November 13 New Moon in Scorpio. And it will be even better after Venus enters Scorpio on the 21st. Create memories as you head into the holiday season, and consider inviting a few friends for dinner around the 24th.

Relationships

The November 28 Full Moon in Gemini, your solar Eleventh House, is ideal for friendship and social events well into December. Before then, Mars in Sagittarius will spark the same. But once again, you could experience some challenges with coworkers as Venus in Libra, your solar Third House, clashes with several planets. The good news is that any incidents will be much less intense than they were earlier in the year.

Money and Success

Expect to move into high gear at work after Mars enters Capricorn, your solar Sixth House, on the 16th. But try not to push yourself or others too hard, especially during the last week of November. A calmer approach will yield better results.

Planetary Hotspots

Mercury begins its retrograde period in Sagittarius, your solar Fifth House, on the 6th. It then retreats into Scorpio, your solar Fourth House, on the 14th, before resuming direct motion on the 26th. The usual cautions regarding mix-ups and misunderstandings apply, especially with social events and family activities. Also put all but the most necessary domestic repairs and purchases on hold. Come December, you're likely to change your mind about decor and furnishings. Retrograde Mercury can also make it tough to mesh family schedules. Be flexible. Adjust as necessary—with a smile.

Rewarding Days

2, 6, 7, 9, 11, 14, 15, 24, 29

Challenging Days

3, 5, 10, 16, 18, 19, 23, 25, 26

Leo | December

Planetary Lightspots

Happy times with family continue with Mercury in Scorpio, your solar Fourth House, through the 9th, and Venus in the same sign through the 14th. Use the creativity of Venus and the ideas of Mercury to decorate your home for the holidays. With smart shopping, you can even do it for less. These two planets also boost your interest in all things domestic. Plan family activities and get the kids involved in decorating cookies.

Relationships

Your social life continues in focus this month, thanks to the December 13 New Moon in Sagittarius, your solar Fifth House. This is also a great influence for time with your kids, and romantic moments with your mate. If you're single, someone new could catch your eye around the 16th. But workplace relationships will be prone to tension at month's end, when major job changes are possible.

Money and Success

The fast pace at work extends through the 24th as Mars advances in Capricorn, your solar Sixth House. And although you might receive recognition for your efforts, a year-end bonus is unlikely. Keep this in mind as you shop for gifts, and don't feel pressured to spend outside your budget.

Planetary Hotspots

Workplace tension and turmoil returns this month as the December 28 Full Moon in Cancer triggers difficult planetary alignments in your solar Sixth House. Just like earlier in the year, you'll want to avoid travel during the last week of the month. Major delays or cancellations, possibly triggered by severe weather, could disrupt your plans. Plan your trip with this timing in mind or better yet, stay home.

Rewarding Days
12, 16, 17, 21, 26, 31

Challenging Days
3, 7, 11, 20, 28, 30

Leo Action Table

These dates reflect the best—but not the only—times for success and ease in these activities, according to your Sun sign.

	JAN	FEB	MAR	APR	MAY	JUN	JUL	AUG	SEP	OCT	NOV	DEC
Move										23–28	28–30	1–5
Start a class									25–29			
Join a club				24, 25				11		4		
Ask for a raise										12		5, 6
Look for work	8–21			21	9, 10				5			
Get pro advice	5, 6											
Get a loan												
See a doctor										8		
Start a diet	21, 22											
End relationship		19		14			5		25			16
Buy clothes												12, 30, 31
Get a makeover				29				16, 17				
New romance												12–31
Vacation												

VIRGO

The Virgin
August 22 to September 22
♍

Element: Earth

Quality: Mutable

Polarity: Yin/Feminine

Planetary Ruler: Mercury

Meditation: I can allow time for myself

Gemstone: Sapphire

Power Stones: Peridot, amazonite, rhodochrosite

Key Phrase: I analyze

Glyph: Greek symbol for containment

Anatomy: Abdomen, gall bladder, intestines

Color: Taupe, gray, navy blue

Animal: Domesticated animals

Myths/Legends: Demeter, Astraea, Hygeia

House: Sixth

Opposite Sign: Pisces

Flower: Pansy

Key Word: Discriminating

Your Strengths and Challenges

Your strength is in the details. Little escapes the attention of your keen, discriminating mind, because you have a knack for seeing what others miss. When compiled, all those bits and pieces of information form a complete picture in your mind that's part knowledge and part intuition. But the details can also be a challenge if you get lost in them and fail to view things from a wider perspective. Remind yourself to periodically step back and take an objective look at the specifics of a situation or project.

Many Virgos are shy in their younger years, a trait that diminishes with life experience and expertise. But even as your overall confidence rises your mutable sign has a tendency to go with the flow, sometimes too much so. Being adaptable is one thing; reluctance to take a stand is another. Don't hesitate. Speak up.

With Mercury as your ruling planet, you also excel at communication, and most Virgos are lifelong learners and avid readers. Practical, commonsense ideas are your specialty, and your sign is noted for its analytical ability. But this also encourages your brain to work overtime, worrying about what could be rather than what is as your imagination runs wild. Rein it in and be realistic.

Ever-efficient, you have a talent for finding the quickest and best way to do just about anything. You also excel at planning and organization. This is true whether you're a neat Virgo or one who prefers an organized mess. Either way, you know where everything is and can reach into a pile and pull out just what you need.

Your Relationships

You prefer a single relationship to playing the field—so much so that some Virgos drift along in a relationship for years without ever feeling the need to commit. All this changes when the right person comes along to stir your passions. As one of the most sensual signs of the zodiac, you're also a sentimental romantic who treasures special events and memories, and delights in elegant, candlelight evenings. You'll know you're truly in love when you leave practical reasoning behind and embrace every magical moment of togetherness. You could make a match with Pisces, your polar opposite, or one of the other water signs, Cancer and Scorpio. Life with a Taurus or Capricorn might bring you happiness, but changeable, free-spirited Gemini and Sagittarius could unsettle you.

Virgo's home environment encourages knowledge and learning, and you probably have books and the latest technology to connect you with the world. Big rooms, big windows, and preferably a big home, appeal to you. Many Virgos are avid do-it-yourselfers who tackle major home improvement projects that can take months to complete. Clutter can get the best of you if you're a messy Virgo, so use your organizational skills and train yourself to put things away. Virgos often get a late start as parents and usually have only one or two children. As a parent, you have high expectations and push your children to succeed in every possible way. While this can build an excellent work ethic for their adult years, children also need time and encouragement to explore their own interests. Balance constructive criticism with praise.

New people come into and out of your life regularly, usually for a purpose. A few become close friends, people you feel are family, especially if you live far away from your roots, as many Virgos do. You're more comfortable with these friends than you are on the meet-and-greet social scene, and enjoy people in the comfort of your own home.

Your Career and Money

Virgo has a reputation for being a workaholic. There's a good reason why: you like to be productive and you enjoy working. It's that simple. Do remember, though, that there's more to life than work, and that balance is as good for you as it is for anyone. Some Virgos push things to the max and have both a career and a side job, such as freelance work. Many choose a career in communications or another field where they can use their communication skills. Your career fluctuates as opportunities come and go, and your flexibility is an asset in adapting to changing conditions. In your job, you need the freedom and independence to manage your own work flow without constant direction. A hands-on boss is not for you. You also do well in a teamwork environment and coworkers often become friends.

Finances benefit from your common sense and practical approach to life—at least most of the time. Occasionally, you have the urge to splurge, especially on loved ones, and can spend on impulse. That's great if you can afford it, which most Virgos can, because you have excellent earning power. Investments will be more profitable if you back decisions with research and think long term. Be somewhat cautious with credit; it's easy to get, but tack on interest and all you have is an expensive bargain.

Your Lighter Side

It can be tough for you to set aside work in favor of leisure. And when you do, the time is usually invested in something productive and practical such as gardening, crafts, household repairs and improvements, and cleaning and organizing. But there are moments, when no one is looking, when you indulge in laziness. Travel brings out this side of you, as does your favorite comfy chair and a good book.

Affirmation for the Year

People inspire me.

The Year Ahead for Virgo

Although 2012 will get off to a slow start, you'll quickly pick up speed after the first several months. Money, people, domestic life, and your career will be in the spotlight, and you also could travel during the first half of the year. A conservative financial path along with planning for the future is the wisest choice in money matters.

Jupiter begins the year in Taurus, your solar Ninth House of knowledge and travel. Both will capture your interest, and if it's financially feasible, this might be the time to take a dream vacation. This influence is equally advantageous for education that can advance your career. A short-term class you can complete before Jupiter moves on to Gemini June 11 could have an amazing influence on your career. Thoughts might also turn to the more philosophical and spiritual aspects of life. You can pursue this in any number of ways from reading to religion to learning about other cultures and their traditions and beliefs.

Your career will benefit from Jupiter's good fortune for about a year as it transits Gemini, your solar Tenth House. This influence, which occurs only once every twelve years, can bring wonderful opportunities for success and advancement. The first of these could come in July, but use your notable common sense when choosing which opportunity to pursue. Also be cautious about taking on more than you can reasonably handle in the allotted time, which is the main downfall of this transit. More often than not you'll be among the favored few at your company, with some influential people backing your efforts.

Saturn spends much of the year in Libra, your solar Second House, before it switches its focus to Scorpio in October. You may have experienced the financial downside of this transit since it entered Libra in November 2009. Or, even if finances are stable, Saturn could have motivated you to save more than you spend and to avoid debt. This is, of course, Saturn's message here, so either maintain the good habits you've developed or put plans in action to adopt them.

Saturn here also encourages you to examine what you value, and is a reminder that you are your most valuable possession. Think about what is most important to you in life, what really matters, and then embrace your priorities. You can also use this Saturn opportunity to get organized while clearing out long-unused possessions and clothing. Profit from them with a yard sale or head to the consignment shop.

Saturn begins a new transit October 5, when it enters Scorpio, your solar Third House. This influence, which will be in effect until 2015, has many possibilities. In addition to an increased focus on the activities of daily life, including errands and communication, Saturn will spark a desire for learning. This could motivate you to continue the studies you began earlier in the year, possibly to complete a degree, or you might choose a series of classes for personal enjoyment. If you've ever wanted to write, now is the time.

This sector is also associated with siblings and cousins. These relationships can deepen, and you can successfully resolve any lingering issues from the past, as well as reunite with any of these people you haven't seen in many years. You could become involved in community activities and possibly even take on a leadership role. Expect more social activities with neighbors.

Uranus continues its multiyear transit of Aries, your solar Eighth House of joint resources. As the planet of the unexpected, Uranus here can just as easily boost your bank account as bring extra expenses, possibly related to your children. This is not the time to put funds at risk. It is the time to save, just as Saturn advises, and to resist the urge to spend on impulse, which will be tempting. Your or your partner's income and benefits could also fluctuate, and you should regularly check your credit reports for errors. Insurance is another area related to this sector, so be sure all policies are up to date and premiums paid. Read the fine print so there are no surprises if you need to make a claim.

An unexpected inheritance is possible but not likely. The same applies to a lucky lottery win. Instead, you can use Uranus to spot money-making opportunities, such as a company bonus program, based on merit or achieving specific goals.

Neptune will complete its transit of Aquarius on February 2. Since it entered this sign in 1998, you've probably experienced all the ups and downs associated with this planet in your solar Sixth House of daily work. Neptune undoubtedly inspired you in these areas at times, but also brought disappointment and difficulty in attracting the recognition you deserved. Set aside time to review what you've learned about service and workplace relationships as well as what you've achieved. Chances are, you'll remember far more positives than negatives, both of which can be beneficial to you later this year when Jupiter is in your career sector.

Neptune enters Pisces, your solar Seventh House, February 3. It will be there until 2025, and during that time, it will put you in touch with many people. Some will enhance your life, while others will attempt to steer you down the wrong path. Knowing the difference is the challenge, so don't be quick to take anyone new at face value. And try not to expect others to live up to your high ideals all the time; after all, people are only human. Neptune is a perfect fit for romance, which can be terrific if you're in a secure relationship. Go slowly, however, if a new romantic interest captures your heart, especially during the year that Neptune connects with your Sun. Only with time will you know for sure that this can be a lasting love. Apply a similar approach if you hire a professional such as an accountant. Check references and keep your options open.

Pluto continues its slow advance in Capricorn, your solar Fifth House, where it encourages you to redefine yourself by getting in touch with your creativity. A good way to get started is to learn a new—and practical—hobby such as home improvement skills, furniture refinishing, or specialized gardening. Or give writing a try. Over time, you'll reap the benefits of increased confidence and self-knowledge, and you might even turn this hobby into a money-making enterprise.

If you're a parent, you'll be more involved in your children's lives as Pluto transits Capricorn until 2024. They too will enrich your life in ways yet to be discovered as you experience the tremendous personal growth parenting can bring. But you should be alert for the tendency to push them too hard or to try to mold them into the people you wish them to be. Give your children the freedom to explore and pursue their interests and talents.

What This Year's Eclipses Mean for You

This year has all the potential to be one of the best for your career, thanks to two of four eclipses in your solar Tenth House in 2012. The other two will spotlight your solar Third and Fourth Houses. Each is in effect for six to twelve months.

May 21 will bring a solar eclipse in Gemini, your solar Tenth House, followed by lucky Jupiter's arrival in the same sign June 11. This sector will be activated again by the November 28 lunar eclipse in Gemini, extending this favorable influence well into 2013. Plan ahead so you make the most of this strong energy. This is important because it will be all too easy to become complacent as success comes your way. Go after this gift from the universe!

With so much energy focused on your career, there may not be much time left for the domestic scene. The June 4 lunar eclipse in Sagittarius (your solar Fourth House), however, has other ideas. Its purpose is to encourage you to strive for a healthy balance of career and family activities. This eclipse could also trigger a desire for home improvements and more involvement with relatives, especially parents.

The year's fourth eclipse, a lunar eclipse in Scorpio, November 13, will complement Saturn in the same sign. This influence will put all forms of communication in the forefront, from social media to writing to public speaking. Hone your skills in these areas and use them to advance your career. Be prepared, though, for the possibility of a vehicle needing significant repairs. A replacement might be a better option.

Saturn

Saturn in Libra, your solar Second House of resources, will contact your Sun **if you were born between September 13 and 22.** This influence will be at its peak in June and July **if your birthday is September 13, 14, or 15.** Otherwise, Saturn will connect with your Sun twice, once before June and again in August or September. Actions taken and decisions made in the earlier period will come up for review during the second contact

Make financial responsibility and security your goal this year. If you don't know where to begin, use Jupiter's transit through your solar Ninth House (January 1–June 11) to educate yourself on everything from budgeting to saving to investing. This, plus a thrifty mind-set can not only save you money but net some great deals on necessities. Also look at resources from another viewpoint: recycle what you have into something useful such as updating your wardrobe with a few items that will create a new look for old outfits.

Saturn's Second House lesson, above all, is learning to effectively manage personal resources, both when money is tight and when things are status quo. Adopt the new habits and attitudes that will be rewarded for many years to come and culminate in about fourteen years when Saturn enters your solar Eighth House of joint resources.

If your birthday is between August 22 and 31, you'll be among the first of your sign to have Saturn contact your Sun from Scorpio after it enters this sign October 5. With Saturn in your solar Third House your mind will be at its best, but you'll also have a tendency to dwell on things and to overanalyze events and opportunities. Step back and get a fresh perspective when you sense yourself slipping into this pattern.

You, more than others born under your sign, should seriously consider the benefits of additional education. Even if you can't see the potential now, it could be the key to maintaining this year's career momentum. Remember that you don't necessarily have to pursue a degree in order to take advantage of this transit. Concentrated, short-term classes to learn a specific skill can be just as valuable.

Uranus

If you were born between August 22 and 31, Uranus in Aries will contact your Sun this year. Keep a close eye on finances with an emphasis on saving rather than spending. Then you can better weather any unexpected downturn or additional expense. The main challenge with this transit, however, is that money matters will be generally unsettled, making it tough to plan and budget.

But it's also possible you could gain from a windfall. Be careful, though, with any form of speculation because what looks like a sure deal under a Uranus transit can backfire well beyond what you can imagine. The Eighth House also governs insurance, so be sure your property is well covered and all premiums are paid. This is not the time to take chances with anything financial, including taking on debt based on anticipated future income. Don't loan money to a friend or relative.

Neptune

If you were born between September 19 and 22, Neptune will contact your Sun from Aquarius before it moves on to Pisces

February 3. With Neptune placed in your solar Sixth House, confusion is possible at work, and it might be tough to zero in on exactly what's happening both with your job and your company. You'll also want to be very cautious about sharing personal information with coworkers, who could use it to their advantage. Double-check your work for errors, which can be overlooked under a Neptune influence. Any workplace issues that arose in 2011 can be resolved now.

If you were born between August 22 and 26, Neptune will contact your Sun from Pisces, your solar Seventh House of relationships. As great as this transit is for love and romance, it's decidedly chancy for commitment. So resist the temptation to enter into what may not be a lasting tie. The romantic interest you think you know may turn out to be someone entirely different. This also applies to new business partnerships and anyone who makes lofty promises. If it sounds too good to be true, it probably is.

Like every planet, Neptune also has its positive side. Help others to help themselves rather than take on responsibilities not your own. Be an inspirational motivator rather than an enabler, and a mentor who guides others in their search for excellence. Also listen to your intuition, which will be strong as Neptune contacts your Sun.

If you're in a committed relationship, Neptune can trigger doubts, possibly because you suddenly realize your mate is not the ideal person of your mind. Although this could trigger thoughts of looking elsewhere, the better choice may be to accept the new reality and the fact that no one belongs on a pedestal. Consider it a lesson in human nature.

Pluto

If you were born between August 29 and September 1, Pluto in Capricorn, your solar Fifth House, will favorably contact your Sun. This may be the year you've been waiting for, the one in which you'll grow into yourself, confident and empowered. Pluto's dynamic energy can help you accomplish this whether you want to get in shape, embrace a new personal direction, or achieve what you never thought possible. Put this powerful planet's willpower and determination to good use.

If you're a parent you can do much to support and encourage your children, guiding them on the right path through life. Listen closely to what they say. Their innocent comments could trigger insights into your own life and how to become the best you can be. Also find a way to express your creative individuality because this too will contribute to the person you are becoming. And be sure to give yourself permission to make mistakes. It really is okay to do that.

There is, unfortunately, a strong negative involving Uranus and Pluto this year. These two planets will clash in June and September, involving your solar Fifth and Eighth Houses. This could trigger unexpected child-related expenses or a sizeable loss through an investment. Entrepreneurial ventures such as starting or investing in a new business are risky at best and should be avoided. There also could be a power struggle involving an inheritance or difficulties settling an insurance claim. Do your best to think ahead even though it is next to impossible to guess the outcome of any alignment involving Uranus. Be sure your property is well insured, and don't sign anything without reading all the fine print. This is not the time to take anyone's word on faith or to cosign a loan for anyone, even a close friend, child, or relative.

Despite all this, however, there's also a chance you could net a nice windfall. The lottery is worth a try the last two weeks of June and around mid-September. Remember that it only takes one ticket to win. Don't invest the grocery money.

Virgo | January

Planetary Lightspots

Venus in Pisces, your solar Seventh House, from January 14 on, is ideal for love, romance, and togetherness. You'll also enjoy time with close friends, and people will be helpful and open to your requests. Return the good will and bring cheer to the lives of others.

Relationships

Fill your calendar with social events as the January 9 Full Moon in Cancer brightens your solar Eleventh House of friendship. This influence also favors teamwork and other group activities, and is a great opportunity for networking. But you'll want to avoid get-togethers or first dates around the 7th, 14th, and 20th, when egos could clash.

Money and Success

The January 23 New Moon in Aquarius, your solar Sixth House, will energize your work life, and could trigger a raise or bonus in addition to praise for a job well done. Business travel is possible, or you could attend (or teach) a training session or conference. If you want to take a class to learn a specific skill, ask your employer about tuition reimbursement. The date of the New Moon is a good choice if you want to apply for a job.

Planetary Hotspots

At times you'll feel as though life is not just on hold but moving backward as Mars travels retrograde in your sign from January 23 to April 12. Frustration will be part of the scenario, as will the desire to try to push matters forward. Take a different view. Use this time to complete unfinished projects and to think about what you want to accomplish between now and when Mars returns to your sign in about two years. Then you'll be fully prepared to embrace new goals in April.

Rewarding Days
3, 12, 13, 17, 21, 22, 25, 31

Challenging Days
1, 7, 10, 14, 18, 20, 26

Virgo | February

Planetary Lightspots

You'll welcome the opportunity to kick back a little, at least some of the time, in the two weeks following the February 7 Full Moon in Leo, your solar Twelfth House. Treat yourself to a massage or spa day, and spend evenings curled up with a book and weekends with family or your mate. Time alone will also appeal to you. Catch up on sleep.

Relationships

Other people, your partner, and friends brighten your life as the February 21 New Moon in Pisces highlights your solar Seventh House. Call out-of-town friends and relatives to catch up on all the latest news, and spend quality time with those closest to you. It's also a good time to get better acquainted with coworkers. But avoid touchy subjects and social events on the 22nd and 24th.

Money and Success

Mercury transits Aquarius, your solar Sixth House, through February 12, and the Sun is in the same sign through the 19th. With this favorable alignment, you can make great strides at work and maybe earn extra cash. If you're job hunting, good news is possible near the 7th, but don't be quick to turn down an offer if it pays less than you're worth. Consider all the factors before making a decision.

Planetary Hotspots

Venus enters Aries, your solar Eighth House, February 8. Although this influence often favors finances, don't depend on it this month. Extra expenses, possibly related to your children, are more likely as Venus clashes with Uranus and Pluto. Don't put funds at risk, and avoid even the safest investments. On the other hand, anything is possible with Uranus involved, so take a chance on the lottery around the 9th.

Rewarding Days

2, 9, 13, 18, 23, 26, 27, 28

Challenging Days

3, 4, 10, 15, 16, 17, 22, 24

Virgo | March

Planetary Lightspots

Venus in Taurus, your solar Ninth House, is great for travel planning, a vacation trip, or out-of-town business conferences and meetings from March 5 through month's end. One small caution: Mercury, your ruling planet, turns retrograde March 12 in Aries, your solar Eighth House, which can trigger mix-ups. Take a carry-on just in case you and your luggage are separated.

Relationships

The March 8 Full Moon in your sign is as much about relationships as it is about you. Reach out to other people, especially your mate, but avoid controversial subjects the first few days of March, when even a casual comment could spark conflict. The 18th is a good choice if you want to get better acquainted with coworkers.

Money and Success

Despite the influence of retrograde Mercury, the March 22 New Moon in Aries, your solar Eighth House, has potential to boost your bank account in an unusual way. But it could just as easily trigger unexpected expenses. The lottery might be worth a try near the New Moon, but remember, it only takes one ticket to win.

Planetary Hotspots

When Mercury, your ruling planet, turns retrograde March 12 in Aries, your solar Eighth House, mix-ups with payments and other money matters can occur. Loan applications should be postponed until late April or May, and do the same with contracts and other legal documents. Relationships are prone to misunderstandings after Mercury retreats into Pisces, your solar Seventh House, on the 23rd. Clarify your comments.

Rewarding Days

8, 11, 12, 16, 18, 21, 25, 26

Challenging Days

3, 4, 7, 9, 13, 15, 17, 27, 30

Virgo | April

Planetary Lightspots

This month's New Moon in Taurus on the 21st accents your solar Ninth House of travel and knowledge. Make both a part of your life. Plan a trip, attend a conference, take a short-term class, or relax at a vacation destination. Any of these will satisfy your desire for adventure, learning, and a change of scenery.

Relationships

Mercury turns direct in Pisces, your solar Seventh House, on the 13th, with Mars doing the same in your sign. Recent relationship challenges will gradually wane, and you'll be able to resolve any difficulties to the point where you can put them behind you and move forward. Prior to that, however, take care to avoid a major misunderstanding with someone close to you.

Money and Success

The April 6 Full Moon in Libra, your solar Second House, reminds you to live within your budget rather than spend if a little extra money comes your way. The week after the Full Moon you could luck into some bargains if you take the time to search out sales and coupons. Look for work clothes for you and your partner, but be sure the store allows returns.

Planetary Hotspots

Your career could get a nice lift after Venus enters Gemini, your solar Tenth House, April 3. Try to maintain a low profile that week, though, because difficult planetary alignments could trigger anything from a misunderstanding to a heated argument. Be sure to confirm all instructions and projects with the source. Don't take a coworker's word for it. If you do, you could get the blame.

Rewarding Days

4, 8, 12, 14, 17, 21, 22, 23, 27

Challenging Days

3, 5, 7, 9, 11, 13, 15, 16, 24

Virgo | May

Planetary Lightspots

With Jupiter in its last full month in Taurus, your solar Ninth House, the timing is ideal for a vacation trip or even a long weekend. If you plan to attend a reunion, however, don't believe everything you hear. Use similar caution if someone approaches you about a business or financial opportunity. Use this Jupiter influence and favorable planetary alignments to take a quick class to learn a sport or how to manage your money in order to achieve financial security.

Relationships

All the relationships in your life will benefit from the May 5 Full Moon in Scorpio, your solar Third House of communication. You'll have a way with words that can charm most anyone, especially because your message will be upbeat and optimistic. Spread cheer and motivate others. This Full Moon also emphasizes spirituality and a strong belief in yourself and your future, which is bright. Get better acquainted with colleagues at an after-work get-together mid-month.

Money and Success

The May 20 New Moon (solar eclipse) in Gemini keeps your career sector in high focus as it energizes your commitment to succeed. Take advantage of any opportunity for self-promotion, share your ideas, and be the first to step up if there's a chance to make a presentation. Creativity is strong this month. Use it!

Planetary Hotspots

A hoped-for promotion or another career endeavor could be put on hold as Venus travels retrograde May 15–June 26, but have faith. This is a terrific career year overall, and what you seek could come about this summer or fall. In the meantime, keep pushing ahead and do all you can to reinforce your position with all the right people.

Rewarding Days

1, 2, 6, 10, 13, 14, 16, 18, 19, 24

Challenging Days

3, 4, 7, 8, 9, 21, 26, 30

Virgo | June

Planetary Lightspots

Home life will be hectic once the June 4 Full Moon (lunar eclipse) in Sagittarius energizes your solar Fourth House. With Mars in your sign aligned with the Full Moon, you'll be in high gear, managing everybody and everything. This is a great period for domestic repairs, cleaning, and getting your garden in shape.

Relationships

Uranus in Aries and Pluto in Capricorn square off this month, and this alignment can trigger difficulties with a friend or a group or organization you're involved in. It's always a good idea to get acquainted with your children's friends and their parents, as well as monitoring their online activities. Be firm if you want your child to end a friendship and then follow through.

Money and Success

You're on your way up in the world, thanks to expansive Jupiter, which enters Gemini, your solar Tenth House, on the 11th. This year-long influence can bring great gains and increased popularity. You could see immediate results in the weeks following the June 19 New Moon in the same sign, possibly as Venus turns direct in Gemini on the 27th. However, don't feel obligated to give what you can't afford even if you feel obligated to support a friend's effort.

Planetary Hotspots

As Uranus in Aries and Pluto in Capricorn transit your solar Eighth and Fifth Houses, this difficult planetary alignment can trigger events related to finances, a romantic interest, insurance, or your children. This is not the time to put funds at risk. Extra expenses involving your children are also possible. And don't let anyone convince you to cosign for a loan, no matter how much pressure is applied.

Rewarding Days

7, 8, 13, 17, 18, 22, 23, 26, 28

Challenging Days

5, 6, 10, 11, 12, 20, 21, 24, 27

Virgo | July

Planetary Lightspots

Although retrograde Mercury periods aren't ones you generally look forward to, it may be different this time. Mercury, your ruling planet, will be retrograde in Leo from July 14 to August 7. Placed in your solar Twelfth House, it will boost your intuition and be an asset if you need to research information. Dreams could also be insightful, so put pen and paper next to your bedside and jot down notes upon awakening.

Relationships

The July 19 New Moon in Cancer spotlights your solar Eleventh House, making this month one of the best for friendship and social events. Involvement in a club or organization can connect you with new people, and you can be an effective team member in a group project at work. Good news could come from a confidential talk with a supervisor in early or mid July, but it may be a while before anything comes of it.

Money and Success

Mars enters Libra, your solar Second House, on the 3rd, the same date as the Full Moon. Even though Mars will initially aggravate the financial crunch, you'll have the opportunity to maximize earnings and could earn a small raise later in July. You could also net some cash by taking unneeded items to a consignment shop, so get motivated and clean out your closet.

Planetary Hotspots

Last month's challenges continue to evolve as the July 3 Full Moon in Capricorn activates Uranus and Pluto. You can expect more financial stress, including a high probability for unexpected expenses, possibly related to your children. But conditions will begin to ease mid-month as solutions start to emerge.

Rewarding Days
7, 8, 12, 22, 26, 27

Challenging Days
2, 4, 9, 17, 24, 30

Virgo | August

Planetary Lightspots

Venus in Cancer, your solar Eleventh House, from August 7 on will have a positive influence on your social life later this month. And when Mercury resumes direct motion in Leo, your solar Twelfth House, on the 8th, you won't lose the intuitive edge it provided, because August 17 brings a New Moon in the same sign. Use the lunar energy to kick back a little. Relaxation time will also enhance your concentration, giving you the ability to tune out the world and focus on the task at hand.

Relationships

You'll be drawn to people and they to you when this month's second Full Moon, in Pisces on the 31st, spotlights your solar Seventh House. This is a great influence for couples and togetherness as well as spending time with family and your closest friends. You'll also have more contact with siblings and neighbors after Mars enters Scorpio, your solar Third House, on the 23rd. But don't chance an accident by talking on the phone while driving.

Money and Success

August begins with a Full Moon in Aquarius, your solar Sixth House, on the 1st. That's sure to please your Virgo work ethic, and it could even trigger a small advancement or raise. At the least you'll be recognized for your efforts. However, be prepared to tighten your budget mid-month.

Planetary Hotspots

Early this month, you can again expect conflict with a friend or romantic interest, especially if things weren't resolved in June. Even though it can be tough for you to cut ties, it might be the best choice because things are unlikely to improve if you wait another month or two or more.

Rewarding Days

3, 4, 8, 9, 11, 14, 18, 19, 22, 27

Challenging Days

6, 7, 13, 20, 21, 24, 26, 28

Virgo | September

Planetary Lightspots

The September 15 New Moon in your sign signals the symbolic start of your new solar year. Tap into this fresh energy and use it to set your personal path for the next twelve months. Luck and communication are strong themes at this New Moon, which will help to boost your success. Plan first and then go into action.

Relationships

People and relationships are emphasized this month, primarily because of the transits of Venus and Mercury. Venus in Cancer, your solar Eleventh House, extends the positive aspects of friendship through September 5, after which its transit of Leo shifts your focus away from the social scene and into memorable moments with your partner. You'll also have the benefit of Mercury in your sign through the 15th, which will encourage people to seek your opinion and listen to your words.

Money and Success

Career progress is steady this month, thanks to many planetary alignments with Jupiter in Gemini, your solar Tenth House. There may be additional talk about your future prospects, which could materialize before year's end. Keep your options open for now.

Planetary Hotspots

Uranus in Aries and Pluto in Capricorn square off again in your solar Eighth and Fifth Houses. You'll experience the strongest effect of this difficult alignment at month's end when the Full Moon in Aries on the 29th targets your solar Eighth/Second House axis. Continue to avoid investments, and be sure to safeguard financial information, especially when you're in public. Also check your (and your family's) credit reports. Take action quickly if you find errors. You might want to consider enrolling in one of the credit monitoring services.

Rewarding Days

1, 5, 6, 8, 15, 27, 28, 30

Challenging Days

2, 10, 11, 16, 19, 23, 24, 29

Virgo | October

Planetary Lightspots

You sparkle and shine with maximum charisma October 3–27, as Venus transits your sign. Turn on the charm and connect with people. Most will be delighted to grant your wishes, and those who can't will direct you to another source. You can also work this magic on your own. Share your desires with the universe and fully expect them to become reality.

Relationships

Family and domestic activities accelerate after Mars enters Sagittarius, your solar Fourth House, on the 6th. The challenge will be to get everyone together long enough to make family plans. Keep trying and you'll succeed. Someone you haven't heard from in years could make contact around the October 29 Full Moon in Taurus, your solar Ninth House. But don't believe everything you hear. At least part of it will be fiction.

Money and Success

Finances enter a more positive period, thanks to the New Moon in Libra, your solar Second House, on the 15th. You may or may not earn more, but expenses will be about average. It's still wise, however, to save for the months ahead.

Planetary Hotspots

Saturn begins a new phase this month when it enters Scorpio, your solar Third House, on the 5th. This is one of the best influences for learning, and a great time to take classes to advance your career. As Saturn progresses through Scorpio during the next two and a half years you'll also either have increased contact with siblings or distance yourself from them. Work to resolve any issues, and don't slip into a pattern of dwelling on the past. Look instead to the future, while benefitting from the knowledge and experience you've gained.

Rewarding Days

2, 3, 5, 8, 13, 16, 21, 24

Challenging Days

4, 11, 14, 20, 25, 27, 31

Virgo | November

Planetary Lightspots

Mercury, your ruling planet, travels retrograde again this month. Despite its retrograde status, your mind will be extra sharp when the November 13 New Moon (lunar eclipse) spotlights your solar Third House. Fill your free time with reading, writing, or games, as well hands-on hobby projects. You'll also have an extra keen knack for research along with the determination to solve puzzling problems.

Relationships

Holiday socializing takes off as Mars enters Capricorn, your solar Fifth House, on the 16th. But you'll want to choose inexpensive destinations because this month could bring yet another unexpected expense. Or invite a group, including a few neighbors, to your place for a casual evening of potluck and cards.

Money and Success

The November 28 Full Moon (lunar eclipse) in Gemini, your solar Tenth House, is filled with luck, promise, and potential for career gains well into next year. Give careful thought to what you want, and then implement your plan to coincide with Jupiter, which will be in Gemini until the end of June 2013. It isn't often you get an opportunity like this, so go for it!

Planetary Hotspots

Mercury begins its retrograde in Sagittarius, your solar Fourth House, on the 6th. It then retreats into Scorpio, your solar Fourth House on the 14th before resuming direct motion on the 26th. Expect more than a few mix-ups and misunderstandings in family matters and communication in general. It's also possible your vehicle or a watch or something else could need a new battery while Mercury is in Scorpio. But if an appliance needs to be replaced, hold off until next month if you can. If not, consider an extended warranty.

Rewarding Days

4, 8, 11, 12, 20, 21, 25

Challenging Days

3, 5, 10, 16, 22, 23

Virgo | December

Planetary Lightspots

Fill your holiday season with special days and memories with family at home. Even if you get a late start, decorate your home as the New Moon in Sagittarius on the 13th accents your solar Fourth House. Even better, the lunar energy gets an extra boost from Mercury in the same sign December 10–30, and Venus there from the 15th on. If you want to host a party, the best choices are the 15th, 22nd, 29th.

Relationships

An active social life continues to be yours as Mars advances in Capricorn, your solar Fifth House, through the 24th. But you don't have to accept every invitation you receive, especially because you'll enjoy socializing at home far more. That's to be expected as family relationships will be at their best this month.

Money and Success

Gear up for a fast pace at work as 2012 ends and 2013 begins. Mars will transit Aquarius, your solar Sixth House, from December 25 to February 1, so this will be an action-packed time with enough work to satisfy even a Virgo. Plan ahead to balance the overload with time for yourself as stress, or even a cold or flu, can quickly put you behind schedule.

Planetary Hotspots

This year's recurring theme pops up again as the December 28 Full Moon in Cancer, your solar Eleventh House, activates Uranus and Pluto. Again this time it can involve finances, your children, a friend, or a dating relationship. Caution continues to apply with investments, as well as standing your ground regarding loans involving others. If you've been anticipating an insurance settlement, expect more delays and an attempt to reduce the award.

Rewarding Days

2, 5, 6, 9, 10, 19, 22, 24, 29

Challenging Days

1, 3, 7, 8, 20, 28, 30

Virgo Action Table

These dates reflect the best—but not the only—times for success and ease in these activities, according to your Sun sign.

	JAN	FEB	MAR	APR	MAY	JUN	JUL	AUG	SEP	OCT	NOV	DEC
Move										29–31		12–31
Start a class										7–27		1–7
Join a club						19		13				1
Ask for a raise										15		
Look for work				14			5		25			
Get pro advice								31				
Get a loan												
See a doctor							5	16, 17	25			
Start a diet				15								
End relationship				16	7							
Buy clothes	12, 13									20		14, 24
Get a makeover										12		6
New romance										20		
Vacation			5–9	20–30	9–23							

LIBRA

The Balance
September 22 to October 22

Element: Air

Quality: Cardinal

Polarity: Yang/Masculine

Planetary Ruler: Venus

Meditation: I balance
conflicting desires

Gemstone: Opal

Power Stones: Tourmaline,
kunzite, blue lace agate

Key Phrase: I balance

Glyph: Scales of justice,
setting Sun

Anatomy: Kidneys, lower back,
appendix

Color: Blue, pink

Animal: Brightly plumed birds

Myths/Legends: Venus,
Cinderella, Hera

House: Seventh

Opposite Sign: Aries

Flower: Rose

Key Word: Harmony

Your Strengths and Challenges

You strive for balance, aiming for the middle ground in everything from relationships to your career to leisure-time activities. When the scales tip one way or the other you're out of sync with yourself and your world. You value cooperation and compromise as well as harmony. But when necessary, you're a master strategist who can out-think most any adversary.

Libras are known for their indecisiveness. This is true of you at times, but not always. It just appears that way to those who fail to understand your mind. Your airy sign makes you a thinker, but it can be tough for you to reach a conclusion because you have the unique ability to see both sides of any question. While this might be an advantage in certain situations, it becomes a challenge if you perpetually sit on the fence.

Ever the diplomat, you have a charming, tactful way with words and can leave people wondering whether your words were intended as praise or criticism. You're also popular on the social scene, and many born under Venus-ruled Libra are attractive. Venus also gives you an eye for beauty and, possibly, artistic talent. You know instinctively how to achieve just the right look in clothing and home décor. Traditional colors and furnishings that create a feeling of calm and serenity are your favorite in décor.

Your sixth sense aids your exceptional people skills, and you're a good listener who can remain emotionally uninvolved. Despite all your grace and charm, however, you can be aloof at times. For one so personable, you maintain a polite distance except with those in your inner circle. And although you dislike controversy, when pushed too far, your temper is unforgettable.

Your Relationships

Born under the universal sign of partnership, most Libras feel incomplete without a partner. Yet for someone who is so attuned to one-on-one relationships, you enjoy group activities with a date and friends. You're drawn to those who share your need for communication, and mental rapport is one quality you seek in a mate. Love can bloom during long late-night talks. But you can mistake infatuation for love and prematurely dash into commitment. So give things a chance to develop and really get to know all sides of your potential mate, both positive and negative. You could feel the sizzle with Aries, your opposite sign, and the other fire signs, Leo and Sagittarius, might spark your interest. You have much in common with your fellow air signs, Gemini and Aquarius, but life could be bumpy with Cancer or Capricorn.

Tradition guides your family life, and you want quality time with loved ones on a daily basis. Dinner and conversation is your ideal, schedules permitting. You keep in touch with elderly relatives, one or more of whom could live with your family at some point. You may have grown up in a highly structured environment with your every moment planned by a parent. Out of that comes a need for private time and space in your own home, as well as encouraging independence in your children, who become more friends than children when they reach adulthood.

You're loyal to your many friends, and take pride in having a wide circle that includes well-connected people. And no small part of your popularity on the social scene is your ability to make each person feel like the center of your universe. You entertain friends in royal style, classy and elegant, whether it's a backyard barbecue or a formal dinner. Many Libras have a large number of acquaintances from their involvement in clubs and organizations, where your leadership skills are at their best.

Your Career and Money

You have wealth potential, and with wise investments and savings you can ensure comfort in your retirement years. Real estate could also be lucrative, so you should aim for home ownership and annual home improvements to increase the value of your property. Many Libras receive an inheritance from a family member, and some gain through collectibles and antiques. But as careful as you can be with budgeting, you also have an eye for the finer things in life. Live within your means and maximize your excellent earning power.

With your people skills you can be successful in most any career, especially those that require working with the public. You're patient and sensitive to clients' or customers' needs, and bring out the best in coworkers, encouraging them to succeed. But loyalty can keep you in a job when it would be in your best interest to move on. A congenial workplace and a pleasant atmosphere are vital to job contentment; anything less can motivate you to send out résumés.

Your Lighter Side

If you're like most Libras, candy and other treats are irresistible. And although many people are unaware of it, you can be the epitome of laziness. Enjoy! Knowing how to relax is a gift and the benefits of kicking back help keep you at your best when job pressure and other stressors rise. So curl up in your favorite chair with a bag of candy and a best seller and savor the moment—guilt free.

Affirmation for the Year Ahead

I have faith in myself.

The Year Ahead for Libra

Travel, money, and learning are in the forefront for 2012, as is the domestic scene. All of these will bring you many opportunities to interact with people, which is another especially active pattern in your life this year. Some will be positive, while others will challenge your diplomatic skills.

Jupiter spends about the first half of the year in Taurus, your solar Eighth House of joint resources. This transit, which occurs only every twelve years, is one of the best for attracting money. The tough part is remembering that it won't last forever. On June 11, when Jupiter moves on to Gemini, this phase will end and life will return to normal, so make saving a priority and you will have something to show for this gift from the universe when the transit is over. You can also use this time to learn more about money management, investing, and how to plan for retirement (whatever your age). Loans are usually easier to get under this influence, but buy less than you can afford if you plan to purchase property this spring.

Jupiter enters Gemini June 11 to begin its year-long tour of your solar Ninth House. Placed here, Jupiter encourages you to widen your horizons through travel, education, self-study, reading, and talking with people. Do as many of these things as you can and be aware of opportunities to learn about other cultures and beliefs. As a result, you'll enjoy a more enlightened perspective and a greater awareness of your role in the world.

Jupiter also encourages you to look toward the future with optimism and to clearly define where you're going and how you plan to get there. This will have the side benefit of reinforcing your faith in yourself and your skills, talents, and abilities as you get in touch with the spiritual side of yourself. If you regularly attend a place of worship, you're likely to get more involved in related activities.

Saturn will conclude its transit of your sign October 5, when it moves on to Scorpio. During its time in Libra, which began in November 2009, you've undoubtedly reflected on the past. This is positive, but it may have come with some regrets. As tough as it is to put these thoughts aside, this is exactly what Saturn wants you to do: learn from the past in order to create a more fulfilling future, which is the only thing you can change. This year you can use Saturn in tandem with Jupiter in Gemini as a self-motivator to prepare and to take the initial steps toward what you will launch in about five years when Saturn enters Capricorn. Saturn does nothing quickly. It's all about planting seeds and nurturing their growth.

Take action now and do what's necessary to resolve any issues within yourself or with other people so you can move on without continuing to carry the baggage. You'll have all the determination you need to accomplish this and much more, thanks to steady Saturn.

Saturn will enter Scorpio, your solar Second House, October 5. You'll have about two and a half years to master Saturn's lessons here, which can lead to greater financial security and stability. It's all about following the rules and being a responsible money manager and consumer. This is the practical side of Saturn in the Second House that encompasses everything from budgeting to saving to minimizing debt and living within your means.

But the Second House encompasses more than money, which is only one of the resources available to you. The most important resource you have is you, including your many strengths and talents. Also a part of you are your attitudes about money and possessions. Now Saturn challenges you to take a close look at these attitudes and to make any necessary changes. Cash or credit? Rich gourmet foods or healthy ones? Pricey designer jeans or comfortable ones at half the cost? Ask yourself these questions and more as you decipher the best use of your resources. Chances are, Saturn here will give you a head start on this path. Take note if you catch yourself passing on a purchase you wouldn't have questioned not too long ago. That's Saturn at work.

Expect the unexpected in relationships as Uranus in Aries continues its trip through your solar Seventh House. A new friend, romantic interest, or mentor could suddenly appear and just as suddenly disappear, having fulfilled a specific purpose. So don't plan on a new relationship to be a lasting one, especially in matters of the heart. Simply enjoy the moment for what it is. Take this caution seriously: avoid legal and financial partnerships.

Change will also touch you and your partner if you're involved in a committed relationship. Because Uranus will be in Aries until 2018, you won't necessarily experience this in a major way in 2012. But there will be ongoing subtle changes, a quick event or comment here and there. It will be easy to perceive this as a negative. However, with a positive attitude and true love in your hearts, you can make the most of this transit to reinvent or revitalize your relationship. It's also possible that this transit will manifest as a change in your family or living environment that requires both of you to adapt.

You'll also meet many exciting, stimulating people in the next few years, even as you say goodbye or distance yourself from others. This is really a reflection of your changing personal needs, interests, and desires. Some people will no longer be a good fit, while others will be an even better one. You can learn much about yourself if you view all these relationships as a mirror image of yourself. The people you're with will be a reflection of you.

Neptune also changes signs this year, switching from Aquarius to Pisces on February 3. Use its brief time in Aquarius to complete any creative projects, even if you started them as long ago as 1998, when Neptune entered this sign. Also devote extra time to your children and their activities. This is one of the best influences for romance, so plan a special evening with your partner or socialize with friends where you might meet someone new. Your sixth sense could lead you to someone fascinating.

Neptune in Pisces will influence your work life for about the next fourteen years as it transits your solar Sixth House. You'll have inspirational periods as well as disappointing ones, periods of illusion and confusion, and compassionate and uplifting moments. The challenge will be to maintain a professional distance with coworkers while you focus on your own work without taking on theirs. However, if you're in sales or a health care or service industry, this transit can increase your job satisfaction.

A great use of Neptune here is creative thinking. A different perspective can help you spot the things others miss, or that you might miss if you're too close to a project. You can accomplish this by freeing your mind with a walk or by switching tasks. Take it a step further and offer your creative ideas in meetings and talks. Even if they're at first perceived as off-base, people will soon appreciate your vision and imagination. Use both in problem solving.

Pluto in Capricorn, your solar Fourth House, will trigger significant changes on the home front at some point during its long transit. (Pluto is in Capricorn until 2024.) They could be positive, such as an extensive remodeling project. Or relocation might be necessary to take charge of a relative's affairs or for a new job or promotion. You also should periodically check your home for any sign of termites and be sure your property is well insured.

On another, deeper level, Pluto challenges you to reflect on your childhood and family life. Deal with unresolved issues and explore the impact these experiences had (and possibly continue to have) on your life. You could also use Pluto's energy to research and discover your family tree and possibly find relatives you never knew or haven't seen in years. With Pluto's powerful focus and determination on your side, you could trace your roots back many generations.

What This Year's Eclipses Mean for You

There are four eclipses this year, two solar and two lunar, and each is in effect for six to twelve months. Three eclipses highlight your solar Third/Ninth House axis; the fourth is in your solar Second House.

The May 21 solar eclipse in Gemini focuses its energy on your solar Ninth House, as does the November 28 lunar eclipse in the same sign. With Jupiter also here from June 11 on, you'll have incentive to travel, expand your knowledge base, return to school or take a class for fun, and to experience another culture in some way. You also could attend a reunion or develop a strong bond with in-laws. Chances are good that at some point you'll be called for jury duty.

Sagittarius and your solar Third House are the site of the June 4 lunar eclipse. This placement, which is opposite Gemini and the Ninth House, also emphasizes learning, along with errands and trips to nearby or familiar locations. It's also your communication sector, so you'll need to budget your time for e-mail, social media, and calls. You'll find this to be a most helpful influence if your job involves a lot of contact with people, meetings, or teamwork. This eclipse could also motivate you to get involved in a community project, and it can benefit relationships with neighbors and siblings.

November 3 is the date of the second 2012 solar eclipse, this time in Scorpio, your solar Second House. This eclipse reinforces Saturn's lessons in thrift, budgeting, savings, and minimal use of credit. The two influences could increase your income, possibly as soon as October. Think carefully, however, if a major domestic purchase or home improvement would require considerable debt. That's the best idea under these planetary alignments.

Saturn

If you were born between October 14 and 22, Saturn in Libra will merge its energies with your Sun before October 5. You'll experience the full effect of Saturn in June and July **if your birthday is October 14, 15, or 16.** For Libras with birthdays on the other dates, Saturn will connect with your Sun between January and May, and again in August or September.

Although this Saturn-Sun connection has a reputation for being difficult—and it can be—there's far more to it. This is a learning experience (one of Saturn's favorite phrases!). The more responsibility you take for yourself and your actions the more successful the outcome. And even though it's not the best time for new endeavors, it is an excellent time to begin to establish new personal directions, goals, and attitudes that will set your course for at least the next fourteen years. Be prepared, though, to feel somewhat held back because achievements probably won't come quite as easily now. Stick with it. Saturn rewards long-term efforts.

Possibly the most important point to remember is that a Saturn-Sun merger nearly always brings exactly what you deserve. This of course can be positive or negative, depending upon the actions you've taken and the decisions you've made. Saturn is, after all, the ultimate karmic planet. Also keep in mind that what you do as Saturn transits your sign will come to fruition in the future. Make other people a key part of the current transit as some of the alliances you form will be invaluable in the future.

You may tire more easily during this period, which makes sleep and relaxation important. You'll also be working harder and may experience instant repercussions if you try to take shortcuts. Anything less than a solid effort is likely to result in difficulties. This too is part of Saturn's role as a teacher. In turn, you can use your knowledge and experience to benefit others by sharing your wisdom.

Uranus

If you were born between September 22 and October 1, Uranus will contact your Sun from Aries, your solar Seventh House. With this planet transiting your relationship sector, unusual people will enter your life and you can also expect the unexpected from some of them. There will be a significant change in at least one close relationship, or an indication that major changes are on the horizon.

On a personal level, the idea of change will be as fearsome as it is attractive because in many ways you are ready to go in a new direction, to be free from perceived yet very real restrictions in your environment or relationships. And the catalyst triggered by Uranus is likely to be sudden and unexpected. But it will in some way set you free with a strong spirit of independence.

One area, however, should be off limits: romantic commitment. Although the thrill of new love can be irresistible, this is not the year to commit or to make a major relationship decision.

Neptune

Neptune will contact your Sun from Aquarius before February 3 **if you were born October 20, 21, or 22.** This connection was also active in 2011, so think back to the events and feelings you experienced last year. A romance could fade away during this final contact, or you could complete a creative project and move on, content in the knowledge that you had the opportunity to express yourself in this way. Your intuition will continue to be active, and if you're part of a couple, this is an ideal time to celebrate your love.

Neptune will advance into Pisces, your solar Sixth House, February 3, where it will connect with your Sun **if you were born between September 22 and 26.** Confusion and chaos are possible in the work place with this transit, and you might feel unsettled about your job or that an indefinable something is going on under the surface at your company. You also could feel disillusioned at times and question whether you're on the best path for you. Finding the answer, however, will be difficult if not impossible because your thoughts and ideas will shift in tandem with illusory Neptune. You'll also want to be very cautious about sharing personal information with coworkers, and be sure to double-check your work for mistakes.

Like every planet, Neptune also has its positive side. In the Sixth House it can inspire you to go above and beyond, to put forth the extra effort that's both personally and professionally rewarding. Creative thinking and approaches can contribute to this success, and you might find yourself thrust into the limelight as a result. You might also want to consider volunteering your time for a charitable organization. This, along with a healthy diet and exercise, can help promote wellness and ease daily stress.

Pluto

If your birthday is between September 29 and October 1, Pluto will contact your Sun from Capricorn, your solar Fourth House of home and family. Be sure your property is fully covered by insurance, especially if you live in an area prone to severe weather. Also regularly check your home for pests and other damage. If you plan to purchase property, make the offer subject to inspection, and carefully check credentials before hiring a contractor for home improvements. This is also the year to get your home in order. You'll have the motivation to clean out closets, storage spaces, basement, garage, and attic, so go to it and enjoy the sense of freedom it provides.

It's also possible your living situation will change because a relative or roommate moves in or out. If an adult child wants to return home, set ground rules in advance and be prepared to enforce them. You might also have issues with your parents or feel the need to resolve events from the past. While this can be healthy, it's also wise to think carefully before you speak your mind.

Family relationships can be rocky this year, especially in June and September when Uranus in Aries, your solar Seventh House, will clash with Pluto. People with control issues will display that side of themselves, and you could be pulled into a family power struggle despite your efforts to remain neutral. This planetary alignment could also trigger damage to your home, so be sure it's insured by a reputable company and for replacement value. Read all the fine print in the policy.

Libra | January

Planetary Lightspots

Although retrograde Mars isn't exactly what you would think of as a lightspot, it certainly can be if you use it well. Mars will spend its entire retrograde period (January 23–April 12) in Virgo, your solar Twelfth House of self-renewal. Use this period to begin and follow through with those things you enjoy but never have time to do. Also listen to your inner voice, both in the intuitive sense and to reflect on your life and your hopes and wishes for the future.

Relationships

Your social life will come alive later this month as the Aquarius New Moon on the 23rd energizes your solar Fifth House. A new dating relationship could spring to life under this influence, and if you're part of a couple, it's an ideal time to celebrate love and romance. Creative projects will also benefit from this New Moon, and you'll be in tune with your children.

Money and Success

The January 9 Full Moon in Cancer highlights your solar Tenth House of career and status. Both will benefit from the lunar energy, and you could have a confidential talk with from someone who thinks you're going places. Don't, however, be tempted to get involved in a workplace romance. That would not be in your best interest.

Planetary Hotspots

The domestic scene will challenge you on several levels this month. Planetary alignments in Capricorn, your solar Fourth House, can trigger conflict with family members, and this is also not the time to invite someone to join your household. If a home repair is needed, check references and get several estimates before proceeding with the work.

Rewarding Days
1, 5, 10, 11, 15, 23, 24, 28, 29

Challenging Days
4, 7, 8, 12, 14, 16, 20, 21

Libra | February

Planetary Lightspots

Quality time with your children will be especially meaningful during the first few weeks of February, and they will appreciate the extra attention. Help with homework, encourage them to express their creativity, and share your pride in their accomplishments. Their wisdom will surprise and inspire you.

Relationships

Friendship takes center stage as the February 7 Full Moon in Leo shines in your solar Eleventh House. Join your friends for evenings out, and meet others for lunch and weekend activities. You can also expand your personal and career networks now. If you're single, a potential romantic interest could enter your life, but if a dating relationship isn't working out, the lunar energy could prompt you to move on.

Money and Success

Your work life is hectic this month with four planets and the February 21 New Moon in Pisces, your solar Sixth House. One of the planets is Neptune, which enters Pisces on the 3rd, providing inspiration and creativity in your daily work. Coworker relationships are generally positive, but one person could try to undermine your efforts mid-month. Be aware and don't share personal information.

Planetary Hotspots

Family or roommate relationships could be a bit rocky at times after Venus enters Aries, your solar Seventh House, February 8. Think calm thoughts and say little because it will be tough to have a reasonable conversation. It's also possible you'll need a domestic repair again this month, for an appliance or weather damage. This too could trigger relationship difficulties.

Rewarding Days

2, 6, 11, 16, 19, 20, 24

Challenging Days

3, 4, 15, 17, 22, 25

Libra | March

Planetary Lightspots

You'll enjoy a momentary retreat from the world under the March 8 Full Moon in Virgo, your solar Twelfth House. The lunar energy could also help you find a missing item or possibly a forgotten collectible that's now worth quite a bit of money. So take advantage of the two weeks following the Full Moon to clean out storage spaces. Look through every box and pocket.

Relationships

Despite the antics of retrograde Mercury, March is an overall positive relationship month. Spend quality time with those you love, and connect with many others at social events in the weeks following the New Moon in Aries on the 23rd. But avoid conflict-prone subjects and entertaining at home on the 29th and 30th.

Money and Success

Finances are favorable this month, with Venus in Taurus, your solar Eighth House, from March 5 on. You could gain through a minor windfall around the 14th, which is also a good date to take a chance on the lottery. A raise for you or your mate is possible, but set a firm budget if you shop for home furnishings. You could easily spend far more than intended.

Planetary Hotspots

Mercury turns retrograde March 12 in Aries, your solar Seventh House, and then retreats into Pisces, your solar Sixth House on the 23rd. Despite your notable people skills, the Aries transit can trigger misunderstandings, so be sure others grasp the points you want to make. Retrograde Mercury could be more problematic in Pisces, where it has the potential to affect workplace projects and communication. Be especially aware of this during the first few days of March.

Rewarding Days

1, 6, 10, 14, 18, 19, 23, 26, 28

Challenging Days

2, 3, 4, 9, 15, 17, 20, 24, 30

Libra | April

Planetary Lightspots

Job-related activities put on hold resume momentum after Mercury turns direct in Pisces, your solar Sixth House, on the 13th. But it's also likely previous decisions will be reversed, so be prepared to adapt as necessary. Take advantage of the days prior to Mercury's direction change to review recently completed projects. Chances are you'll find errors that can be easily corrected.

Relationships

The April 6 Full Moon in your sign is as much about you as it is about the close relationships in your life. Reach out to loved ones, and spend quality time with your partner. You could hear surprising and very unexpected news from someone near the 22nd. However, expect challenges with someone close to you around the 15th and the last full week of April, when it will be tough to compromise on anything.

Money and Success

Your bank account could get a boost from the April 21 New Moon in Taurus, your solar Eighth House. The source could be anything from an inheritance to a property sale, lucky find, or a raise for you or your mate. If necessary, put it toward a home repair, but don't let the free flow of money encourage you to incur debt. Take care in early April to protect valuables from loss.

Planetary Hotspots

Difficult planetary alignments the first week of April caution against travel, meetings, and contact with in-laws or people at a distance. It will be tough to get anyone to listen to you or understand your point, and it's also possible someone could try to undermine your position or efforts.

Rewarding Days

1, 2, 10, 14, 19, 22, 25, 27, 28, 30

Challenging Days

3, 5, 9, 11, 13, 15, 18, 20, 24, 26

Libra | May

Planetary Lightspots

The May 20 New Moon (solar eclipse) in Gemini triggers your curiosity. Since travel is prone to difficulties this month, find a good substitute to widen your horizons and your knowledge. Take a class for fun, stock up on books, tour local museums or historic spots, or explore your creativity through a hobby.

Relationships

Relationships aren't a strong theme this month, but Mercury in Aries, your solar Seventh House, through the 8th favors one-on-one interaction with people, especially your partner. But avoid controversial topics and serious discussions on the 3rd and 4th. It will be tough to agree on much of anything then, and both of you will be unwilling to compromise.

Money and Success

Again this month, you could end up with considerably more money than you had on the first. Luck is definitely with you in financial matters as the May 5 Full Moon in Scorpio, your solar Second House, activates Jupiter in Taurus, your solar Eighth House. This emphasis on your money sectors has great potential to trigger a windfall, raise, or bonus for you or your mate. Take a chance on the lottery around the 22nd and 27th, and cross your fingers. Remember, though, it only takes one ticket to win.

Planetary Hotspots

Venus turns retrograde in Gemini, your solar Ninth House, May 15. Lost luggage is a strong possibility if you travel, and you can expect misunderstandings with people at a distance, especially work-related communication. A lost pet is also possible, so take extra precautions to prevent your cat or dog from making a dash for freedom.

Rewarding Days

8, 11, 12, 15, 17, 20, 22, 26, 27, 31

Challenging Days

3, 4, 7, 9, 16, 21, 23, 29, 30

Libra | June

Planetary Lightspots

Jupiter arrives in Gemini, your solar Ninth House, on the 11th. This marks the start of a year-long emphasis on travel, education, and spirituality. All of these will influence your life in some way, and this month's New Moon in the same sign on the 19th could motivate you to make reservations, take off on vacation, or enroll in school. If the latter, focus your studies on a short-term program that can benefit your career when Jupiter moves on to Cancer next year.

Relationships

Your intuition will be active under the June 4 Full Moon (lunar eclipse) in Sagittarius, your solar Third House. This can come in handy in conversation because you'll sense what people are thinking but not saying. Ever the diplomat, you're unlikely to let your irritation with a sibling or neighbor emerge. That's best, anyway, because it will be short-lived.

Money and Success

You'll need to be cautious about what you say and do at work because of the Uranus-Pluto alignment. Even a casual comment could trigger conflict, and it's unwise to put your trust in coworkers even though they'll encourage you to open up. Silence is a better choice.

Planetary Hotspots

Expect challenges with relationships and home life as Uranus in Aries squares off with Pluto in Capricorn. With these two planets in your solar Seventh and Fourth Houses, and triggering planets in Cancer, your solar Tenth House, career difficulties could set things off. Also check your home for termites, and be sure all property and possessions are fully insured against weather damage. The need to relocate is also possible.

Rewarding Days

7, 8, 13, 17, 18, 19, 22, 23 26

Challenging Days

5, 10, 11, 12, 20, 21, 24, 28, 29

Libra | July

Planetary Lightspots

There's no time like now to take off for a few days to delight in a long weekend with your partner. Romance and fresh scenery go together with Venus and Jupiter in Gemini, your solar Ninth House of travel. Expect a few pleasant surprises in addition to the ones you have in mind.

Relationships

If you let it, retrograde Mercury in Leo from the 14th on can trigger mix-ups in your social plans. There's a simple solution as this planet transits your solar Eleventh House: confirm times, dates, and places before you go. However, family life may not be quite so enjoyable around the July 3 Full Moon in Capricorn, your solar Fourth House. The lunar energy could trigger conflict with a family member, possibly as a result of domestic repairs or the needs of an elderly relative.

Money and Success

Career success can be yours under the July 19 New Moon in Cancer, your solar Tenth House. Expect it to come with a price, however. It'll be hard work. But you already know that. Even so, between the lunar energy and Mars in your sign, remember not to push yourself too hard. Know when to quit, and when to relax. This is also a good month to get better acquainted with colleagues at an after-work get-together. You could pick up some valuable information for the future.

Planetary Hotspots

Mars arrives in your sign July 3, where it will give you all the incentive and initiative to achieve whatever you focus on. But you'll need to calm your mind well before bedtime in order to get the solid night's sleep you'll need to maintain a fast pace. Also take care in the kitchen and when working with tools as Mars can trigger accidents.

Rewarding Days

1, 5, 10, 14, 15, 16, 20, 23, 28

Challenging Days

3, 9, 13, 17, 19, 24, 30

Libra | August

Planetary Lightspots

Put fun at the top of your priority list when you're not working. That will be a snap, thanks to this month's first Full Moon, on the 1st in Aquarius, your solar Fifth House. Plan a family outing, spend time with a favorite hobby, and enjoy outdoor activities. Or opt for a day trip or another long weekend at a recreation destination.

Relationships

Friendship is featured under the August 17 New Moon in Leo, your solar Eleventh House. Expect your social life to pick up in the following weeks. But this influence is just as good, maybe even better, for job-related teamwork, with you as the leader. If you plan to attend a conference or travel on business, consider it an opportunity to widen your circle of career contacts.

Money and Success

Earning potential increases after Mars shifts into Scorpio, your solar Second House, on the 23rd. You could see income rise during this seven-week transit, but you'll need to control spending in order to realize a net gain. The work pace will accelerate into September after the second August Full Moon, on the 31st in Pisces, activates your solar Sixth House. Time management is your best ally.

Planetary Hotspots

Career commitments could interfere with family and partnership time after Venus enters Cancer, your solar Tenth House, on the 7th. Be proactive. Explain and ask for their support beforehand. This will help ease the tension that will peak around the 16th. After that you'll benefit from the extra popularity that comes with Venus moving through this sector.

Rewarding Days

2, 5, 9, 11, 15, 17, 25, 29

Challenging Days

6, 7, 13, 16, 20, 21, 26, 28

Libra | September

Planetary Lightspots

You can enjoy some precious hours alone to pursue your own interests around the September 15 New Moon in Virgo, your solar Twelfth House of self-renewal. Slow the pace a little, look inward, and listen to your subconscious. Then you'll be ready to move into your new solar year with confidence when next month's New Moon highlights your sign.

Relationships

Despite relationship challenges in other areas, you'll enjoy upbeat times with friends after Venus enters Leo, your solar Eleventh House, on the 6th. Don't be surprised, though, if a close pal presents a different perspective on other events going on in your life. Listen and think. Although what you hear may not be entirely on target, it will offer new insights.

Money and Success

Your career remains in the spotlight through September 5 as Venus transits your solar Tenth House. The pace will ease after that and you'll be able to catch up and even work ahead. Mars continues to advance in Scorpio, your solar Second House, accenting income and spending. You could find a bargain on household items if you shop around the 3rd.

Planetary Hotspots

The clash between Uranus and Pluto will be activated again by the September 29 Full Moon in Aries, your solar Seventh House. So relationships will be central to the challenges you'll experience. Disagreement over a family matter is likely, and it will be difficult for you and your partner to find a compromise. In time, though, you will work things out. Again, be sure your home is well insured, especially if you live in an area prone to severe weather.

Rewarding Days

3, 6, 9, 13, 17, 21, 25, 30

Challenging Days

2, 10, 11, 16, 20, 23, 24, 29

Libra | October

Planetary Lightspots

Look to the future with optimistic enthusiasm as the October 15 New Moon in Libra puts you in the spotlight. Balance fun, and possibly travel, with thoughts of where you want to be a year from now and how best to maximize your talents. Include career goals on your to-do list because you'll have opportunities in this area in 2013.

Relationships

Expect the daily pace to be hectic between October 6 and November 15 as Mars advances in Sagittarius, your solar Third House. With it will come increased communication, much of it reflecting this positive relationship period. But early October could bring confusion or even deception involving a coworker, and questions concerning a project. Intuition will help guide you to answers.

Money and Success

Although family income could rise this month, it may be less than hoped for. The Full Moon in Taurus, your solar Eighth House, on the 29th, could also trigger the need for a domestic or vehicle repair or replacement.

Planetary Hotspots

Money and values will be a main focus as Saturn transits Scorpio, your solar Second House, during the next two and a half years. You could earn a raise soon after it enters this sign on October 5, or be offered another opportunity to increase your paycheck. Saturn here is all about becoming a better money manager and taking a long-term financial view rather than one that's month to month or year to year. Part of this is will be due to your changing values about materialism, and you'll gradually realize there are many things you don't really need, or even want.

Rewarding Days

5, 6, 10, 13, 18, 22, 28, 31

Challenging Days

1, 4, 7, 9, 14, 20, 23, 27

Libra | November

Planetary Lightspots

The November 28 Full Moon (lunar eclipse) in Gemini re-energizes your solar Ninth House of travel and knowledge. With this eclipse influence extending well into 2013, it might be time to plan a dream trip, or to immerse yourself in learning another language or a subject that's always been of interest. Any of these will satisfy your spirit of adventure and your curiosity.

Relationships

Early and late November could bring more stress involving family relationships. The triggering event could again be a relative who disrupts family harmony when you and your partner disagree over the best course of action. There also could be issues related to home improvements or renovations, possibly because they aren't progressing as they should be.

Money and Success

Despite retrograde Mercury, the November 13 New Moon (solar eclipse) in Scorpio has the potential to boost your bank account not only this month but in 2013. Spending can rise as well. Set a budget and live within it while adding to savings.

Planetary Hotspots

November brings another retrograde Mercury period that begins on the 6th in Sagittarius, your solar Third House. Mercury slips back into Scorpio, your solar Second House, on the 14th, before resuming direct motion on the 26th. Misunderstandings and confusion can alter plans while Mercury is in Sagittarius. Once it returns to Scorpio, however, the potential for mix-ups centers on money matters. Check statements for errors, be sure deposits are made to the correct account, and allow plenty of time for payments to reach their destination. A watch or car battery may need to be replaced.

Rewarding Days

2, 6, 7, 11, 14, 15, 24, 29

Challenging Days

3, 10, 12, 16, 23, 25, 26, 30

Libra | December

Planetary Lightspots

You're in luck if your New Year's resolution involves exercise and a healthier lifestyle. Mars in Aquarius, your solar Fifth House, from December 25 to February 1 can get you off to a fast start and provide the incentive and determination to stick with the plan. Join a gym or a mall walkers group. Probability of success rises even more if you do this in partnership with your mate or a close friend.

Relationships

Quick, creative thinking and increased communication accompany the New Moon in Sagittarius, your solar Third House, on the 13th. And with Mercury in the same sign from the 10th to the 30th, and Venus there from the 15th on, you'll instantly put others at ease. But your notable, if seldom seen, temper could spark to life at month's end. Take a time-out rather than say what you'll later regret.

Money and Success

Money matters continue to be positive this month with Mercury and Venus in Scorpio, your solar Second House, before they advance into Sagittarius. Holiday shopping will yield bargains if you take your time and watch for sales.

Planetary Hotspots

Although domestic and relationship issues will be minimal much of the month, the December 28 Full Moon in Cancer will fuel these ongoing challenges. The trigger could be career-related relocation or major structural changes and downsizing in your company. However, if you're just frustrated with your job, resist the urge to act impulsively. Conditions will ease with time. Also discard thoughts of a home-based business, which is unlikely to be successful in the next few years.

Rewarding Days

9, 12, 15, 16, 17, 21, 26, 31

Challenging Days

1, 7, 8, 10, 14, 20, 28, 30

Libra Action Table

These dates reflect the best—but not the only—times for success and ease in these activities, according to your Sun sign.

	JAN	FEB	MAR	APR	MAY	JUN	JUL	AUG	SEP	OCT	NOV	DEC
Move	12–19									20, 21		23, 24
Start a class					7, 8			24, 25				11, 17
Join a club							19–31	1–21				
Ask for a raise	16									16		10
Look for work										24	30	
Get pro advice												20
Get a loan									4, 5			
See a doctor									14	12		5
Start a diet				16				31	3			
End relationship				19, 20								
Buy clothes				14								
Get a makeover									16			16
New romance									25, 26			16
Vacation								1–6				

SCORPIO

The Scorpion
October 22 to November 21
♏

Element: Water

Quality: Fixed

Polarity: Yin/Feminine

Planetary Ruler: Pluto (Mars)

Meditation: I can surrender
my feelings

Gemstone: Topaz

Power Stones: Obsidian,
amber, citrine, garnet, pearl

Key Phrase: I create

Glyph: Scorpion's tail

Anatomy: Reproductive system

Color: Burgundy, black

Animal: Reptiles, scorpions,
birds of prey

Myths/Legends: The Phoenix,
Hades and Persephone, Shiva

House: Eighth

Opposite Sign: Taurus

Flower: Chrysanthemum

Key Word: Intensity

Your Strengths and Challenges

Your determination is relentless and you'll push yourself to the point of exhaustion to achieve a goal. Obstacles are irrelevant to you and your willpower is in a class of its own. Anyone who tries to circumvent your efforts soon learns you will not be deterred, sometimes to the point of ruthlessness. But it's also wise to know when to quit rather than put your health at risk.

You take life seriously, and at times feel as though you're on a path of destiny as you pursue your life purpose. Your soul runs deep and you have an innate understanding of both the light and dark sides of life.

You have a magnetic, mesmerizing charisma that intrigues those around you. Yet, you're cautious about expressing your views. When you do, you need only a few words to say it all. This adds to your mysterious aura, as does your classic poker face that reveals nothing—even when you're seething inside. Your steely mask can also be an advantage when you want to keep people guessing.

You're intuitive (and possibly psychic), perceptive, and shrewd. These traits definitely give you an edge in life. Besides being a step ahead of most everyone, you watch and wait and take action only when the timing is to your advantage.

But you also can be intense, and some Scorpios are controlling and manipulative, using their personal power to dominate others rather than to better themselves and their own lives. Of all the signs, Scorpio is the one with the greatest potential and willpower for self-transformation.

Your Relationships

People place their trust in you because they recognize your honesty and integrity. They also share secrets because they know you respect a confidence. Your circle of friends and acquaintances is wide, but you know them far better than they know you. This gives you a distinct advantage in just about every area of life.

You're a romantic with a big heart. But you're hesitant to express your emotions until you're sure the feeling is mutual. It's a matter of self-protection; only those who know you well are aware of your sensitive soul. Your passion runs deep once you find your soul mate, but you can be possessive and even jealous, as can your mate. Trust, however, is what builds a foundation for lasting love. You could find happiness with one of the earth signs—Virgo, Capricorn, and especially Taurus, your opposite sign. Compatibility runs high with your fellow water signs, Cancer and Pisces, but you could clash with dramatic Leo or independent Aquarius.

You like to be in control of your environment, and can achieve this in some arenas, but probably not in your home life. There anything goes and the unexpected is often the norm rather than the exception. Many Scorpios opt for contemporary home décor or an eclectic mix that makes a statement. Family communication is also important to you, and there are impromptu gatherings of friends in your home. As a parent you're protective of your children and can be a powerful motivational force in their lives. But you also tend to see the best in them when a more realistic view would be to their advantage. Find a balance between spoiling them and giving them the life skills they need.

You're choosy about your friends. You have many acquaintances, some of whom are business colleagues, but your inner circle is small and select. The social circuit isn't your scene; you much prefer casual evenings and lively conversation with people you know well. And more than a few Scorpios cherish their pets as best friends. You also might develop good friends through involvement in a charitable or service organization, which is a great way for Scorpios to network and meet new people.

Your Career and Money

Your earning power is among the best of the zodiac. You also go on occasional spending sprees. That's great when you can afford it, but don't go into debt to get what you want. Despite your financial savvy, income and expenses fluctuate somewhat, so it's wise to plan ahead. You could do well with investments if you take the time to do thorough research, and can often find the best interest rates. Always read the fine print being signing any contract, even those that appear to be routine.

You have great potential to achieve a top career spot where you can grab more than a little of the limelight. Develop your leadership skills on the way up as you encourage others. Then, you'll have the supporters you need when you need them. You prefer a fast-paced work environment where your initiative is valued. Endless meetings are not for you. Neither is sitting behind a desk. If your career requires an office workplace, be sure any job comes with enough freedom to structure your work so you don't feel hemmed in.

Your Lighter Side
Scorpio is the sign of transformation, something you do almost unconsciously. You can take someone else's junk and transform it into something beautiful or useful, or resurrect what others have written off as a lost cause. Personally, you have the inner strength to reinvent yourself physically and mentally. What others call hurdles, you call possibilities.

Affirmation for the Year

My mind is my greatest asset.

The Year Ahead for Scorpio

Money is a strong theme this year and into 2013, at the end of which your net worth could be considerably more than it is now. You'll connect with many people and may see changes in your workplace and community. At year's end, you'll begin a new phase that includes assessing and defining your personal goals, what you've learned, what you value, and where you want to go in the future. Opportunities await!

Jupiter spends about half the year in Taurus, your solar Seventh House of relationships, before moving on to Gemini in June. Other people can bring you luck during the Taurus transit, which occurs only once every twelve years. It's also one of the best for couples and those who would like to meet someone special. But be wary of mixing finances with anyone other than a legal partner. Jupiter here can also put you in touch with a wide variety of people, from new friends to coworkers to professionals such as an accountant. Most of all, take advantage of this period. You'll attract positive energy and many opportunities, some of which could bring you added income within the next few years.

Jupiter advances into Gemini on June 11, to begin its year-long transit of your solar Eighth House. Make the most of it! This time frame can be a lucrative one, even to the point where you'll feel as though the flow of money coming your way will never end. Think long term to avoid the trap of complacency. In a year, Jupiter will move on, so plan ahead to have something to show for the universe's financial gift. Also take time to update insurance policies, review your retirement plans (even if it's years away), and pay off existing debt while building savings.

Saturn completes its Libra transit October 4, and then moves on to Scorpio. While this serious planet is in Libra, your solar Twelfth House, take the time to think about where you've been and what you've accomplished in the past twenty-eight years. Also give considerable thought to what you learned during those years as well as the personal issues that hold you back. These memories and realizations will be helpful to you as Saturn transits your sign for several years.

Because the Twelfth House is the self-renewal sector, this is also the time for an honest self-assessment of your lifestyle, including diet, exercise, and general health. You can draw on the strength of Saturn to make necessary changes that will be especially beneficial as Saturn transits your sign.

You might also be involved in helping to care for someone, possibly an elderly relative, who is hospitalized or otherwise confined. Or you could experience the rewards of contributing your time and talents to a charitable organization or cause that would benefit your neighborhood or community.

Uranus spends the entire year in Aries, your solar Sixth House of daily work, health, and service. While Saturn gives added determination, Uranus, the ultimate planet of change, provides added incentive to adopt a healthier lifestyle, and possibly to get involved in a group effort for a good cause.

Changing conditions can also surround your work life, especially during the year that Uranus contacts your Sun. Nevertheless, an element of change and the unexpected will be more the norm than the exception until this planet completes its Aries transit in 2018. Some changes will be exciting opportunities that pop up in an instant, while others will challenge your strong need to maintain the status quo. Shift your perspective. You can be the initiator of positive change now because you're uniquely placed to take the lead and guide a group to success.

The Sixth House also governs wellness, so you may be especially prone now to nervous tension. Find an outlet that works for you—

exercise, walking, meditation, hobbies—and that can ease work-related stress. In tandem with Saturn in your solar Twelfth House, Uranus here can help you change your diet, end bad habits, and adopt an overall healthier lifestyle.

Home and family life have been influenced by Neptune since it entered Aquarius, your solar Fourth House, in 1998. This year it completes that transit, moving on to Pisces on February 3. Use the weeks before it shifts signs to finish any domestic projects, even those begun long ago, or give a room a quick creative and inexpensive update. On another level, take time to think about how your perspective of family and your relationship with relatives has changed. You can successfully resolve any lingering issues now, mostly because your outlook regarding family members has shifted. Don't be surprised if this review motivates you to move forward with greater confidence.

Neptune will switch its influence to your solar Fifth House when it moves on to Pisces, the sign it will transit for many years. Here, Neptune will focus all its traits on romance, children, creativity, speculation, and leisure-time activities. You'll undoubtedly experience both the positive and negative sides of this planet during the years ahead. At its best, Neptune signifies inspiration, spirituality, and compassion, while its flip side can trigger disillusionment, disappointment, and a lack of clarity.

So you'll want to be somewhat wary in matters of the heart, because it will be easy to mistake real love with being in love with love. Likewise, a promising investment could pay off handsomely or leave you wondering how such a "sure thing" could fail. It's also wise during this transit to be aware of what your children are doing in their free time and who their friends are because substance abuse is a possibility. On the upside, you can inspire your children and they might do the same for you. Also be sure to explore your creativity through a hobby such as crafts, painting, or music.

Pluto continues its long transit in Capricorn, your solar Third House. At times you'll find yourself lost in deep thought about anything and everything from the meaning of life to how you can maximize personal potential. Pluto here is about looking within to discover the hidden side of yourself, and self-help books can spur your thinking and be an asset in dealing with any issues that limit you. This powerful planet could also motivate you to study a subject on your own or in school, or even to write a book.

The third house is also associated with siblings and neighbors. You'll be more involved with these people, and you could get involved in a community cause or project to improve your surroundings. As a catalyst for change, the effort you put into any such effort will be rewarded many times over. You're also in a position to influence people one on one, to be the person who makes a difference and ultimately changes someone's life for the better.

What This Year's Eclipses Mean for You

There are four eclipses this year, two solar and two lunar, with one in your sign and the other three highlighting your financial sectors. Each is in effect for six to twelve months.

The May 21 solar eclipse in Gemini, your solar Eighth House, is followed by a lunar eclipse in Sagittarius, your solar Second House, June 4. As the year draws to a close, another lunar eclipse will occur in Gemini. Together, these three, along with Jupiter in Gemini, have the potential to boost income both from earnings and other sources such as investments, an inheritance, a windfall, or your partner's income. Be especially cautious with investments in June and September, and avoid major purchases in July and December.

Scorpio is the sign of this year's fourth eclipse on November 13. Use this solar eclipse to set new personal goals and then let it and Saturn, also in your sign, motivate you to achieve them. You might choose to set your sights on career gains, financial security, getting in shape, or something else entirely. What is important is that you take full advantage of this strong solar energy to make great strides in one or more areas into 2013. You have all the determination to do exactly what you wish.

Saturn

If you were born between November 13 and 22, Saturn will contact your Sun from Libra, your Solar Twelfth House, before it advances into Scorpio. June and July will be particularly significant months **if your birthday is November 13, 14, or 15**. For Scorpios born on the other dates, Saturn will contact your Sun once between January and May, and again in August or September.

Saturn in your sector of self-renewal encourages you to be of service to others. This might be as a volunteer for a community organization, helping people learn to read, or organizing an adopt-a-highway team at your company. Whatever you choose will in some way change your perspective of daily life, leading to a greater appreciation of yourself, others, and your role in the world.

This is also the time to complete unfinished projects, to clear the slate for the new beginning that is on the horizon. Take this a step further with a step into the past. Clean out storage spaces, organize everything, use your creativity to compile photos and mementoes in digital or paper scrapbooks, or ask relatives to compile an oral family history. You'll especially enjoy activities that offer the bonus of time alone. But don't dwell on the past and regrets. See this time instead as preparation for the future.

If your birthday is between October 22 and 31, Saturn in Scorpio will join forces with your Sun between October 5 and year's end. Although this is not the time to begin a major new endeavor such as a significant job or career change, it is the time to reap personal rewards for what you have earned. Of one thing you can be sure: Saturn will bring you what you deserve when it contacts your Sun. Whether the outcome is positive or negative or a combination of the two, look inward and reflect upon and learn from it. Then you'll be better prepared to strive toward earning Saturn's rewards seven years from now and again in fourteen years.

Saturn's alignment with your Sun can reflect lowered vitality so you'll want to get enough sleep and rest. This is not the time to push yourself to your physical limits. You may also feel somewhat lonely at times, almost as though there's an indefinable distance between you and other people. Rather than viewing this as a negative, see it as Saturn encouraging a time of introspection so you can better know yourself. And do try to motivate yourself to be with people. You'll have a great time once you get there.

Uranus

If you were born between October 22 and 31, Uranus in Aries, your solar Sixth House, will align with your Sun this year. You can expect change on some level in your job or work environment. This could take the form of different responsibilities, the departure of coworkers and/or the arrival of new employees or supervisors, or a job change. Adaptability will be one of your greatest assets this year, so do your best to go with the flow rather than resist the inevitable. Also be wary and avoid anyone in the workplace who could try to shift blame to you.

Restlessness will be a challenge at times, making it difficult to focus on the current task. Take a few deep breaths or a quick walk to dispel the energy. This will also help take the edge off the tension associated with Uranus in contact with your Sun. Uranus could also prompt the desire to—uncharacteristically—initiate workplace change. That is not the best idea this year as others might feel threatened. Satisfy the urge instead with a productive domestic project.

A pet may require extra attention this year as well as one or several trips to the veterinarian. Think carefully, though, if you want to adopt a pet, because the adjustment will be difficult at best.

Neptune

Neptune in Aquarius, your solar Fourth House of home and family, will contact your Sun before February 3 **if you were born between November 19 and 22**. This will be the third contact; the first and second occurred in the spring and fall of 2011. Relationship matters left unfinished at that time can be concluded now. But you may not fully appreciate and understand the significance of what you've experienced until Neptune leaves this sector. Keep this thought in mind: Neptune is the planet of compassion and spirituality.

During Neptune's final weeks in Aquarius, you'll want to check your home for leaks, and take precautions to prevent pipe breakage if you live in a cold climate. Also consider giving your bathroom a fresh look with paint or wall-covering and new towels.

If you were born between October 22 and 26, Neptune will favorably contact your Sun after it enters Pisces, your solar Fifth House, February 3. You can easily tap into the creativity represented by this mystical planet, which will also inspire you with hope. However, be sure to blend these feelings with your innate Scorpio skepticism rather than let uplifting thoughts become blind faith.

Find a new hobby outlet to express your creativity, or revitalize one from the past. If you're a parent, you may discover a child has a hidden talent that you can nurture. But it will be much easier now for your children to charm you, simply because you'll tend to see and hear what you want to see and hear. And they'll try to convince you to fulfill their every wish and desire.

Neptune will also enhance your mysterious aura, attracting people and giving you the ability to easily adapt and blend in with your environment and those you're with. This can be a real plus in any situation where persuasion is required, including romance. Be cautious with investments, however, because it will be tough to be completely objective.

Pluto

Pluto will contact your Sun from Capricorn, your solar Third House, **if you were born between October 29 and November 1**. This favorable connection will multiply your already significant willpower and determination to change whatever you wish about yourself this year. Get a new look, or polish your public speaking and communication skills.

Pluto's influence this year also include relatives, especially siblings. Make an effort to resolve any longstanding issues with these people, or simply take the time to learn more about them, their current lives, and the depth of their personalities. You also could be a positive force for change in your community, and neighbors will in some way have greater significance in your life.

Learning has a role with Pluto in your solar Third House. Your powers of concentration will be strong and you'll be able to focus and master whatever you study. Just be cautious about letting a new subject of interest become all-consuming.

Although Pluto's influence will be generally positive, its clash with Uranus in June and September could trigger difficulties at work. Power struggles and a communication breakdown are possible. Tread softly and say less rather than more, no matter how you feel. This is not the time to challenge the powers that be. The Uranus-Pluto alignment could also indicate a problem with a pet or one related to a family member or your home. Be sure property or renter's insurance will cover any eventuality.

Scorpio | January

Planetary Lightspots

A vacation, or even a quick weekend trip, would be a nice getaway around the January 9 Full Moon in Cancer, your solar Ninth House. If that's not realistic, use the lunar energy to learn. Visit the library or bookstore, or sign up for a community class to learn a new hobby or advanced computer skills that can benefit your job performance

Relationships

Home, family, and all things domestic will capture your attention under the January 23 New Moon in Aquarius, your solar Fourth House. Enjoy time with loved ones, begin a decorating project, entertain friends, and simply enjoy time in your own space. Romance is also in the forecast if you're part of a couple. Plan a special evening for two around on the 12th or 13th.

Money and Success

Mercury advances in Sagittarius, your solar Second House, through January 7. Use this time to organize financial records, and shred documents you no longer need. Then develop a budget for 2012. Base it on 2011 income and emphasize saving rather than spending. Bank or invest the extra income that should come your way the second half of the year.

Planetary Hotspots

At least one friendship will be rocky as Mars travels retrograde in Virgo, your solar Eleventh House, from January 23 to April 12. The same could apply to any group endeavor you're involved in. Be especially cautious if it's a work-related project. Back off no matter how much you want to take control or how strongly you feel the group is headed in the wrong direction. Anything else could bring repercussions. On another level, take time to think about your job, what you want from it, and whether this is the best place for you.

Rewarding Days

3, 4, 8, 12, 13, 1, 25, 31

Challenging Days

7, 14, 15, 20, 26, 27, 30

Scorpio | February

Planetary Lightspots

Last month's emphasis on domestic life continues with Mercury in Aquarius, your solar Fourth House, through the 12th, and the Sun there until the 19th. Both are great for family talks, and around the 7th and 13th, you can make great progress on a home improvement project or routine tasks. You might even find a long-forgotten treasure if you start digging through boxes.

Relationships

February brings the New Moon in Pisces, your solar Fifth House, on the 21st, and Neptune's arrival in the same sign on the 3rd. Together, they hold much promise for boosting your social life as well as romantic opportunities. Expect a challenge with your children, however, around the 22nd and 24th, when the same could be true of you and a friend. Harmony returns at month's end.

Money and Success

You can command much attention under the February 7 Full Moon in Leo, your solar Tenth House of career and status. The lunar energy aligns favorably with Mercury then, making that week a good choice if you need to schedule a meeting or important talk. People will listen closely to what you say, and a family member's comment could help you solve a tricky problem at work.

Planetary Hotspots

Expect a surprising development at work around the 9th, when Venus aligns with Uranus in Aries, your solar Sixth House. Although you'll feel unsettled, accept that change is inevitable and go with the flow. The following week could bring a power play when Venus clashes with Pluto, and controlling people will be at their worst. Also drive with extra care on your morning and evening commutes.

Rewarding Days

8, 9, 13, 21, 23, 26, 27, 28

Challenging Days

3, 10, 15, 17, 22, 24

Scorpio | March

Planetary Lightspots

Love the one you're with after Venus enters Taurus, your solar Seventh House, March 5. Positive planetary alignments favor togetherness, and you can also use this energy for professional consultations such as with an accountant. If you plan to hire someone new, check references rather than rely solely on a friend's recommendation.

Relationships

The March 8 Full Moon in Virgo, your solar Eleventh House, will boost your social life during the following two weeks. See friends, meet new people. If you're single, the lunar energy could bring a new romantic interest through a friend. But avoid the first few days of March, when conflict is possible even with someone you know well. Find another weekend to socialize.

Money and Success

Expect your workload to pick up as the March 22 New Moon in Aries energizes your solar Sixth House. Although retrograde Mercury will move into Pisces the next day, details still need attention as errors can come to light in late April. The third full week of March is a good choice if you need to schedule an important meeting or presentation.

Planetary Hotspots

Both your solar Fifth and Sixth Houses will be affected by Mercury's retrograde period, which begins March 12. Set aside time to double-check all work output and be sure you fully understand instructions. This period can also bring indecision about projects and misunderstandings on the job. On the 23rd, Mercury retreats into Pisces, where it can trigger mix-ups involving social events and your children's schedules. Confirm dates, times, and places, and clarify your thoughts rather than assume others understand what you're saying.

Rewarding Days

5, 11, 12, 16, 18, 21, 25, 26

Challenging Days

2, 3, 4, 7, 9, 13, 15, 30

Scorpio | April

Planetary Lightspots

Mercury turns direct in Pisces, your solar Fifth House, on the 13th, as Mars does the same in Virgo, your solar Eleventh House. The dual influence will stimulate your social life, so plan ahead to see friends, especially where you can meet other people. If you're single, someone who caught your eye a few months ago could make another appearance.

Relationships

The April 21 New Moon in Taurus, your solar Seventh House, is designed for love and togetherness. Delight in your partner's company, both alone and with friends, and set aside time before month's end for a relaxing evening with talk, laughter, and much more. The lunar energy also favors time with your closest friends. Do lunch and go somewhere fun and different for the day. Make it an adventure.

Money and Success

Mercury returns to Aries, your solar Sixth House, on the 16th, where it could trigger unexpected news. You'll also need to be wary of coworkers who could be talking behind your back. The last week of the month could bring a difficult talk or meeting with someone who's more interested in power and control than progress.

Planetary Hotspots

Venus enters Gemini, your solar Eighth House, April 3. Although this will be a plus for finances later in the month, the first week will be the opposite. Expect extra expenses, possibly involving your children, taxes, a friend, or social event. Avoid the latter, which could be pricey, as well as investments, and don't hesitate to say no to a friend who's looking for a loan.

Rewarding Days

4, 8, 10, 12, 17, 21, 22, 23, 27, 28

Challenging Days

3, 5, 7, 9, 13, 15, 18, 20, 24, 26

Scorpio | May

Planetary Lightspots

You'll attract the attention of many in the two weeks following the May 5 Full Moon in your sign. Among them could be someone who turns out to be your lucky charm, opening a door to money and prestige. Most of all, you'll simply enjoy being with people, especially those closest to you.

Relationships

In addition to the Full Moon, which encourages you to reach out to others, you'll be on the same wavelength with most everyone as Mercury transits Taurus, May 9–23. This planetary influence could bring exciting news the third week of May that calls for a celebration. Couples will be reminded of all the reasons they fell in love, but hold off if you want to take a romantic relationship to the next level. With Venus retrograde, you could change your mind in late June or July. If you're planning a wedding, avoid the retrograde Venus period.

Money and Success

Despite retrograde Venus, the May 5 Full Moon in Gemini, your solar Eighth House, has much potential for financial gain. You or your partner could earn a nice raise or receive a windfall. Venus's status, however, could indicate a delay in receiving the funds. Don't share secrets with coworkers the first week of the month.

Planetary Hotspots

Finances require close attention as Venus in Gemini travels retrograde May 5–June 26. Pay bills early, confirm payments, and be cautious with investments. This is not the time to apply for a loan, sign documents, or enter into a partnership. It is the time to be sure your property and possessions are well insured. If you need to make an insurance claim for a lost valuable, the settlement could be delayed.

Rewarding Days

1, 6, 10, 13 14, 18, 19, 24, 25

Challenging Days

3, 4, 7, 9, 16, 17, 28, 30

Scorpio | June

Planetary Lightspots

Enjoy the final ten days of Jupiter in Taurus, your solar Seventh House of relationships. That's all the reason you need to celebrate togetherness with your partner and to tell all the loved ones in your life how important they are to you. Give hugs and feel the warmth you receive in return.

Relationships

Mars continues to advance in Virgo, your solar Eleventh House. Although not a major influence, it will connect you with friends. Aim for quiet evenings out where you can really talk, especially with your best pal. You'll enjoy these far more than the party scene.

Money and Success

Finances are in high focus this month as lucky Jupiter enters Gemini, your solar Eighth House, on the 11th. You'll also get the benefit of the June 4 Full Moon (lunar eclipse) in Sagittarius, your solar Second House, and the New Moon in Gemini on the 19th. Together, all these influences have the potential to expand your bank account by month's end. Take a chance on the lottery on the 4th and the 19th.

Planetary Hotspots

You'll experience the effects of this month's difficult alignment between Uranus in Aries and Pluto in Capricorn in your solar Third, Sixth, and Ninth Houses. Avoid travel if at all possible, especially near the 11th and 29th. And be very cautious on your daily commute and anytime you're behind the wheel. If you socialize, catch a ride or go with a designated driver. Workplace changes are also likely, which may or may not directly affect you. This is not the time to initiate legal action or to put yourself in a position where that's possible. Be cautious and safe.

Rewarding Days

1, 2, 9, 14, 15, 16, 19, 25, 30

Challenging Days

5, 10, 11, 12, 20, 24, 27, 29

Scorpio | July

Planetary Lightspots

Venus and Jupiter in Gemini, your solar Eighth House, add luck to money matters again this month. You or your mate could gain through a raise or added benefits, which could come in handy as unexpected expenses are also possible. The 21st is a particularly lucky day, so take a chance on the lottery that week.

Relationships

Mars in Libra, your solar Twelfth House, from the 3rd on will trigger both upbeat and challenging discussions with people, as will the Full Moon of the same date. News received around the 11th brings optimism, but the 17th and 18th are more inclined to conflict. Much of this will occur behind the scenes, away from others. Even so, you'll need to use your powerful self-control. Think calm thoughts and say little, no matter how you feel.

Money and Success

Career-related decisions are likely to be delayed or reversed after Mercury turns retrograde in Leo, your solar Tenth House, on the 14th. Projects can also be affected because you'll lack all of the needed information. Patience is your best ally. Limit frustration by letting things evolve in their own time.

Planetary Hotspots

Travel continues to be inadvisable, especially during the first three weeks of the month. Much of this is due to the July 3 Full Moon in Capricorn, which will reactivate last month's difficult planetary alignment. Also avoid controversial topics at work, where more changes are possible. This is not the time to challenge a supervisor or coworker. Be especially cautious near the 3rd and 13th, both on and off the road.

Rewarding Days

7, 8, 11, 12, 14, 21, 27

Challenging Days

4, 9, 10, 13, 17, 18, 24, 30

Scorpio | August

Planetary Lightspots
Family life is at its best under this month's first Full Moon on the 1st, and you might even enjoy spending your vacation days at home this year. With the lunar energy in Aquarius, your solar Fourth House, the time is also ideal for domestic projects and entertaining friends. If you want to host a party, the 3rd and 4th are good choices.

Relationships
Relationships are mostly easygoing this month, especially in your personal life. Again this month, however, there could be challenges with a coworker. Rise above it, knowing you have plenty of support behind you. Later in the month, the August 31 Full Moon in Pisces, spotlights your solar Fifth House. Your children and your own activities will have you on the run in the following two weeks. Plan ahead in order to keep everyone on schedule.

Money and Success
The timing is ideal to clear up any recent career-related mix-ups. When Mercury in Leo, your solar Tenth House, turns direct on the 8th, use the time between then and the New Moon in the same sign on the 17th to be an attention-getter. A promotion is a possibility, as is a job offer, and with a little luck, you could see a bigger paycheck. You'll also have many opportunities to interact with coworkers, both on the job and after hours. Cultivate these ties as they could be invaluable in the future.

Planetary Hotspots
Again this month, you'll have a desire for a change of scenery after Venus enters Cancer, your solar Ninth House, on the 7th. Resist the urge until after the 16th. Before then you could encounter delays and cancellations because of severe weather, as well as an increased chance for lost luggage.

Rewarding Days
3, 4, 9, 14, 18, 19, 22, 23, 31

Challenging Days
6, 7, 13, 16, 20, 21, 26, 28

Scorpio | September

Planetary Lightspots

Your sixth sense will be especially active from the 16th on when Mercury is in Libra, your solar Twelfth House. This can help you sense what's happening in your workplace as well as give you access to confidential information. On another level, you can use this time for meditation or quiet activities, either of which can be an excellent stress reliever. Your dreams could be insightful.

Relationships

Friends and socializing also offer stress relief this month as both the Sun and Mercury spend part of the month in Virgo, which is also the site of the New Moon on the 15th. With all this energy focused on your solar Eleventh House, you'll also enjoy group outings. But be choosy about the people you see. Anyone who hasn't exactly been a true friend in the past is likely to be even less so this month.

Money and Success

This month's planetary alignments favor financial stability, and possibly some extra cash. It could come from an unlikely source, an investment, or an increase in your partner's earnings. This is not the month, however, for major purchases or loan applications.

Planetary Hotspots

Workplace changes are in the forecast as Uranus and Pluto square off again this month. You'll see the first signs of what's on the horizon within a few days of their alignment on the 19th. But difficulties will be most apparent when the Full Moon in Aries on the 29th activates both planets. Challenges with coworkers are also possible, and other changes could involve restructuring or downsizing. Even if this doesn't directly affect you, it could change the scope of your job. Be very careful on your daily commute all month.

Rewarding Days

1, 5, 6, 9, 13, 15, 21, 27, 28

Challenging Days

2, 10, 11, 16, 19, 20, 23, 26, 29

Scorpio | October

Planetary Lightspots

Your social life benefits from Venus in Virgo, your solar Eleventh House, October 3–27. Connect with friends and plan outings where you can meet other people. This is a great opportunity to widen your circle of acquaintances, both at social events and through a community project or organization.

Relationships

The October 29 Full Moon in Taurus, your solar Seventh House, encourages you to reach out to people and to spend quality time with your partner. So even though you're wrapped up in your own activities, make the effort to share yourself with your partner and other loved ones. Earlier in the month, plan a romantic evening for two around the 8th, which is also a good date to entertain friends.

Money and Success

Get ready to invest more of your energy in making money after Mars enters Sagittarius, your solar Second House, on the 6th. Good opportunities to do this could come around the 16th. But keep your budget in mind around the 28th, when you'll have the urge to splurge. Avoid shopping on the 7th. What appears to be a bargain could instead be a poor value and an expensive lesson.

Planetary Hotspots

October 5 is an important date for you. That's when Saturn arrives in your sign, where it will be for the next two and a half years. This is not the time for new endeavors. Rather, it's a time to reflect on what you've achieved as a first step to preparing for the future. Regrets are also a part of this process, but don't let yourself dwell on them. Instead, learn from them. Also make sleep a priority while Saturn is here, and know when to quit. Don't push yourself too hard.

Rewarding Days

2, 3, 8, 12, 16, 21, 24, 30

Challenging Days

1, 4, 7, 9, 20, 27, 31

Scorpio | November

Planetary Lightspots

Despite the effects of retrograde Mercury, you'll enjoy time in the spotlight, thanks to this month's New Moon (solar eclipse) in your sign on the 13th. Use the days between the New Moon and the 26th, when Mercury turns direct, to reflect on the past twelve months and what you want to accomplish in the next year. Then you'll be set to go at month's end, ready to make your mark on the world.

Relationships

Some relationships benefit from Mars in Capricorn, your solar Third House, from the 16th on. Others, however, require careful handling. Avoid touchy subjects on the 3rd and 23rd, especially with coworkers and siblings, and the next day is a good choice if you need to make a strong but congenial point with someone.

Money and Success

Your or your partner's income could get a boost from the November 28 Full Moon (lunar eclipse) in Gemini, your solar Eighth House. Also use the lunar energy to establish a firm holiday budget within limits, even if you can afford more. You'll find it surprisingly easy because the two of you will be on the same wavelength.

Planetary Hotspots

Mercury travels retrograde for the final time this year, from the 6th to the 25th. It begins in Sagittarius, your solar Second House, and retreats into your sign on the 14th before resuming direct motion on the 26th. Mix-ups will center around money matters while Mercury is in Sagittarius, so be sure to check statements for errors and then be sure all payments are received on time. Avoid major purchases, credit applications, and contract signing. Be prepared to be frustrated at times when Mercury is in your sign. Personal plans won't unfold as expected and others will stall. Patience is the lesson.

Rewarding Days

4, 8, 20, 21, 22, 27

Challenging Days

3, 5, 10, 16, 18, 23

Scorpio | December

Planetary Lightspots

You'll be among the most popular guests at holiday social events. For this you can thank Mercury in your sign through the 9th, and Venus there through the 14th. Both will take your natural charm and charisma to a higher level, which will intrigue and attract many. You'll also be able to stay a step ahead of just about everyone as Mercury sharpens your focus and your thinking.

Relationships

Workplace relationships will be challenging at times, particularly later in the month. Refuse to engage in debate or to be pulled into a power struggle. If you can convince others to listen, which is iffy at best, they'll benefit from your knowledge and experience. Scorpio couples will have many reasons to celebrate their love this month, but if you're single, remember that first impressions can be off base. The reality may be far different from the illusion.

Money and Success

Money flows your direction in the weeks following the December 13 New Moon in Sagittarius, your solar Second House. Splurge a little on gifts for loved ones while remaining true to your budget, and also treat yourself to something on your wish list.

Planetary Hotspots

As at other times during the year, this month's planetary alignments caution against travel, and emphasize the need to drive with extra care. This especially applies to the days surrounding the December 28 Full Moon in Cancer, your solar Ninth House. Weather-related delays and cancellations are possible, so the best choice might be to stay home for the holidays. If you want to visit relatives, schedule the trip to avoid the last week or so of December and the first few days of January.

Rewarding Days

1, 2, 5, 10, 15, 19, 24, 29

Challenging Days

3, 4, 7, 20, 28, 30

Scorpio Action Table

These dates reflect the best—but not the only—times for success and ease in these activities, according to your Sun sign.

	JAN	FEB	MAR	APR	MAY	JUN	JUL	AUG	SEP	OCT	NOV	DEC
Move	28-31	1-12			11, 12							
Start a class	8-19									20		
Join a club					8, 9				1-15			
Ask for a raise				29					21			
Look for work							24, 28	16, 20				
Get pro advice									5			
Get a loan				24						15		
See a doctor										15		
Start a diet				19								
End relationship							12		4, 5			
Buy clothes								31	1			
Get a makeover								22		16		
New romance		21, 22										10
Vacation						20-25		24-31	1-5			

SAGITTARIUS

The Archer
November 21 to December 21

Element: Fire

Quality: Mutable

Polarity: Yang/Masculine

Planetary Ruler: Jupiter

Meditation: I can take time to explore my soul

Gemstone: Turquoise

Power Stones: Lapis lazuli, azurite, sodalite

Key Phrase: I understand

Glyph: Archer's arrow

Anatomy: Hips, thighs, sciatic nerve

Color: Royal blue, purple

Animal: Fleet-footed animals

Myths/Legends: Athena, Chiron

House: Ninth

Opposite Sign: Gemini

Flower: Narcissus

Key Word: Optimism

Your Strengths and Challenges

Sagittarius is the adventurer of the zodiac, and each day brings new horizons to explore in your perpetual quest for truth and knowledge. Thus, travel is a high priority for many Sagittarians, while others prefer mental journeys to expand their worldview. What you seek is not just information but understanding. The questions intrigue you—everything from how the pyramids were built to the psychology of human nature. But as open-minded as you are, at times you're just the opposite and quick to judge something as pure nonsense rather than listen objectively to other opinions.

You're optimistic and outgoing, enthusiastic about life and your daily pursuits. With expansive Jupiter as your ruling planet, more is nearly always better in your mind. If only life weren't so short! Jupiter is also the planet of luck, which most Sagittarians have in abundance. You could win the lottery; however, your good fortune is linked more to opportunities and your knack for spotting and seizing them. Just be sure to put your idealism on hold and look at the realistic facts before jumping in.

You're generous and sincere, friendly and confident. But you also can be blunt and speak the plain truth when a more tactful approach is needed. Learn to soften your message with kind and supportive words that will endear you to others and advance your aims.

Your Relationships

You're popular with friends, coworkers, and just about everyone you meet. They're attracted to your sense of humor, and you have a sixth sense about what makes people tick. As much as you enjoy your wide social circle, you treasure your best friends and would find life incomplete without them. These are the people you share your inner feelings with, the ones who are always there for you, as you are for them. You prefer going places and doing things with a friend to spending leisure-time alone. Love grows out of friendship for many Sagittarians who need and want a mate who's also a best friend.

You delight in playing the field, and to you, love, like life, is an adventure to be explored to the fullest. You're passionate and spontaneous, and can fall in and out of love in a flash—at least until you meet someone who's as lively and free spirited as you are. Mental rapport is also a must, and you bypass anyone who doesn't share your thirst for knowledge and information. You could feel the zing of true love with Gemini, your opposite sign, and Sagittarius is compatible with the other air signs, Libra and Aquarius. Fiery Aries and Leo have much in common with you, but Virgo and Pisces are likely to lack the spontaneity you desire.

You have a strong spiritual connection with family, even the people you're not particularly close to, and strive for a home life that's peaceful and serene—the place where you can escape the stresses and strains of daily life. Ocean colors can help you achieve this goal. As a parent, you're actively involved in your children's lives, pushing them to succeed in everything from sports to school. But consistency can be a challenge, so remind yourself to deliver the same values-based message day in and day out. Your children will benefit from it and both you and they will doubly enjoy those moments when you give in and spoil them.

Your Career and Money

You're likely to change careers at least once during your lifetime and probably several times. With so many interests, skills, and talents, it's only natural to expect your career life to evolve to keep pace with your ever-increasing knowledge. You're a natural teacher even if that's not your profession. So you need the flexibility in your career to share what you know, formally or informally. But you should also take care not to lose sight of the big picture. The search for the perfect career, which doesn't exist for you or anyone else, can encourage you to leap from one to another. Try to limit major shifts in career direction to those that will contribute to lifetime success. A comfortable, stable work environment is a must. And despite your energy, you're happiest in a job where you can work at your own pace, handling each task thoroughly and completely. A high-pressure job isn't the best option for you.

You can stretch a dollar further than most people when necessary. An extravagant spender at times, and conservative at others, the sooner you learn to save and invest for the long term, the greater your wealth potential. Doing this will also minimize the impact of tight financial periods because you'll have savings to fall back on. Home-ownership could net you sizeable gains, and you might also receive a family legacy. If you're handy, you could profit from owning rental properties.

Your Lighter Side

Although you're known for your adventuresome, action-oriented approach to life, you're also a lover of peace and harmony who's far more sensitive than most people realize. This, plus your understanding of human nature, makes you a fine negotiator and consensus-builder. You want people to get along and thus emphasize cooperation and compromise, both of which can also advance your personal goals.

Affirmation for the Year

People are my pathway to the future.

The Year Ahead for Sagittarius

People will have a prominent place in your life this year as several planets highlight your friendship, partnership, and family sectors. The universe will encourage you to assess your own life, your goals, your career direction, and what you value most in yourself and in others.

The year begins with Jupiter, your ruling planet, in Taurus. As it transits your solar Sixth House through June 10, you can gain great satisfaction from your job. It will fulfill your need to be of service to others while establishing a niche of your own. Relationships with coworkers will be generally upbeat, partly because of your enthusiastic optimism. You could earn a nice raise, but don't expect a promotion. All of this motivation could prompt you to take on additional tasks. That's okay as long as you balance it with time for yourself and the people in your life. This will promote wellness, as will exercise and a healthy diet. Plan ahead so you're less tempted to eat fast food on the run.

Jupiter advances into Gemini, your solar Seventh House, June 11. During the following twelve months, relationships will be an ongoing theme in your life, and you'll connect with a wide variety of people. They'll fill your life with everything from luck to laughter to opportunities. At times, it will be tough to schedule dates with all those you want to see and who want to see you. This Jupiter transit is among the best for couples, as well as those looking for a mate. Most of all, though, you'll simply enjoy the company of the ones you're with.

Saturn spends much of the year in Libra, your solar Eleventh House, before beginning its two-and-a-half year transit of Scorpio. In Libra, Saturn focuses its energy on friendship and groups, both of which will be learning experiences for you. Some friendships may fall by the wayside as you realize their lives no longer mesh well with yours. New people will arrive to take their places, and some of these will arrive for a purpose: to teach you something, to motivate you, or to provide a networking connection.

A teamwork setting through your job or an organization can help you polish your leadership skills, and you could be asked to take on such a role. Be careful. With Saturn here you could find yourself doing all the work, either because people believe or expect you will or because you feel you're the only one who can do things right. Get past this. Part of Saturn's lesson is to learn to share the load.

The Eleventh House is also your sector of hopes and wishes, goals and objectives. Give some thought to this and make a wish list. Pare it down to what you can realistically accomplish by this year and then set your plan in motion.

Saturn moves on to Scorpio, your solar Twelfth House, October 5. This influence is quite different from your Eleventh House, as this sector represents self-renewal, the hidden side of life, and secrets. It also represents institutions such as hospitals, as well as humanitarian organizations and activities, which you may want to support.

Saturn's purpose here is to encourage you to look inward, to examine your life: what you've accomplished and what you hope to do in the future. This is all in preparation for several years from now when Saturn will enter your sign. Regrets are likely to emerge in your thoughts. Recognize them and move on, appreciating where you are today. To dwell on them is to take a step backward. Similarly, you're likely to realize you have issues related to people and events from the past. Make every effort to resolve these as well, even if only in your own mind. Self-help books can be invaluable in this process.

This is the time to complete unfinished projects. Look around your house, room by room, and find all those things you put off until another day—personal projects, hobby projects, home improvement projects—and while you're at it, discard or recycle unwanted items and those that are no longer useful. Your to-do list could be long or short, or somewhere in between. Whatever it is, get started. You have until 2015 to complete it all.

During Saturn's time in Scorpio, you also could volunteer your time and talents for a good cause, which could be a great learning experience and one that brings you countless intangible rewards. It's also possible that at some point during Saturn's transit you'll be involved in the care of a relative.

Uranus continues to move through Aries, your solar Fifth House, where it will be until 2018. You can successfully combine creativity and invention in leisure-time interests, hobbies, and projects, and might even develop a new technique or employ a new approach in gardening, computer graphics, sports, or something else. This is also a great influence for team sports such as a softball league. You can be sure your evenings and weekends will be filled with many activities, including socializing and romance. If you're single, you'll enjoy dating but might be reluctant to settle on one romantic interest. Uranus is after all the ultimate planet of independence.

If you're a parent, your children will surprise you as they reveal hidden talents and interests. Get involved in their activities. Don't be a stage parent, though. If you have teens, you'll want to keep a close eye on them and maintain rules without being overly restrictive. They will assert their independence in ways you cannot begin to imagine.

This Uranus transit can trigger your sixth sense in the form of hunches. Use them to advantage, but be careful if you plan to invest. With the planet of the unexpected involved, sizeable losses are as possible as gains. Be conservative.

Neptune in Aquarius completes its trip through your solar Third House on February 2. Since 1998, when Neptune first entered this sign, you've experienced its influence on communication, sibling relationships, and learning. This creative planet has surely helped you to think this way, coming up with ideas that have amazed even you. It may also have enhanced your intuition and helped you sense what other people were thinking but not saying.

Neptune begins its next journey February 3, the date it enters Pisces and your solar Fourth House. Here it will focus on home, family, and all things domestic. At some point during this long transit, which lasts until 2025, you'll get the urge to redecorate a few rooms or your entire home. Add a water feature, such as a fountain, which can surround you with calming energy. Be aware of the possibility for pipe or appliance leaks.

Family communication will reflect Neptune's reputation for confusion as well as inspiration, and at times it will be difficult to understand the intention behind the words. Sometimes it will be honorable, and sometimes not. With this transit you have an opportunity to sort through family and childhood issues. Careful thought could lead you to the realization that although these issues have in some way shaped your life, you don't have to take ownership of what you didn't create. In the process, you can become more compassionate and accepting.

Pluto continues in Capricorn, your solar Second House, emphasizing a conservative financial approach even though gains can come as easily as losses. With Pluto, though, it's wise to play it safe. Take a close look at your financial attitudes and habits. If you find them lacking, or not as effective as they should be, Pluto's transformative powers can help you make necessary changes. Don't hesitate. Do it. Otherwise, Pluto could trigger events that will force the change. Save, invest for the long term, and do all you can to maximize income. Also be sure your possessions and property are fully insured as this is not the time to gamble.

Pluto also urges you to clearly define (or redefine) your values, both personal ethics and your attitudes about possessions. Ask yourself some thought-provoking questions about what is most important in your life, and examine your materialistic views. The answers could surprise you, and you could discover that things are not nearly as valuable as your skills, talents, and relationships.

What This Year's Eclipses Mean for You
There are four eclipses this year, two solar and two lunar. Together, they highlight your solar First, Seventh, and Twelfth Houses, emphasizing you, your relationships, and self-renewal. Each is in effect for six to twelve months.

The first eclipse of 2012 is May 21 in Gemini, the sign that Jupiter, your ruling planet, will enter June 11. Later in the year, on November 28, a lunar eclipse will shine brightly in the same sign. This makes relationships a strong theme in 2012, along with the opportunity to greatly expand your circle. If you're in a couple relationship, get ready for a memorable year of love, romance, and togetherness. But if someone captures your heart, it might be best to wait until summer 2013 before making a commitment decision. The same applies if you're interested in forming a business partnership. What initially looks good could turn into a very expensive mistake.

The year's first lunar eclipse is in your sign on June 4. You'll be an attention-getter and a popular guest. But this eclipse is also about relationships, so your aim should be to learn more about human nature as you interact with others. In turn, you'll also gain new insights into yourself and how you approach relationships.

November 13 will bring the second solar eclipse of 2012. Placed in Scorpio, your solar Twelfth House, it will reinforce the message of Saturn, which enters Scorpio on October 5. Together, Saturn and the eclipse can empower you to look more deeply into what motivates you and why you are the way you are. Use it to access your subconscious.

Saturn

If you were born between December 12 and 21, Saturn will favorably contact your Sun from Libra, your solar Eleventh House. You'll experience Saturn's influence June or July **if your birthday is December 12, 13, or 14.** For other birthdays, Saturn will connect with your Sun between January and May, and again in August or September.

Transiting your solar Eleventh House, Saturn can bring seemingly endless meetings, at times surrounded by much indecision, but also dynamic interaction with people and groups in both your personal life and job. Your challenge will be to keep others on track and to lead by example, with every group member contributing a fair share of work. Job-related teamwork projects can enhance your value to the company and give you valuable experience that will pay off in future years. You can be just as effective in a leadership position with a professional organization or one that supports a good cause. Saturn will also give you extra stamina and determination, as well as patience.

You'll take friendships more seriously as Saturn contacts your Sun from Libra. Some of these relationships will deepen, but you'll drift away from others, primarily because you no longer have much in common. You might also form strong ties with a mentor, someone who can advise you on life and your career. This could be an older person, or someone with much experience that can beneficial to you. Even if not a mentor, you may form a fond friendship with an elderly person this year, possibly a neighbor or a friend of a relative.

If your birthday is between November 21 and December 1, Saturn will connect with your Sun after it enters Scorpio October 5. Placed in your solar Twelfth House, Saturn will encourage self-understanding through introspection. This is the first step in this process, which will come full circle in 2013 when Saturn again contacts your Sun. You'll also want to spend more time alone, which can be both positive and negative. While it will give you the opportunity to reach into your subconscious, you will gain as much if not more from being with people and long talks with your partner or best friend.

You should also consider getting involved in a charitable organization or another similar activity that would benefit from your supportive efforts. This too will add to your self-understanding as it widens and deepens your perspective of life, people, and today's world. You could reap the greatest satisfaction from involvement in a community project, both hands-on and raising funds to advance the cause.

Uranus

Uranus in Aries, your solar Fifth House, will contact your Sun **if you were born between November 21 or 30**. This favorable alignment with your Sun gives you all the tools necessary to initiate positive, lasting change. You can remake yourself almost any way you choose, whether your goal is a firmer body, a new look, a new skill, or a healthier diet. Your ideas will be innovative, and a flash of insight could encourage you to develop a latent talent. A chance encounter could trigger a fabulous love-at-first-sight romance, or you might suddenly discover that a friend is the partner you've been searching for. If you're part of a couple, surprise your partner from time to time with an impromptu night of romance.

Expect the unexpected from your children, whatever their age. If you have youngsters, do all you can to encourage them to explore their interests. This could reveal a hidden talent that's well worth nurturing. Teens, however, could be a major challenge at times because they'll want an unreasonable level of freedom and independence. So it's wise to get to know their friends and to monitor their activities, both on- and off-line. Take swift action if necessary, rather than hope for the best, and view this as an opportunity to both teach and learn from your children. Listen closely to what they say and keep an open mind. You may ultimately gain more from the experience than they do. It's also possible you could have an unexpected addition to the family.

Neptune

If your birthday is December 19, 20, or 21, Neptune will contact your Sun from Aquarius, your solar Third House, before it advances into Pisces February 3. This is the final contact to your Sun, the first having occurred in 2011. Reflect on last year's events, especially those involving siblings and neighbors, and what you learned from interacting with people. The creative thinking and intuition you developed will stay with you, but the periodic confusion and disappointment in others will be left behind as Neptune enters a new phase.

If you were born between November 21 and 25, Neptune will contact your Sun from Pisces, your solar Fourth House of home and family. On a practical level, your home could suffer damage from a leaky pipe or appliance, or from severe weather. Flooding is possible, so be sure you have adequate homeowner's or renter's insurance. Check your policy. Read the fine print.

Communication with some family members will be difficult and confusing at times. You'll also find it tough to understand their perspective and grasp their motivations. Be cautious if you're looking for a roommate, which isn't the best idea this year. Someone who appears to be a perfect fit could turn out to be far different from your perception.

This transit is also about you and your identity. Family and childhood are key components here, and you can learn much about yourself by examining their influence on your life, personality, needs, goals, and desires. This will help you to replace disillusionment with faith and inspiration. You may lack direction or goals under this transit. If so, be patient. This too is part of the Neptune-Sun contact. Question why, explore the issue, and begin your quest for answers this year, knowing that you'll find the solution in 2013. Then your new direction will emerge. For all these reasons, it's wise to postpone major life decisions rather than push yourself to get back on track. Take note of your dreams. They can be insightful.

Pluto

If you were born between November 29 and December 1, money matters will be in the forefront as Pluto contacts your Sun from Capricorn, your solar Second House. Expenses may rise and income fall, so do all you can to build up savings.

The Second House is also about possessions and what you value. Both will be prominent themes in your life this year and you'll be motivated to clean out junk, restore order, and eliminate what is no longer useful. Sell the best at a yard sale or consignment shop, and donate the rest to a good cause. Clearing your space will bring fresh energy into your home and mind, and bring you great satisfaction. This is a very positive use of Pluto's transformative power.

However, Pluto will clash with Uranus in Aries in June and September, with both planets contacting your Sun. The alignment could trigger extra expenses involving your children, the need for a new vehicle, or severe weather that damages your home. Avoid investments or other speculative ventures, especially those you believe, or that someone tells you, are a sure thing. You also could find yourself in a power struggle with a relative or one of your children.

As difficult as the Uranus-Pluto contact can be, it will ultimately result in positive change and a sense of freedom never before experienced. View it as a growth opportunity and one of enlightenment that can strengthen your faith in yourself and the close relationships in your life.

Sagittarius | January

Planetary Lightspots

Here, there, and everywhere sums up your life under the January 23 New Moon in Aquarius, your solar Third House. The daily pace will be hectic but also satisfying, and you can be an effective communicator in your job. But stop short of overloading yourself with too many projects or commitments. Enthusiasm is great as long as you recognize your limits.

Relationships

Venus in Aquarius through January 13 adds an extra level of charisma as it helps you promote your ideas and viewpoints. This is especially favorable in job-related meetings and talks, and you'll connect with some people who can be excellent networking contacts. Family ties get a boost after Venus moves on to Pisces, your solar Fourth House, on the 14th. Treat loved ones to a special evening at month's end.

Money and Success

Your attention will focus on money matters as the January 9 Full Moon in Cancer highlights your solar Eighth House of joint resources. Use this lunar energy to create a budget for the year ahead and include a savings goal as well as a plan to pay down debt, if necessary. If you're part of a couple, include your partner in financial discussions. Joint resources benefit from mutual decisions.

Planetary Hotspots

Expect career-related delays and frustration at times as Mars travels retrograde in Virgo, your solar Tenth House, January 23 to April 12. Take care not to assert yourself too much, though, as this could create difficulties with a supervisor. This is a time instead to focus on daily tasks, which you'll enjoy, and to postpone any plans to elevate your position or status. Good things will come if you're patient.

Rewarding Days

10, 11, 15, 18, 19, 23, 24, 27, 29, 30

Challenging Days

1, 2, 6, 7, 13, 14, 16, 20, 22, 26

Sagittarius | February

Planetary Lightspots

Family ties are upbeat this month, thanks to Neptune's arrival in Pisces, your solar Fourth House, February 3, and the New Moon in the same sign on the 21st. Plan some fun family activities, and also set aside time to connect with relatives, who will appreciate hearing from you. If you want to host a get-together for friends, aim for the 11th or 25th. These dates are also favorable for domestic projects.

Relationships

Relationships benefit from the February 7 Full Moon in Leo, opposite the Sun in Aquarius, spanning your solar Ninth-Third House axis. You could hear from someone from the past, possibly an old school friend, mid-month. Use the same timing if you need to call customer service about an appliance or rebate, or to search online for a better price for upcoming vacation travel.

Money and Success

Last month's career-related challenges continue as several planets clash with retrograde Mars in Virgo, your solar Tenth House. Conflict is more likely to erupt early in February and again during the last full week of the month, so be aware and do your best to stay out of it. You'll also feel pushed this month to generate high output, which can increase your overall stress level. Erase the day with moderate exercise, a favorite hobby, a book, or video.

Planetary Hotspots

A dating relationship or friendship could end around the 9th or 15th as Venus in Aries, your solar Fifth House, forms difficult planetary alignments. Money and values could be the trigger, or you might suddenly realize life is too short to try to maintain a less than satisfying relationship. The same dates could bring an unexpected expense related to your children.

Rewarding Days
2, 6, 11, 16, 19, 20, 25

Challenging Days
3, 4, 15, 22, 24

Sagittarius | March

Planetary Lightspots

You'll be among the favored few after Venus enters Taurus, your solar Sixth House, March 5. Positive planetary alignments signal good news mid-month, including a possible raise. Or you could be asked to take charge of an important project.

Relationships

Despite retrograde Mercury, March favors socializing and romance. Just plan ahead so you don't miss out on an opportunity to see friends and meet someone new. If you're part of a couple, plan a special evening for two after the March 22 New Moon in Aries spotlights your solar Fifth House. Also set aside evening or weekend hours for your children and your favorite leisure-time interests.

Money and Success

You'll be an attention-getter under the March 8 Full Moon in Virgo, which shines brightly in your solar Tenth House. Although this influence complements Venus in Taurus, you'll need to get past the first few days of March in order to reap its benefits. Before then, conflict with a supervisor could bring a setback. Keep thoughts to yourself.

Planetary Hotspots

Confirm dates, places, and times for social events after Mercury turns retrograde in Aries, your solar Fifth House, March 12. You can also expect mix-ups involving your children's activities and homework, and this is not the time for investment decisions. Retrograde Mercury retreats into Pisces, your solar Fourth House, on the 23rd, when it could trigger an appliance problem or the need for a home repair. Postpone home improvement projects until late April.

Rewarding Days

1, 5, 6, 12, 14, 16, 18, 23, 26

Challenging Days

3, 9, 10, 13, 15, 20, 27, 30

Sagittarius | April

Planetary Lightspots

Relief arrives in the form of Mercury and Mars turning direct on the 13th. Although it will take a couple of weeks to iron out any mix-ups that occurred during the retrograde periods, you'll gradually see things begin to come together on the domestic scene and in your career. Be glad for the progress and look forward to more.

Relationships

Friendship is in the spotlight as the April 6 Full Moon in Libra shines on your solar Eleventh House. Make plans to see friends and also to take your kids to a sporting event or museum. With Mercury in Aries from the 16th on, you could encounter a former friend or romantic interest. Move on while remembering all the reasons you're no longer together.

Money and Success

Your work life will be stimulating and upbeat under the April 21 New Moon in Taurus, your solar Sixth House. You could even earn some extra money and well-deserved recognition. If a new job is your goal, submit your resume the day after the New Moon.

Planetary Hotspots

Tension could surround a close relationship within days of Venus's arrival in Gemini, your solar Seventh House. The issue is likely to be focused on the need to balance career ambitions with family time. You also could have difficulties with someone at work over what is essentially a misunderstanding. Convincing anyone of that, however, will be a challenge.

Rewarding Days
1, 2, 10, 12, 14, 17, 19, 22, 25, 28

Challenging Days
3, 5, 7, 9, 13, 15, 16, 23, 24, 26

Sagittarius | May

Planetary Lightspots

The May 5 Full Moon in Scorpio, your solar Twelfth House, offers the ideal opportunity to briefly step out of the social whirl in order to focus on some of your other interests. You'll also value time alone and a chance to catch up on sleep. Dreams can be insightful with this lunar influence and your sixth sense unusually active.

Relationships

Despite Venus's retrograde status, the New Moon (solar eclipse) in Gemini on the 20th is one of the best of the year for relationships. If you're in a serious dating relationship, however, hold off if you want to take things to the next level. Your feelings could change after Venus resumes direct motion, and in any case, weddings are inadvisable during the retrograde period. Month's end could bring a few challenging days with a supervisor, and you and a friend could disagree in early May. Say little rather than aggravate the situation.

Money and Success

Your work life continues to be on the upswing as Mercury in Taurus, your solar Sixth House, stimulates ideas, optimism, and enthusiasm. Look for a chance to casually connect with a decision-maker the second week of May. You could hear good news around the 22nd, but be sure you can handle the extra work if you're offered an opportunity to do more.

Planetary Hotspots

Tactful words are even more important while Venus is retrograde in Gemini, your solar Seventh House, May 15–June 26. Listen closely in conversation, especially with your partner and other loved ones, and be aware of body language. Then you can quickly clarify your comments, if necessary.

Rewarding Days

4, 8, 11, 12, 17, 20, 22, 26, 27, 31

Challenging Days

3, 9, 13, 21, 28, 29, 30

Sagittarius | June

Planetary Lightspots

You could hear good news from an out-of-town friend or relative after Mercury enters Leo, your solar Ninth House, on the 25th. But there's no reason to wait for others to contact you. Call or e-mail your favorite people and catch up on all the latest.

Relationships

Jupiter enters Gemini, your solar Seventh House, on the 11th, to begin its year-long emphasis on relationships. You'll connect with many people, and many of them will bring you luck as they fill your life with optimism and good cheer. And you'll do the same for others. Take note of the days surrounding the New Moon in Gemini on the 19th, as well as the 27th, when Venus in the same sign turns direct. Both will offer clues to what you can expect as the next twelve months unfold. Some Sagittarians will fall in love, and others will form beneficial partnerships.

Money and Success

Career motivation is strong under the June 4 Full Moon (lunar eclipse) in your sign, which aligns with Mars in Virgo, your solar Tenth House. Forge ahead, but slow down enough so you don't miss important details.

Planetary Hotspots

Financial challenges could be triggered by a difficult alignment of Uranus in Aries and Pluto in Capricorn. Unexpected expenses are again possible involving your children, and you should steer clear of investments. This is also not the month to apply for a loan. Protect valuables, especially your credit cards and other financial information. Check credit reports and take swift action if you find errors, and be sure your property and possessions are well covered by insurance. All of these precautions are wise and can help prevent loss.

Rewarding Days

7, 8, 13, 17, 19, 22, 23, 26

Challenging Days

5, 6, 10, 11, 12, 20, 24, 27, 29

Sagittarius | July

Planetary Lightspots

Venus and Jupiter in Gemini, your solar Seventh House, accent love, romance, and togetherness for couples. If you're single, a new romantic interest could appear at the least expected moment around the 5th or 20th. But let things develop at their own pace. It may or may not last.

Relationships

Some other relationships in your life won't be nearly so positive. You and a friend could have major issues near the 17th when you realize your values are quite different. The best choice is probably to move on because the chances of repairing the friendship are slim. It might be wise to monitor your children's online activities this month and also to get to know their friends.

Money and Success

Expenses rise again when the July 3 Full Moon in Capricorn, your solar Second House, activates Uranus and Pluto. This will ease somewhat after the New Moon in Cancer on the 19th in your solar Eighth House. But your budget will still be tight, so you'll need to monitor spending all month. You could get lucky, though, with Uranus involved. Try the lottery in the few days around the New Moon, and remember it only takes one ticket to win.

Planetary Hotspots

You'll have to contend with retrograde Mercury from the 14th on. Although generally not more than a minor irritation, this time Mercury changes direction in Leo, your solar Ninth House. This can trigger delays, cancellations, and lost luggage if you travel. For students, it will be all too easy to forget or misplace an assignment, and to include incorrect information. Check the details.

Rewarding Days

1, 5, 6, 10, 14, 16, 20, 25

Challenging Days

2, 3, 17, 18, 24, 30, 31

Sagittarius | August

Planetary Lightspots

You'll be quite content to spend more time at home when this month's second Full Moon, August 31 in Pisces, shines brightly in your solar Fourth House. You can also take advantage of this period to get caught up on all those domestic tasks you intended to do this summer. If you want to host a party, the September 3 holiday is a good choice for a final outdoor get-together.

Relationships

Life will be hectic and you'll be on the go and on the phone in the two weeks following the August 1 Full Moon in Aquarius, your solar Third House. The more people you connect with, the better, because someone you encounter could be your lucky charm. You'll also delight in the company of your partner. If you can manage the time, take off on a romantic getaway to a nearby destination.

Money and Success

Use the days after the Sun enters Virgo, your solar Tenth House, on the 22nd to lay the groundwork for career achievements in September. Month's end could bring an opportunity to talk with someone important who could be your ally. But this is not the time to ask for a raise. The odds shift more in your favor if you wait until next month.

Planetary Hotspots

Money matters are in focus again this month with yet more unexpected expenses possible. This could be connected with a trip, which isn't the best idea, especially if you plan to travel with friends. But with beneficial Venus in Cancer, your solar Eighth House, from the 7th on, the challenges will be manageable. And once past mid-month, Venus could actually help you make up any financial shortfall.

Rewarding Days
2, 11, 12, 14, 17, 25, 29, 30

Challenging Days
6, 13, 20, 21, 24, 26, 28

Sagittarius | September

Planetary Lightspots

Venus in Leo, your solar Ninth House, gives you an outlet when you need to get away from it all. Take a day trip, see a movie, or escape into the pages of a good book with the goal of in some way expanding your knowledge.

Relationships

Your partner will be especially supportive this month, and you can easily seek the information you need by talking with people. Do your own research, however, if you need to hire a professional such as an accountant or financial advisor. A relative's or friend's recommendation could be off-base and even detrimental. Ignore the pressure and pleas of anyone who looks to you for a loan or to cosign for one.

Money and Success

Your career and worldly status are high points this month, thanks to Mercury in Virgo, your solar Tenth House, through the 15th, the date of the New Moon in the same sign. A promotion or job offer is as possible as a raise or bonus. Do all you can to impress decision-makers, especially during the first two weeks of September.

Planetary Hotspots

Uranus and Pluto form an exact alignment this month, on the 19th, when matters related to this summer's financial stress will again be active. The events will peak at month's end as the September 29 Full Moon in Aries activates both planets. Challenges could involve your children or a friend, or your children's friends. If you have teens, expect them to assert their independence to a greater or lesser degree. Above all, continue to monitor your children's online activities as well as who their friends are, and be ready to take action if necessary.

Rewarding Days

3, 7, 12, 13, 17, 21, 25, 30

Challenging Days

2, 10, 11, 16, 19, 20, 23, 29

Sagittarius | October

Planetary Lightspots

Your popularity continues to rise this month, thanks to Venus in Virgo, your solar Tenth House, October 3–27. Enjoy the praise and recognition, but also keep things in perspective. The second week of October could bring an opportunity to connect with someone important who could be a valuable ally at month's end.

Relationships

Fun and friendship mix beautifully in the weeks following the October 15 New Moon in Libra, your solar Eleventh House. A serious talk with a friend around the 5th can help you resolve regrets and inspire you to envision a bright future. You and your mate will be on the same wavelength much of the month, with the 10th being a high point for love, romance, and togetherness. But don't believe everything you hear from a family member at month's end.

Money and Success

You'll be wrapped up in work during the weeks following the October 29 Full Moon in Taurus, your solar Sixth House. So much so that you'll feel cut off from the world at times. Counteract this with quality time with friends and family. It will be fun and a good stress-reliever even if you think not.

Planetary Hotspots

You'll have all the initiative and energy you need to accomplish most anything after Mars advances into your sign on the 6th. That's a good thing. But you'll be more impatient than usual, and short-tempered at times. Mars here can also trigger accidents just because you're in a hurry. Take care in the kitchen, on the road, and when working with tools, as well as when working out or playing sports. And be sure to calm your mind before bedtime so you can get the rest you need.

Rewarding Days

5, 6, 10, 19, 22, 28, 30

Challenging Days

1, 4, 7, 11, 14, 20, 31

Sagittarius | November

Planetary Lightspots

The November 13 New Moon (solar eclipse) in Scorpio and retrograde Mercury send the message to retreat briefly from your hectic life to enjoy family time and to catch up on sleep. You can also put the lunar energy to work for you around the house. Organize drawers and closets, and keep an eye out for anything that's been missing for a while. Retrograde Mercury could lead you right to it.

Relationships

Relationships are in the spotlight under the November 28 Full Moon (lunar eclipse) in Gemini, your solar Seventh House. This is a real plus for close relationships, especially romantic moments with your partner. Some Sagittarians will take a dating relationship to the next level. You'll also have plenty of opportunities to see friends as Venus transits your solar Eleventh House through the 20th. However, the 3rd could bring challenges with a friend or romantic interest.

Money and Success

Mars leaves your sign on the 23rd, when it enters Capricorn, your solar Second House. An unexpected expense is possible around the 23rd, but money matters will otherwise benefit from this transit. Earn more. Spend less.

Planetary Hotspots

Your sense of humor will be your greatest asset during this retrograde Mercury period that begins on the 6th and ends on the 26th. Just as life seems to be moving forward, Mercury turns retrograde in your sign before slipping back into Scorpio, your solar Twelfth House, on the 14th. Try not to let the frustration get to you when delays and indecision on the part of others limit your progress. It's actually all to the good. Use the time to review and revise current plans and directions.

Rewarding Days

2, 6, 7, 11, 15, 24, 29

Challenging Days

3, 8, 10, 16, 22, 23

Sagittarius | December

Planetary Lightspots
The universe brings you fresh energy in the form of this month's New Moon in your sign on the 13th. Embrace your new solar year with optimistic enthusiasm and positive change, along with increased faith in you and your skills, talents, and abilities. Someone close to you will be your greatest cheerleader in your new endeavors.

Relationships
You'll be an attention-getter as Venus travels in your sign from the 15th on. And with Mercury there from the 10th to the 30th, you'll have a way with words that will draw people into your orbit. Share your bright ideas and listen to the feedback. You'll gain new insights into yourself, human nature, and the special people in your life. Choose the 15th or 21st if you want to host a holiday get-together.

Money and Success
Mars continues to advance in Capricorn, your solar Second House, through the 25th, where it can bring opportunities to increase earnings, as well as spending. Venus in your sign can also add to your bank account because it enhances your powers of attraction. Wish for what you want and then truly believe it can be yours.

Planetary Hotspots
This year's ongoing financial challenges will require yet more attention as the December 28 Full Moon in Cancer, your solar Eighth House, activates Uranus and Pluto. With luck, however, and a favorable Saturn-Pluto alignment two days before the Full Moon, you could finally bring these matters to a conclusion. Push forward, gather all the information you need, and let your determination prevail.

Rewarding Days
3, 6, 12, 15, 16, 21, 26, 31

Challenging Days
5, 7, 14, 20, 28, 30

Sagittarius Action Table

These dates reflect the best—but not the only—times for success and ease in these activities, according to your Sun sign.

	JAN	FEB	MAR	APR	MAY	JUN	JUL	AUG	SEP	OCT	NOV	DEC
Move			24, 25							1, 2	7–22	
Start a class		2–17					16			5, 6, 7		
Join a club									23–30	1–12		
Ask for a raise	13, 14	28									1	
Look for work					2, 3, 16–20, 30, 31							
Get pro advice					5	28, 29	18, 19					
Get a loan												
See a doctor					24, 25, 30, 31					27		
Start a diet					30, 31							
End relationship						29		18				
Buy clothes		6	25–30	25–30	5, 6, 9, 10							
Get a makeover	28, 29									1		
New romance				30	30							
Vacation					9–11		23–31					10

CAPRICORN

The Goat
December 21 to January 20

♑

Element: Earth

Quality: Cardinal

Polarity: Yin/Feminine

Planetary Ruler: Saturn

Meditation: I know the strength of my soul

Gemstone: Garnet

Power Stones: Peridot, diamond, quartz, black obsidian, onyx

Key Phrase: I use

Glyph: Head of goat

Anatomy: Skeleton, knees, skin

Color: Black, forest green

Animal: Goats, thick-shelled animals

Myths/Legends: Chronos, Vesta, Pan

House: Tenth

Opposite Sign: Cancer

Flower: Carnation

Key Word: Ambitious

Your Strengths and Challenges

Worldly ambition defines you, although many Capricorns don't fully discover their niche in life until reaching their late twenties. But even in childhood, Capricorns feel the urge to in some way make their mark in the world. That's most likely to occur after age forty, when you and your success potential suddenly take off. Being a late bloomer is to your advantage, however, because you get the benefit of years of knowledge and experience, which can help you dash ahead of the competition.

Capricorn is an earth sign, so you're practical, sensible, and patient. You're also responsible and conscientious, and with serious Saturn as your ruling planet, you can be overly cautious when a calculated risk could be a better choice. Start slowly with inconsequential matters. Then you'll feel more at ease when faced with major life decisions.

You're efficient, organized, and thorough, and at times can be intolerant of those who fail to measure up to your high standards. Try to remember that not everyone has your drive and ambition. Some people are content to simply drift through life even though this is beyond your understanding.

Yet for all the caution you exercise in certain situations, decisiveness is one of the strengths associated with your cardinal, action-oriented sign. Your vast storehouse of knowledge and excellent memory give you the ability to quickly weigh the pros and cons in almost any situation. When presented with an opportunity that feels right, nothing holds you back.

Your Relationships

Your practicality extends to dating relationships, where you're attracted to people who are level-headed. You can be so content in a relationship that you're reluctant to move on, preferring the known to the unknown. Although that might be comfortable, you'll need to break out of this pattern in order to find someone who makes your heart zing. When you do, your sensual side emerges along with your flair for romance. You could make an ideal match with Cancer, your opposite sign, which shares your need for emotional and financial security in a warm family setting. The other water signs, Scorpio and Pisces, might interest you, as could your fellow earth signs, Taurus and Virgo. But life with Aries or Libra could be unsettling.

Home life is fast-paced for most Capricorns, with people coming and going and many family activities. But it also comes with a challenge: the need for balance. You can be so focused on your career that you dash home to sleep and dash out to work. Remind yourself that your mate needs quality time and support, and that children grow quickly. You'll also be much happier and more productive when you have a well-rounded lifestyle. As a parent, you're warm and loving but also expect rules to be followed. This no-nonsense attitude is tempered by reasonable expectations, however, and you excel at encouraging your children to explore their interests and creativity within a stable, tradition-based home environment.

Your wide circle of acquaintances includes people who are financially successful and those who can benefit your career. You're also an excellent judge of character and quickly spot people who share your values. Some of these become your closest friends and you'll develop a deep emotional bond with them. Yet these friends don't necessarily know each other. You tend to compartmentalize them because each fulfills a different need in your life.

Your Career and Money

Only those who know you well realize how truly ambitious you are. And that keeps you a step ahead of the competition, because you're able to strategize, plan, and implement your next move—all without tipping your hand. You relate well with supervisors and VIPs and can successfully develop positive give-and-take relationships with those who can further your goals. Although your timing is usually on target, impatience can get the best of you, so step back and rein yourself in when necessary. In your daily work you need a lot of variety, communication, organization, and people contact. When that's in place you can be happy and successful in any work environment. You also need the freedom to multitask and structure your own work in order to keep yourself interested and involved.

You can amass considerable assets as long as your ego doesn't interfere with financial decisions. That's particularly important with investments, credit, and spending because you equate materialism with success. Rely on the same practical approach you use in other areas of your life. Otherwise, and despite your cautious nature, payments could stretch your resources. Although your income and expenses fluctuate somewhat, you can be thrifty and use money and credit to advantage. Capricorns often luck into special deals and other money-saving bargains.

Your Lighter Side

You're a hard worker, but you also know how to relax when you let yourself do that. Tap into your lazy, comfort-loving side and fill some of your evenings and weekends with practical, productive hobbies such as gardening, woodworking, furniture refinishing, and artistic pastimes. Many Capricorns also enjoy photography, movies, and reading fantasy novels.

Affirmation for the Year

Balance and moderation guide my life.

The Year Ahead for Capricorn

This year brings an emphasis on job and career, leisure-time activities, friends, and your community. You'll be involved in all of these and much more, including family life and the domestic scene.

Jupiter highlights the lighter side of life as it transits Taurus, your solar Fifth House, through June 10. Fill your evening and weekend hours with all the fun things you enjoy doing when not pursuing your ambitions. Your social life gets a boost from this transit, and whether you're single or part of a couple, Jupiter could bring you an abundance of romantic moments. Hobbies can bring many satisfying hours, especially those that free your creativity, as can time with your children and their activities. Learn a new sport, join a gym, or get involved in a community sports league. Overall, this transit represents a gift from the universe to kick back a little and enjoy life.

Jupiter will enter Gemini, your solar Sixth House, June 11, to launch an upbeat job year. Work will be especially pleasurable even when it's tough to keep up with it all. Remember this when you're tempted to take on more. Even you can do only so much, and it's more important to deliver top-quality work on time without pushing yourself to the max. The Sixth House is also a wellness sector, so try to maintain all the good leisure-time habits you developed when Jupiter was in Taurus. Exercise will help keep the pounds off when you drive in for fast food because you're too busy to plan ahead.

Saturn changes signs this year, spending the first nine months in Libra, your solar Tenth House, before moving on to Scorpio. Do all you can to make the most of Saturn's final months in your career sector, which represents a significant pinnacle that occurs only every twenty-eight years. You could be offered a promotion this spring or summer, but be sure you fully understand the scope of the job before you accept. It may or may not be the best option to advance your career. You also could send out resumes in June and see what develops.

The Tenth House represents status, so it can be tempting to go after any opportunity solely to improve your presence. The same is true of things. To you, luxury vehicles, top-quality furnishings, a substantial home, and the latest technology are tangible proof of your success. What will serve you better now is hard work, connections with the right people, and exceeding expectations.

Networking will be especially valuable to your career ambitions after Saturn enters Scorpio, your solar Eleventh House, October 5. During the two and a half years that follow, you can widen your circle of career and personal contacts through friends and group activities. This is a great time to get involved in a professional organization or a teamwork environment in your job. Both will put you in touch with new people and give you the opportunity to strengthen some of these ties. But some friends will gradually fade from your life during this transit, primarily because your interests and aims are changing. Others who have more relevance will replace them, and some of these can become life-long friends.

The Eleventh House is also associated with hopes and wishes, goals and objectives. Use this influence to identify your next career goals, as well as your personal and life wish lists. Then you can begin to implement these with the help of those you meet through your job, at social events, and in your community. If you're involved in an organization or a team project at work, you could be asked to accept a leadership role. This can be a rewarding experience, but be sure to share the load rather than do it all yourself. Otherwise, you could quickly become overloaded.

Uranus continues to advance in Aries, the sign it will occupy until 2018. During these years you can expect many domestic changes, including relocation, family members moving in or out, home improvements and possibly significant repairs. The Uranus energy will be strongest in the year it contacts your Sun, although more often than not you'll feel like the domestic scene is in a perpetual state of flux. And it will be, with visitors coming and going, your children's activities, and entertaining friends. Don't be surprised if a periodic strong urge for change has you rearranging furniture or painting a wall. Be cautious, though, with all things electrical and take care not to overload circuits.

Uranus here can also spark an interest in discovering your ancestral roots. Your curiosity could be triggered by the revelation of an old family secret, or an elderly relative's stories. If you dig deeply enough, you'll find plenty that surprises you. But it will also be enlightening, and in some way enhance your independence. A good use of this energy and Jupiter in Taurus the first half of the year would be to organize old family photos and create scrapbooks to be passed on to your children.

Neptune will complete its time in Aquarius, your solar Second House, when it advances into Pisces on February 3. Since Neptune entered Aquarius in 1998, it has influenced your personal resources, including what you value, your income, your spending habits, and your attitude toward debt. Confusion and disillusionment prevailed at times, while at others you were inspired to do more in order to earn more. In all, both the positive and negative experiences were a learning experience in money management that will serve you well in the future. Keep these in mind as you move forward in life.

Neptune will transit Pisces, your solar Third House, until 2025, influencing relationships with siblings and neighbors, and focusing its energy on communication. Creative thinking will be a strength during this time, enhanced by the ability to view situations and events from a slightly different perspective. This will be an asset in problem solving and in sensing what people are thinking but not necessarily saying. But as much as your sixth sense nudges you, it's also important to rely on your notable common sense. Remind yourself that although Neptune is the planet of faith and inspiration, it's also known for illusion and confusion. All of these will color your relationships with siblings and other people you come in contact with on a regular basis.

The Third House is also associated with errands, vehicles, and quick trips. Try to plan occasional weekend getaways or day trips to nearby locations. The change of scenery will refresh your spirit. Be sure to schedule routine maintenance for your vehicle, and don't ignore any suspected problem. It will only get worse, not better. Also take precautions to protect valuables because it will be much easier now to lose things as you dash through your day.

Pluto continues its slow trip through your sign this year, and you'll be influenced by its transformative energy until 2024. As the planet of willpower, you can use Pluto's determination and drive to accomplish almost anything. But step back periodically and view your mission from a wider perspective. Otherwise, what is potentially positive could become obsessively negative. Pluto in your sign will operate on a more subtle level most of the time, gradually changing your life direction and re-shaping your attitudes about life and your role in relationships. As much as this transit is about you, it's also about those closest to you, especially your partner. Empower the one you love to pursue his or her own interests even if they differ from your own. In return, you'll experience a stronger, deeper relationship that enhances your growth.

What This Year's Eclipses Mean for You

There are four eclipses in 2012, two in Gemini, one in Sagittarius, and the fourth in Scorpio. Each is in effect for six to twelve months, so their influence will extend into 2013.

The year's first solar eclipse, May 21 in Gemini, highlights your solar Sixth House of daily work. Later in the year, on November 28, there will be a lunar eclipse in the same sign. Your job is, therefore, a major focus the second half of 2012, as the eclipse energy combines with Jupiter in Gemini from June 11 on. You'll enjoy work so much that all else in your life can become a distant second. Aim for balance as you'll be more productive and more effective in all areas of life. You also could find yourself in the role of workplace cheerleader, encouraging others to do their best, and you'll have many opportunities to get better acquainted with coworkers at social events.

Let the June 4 lunar eclipse in Sagittarius, your solar Twelfth House, be an ongoing reminder of the importance of healthy living, a balanced lifestyle, and time for yourself and your favorite leisure-time interests. This won't be nearly the challenge you might envision. The November 3 solar eclipse in Scorpio will accent your solar Eleventh House of friendship and reinforce Saturn's emphasis on this sector. Time with friends and social events will get a boost from the eclipse, as will your stature as a leader in group activities.

Saturn

Saturn will contact your Sun from Libra, your solar Tenth House of career and status, **if you were born between January 12 and 20.** You'll experience Saturn's influence in June or July **if your birthday is January 12, 13, or 14.** If you were born on any of the other dates, Saturn will contact your Sun between January and May, and again in August or September.

Hard work can lead to lowered vitality with this Saturn contact, so be sure to get enough sleep. This will help maintain your immune system and high energy during stressful career periods. Stellar achievements are also possible now with Saturn, your ruling planet, in your achievement sector. The determining factor is whether you've lived up to Saturn's expectations by fulfilling responsibilities and following the rules. Saturn rewards these efforts, and when it contacts your Sun, it always brings what you deserve.

If you're ready for a career boost, what you seek could appear later this year after Jupiter enters your job sector June 11. This won't necessarily be a promotion, but it will expand your influence and re-energize your career commitment. July could bring an exciting opportunity with great income potential, but be sure to weigh all the pros and cons in your decision-making process. Also consider how it will fit with your long-term goals because career decisions made now will guide you for the next fourteen to twenty-eight years.

If you were born between December 21 and 30, Saturn will connect with your Sun after it enters Scorpio October 5. This favorable contact to your Sun will give you free access to Saturn's steadying influence and the ability to do more with less effort. But you also could fall into the trap of doing everything yourself. Don't go there. Instead, let your leadership ability prevail and motivate and empower others to succeed. In many ways, this transit is about becoming a skillful leader. In the process you'll sense that some of your goals are changing and evolving as you realize you're capable of even greater achievements. Be patient with yourself. All of this is a work in progress as Saturn will contact your Sun from Scorpio again in 2013.

You may become fond friends with an elderly person under this influence, and you could also gain through a mentor who can offer valuable advice. Listen closely when knowledge and experience talk. This can give you the edge you need for advancement, especially in an organization or teamwork setting.

Uranus

If you were born between December 21 and 30, Uranus will contact your Sun from Aries, your solar Fourth House of home and family. Domestic changes will occur this year, partly because you have the urge for change. You could launch a major home improvement or redecorating project, or look for a new home. Relocation to another area is also possible. An adult child could move in or out, and you may need to deal with a parent's changing circumstances. Try to find an alternative if a parent wants to join your household, because this could be extremely disruptive. You could be faced with domestic repairs and the need to replace appliances, and it's vital to be very careful with anything electrical. Better yet, call an expert.

On a personal level, this Uranus-Sun contact will ignite a strong urge for freedom and independence. This can be positive if you use it to change those things about yourself that need changing. Look inward rather than outward. A change in your physical surroundings might temporarily satisfy this urge, but it won't be long-lasting.

Neptune

If you were born January 18, 19, or 20, Neptune will contact your Sun from Aquarius, your solar Second House, before February 3. Reflect on the financial lessons you learned in 2011, when Neptune also contacted your Sun. Then use this final transit to think about how your attitudes about money and value have evolved. What is most important to you now is probably vastly different from your attitudes prior to this contact. Carry this forward, along with an increased faith in yourself and your abilities.

If you were born between December 21 and 24, Neptune will contact your Sun after it enters Pisces February 3. This easy connection from your solar Third House will enhance your intuition, so listen when your inner voice speaks, and test it in small ways if this is a new experience for you. Your confidence in your sixth sense will gradually grow and become stronger.

This sector is also associated with learning, so consider taking a community class to learn a new hobby or creative writing skills. If you're inexperienced at public speaking, this transit can not only help you learn these skills but take you to a high level, where you're among the best. However, communication on some levels and with some people can be confusing, leading to misunderstandings. This could happen with a sibling or in workplace meetings, almost as though you're speaking two different languages. Cover yourself when necessary by documenting your ideas and opinions.

Get a second opinion if your vehicle or an appliance requires an expensive repair. It may not need it at all, or your best option might be replacement. If you purchase a new vehicle this year, read all the fine print after shopping around for the best deal.

Pluto

Pluto will merge with your Sun **if you were born between December 27 and 30**. Although this can be a difficult transit that occurs only once in a lifetime, it does have its up side. Pluto transforms whatever it touches, which means you or someone close to you will undergo major change in the coming year. A relationship could deepen or end, or you could suddenly recognize that you're caught up in an unhealthy one. At the same time you can learn much about human nature and relationships, thereby transforming yourself and your attitudes. You can also use Pluto to revamp yourself through diet, exercise, and an overall healthier lifestyle. Use this powerful planet to replace bad habits with good ones.

Take care not to become involved in any power struggles, especially at work. This could be difficult to do at times because others will try to pull you into the conflict while pressuring you to choose sides. The more neutral you can remain, the better. But here again you'll expand your knowledge of people and what motivates them.

The most challenging Pluto period will come when it clashes with Uranus in Aries, your solar Fourth House, in June and September. Be sure your home and property are well insured, especially if you live in an area prone to severe weather. Read the policy even if your agent assures you that every eventuality is covered. If major home improvements are your goal, it would be wise to postpone them as the positive results you expect are unlikely. It's also possible a family rift could develop. Relatives could look to you to settle the issue.

Capricorn | January

Planetary Lightspots

Your mind moves into high gear as Mercury transits your sign from the 8th through the 20th. Direct your thoughts to the year ahead, what you plan to accomplish and how best to achieve your goals. Concentration peaks mid-month, along with bright ideas, so use this time to get up to speed on a work-related project. Gain the knowledge you need to succeed.

Relationships

Your attention will focus on people and relationships in the two weeks following the January 9 Full Moon in Cancer your solar Seventh House. This lunar energy favors love and romance, especially around the 13th. But be cautious if you plan to consult a professional such as a financial advisor or attorney. Ask pointed questions, check references, and be sure you understand the potential losses as well as gains.

Money and Success

Money will flow your way under the influence of the January 23 New Moon in Aquarius, your solar Second House. You could profit through a raise, bonus, or investment, or receive a beautiful gift. Spending could rise at month's end when the latest tech gadget catches your eye or your children mount a campaign for a coveted item. Go for it if you can afford it, but avoid buying on credit.

Planetary Hotspots

Travel plans can be disrupted at any time from January 22 to April 12, while Mars is retrograde in Virgo. Try to schedule vacation or business trips before or after this period. If that's unrealistic, confirm reservations and prepare for delays. As Mars moves through your solar Ninth House, you also could find yourself in the midst of family turmoil involving a relative or in-law, as well as delays in legal matters.

Rewarding Days

3, 4, 8, 13, 17, 21, 25, 30, 31

Challenging Days

1, 7, 12, 14, 22, 27, 28

Capricorn | February

Planetary Lightspots

If you can manage the time for a quick weekend trip, take advantage of several planets and the February 21 New Moon in Pisces, your solar Third House. If not, plan a day trip instead. Either one will refresh your spirit and provide a nice break from everyday stress. But avoid the first weekend of February and dates around the 23rd, when planets will clash with retrograde Mars.

Relationships

Mercury makes many favorable planetary alignments this month, first in Aquarius, and then in Pisces. The first full week of February could bring positive career news, including a chance for a raise. Choose the 18th or 19th for a meeting, especially if you need to sell an idea. Creative ideas and approaches will come to you then, and you'll also be able to charm even the most stubborn client or coworker.

Money and Success

February 7 brings the Full Moon in Leo, your solar Eighth House of joint resources. This is a positive influence for all money matters, including financial decisions, loan applications, and family financial planning. Include your partner in discussions and use the lunar energy to find the budgeting compromise that makes you both happy. Then get started on your taxes.

Planetary Hotspots

Family relationships could be challenging after Venus enters Aries, your solar Fourth House, February 8. Difficult planetary alignments can spark conflict and domestic disruption, possibly because of a needed household repair or simply a battle of wills involving a family member. Be sure your home and property are well protected and insured, especially if you live in an area prone to severe weather.

Rewarding Days

8, 9, 12, 13, 18, 21, 26, 27, 28

Challenging Days

3, 4, 10, 15, 17, 22, 24, 29

Capricorn | March

Planetary Lightspots

Despite the potential downside of retrograde Mercury in Aries, the March 22 New Moon in the same sign will offer a bright spot, including quality family time. If you want to host a get-together, aim for the 24th or 25th, when family members are also likely to pitch in on spring cleaning and other domestic tasks.

Relationships

Your love life and your social life benefit from Venus in Taurus, which enters your solar Fifth House March 5. Positive planetary alignments enhance the influence, and if you're single, you could launch an exciting relationship. It might not be long-lived, but you'll enjoy the moment in the meantime. If you're a parent, one of your children could receive good news, including the possibility of a scholarship or an award.

Money and Success

Your career life is mostly status quo this month, but you can expect some challenging days, particularly in early and late March. Try to maintain a low profile at these times, and also be sure your work is up to date and accurate.

Planetary Hotspots

Family life and all things domestic will be affected by Mercury, which turns retrograde in Aries, your solar Fourth House, March 12. Laughter is a good antidote when misunderstandings occur, but an appliance breakdown or needed home repair won't be quite so amusing. It also will be late April or May before any current family or domestic events are resolved. Unexpected or surprising family news could arrive mid-month, or you could receive an offer if your home is for sale.

Rewarding Days

7, 11, 12, 16, 18, 21, 25, 26

Challenging Days

2, 3, 4, 9, 13, 15, 22, 30

Capricorn | April

Planetary Lightspots

Be happy! And look forward to April 13. That's the date both Mercury and Mars turn direct. The pressure you've experienced in your solar Third and Ninth Houses will soon ease, freeing the energy for effective communication, travel, and decision-making. Take the initiative to smooth over any recent relationship challenges.

Relationships

April's New Moon in Taurus on the 21st is all you need to energize your social life and your love life. With this influence in your solar Fifth House, you'll also enjoy time with your children and friends. Even better, pack your bags and take the family on vacation, even for a few days. The lunar energy will trigger a new romance for some Capricorns, possibly while traveling on business.

Money and Success

Expect some workplace issues to arise the first week of April, primarily because of miscommunication. If at all possible, try to postpone important talks and meetings until late in the month. But you'll also get the benefit of the April 6 Full Moon in Libra, your solar Tenth House. This can be a plus for your career, and bring you to the attention of someone important.

Planetary Hotspots

Family life could be a bit rocky at times this month as difficult planetary alignments influence your solar Fourth House. The issue may be family time versus career time. Take a close look at priorities and re-balance as necessary. You also could be faced with an appliance or home repair the last week of April. Don't attempt it yourself. The result will be aggravation and frustration, as well as additional expense. Call a pro.

Rewarding Days

4, 8, 12, 17, 21, 22, 23, 27, 29

Challenging Days

3, 5, 7, 13, 15, 18, 20, 24, 26

Capricorn I May

Planetary Lightspots

The May 5 Full Moon in Scorpio, your solar Eleventh House, is as much about creativity as it is about friendship and group activities. With the lunar energy activating Jupiter in Taurus, your solar Fifth House, you could be tapped for a leadership position in a teamwork project or organization. Then set yourself apart from the crowd with creative thinking and ideas. Also reserve some of your free time to enjoy a hobby or attend a sporting event.

Relationships

Mercury transits your Aries, your solar Fourth House, through the 8th, and then advances in Taurus, your solar Fifth House, May 9–23. While in Aries, you can expect tension involving a family member or supervisor, because both will want your full attention. Once Mercury enters Taurus, however, relationships will be upbeat, with plenty of opportunities to socialize with friends and spend quality time with your kids. A new romance is possible, but don't take things too seriously until Venus turns direct the end of June.

Money and Success

Despite retrograde Venus, you'll experience satisfying hours at work after the May 20 New Moon (solar eclipse) energizes your solar Sixth House. Be the spark and the cheerleader, the one who motivates others to do and be their best. But curb a tendency to push others to be more productive around the 25th.

Planetary Hotspots

Workplace projects will be error prone, and a few challenges with coworkers pop up as Venus travels retrograde May 15–June 26, although these will be mostly because of misunderstandings. Play it safe. Keep personal information and career plans to yourself. Someone could try to use shared information to undermine you.

Rewarding Days

1, 6, 13, 14, 18, 19, 20, 31

Challenging Days

3, 4, 8, 9, 16, 17, 23, 30

Capricorn | June

Planetary Lightspots

Mercury enters Leo, your solar Eighth House, on the 25th, where it could trigger a small raise or bring an opportunity to earn some extra cash. Splurge a little if you realize a gain and treat your family to a special outing. Let the kids pick the restaurant and the movie. Or do the same with your best friend.

Relationships

Challenges will surround a close relationship as Mercury transits Cancer, your solar Seventh House, June 7–24. It will be tough to find a compromise, and other stressful events in your lives could be the trigger that sparks conflict. A warm, supportive, and understanding approach will help ease the tension.

Money and Success

Circle June 11 on your calendar. That's the date lucky Jupiter enters Gemini, your solar Sixth House. Your work life benefits from this year-long influence, which begins with the New Moon in the same sign on the 19th. On the 27th, Venus turns direct in Gemini to boost your popularity another notch. Expect great things of yourself in the next twelve months. If you're job hunting or want to see what's available, submit résumés near the New Moon.

Planetary Hotspots

Pluto in your sign clashes with Uranus in Aries, your solar Fourth House, this month. Between these two planets and others in Cancer, your solar Seventh House, related events will concern you, your home, and those closest to you. Relocation or someone moving in or out of your household are possibilities. Be very sure your property and possessions are fully insured. Be especially cautious with anything electrical in your home, and be alert to severe weather. Try to find another option if a parent wants to move in with you.

Rewarding Days

1, 2, 9, 14, 15, 16, 19, 25, 26, 30

Challenging Days

5, 6, 10, 11, 12, 20, 21, 24, 27, 29

Capricorn | July

Planetary Lightspots

Your work life continues to be upbeat this month, thanks to Venus and Jupiter in Gemini, your solar Sixth House. Coworkers will be helpful and friendly, and you'll feel as though you're making solid progress on projects. Double-check details, though, while Mercury is retrograde.

Relationships

Close relationships benefit from the July 19 New Moon in Cancer, your solar Seventh House. You'll feel drawn to other people, and they to you. But the best of all will be special moments with your partner and others you love. But the July 3 Full Moon in your sign could bring tension with a family member (similar to last month), and it might be necessary for you to take charge of an elderly relative's affairs.

Money and Success

Mars dashes into Libra, your solar Tenth House, on the 3rd, initiating a seven-week emphasis on your career. You can make great strides in the weeks ahead, but be prepared for some challenges around the 17th, when you should tread carefully with supervisors. It's also possible you could be pulled away to deal with family matters.

Planetary Hotspots

Mercury travels retrograde in Leo, your solar Eighth House, July 14–August 7. Although its impact on money matters is likely to be minor, it's still wise to check statements for errors as soon as they arrive, pay bills early, and be sure payments are received on time. Also avoid loan applications and signing contracts or other legal paperwork. It will be all too easy to miss an important clause. If you're expecting a check or other funds, it's likely to be delayed.

Rewarding Days

7, 8, 12, 21, 23, 25, 27

Challenging Days

3, 4, 9, 17, 18 24, 30

Capricorn | August

Planetary Lightspots

You'll be dashing here, there, and everywhere in the weeks following this month's second Full Moon, on the 31st in Pisces, your solar Third House. Remember to charge your phone because communication will match the daily pace. Enjoy all the activity, and take time out to touch base with siblings. They'll be glad to hear from you.

Relationships

Mars moves on to Scorpio, your solar Eleventh House, on the 23rd. In the following weeks you'll have plenty of opportunities to see friends and socialize. This is also an ideal time to take the lead in a work-related team project or to get more involved in your community. Consider an organization or good cause in which your entire family can participate.

Money and Success

Money is a featured theme this month with the Full Moon on the 1st in Aquarius and the New Moon on the 17th in Leo, your financial sectors. You or your mate could earn a raise or bonus, or gain through a small windfall. This dual influence also makes August a good month for financial planning after Mercury turns direct in Leo on the 8th. Bargain shopping is at its best during the first few days after the Full Moon, when you could luck into some super buys on clothing.

Planetary Hotspots

Venus enters Cancer, your solar Seventh House of relationships, August 7. You'll need to get past the 16th, however, before you experience the upside of this transit. Before then you can expect further challenges involving a family member, but they'll pass as fast as they appear.

Rewarding Days

3, 4, 9, 14, 19, 22, 23, 27

Challenging Days

6, 7, 13, 16, 20, 21, 26, 28

Capricorn | September

Planetary Lightspots

Give yourself the gift of a short break as several planets transit Virgo, your solar Ninth House, prior to the New Moon on the 15th. A vacation trip with friends would be ideal, but if that's not realistic, opt instead for a long weekend where you can relax and refresh yourself, body and soul.

Relationships

This month's relationship challenges will of course be strongly linked to family and career. But you'll also have opportunities to see and socialize with friends as Mars continues to advance in Scorpio, your solar Eleventh House. Your partner will fill your heart with love and invaluable support as Venus transits Cancer, your solar Seventh House, the first five days of September.

Money and Success

Finances benefit from Venus in your solar Eighth House after it moves on to Leo September 6. However, major career changes linked to Uranus-Pluto could be on the horizon as a result of company restructuring or a management shift. These may affect others more directly than you, and it's even possible you could be rewarded for your past efforts.

Planetary Hotspots

Although Uranus in Aries and Pluto in your sign square off September 19, the challenges associated with these two planets will peak at month's end under the Full Moon in Aries on the 29th. You'll be pulled in two directions, dealing with domestic and career concerns, with both demanding your full attention. Your career or family matters could trigger the need to relocate, or stress could be related to someone moving in or out of your household. Again, be alert for severe weather that could damage your home.

Rewarding Days

1, 3, 5, 6, 9, 13, 14, 18, 27, 28

Challenging Days

2, 10, 11, 16, 19, 20, 23, 24, 26, 29

Capricorn | October

Planetary Lightspots

If you didn't manage to get away for a few days last month (or even if you did), Venus in Virgo, your solar Ninth House, brings another opportunity to do just that. If work-related travel is on your agenda between October 3 and 27, take your partner along and mix business with pleasure. Or surprise your mate with a romantic weekend designed for two.

Relationships

Relationships are generally upbeat and easygoing this month, with a focus on friendship. But at times it will be tough to know who's stretching the truth and who's telling you what you want to hear. Be wary of confidential information and enthusiasm that doesn't quite ring true. You intuition will be helpful after Mars enters Sagittarius, your solar Twelfth House, on the 6th.

Money and Success

You're a shining star under this month's New Moon in Libra, your solar Tenth House, on the 15th. Catch the incentive and initiative of the lunar energy to outshine the competition and strengthen relationships with decision-makers. Although you could gain through a promotion, this influence is more about reinforcing your position for the future. Indicate your interest in advancement if you have the opportunity.

Planetary Hotspots

Saturn enters Scorpio, your solar Eleventh House, October 5. As it transits this sign for the next two and a half years you'll form lasting friendships and see others fade away. Work-related group activities, or those you're involved in on your own time, can help to advance your career. But resist the urge to do more than your fair share, or even to do it all yourself, and focus, instead, on the value of teamwork.

Rewarding Days

2, 3, 5, 8, 10, 16, 21, 24

Challenging Days

1, 4, 7, 11, 14, 20, 27, 31

Capricorn | November

Planetary Lightspots

You'll be at your dynamic best from the 16th on, with Mars in your sign. At times it will be tough to keep up with yourself and all you have going on, but the effort will pay off for a long time to come. Just be sure to get enough sleep, which will be a challenge at times. Also slow down and focus when working in the kitchen or with tools. Mars can spark a mishap in a flash.

Relationships

As long as you're aware of the downside of retrograde Mercury, this can be one of the best social months of the year. You'll hear from many friends in the weeks following the November 13 New Moon (solar eclipse) in Scorpio and initiate contact with others. Get together with as many as you can, and accept invitations that come your way. Each will provide excellent networking opportunities as well as a good balance for this high-powered month.

Money and Success

Your status and popularity continue on the upswing, thanks to Venus in Libra, your solar Tenth House, through the 20th. Equally favorable is the November 28 Full Moon (lunar eclipse) in Gemini, your solar Sixth House of daily work. Go all out to impress those who count. Luck is on your side.

Planetary Hotspots

Listen to your sixth sense again this month. It will be active while Mercury is in Sagittarius, your solar Twelfth House, and especially after this planet turns retrograde on the 6th. Once it retreats into Scorpio, your solar Eleventh House, on the 14th, you'll want to confirm times, dates, and places for outings with friends and social events. Misunderstandings can also occur, but you'll be able to quickly clear the air after Mercury resumes direct motion on the 26th.

Rewarding Days
4, 8, 9, 11, 12, 15, 20

Challenging Days
3, 10, 16, 18, 23, 30

Capricorn | December

Planetary Lightspots

When everyone else is out socializing, you'll welcome a much-needed break under the New Moon in Sagittarius on the 13th. With this fresh energy in your solar Twelfth House of self-renewal, you'll enjoy time alone and at home with those closest to you. This will also give you an opportunity to review the past year and what you've accomplished. Use this knowledge to prepare for the symbolic fresh start represented by next month's New Moon in your sign.

Relationships

Quieter social events such as dinner with a few friends will suit you well as Mercury transits Scorpio, your solar Eleventh House, through the 9th, and Venus in the same sign through the 15th. After that you'll be more interested in family. It's also possible you could spend considerable time involved in the care of a relative later this month.

Money and Success

Finances enter positive territory when Mars arrives in Aquarius, your solar Second House, on the 25th. This influence, which will extend into February, has the potential to boost your bank account. Or it will if you can limit a temporary urge to spend on impulse. Year's end could bring some extra cash.

Planetary Hotspots

You'll feel like your life is a rerun when the December 28 Full Moon in Cancer sparks relationship, personal, and domestic tension. On the positive side, it won't be as intense as what you experienced last summer, and your inner strength will help you to weather it all. Just be cautious about becoming so focused that you fail to see the big picture. Accept the help of the many supportive people around you.

Rewarding Days

2, 5, 6, 10, 15, 19, 22, 24, 29

Challenging Days

1, 3, 7, 8, 14, 20, 28, 30

Capricorn Action Table

These dates reflect the best—but not the only—times for success and ease in these activities, according to your Sun sign.

	JAN	FEB	MAR	APR	MAY	JUN	JUL	AUG	SEP	OCT	NOV	DEC
Move				25–30	1–14							
Start a class		22–28	1–5									
Join a club		22, 23								13–31		
Ask for a raise										6, 7		
Look for work					1–6	1–15	26, 27					
Get pro advice										18, 19		
Get a loan												
See a doctor						1						
Start a diet						28						
End relationship	18, 19						28			18		
Buy clothes					16–31	1						
Get a makeover		28								31	1	
New romance				2, 24, 25, 30				29–31	1–21			
Vacation												

AQUARIUS

The Water Bearer
January 20 to February 19

Element: Air

Quality: Fixed

Polarity: Yang/Masculine

Planetary Ruler: Uranus

Meditation: I am a wellspring
of creativity

Gemstone: Amethyst

Power Stones: Aquamarine,
black pearl, chrysocolla

Key Phrase: I know

Glyph: Currents of energy

Anatomy: Ankles,
circulatory system

Color: Iridescent blues, violet

Animal: Exotic birds

Myths/Legends: Ninhursag,
John the Baptist, Deucalion

House: Eleventh

Opposite Sign: Leo

Flower: Orchid

Key Word: Unconventional

Your Strengths and Challenges

You're a fascinating mix of traits, sometimes traditional, conventional, and friendly. Just when people think they know you, you present the other side of Aquarius, and can be progressive, eccentric and aloof. All of this makes you an intriguing puzzle that keeps people guessing.

Aquarius is a fixed sign, which gives you great stamina and follow-through. Often you're described as determined and independent, but you also can be frustratingly stubborn with a strong will that sees you through life's challenges and motivates you to succeed. Uranus, your ruling planet, shares the uncommon mix of your sign, insightful at times and delivering the unexpected at others. You thus welcome change, but only when it's your idea. Then it can't happen fast enough because you like to shake things up. This can be invigorating, but remember that change for the sake of change isn't always the best idea.

Aquarius is the sign of friendship and the humanitarian, so you're generous with your time and money. You support those in your inner circle as well as organizations whose mission you value. The original networker, you get great satisfaction from connecting people with people and people with opportunities, and you nearly always know someone to contact for help or information when you need it.

Because Aquarius is an air sign, you're a communicator, albeit one who prefers to maintain at least some distance. And thus you're at times perceived as aloof when in reality you're uncomfortable with emotional expression. The intellect is your arena.

Your intuitive, insightful mind is geared to the future, and you have a knack for spotting trends, sometimes years in advance. Many Aquarians are also innovators and some are brilliant inventors. But remind yourself to also enjoy the moment while anticipating and looking forward to the next adventure or accomplishment.

Your Relationships

You're a flirt who plays the field, believing that variety keeps things lively as you search for a partner. Long talks and walks keep you interested and you can fall in love with someone's mind. Communication is just as important once you settle into a committed relationship because you know it keeps your hearts and minds connected. Only a very special person, however, can capture your independent heart. Love could sizzle with a dramatic, outgoing Leo, your opposite sign, and you might be compatible with Aries or Sagittarius. Your fellow air signs, Gemini and Libra, share your need for communication, but you could clash with Taurus and Scorpio, both of whom are possessive.

Family life brings out your more traditional side and you stay in close touch with relatives. You're protective of them, and probably grew up in a loving, affectionate, and comfortable home. The same is true of your own home, although some Aquarians have difficulty letting go of things and live with clutter—collectibles on every surface, stacks of books, and stuffed closets and storage spaces. If this describes you, ask yourself why you find security in the things rather than the people in your life. Most Aquarians have only one or two children and some have twins. You're fond of your children, encouraging them to explore their talents and develop their curiosity. This encourages an easygoing relationship, but remember you're a parent first and a pal second, at least until they reach adulthood.

Aquarius is the universal sign of friendship so it's only natural that you surround yourself with many acquaintances and only a few close pals. Group activities appeal to most Aquarians, and you may be involved in clubs or organizations that satisfy your humanitarian goals. You can be the social butterfly working your way through a room full of people, or find a like-minded soul and talk away the evening, exchanging knowledge and information. You accept people for what they are and have male and female friends from all walks of life. Only one requirement is necessary: they must be or different in some way. "Normal" people don't interest you; in fact, they bore you.

Your Career and Money

Most Aquarians are content to remain in one career throughout their lifetimes. You might switch your emphasis or branch out into a related field, but your desire is to stick with a main area of interest. Fortunately, you have the staying power to do just that if you plan and strategize how to achieve this goal. It's wise, however, to keep your grand plan to yourself rather than risk tipping off a competitor. You have the ability to rise to a powerful position, to network your way into a spot where you can be in charge. In your everyday work life you're happiest in a family-like atmosphere and might even work in a family business. A calm working environment is a must for high productivity, as is the opportunity to initiate change and to revamp procedures, policies, and even your work space. Your ideal would be to overhaul an entire department or company, or to take the lead in resurrecting a faltering enterprise.

In money matters you're both practical and naïve, creative and analytical. At times money slips through your fingers almost as if it disappears into thin air. You also attract what you need when you need it. Even so, it's wise to train yourself to live within a realistic budget that includes necessities, savings, investments, and fun money. Then you'll always have savings to fall back on. Study facts and figures before you invest and double-check all details in loan documents before you sign. Overall, you can do well financially if you plan, think long term, and look at the big picture. Real estate can be especially profitable, and you could receive a sizeable family inheritance.

Your Lighter Side
There's a certain electrifying something about you that fascinates people. They're drawn to your magnetic charm and uniqueness and intrigued by your ability to say a lot but reveal almost no personal information. Only a select few ever learn your full story, which keeps people wondering about the mysterious you and what makes you tick.

Affirmation for the Year
My future sparkles with opportunity.

The Year Ahead for Aquarius

Fun, friendship, learning, and people are all featured in 2012, and later in the year you'll take the first steps toward new career achievements. Money and creativity are also themes in 2012, and a lucky moment this summer could bring you a small windfall.

The year begins with Jupiter in Taurus, your solar Fourth House of home and family. This positive influence in your domestic sector through June 10 is great for home improvement projects, memorable times with family, and entertaining friends. Most of all, you'll simply enjoy being home, where you can relax in comfort and be yourself. However, Jupiter is the planet of expansion so it will be all too easy to spend freely on a wide variety of things for your home. You don't really need most of them as much as you just want to have them. Establish a budget, and use Jupiter to help you organize your space, eliminate clutter, and sell or donate what you no longer need. Take the plunge in May when it will be much easier to let go of unwanted items.

Jupiter moves on to Gemini, your solar Fifth House, June 11, where it spends the rest of the year and the first half of 2013. Then your interest will switch from the domestic scene to socializing, leisure-time interests, hobbies, and sports. If you're a parent, you'll create fond memories with your children if you emphasize quality time instead of indulging your desire to spoil them with gifts. A nearby location will be more enjoyable for a summer vacation.

Saturn also transits two signs in 2012, spending most of the year in Libra, your solar Ninth House of knowledge, travel, legal matters, and life philosophy. Meditation is a good outlet for this energy as you review the past and explore your spirituality. Saturn here encourages you to refine your beliefs so they better reflect your individuality and the person you are today. This might mean stepping away from some of your childhood or family traditions. You also could gain a new perspective through travel and exposure to other cultures.

Consider taking a class to boost your career skills, or complete the program you began two years ago when Saturn entered this sector. Knowledge gained will begin to pay off as Saturn moves on to Scorpio, your solar Tenth House of career and status, October 5. This can be a life pinnacle, a step up that reaffirms all the effort you've invested in your career during the past fourteen years. It may be 2013 before you see real gains, but you could earn a raise soon after Saturn enters Scorpio.

Meeting and getting to know the right people is important as Saturn transits your solar Tenth House. Target those who could speed your path up the ladder and then let them see you at your best. Take responsibility for all you do and go out of your way to turn out high-quality work, day after day. Remember, serious Saturn rewards a solid effort.

Uranus continues its seven-year transit of Aries, the sign it will occupy until 2018. As it moves through your solar Third House, your ruling planet will trigger everything from surprising news to flashes of insight. In addition to communication and thinking, this sector governs siblings, cousins, neighbors, and quick trips. Life will be full of the unexpected during these years, and at times you'll find yourself dashing off for the day, a weekend, or just a few hours in order to satisfy your need for a change of scenery.

This transit is great for community involvement and getting acquainted with neighbors in order to widen your circle. Among them could be just the networking contact you've been looking for, and someone could spark thoughts that change your self-perspective and ideas, as well a shift in your life direction. You can do the same for them. You can also use this transit to start a blog or a book, to master your public speaking skills, or to take a class to learn more about a subject that interests you.

Neptune completes its long transit of your sign February 2, and then moves on to Pisces, where it will be until 2025. Use Neptune's final weeks in Aquarius to reflect on what you've learned about yourself, life, relationships, and what you value most in yourself and others. Then you'll be ready to apply all of these inspirational thoughts as Neptune transits your solar Second House of personal resources.

In your solar Second House, Neptune influences your income and saving and spending habits. This will be a challenge at times because money can disappear as if into thin air. Also monitor credit card use or you could get a big surprise when the bill arrives. For all these reasons and more it will be important during these years to establish a budget and live within it. Keep bills and financial records organized in order to avoid late payments and Neptune's characteristic confusion. But this transit can also be a blessing because Neptune can provide just what you need when you need it. Don't depend on it to come through all the time, though. Dream big and then follow through with a practical, commonsense plan to achieve your desired wealth.

Pluto, the slowest moving planet in the Zodiac, continues in Capricorn, your solar Twelfth House, through 2024. Its influence in your self-renewal sector will be subtle yet profound as it works through your subconscious. Memories, regrets, and unresolved issues will emerge for one purpose: so you can come to terms with them. Some will be positive and others will be negative. All, however, will have a meaning in the context of your current life.

This transit will push you to examine your psychological motivations, including self-limiting behaviors. Think about how you react in stressful situations, especially those involving other people, in order to find the reasons behind your responses. You will learn much about yourself and this will help you become the best you can be. A self-help book could trigger your thinking.

What This Year's Eclipses Mean for You

There are four eclipses in 2012, two lunar and two solar. The influence of each is in effect for six to twelve months.

The May 21 solar eclipse in Gemini and the November 28 lunar eclipse in the same sign favorably contact your Sun sign. With Jupiter in Gemini the second half the year, your solar Fifth House will sizzle with activity. The emphasis here is on socializing, romance, children, fun, hobbies, and all the things you enjoy doing in your free time. It's even possible you could turn a special interest or hobby into a sideline money-making endeavor. Go for it as long as it doesn't require a sizeable investment.

June 4 will bring a lunar eclipse in Sagittarius, your solar Eleventh House. This sector emphasizes friendship, groups, organizations, and networking, so it's a nice complement to this year's Gemini influence. A professional organization could increase your circle of acquaintances, and you could get positive results from involvement in a community organization or your children's sports or school activities. But this sector is also about goals, and what you hope to achieve. If career gains are on your list, the timing is ideal because Saturn enters Scorpio, your solar Tenth House in October. Soon after, on November 13, Scorpio will be the sign of a solar eclipse. The combination is very promising for career success into 2013, so to take advantage of all this planetary energy and earn the success you deserve.

Saturn

If you were born between February 11 and 19, Saturn will contact your Sun from Libra, your solar Ninth House, before it moves on to

Scorpio October 5. This easy connection can give you extra stamina and determination, and at times you'll have a more serious outlook on life. That's okay. Saturn's purpose here is to encourage you to look to the future in the context of the past, and to discard belief systems that no longer work for you. Retain those that are viable and say goodbye to the rest.

On a practical level, Saturn in this sector encourages you to broaden your world view, whether through reading, travel, or education. The goal is knowledge. The most effective and productive way to achieve this could be additional schooling. Complete a degree, take classes that will enhance your job expertise, or attend a few conferences. Consider online learning to maximize your time. The knowledge you gain can open up new avenues for career success in the next few years.

Saturn enters Scorpio, your solar Tenth House of career and status, October 5, and will contact your Sun before year's end and again next year **if you were born between January 20 and 31**. Transiting this sector, Saturn will bring exactly what you deserve. So if you've worked hard and earned recognition and success, the odds are that Saturn will deliver a nice reward. This time is a pinnacle of your involvement in the outer world, and for many it represents a time of maximum career achievement. Saturn's influence is even stronger here because of the November eclipse energy, so take time for a self-assessment before this period arrives. Then you'll be better prepared to seek a promotion or new position that reflects your skills, talents, and abilities.

However, all this hard work can result in less stamina and lowered vitality, which can do the same to your immune system. This is only Saturn's way of reminding you that a balanced lifestyle adds to success. Get enough rest and sleep, and fill your evening and weekend hours with friendship, family time, hobbies, and social events. You'll be far more effective at work, and that can get you noticed.

Uranus

If you were born between January 20 and 29, Uranus will favorably contact your Sun from Aries, your solar Third House. If you've ever wanted to write, give it a try this year when Uranus can provide the inspiration. Or study astrology. At the least you'll gain fresh insights into yourself and your mind. This contact is also one of the best for learning, whether for the fun of it, in online classes, or as a way to boost job skills. You can also expect flashes of insight at the oddest times. Pay attention. Your intuition will be strong during this time.

Restlessness can accompany this transit, so don't be surprised if you're more than usually inclined to take impromptu trips or to suggest spur-of-the-moment outings with friends. But pay close attention while driving because Uranus can trigger a mishap at the least expected moment. Put your phone in the back seat so you won't be tempted. Be extra alert, especially in July, August, October, and November. The same periods could bring a clash with a neighbor or relative. If so, listen closely. The underlying message may be a learning experience.

Neptune

If your birthday is between February 16 and 19, Neptune in Aquarius will join forces with your Sun before moving on to Pisces February 3. This inspirational contact can help you see yourself from a new perspective, with an emphasis on boosting your self-esteem. What you see now may have been obvious to others in the past, but with the help of enlightening Neptune, you'll cherish who you are and who you've become during this planet's long transit of your sign. No small part of this is the intuition, compassion, and creativity you've developed along the way, all of which are very much a part of you and your life.

Neptune will contact your Sun after it enters Pisces February 3 **if your birthday is between January 20 and 23**. This transit through your solar Second House emphasizes personal finances, spending, bills, and budgeting. You could receive a nice raise in October, along with an ego boost from positive feedback. But don't go on a shopping spree because you could spend far more than you intend. Instead, track expenses the first month or two of this transit in order to find out exactly where your money goes. A little bit here and a little bit there can add up to a mysteriously depleted bank account and leave you wondering why. From this you can set a realistic budget to cover your needs and a few luxuries—and increase savings.

This transit is about far more than money, however. It's about your most prized possession: you! Use Neptune to explore your strengths and challenges, your talents and skills, your best traits and those you'd like to change. You'll find the exercise inspiring because you'll realize you have a lot going for you. In fact, you may see yourself in a whole new self-empowering light.

Pluto

If you were born between January 26 and 29, Pluto in Capricorn, your solar Twelfth House, will contact your Sun this year. Transiting your self-renewal sector, Pluto encourages you to assess your life and lifestyle—what works and what doesn't, what do you want to change and what do you want to retain. Be honest with yourself. Are you as healthy as you could be? With Pluto in place, you'll have the willpower to change almost anything you wish, even long-standing habits.

Pluto here also operates on a mental level, targeting your subconscious, especially in June and September, when it will clash with Uranus in Aries, your solar Third House. So don't be surprised if memories and long-dormant wishes and desires emerge into your daily thoughts. Explore each one, resolve regrets, and take action to pursue the dreams that capture your interest.

On another level, you may receive unexpected news regarding a sibling, or find it necessary to purchase a new vehicle. If you take daily walks, go with a friend and stick to safe neighborhoods. Better yet, join a group of mall walkers. Take similar precautions when you're out and about running errands, and try to postpone travel, including road trips.

Aquarius | January

Planetary Lightspots

The January 23 New Moon in Aquarius marks the symbolic start of your new solar year. Use this strong energy to set your path to success for the year ahead. Dream big! There is much you can accomplish in 2012, especially on the domestic scene and, later this year, in your career. This year also brings an opportunity to access the hidden recesses of your mind, including your sixth sense. The more you listen, the stronger your intuition will become.

Relationships

Your charming ways will attract people as Venus transits your sign through the 13th. Romance your mate, or flirt with someone new. It's also possible a former romantic interest could express interest in rekindling a relationship. Think carefully and remind yourself why you're no longer together.

Money and Success

Your work life is highlighted by the January 9 Full Moon in Cancer, your solar Sixth House. Expect the pace to be hectic and pressure to build at times. That's a good reason to balance long hours with time for yourself, sleep, and mild exercise. All will help you maintain a healthy lifestyle so you're at your most productive. Extra effort will pay off, although not until later this year.

Planetary Hotspots

Money matters will require careful management as Mars in Virgo, your solar Eighth House, travels retrograde January 23–April 12. But rather than see this as a negative or a setback, you can use it to learn or improve your financial skills, including budgeting, savings goals, debt reduction, and investing for the future. During the retrograde period, however, double-check that bills are paid on time and set aside a few hours to organize financial records.

Rewarding Days

1, 5, 6, 10, 11, 15, 19, 23, 24, 27

Challenging Days

2, 8, 12, 13, 14, 16, 20, 22, 26

Aquarius | February

Planetary Lightspots

January's spotlight on you continues this month with Mercury in your sign through February 12, and the Sun there until the 19th. Take advantage of these planetary influences to gather and share information. Your mind and memory will be especially sharp, as will your intuition and your ability to clearly present ideas. Students will excel.

Relationships

The February 7 Full Moon in Leo, your solar Seventh House, accents all the close relationships in your life, from partner to family to your best friends. Plan ahead so you can spend quality and quantity time with all of them. This lunar energy is especially nice for couples in love, and will trigger an engagement for some Aquarians. Be sure, though, to listen more than you talk. Chances are, you'll learn some interesting information.

Money and Success

This month's New Moon in Pisces on the 21st highlights your solar Second House. The lunar energy could bring you a raise, but there could be a delay before it goes into effect. You'll also be able to find bargains on clothing and household decor if you take your time and shop around rather than buy the first thing you see. Set a budget first, though, as you'll be in the mood to spend.

Planetary Hotspots

Venus advances into Aries, your solar Third House, February 8, where it forms difficult planetary alignments. Be especially cautious when driving, and don't take chances in bad weather. Take your vehicle in for routine maintenance prior to this period. The same time frame could trigger a problem with an appliance, so be sure to ask someone to check your home if you're away for a few days.

Rewarding Days

1, 2, 11, 12, 16, 19, 20, 25

Challenging Days

3, 4, 15, 17, 22, 24

Aquarius | March

Planetary Lightspots

Home life will be upbeat after Venus enters Taurus, your solar Fourth House, March 5. Entertain friends on the 10th or 18th, which are also good days for simply enjoying family time. With Mercury turning retrograde this month, however, it's unwise to begin domestic projects. But you can begin making a to-do list.

Relationships

Relationships are generally upbeat this month, although you'll want to confirm dates, times, and places for meetings, seeing friends, and community activities. Try not to let a controlling person get to you at month's end, and do your best to avoid contact with relatives, including in-laws, the first few days of March. Good news could come your way the third week of the month.

Money and Success

The March 8 Full Moon in Virgo, your solar Eighth House, has more potential to trigger extra expenses than income. Don't be hasty, though, if you absolutely must replace an appliance, for example. Also be wary of incurring debt, or even applying for credit or a loan, because Mars is still retrograde in Virgo.

Planetary Hotspots

Be prepared for some aggravation after Mercury turns retrograde in Aries, March 12. With the planet of communication affecting your communication sector, you can expect everything from mix-ups and misunderstandings to mechanical problems. Try to take your vehicle in for routine maintenance before the retrograde period begins, and if it all possible, postpone major purchases. Also hold off until late April or May if you need a new cell phone or computer.

Rewarding Days

1, 5, 6, 10, 14, 16, 18, 23, 26, 28

Challenging Days

2, 3, 4, 9, 13, 15, 22, 27, 30

Aquarius | April

Planetary Lightspots

Time with family and at home are favored when the April 21 New Moon in Taurus accents your solar Fourth House. Kick back and enjoy your space again this month, and put off those projects until June. But you could fill your home with fresh energy by getting the entire family involved in spring cleaning.

Relationships

Just in time for spring, Venus enters Gemini, your solar Fifth House, April 3. Fill your free time with outdoor activities, social events, and family outings the last two weeks of the month. Before then, you could unknowingly make plans for a fun event that ends up being a very expensive one. Invite friends for a casual evening on the 10th, instead.

Money and Success

Financial challenges begin to fade after Mercury and Mars resume direct motion on the 13th. All will not return to normal, however, for another month or so. But at least you'll feel as though you're making progress in unraveling any problems that arose in the past few months, and income will begin to flow your way. Remember this when frustration mounts during the first full week of April.

Planetary Hotspots

Although the urge for fresh scenery could be strong under the April 6 Full Moon in Libra, your solar Ninth House, this isn't the time for travel. Difficult planetary alignments signal a high potential for delays, changes, and lost luggage. Mid-April could bring the need for a repair. If so, find a highly recommended mechanic so you don't have to repeat the process next month.

Rewarding Days

1, 2, 10, 12, 14, 17, 19, 22, 25, 29

Challenging Days

3, 5, 7, 9, 11, 13, 15, 16, 24, 26

Aquarius I May

Planetary Lightspots

Family ties and communication will be upbeat as Mercury advances in Taurus, your solar Fourth House, May 9–23. Take advantage of this time to catch up on what's going on with relatives, and also with your immediate family. You can also use Mercury's mental focus to plan a home improvement project before getting started after Venus turns direct the end of June.

Relationships

The May 20 New Moon (solar eclipse) in Gemini highlights many of the relationships in your life. Fun with friends and family activities will be among the best, but a romantic relationship could cool after Venus turns retrograde. If you meet someone new, take it slowly as it may not last. But you'll want to avoid workplace meetings, travel, and talks with people at a distance in early May when Mercury is in Aries, your solar Third House.

Money and Success

The May Full Moon in Scorpio on the 5th could trigger exciting career developments as it brightens your solar Tenth House. A promotion is as possible as a raise, or you could receive an offer if you're job hunting. The latter would be wise if your company is having financial problems.

Planetary Hotspots

Your social life will slow somewhat while Venus is retrograde in Gemini, your solar Fifth House, May 16–June 26. Devote the time instead to your children, who will appreciate the attention during this period. Be cautious, though, with investments, because even the most promising ones could leave you with a net loss. Creative projects can be fulfilling now, but don't do anything you can't undo after Venus resumes direct motion.

Rewarding Days

8, 10, 11, 12, 17, 20, 22, 26, 31

Challenging Days

3, 4, 9, 16, 21, 23, 24, 28, 30

Aquarius | June

Planetary Lightspots

Jupiter moves into Gemini on the 11th to begin its year-long transit of your solar Fifth House. An addition to the family is possible, but this influence is more likely to energize your social life and your love life. Creativity is another element here, so explore possibilities and find the best outlet for you and your talents. Crafts and writing are two possibilities. Your children, whatever their age, will make you proud.

Relationships

A week before Jupiter changes signs, the June 4 Full Moon (lunar eclipse) in Sagittarius shines brightly in your solar Eleventh House. This, too, is a great influence for socializing and seeing friends, as is Venus returning to direct motion in Gemini on the 27th. Fill your calendar with summer outings where you can meet people, and look to the June 19 New Moon in Gemini for romance and possibly a new romantic interest.

Money and Success

Mercury enters Leo, your solar Sixth House, on the 25th, to set the pace for July, which will be a busy one at work. Work ahead as much as possible the last week of June so you can get off to a fast start next month.

Planetary Hotspots

Uranus in Aries and Pluto in Capricorn square off June 24, as they do again in September. This month's challenges could be conflict with coworkers. Do your best to avoid them, or refuse to engage in a battle. There also could be developments regarding income and benefits, which could be reduced because of economic conditions. Either situation will be most apparent in the second week of June, followed by more at month's end.

Rewarding Days

7, 8, 13, 17, 18, 19, 22, 23, 26

Challenging Days

5, 6, 10, 11, 12, 20, 24, 27, 29

Aquarius | July

Planetary Lightspots

Favorable planetary alignments involving Venus and Jupiter in Gemini, your solar Fifth House, make July a good month to see cousins and siblings and to get better acquainted with neighbors. Among them could be someone who will become a longtime friend or who will connect you with an opportunity. Consider getting involved in a project that would better your community.

Relationships

Relationships are prone to confusion and miscommunication after Mercury turns retrograde on the 14th. Confirm times, dates, and places, and be sure others, especially your partner, understand what you're saying. Don't assume, as thoughts can be jumbled during this period. More information regarding news received around the 4th will be forthcoming near the 14th and the 28th.

Money and Success

The July 19 New Moon in Cancer, your solar Sixth House, is all about hard work, and it might be tough to please the boss. Stick with it. What you do now will be rewarded in several months, if not sooner.

Planetary Hotspots

Last month's challenges make a rerun as the July 3 Full Moon merges with Pluto in Capricorn and clashes with Uranus in Aries. This two-week influence will be apparent in your job, communication, and travel sectors. This is not the month to travel, whether on business, vacation, or even a long weekend at a nearby destination. Your vehicle could need a repair mid-month, when you should also drive with the utmost care. Catch a ride if you socialize.

Rewarding Days

1, 5, 6, 10, 11, 14, 15, 20, 25, 28

Challenging Days

9, 12, 13, 17, 18, 24, 29, 30

Aquarius I August

Planetary Lightspots

The second August Full Moon, on the 31st, focuses its energy on your solar Second House of income, spending, and possessions. Its alignment with Pluto is all the reason you need to clean closets, storage spaces, drawers, and more. Dig deep and you'll find things you haven't seen in years. Some of them could net a profit, but most of all this exercise will free your mind and fill your space with fresh energy.

Relationships

The August 1 Full Moon in your sign and the August 17 New Moon in Leo, your solar Seventh House will work in tandem, spotlighting the relationships in your life. Your goal is to reach out to others in order to learn all you can about human nature and how you interact with others. This will be all the easier after Mercury turns direct in Leo on the 8th. Someone will bring you luck.

Money and Success

Mars zips into Scorpio, your solar Tenth House, on the 23rd. During the following seven weeks you'll have many opportunities to connect with people through your career, and possibly earn well-deserved recognition along with a raise.

Planetary Hotspots

Venus enters Cancer, your solar Sixth House, on the 7th, but you won't feel the beneficial influence of this planet until the second half of August. Until then you can expect periodic challenges with coworkers and projects as well as sudden, unexpected changes in decisions and projects. Also be cautious what you say as someone could use the information against you. Choose another venue if you're looking for a new romantic interest. An office romance would not end well.

Rewarding Days

2, 9, 11, 15, 16, 17, 25, 29

Challenging Days

6, 7, 13, 20, 21, 24, 26, 28

Aquarius | September

Planetary Lightspots

Easy planetary alignments with Jupiter in Gemini, your solar Fifth house, add a lightspot to the month, bringing optimism and fun times with friends, your children, and your favorite leisure-time activities. Enjoy!

Relationships

Venus transits Leo, your solar Seventh House, from September 6 on. This is one of the best influences for relationships. If you're part of a couple, plan a special evening at home with your mate around the 13th or 21st. Talk, laugh, and enjoy a takeout gourmet dinner as you celebrate your love. Overall, you'll find people to be helpful and ready to grant favors this month.

Money and Success

The September 15 New Moon in Virgo, your solar Eighth House, has potential to boost your bank account. Not a lot, but to the point where you'll be pleased. Earlier in the month you can take advantage of Mercury in Virgo through the 15th. Use it for budgeting, financial planning, and learning how to better manage your money.

Planetary Hotspots

Uranus in Aries and Pluto in Capricorn clash again on September 19, but the major effect of this alignment will be triggered by the September 29 Full Moon in Aries, your solar Third House. Avoid travel unless absolutely necessary, and also be very careful when driving or even walking in your neighborhood. If you need to purchase a new vehicle, try to hold off until next year. If that's impossible, read all the fine print and buy nothing without at least a year's full warranty. Do the same if you need an appliance.

Rewarding Days

3, 6, 7, 9, 13, 17, 21, 25, 30

Challenging Days

2, 10, 11, 16, 19, 23, 24, 26, 29

Aquarius | October

Planetary Lightspots

Favorable planetary alignments and the October 15 New Moon in Libra, your solar Ninth House, favor travel, unlike last month. Take a quick vacation with the family or plan a winter getaway. The lunar energy is also positive for visits or talks with out-of-town relatives. Traveling singles could launch a new romance.

Relationships

Mars arrives in Sagittarius, your solar Eleventh House, on the 6th and continues there until mid-November. This is a plus for holiday socializing with friends. You could kick things off this month by hosting a get-together after the October 29 Full Moon in Taurus, you solar Fourth House of home. Around the same time, though, and also near the 7th, don't believe everything a friend tells you.

Money and Success

Money flows your way October 3–28, as Venus transits Virgo, your solar Eighth House. You could earn a raise soon after Saturn enters Scorpio, or make a lucky find. But don't let anyone convince you to invest or make a loan. Ignore promises. They're likely too good to be true. Take a chance on the lottery mid-month, and also look where you walk. A lucky find could be yours.

Planetary Hotspots

Saturn begins its transit of Scorpio, your solar Tenth House, October 5. With it comes an opportunity to reach a career peak, building on the experiences and successes of the past as you make the most of your knowledge. Aim for a promotion during the next two and a half years, live up to your responsibilities, and set an example for others.

Rewarding Days

5, 6, 10, 18, 22, 23, 24

Challenging Days

1, 4, 7, 11, 14, 20, 27

Aquarius | November

Planetary Lightspots

Mars transitions into Capricorn, your solar Twelfth House, on the 16th, where it will activate your sixth sense. Listen to hunches, especially the last two weeks of the month. They can help you in everything from your career to finding bargain gifts while Mercury is retrograde. It's also possible you'll hear some secrets or confidential information that can give you an edge at work.

Relationships

Your social life gets a burst of energy under the November 28 Full Moon (lunar eclipse) in Gemini, your solar Fifth House. The influence extends into December, when other planetary alignments will continue the trend. However, you can expect a few minor challenges in early November, when it's wise to avoid difficult people.

Money and Success

Your career gets a strong push from the November 13 New Moon (solar eclipse) that can put you in the spotlight well into 2013. This month, beneficial Venus adds its energy to the mix when it enters Scorpio on the 21st. Push forward, remembering to double-check work and details while Mercury is retrograde. Listen to advice you hear during the last ten days of the month, but make your own final decision.

Planetary Hotspots

Mercury turns retrograde in Sagittarius, your Eleventh House, on the 6th, so plan ahead to confirm details before you head off to a social event or to see friends. Mix-ups will be more the norm than the exception. Do the same with career-related meetings and deadlines after retrograde Mercury slips back into Scorpio, your solar Tenth House, on the 14th, before turning direct on the 26th.

Rewarding Days

2, 6, 7, 9, 11, 14, 15, 24, 29

Challenging Days

3, 5, 10, 16, 18, 19, 23, 25

Aquarius | December

Planetary Lightspots

Mars enters your sign on the 25th, so you'll be ready to dash into the new year with high energy. That's great, but slow down enough to prevent accidents, which can happen in a flash. Be especially careful in the kitchen and when working with tools.

Relationships

The timing and placement of this month's New Moon on the 13th is ideal for holiday fun. Placed in Sagittarius, your solar Eleventh House, your social life will be filled with friendship, parties, and more. You also get the benefit of Mercury in the same sign December 10–30, and Venus there from the 15th on. All of this also favors evenings in or out for couples making romantic memories. If you want to host a get-together, the 17th is a good choice.

Money and Success

Your workplace popularity continues with Mercury and Venus in Scorpio, your solar Tenth House, the first part of December. Both these planets can help you get the attention of decision-makers, but the real work begins just before year's end when the Full Moon in Cancer on the 28th lights up your solar Sixth House. Try to grab a relaxing few days so you're ready to keep up the pace in January.

Planetary Hotspots

Try to slow the pace a little during the last ten days of the year. With several planets in Capricorn, your solar Twelfth House, and some difficult planetary alignments, you could end up with a cold or flu. And that would interfere with holiday gatherings and what will be a busy month at work. Sleep, eat healthy, dress warmly, and treat yourself well.

Rewarding Days

9, 12, 15, 16, 17, 21, 26, 31

Challenging Days

3, 4, 7, 14, 20, 23, 28, 30

Aquarius Action Table

These dates reflect the best—but not the only—times for success and ease in these activities, according to your Sun sign.

	JAN	FEB	MAR	APR	MAY	JUN	JUL	AUG	SEP	OCT	NOV	DEC
Move					16–31							
Start a class			21–25	25–30								
Join a club										1	2–17	
Ask for a raise		12, 28	4									
Look for work						22–30	5–21			18, 19		
Get pro advice												
Get a loan												
See a doctor		1, 28			20						1	
Start a diet	19							24				
End relationship		17	16		10							
Buy clothes			11			10, 18			18			
Get a makeover										6, 7		
New romance						1						
Vacation									23–30	1–12		

PISCES

The Fish
February 19 to March 20

♓

Element: Water

Quality: Mutable

Polarity: Yin/Feminine

Planetary Ruler: Neptune

Meditation: I successfully navigate my emotions

Gemstone: Aquamarine

Power Stones: Amethyst, bloodstone, tourmaline

Key Phrase: I believe

Glyph: Two fish swimming in opposite directions

Anatomy: Feet, lymphatic system

Color: Sea green, violet

Animal: Fish, sea mammals

Myths/Legends: Aphrodite, Buddha, Jesus of Nazareth

House: Twelfth

Opposite Sign: Virgo

Flower: Water lily

Key Word: Transcendence

Your Strengths and Challenges

Born under the mutable water sign of the zodiac, you're known for your flexibility. You can adapt in most any situation, changing your approach and demeanor as necessary in order to achieve a goal or gain acceptance. This trait also gives you the ability to blend in or stand out and to quickly get in sync with other people and your environment. This can be a plus or a minus, depending upon the situation. There are times when the best choice is to take a stand, something you're reluctant to do if it might spark controversy. Accept that healthy disagreements are a necessary part of life.

Sensitive and compassionate, you're interested in the welfare of others, and some with a Pisces Sun are actively involved in charitable organizations that help the less fortunate. If you find yourself consistently putting the needs of others first, however, remember to look out for yourself; no one else will.

Creativity is another of your strengths. Whether it takes the form of artistic endeavors, ideas, or something else, you envision possibilities that others miss. Neptune, your ruling planet, also encourages you to inspire others and to follow your own spiritual path. Your strong faith sees you through hurdles, although you have a tendency to turn inward when worries dominate your thoughts. Meditation can re-center you, body and soul, during these times.

Idealistic and trusting, you strive to see the best in everyone. While that's admirable, you'll benefit from asking questions and taking less for granted. Your sixth sense can steer you in the right direction here and in other life situations. Listen to your inner voice. It's an asset, and the more you listen the stronger it will become. Some people with a Pisces Sun are psychic. But keep in mind that you're also impressionable and can pick up vibrations, both positive and negative, from other people and your environment. Get in the habit of surrounding yourself with a positive energy field.

Your Relationships

You're a romantic with a heart of gold, kind and sentimental. Most people with a Pisces Sun dislike being alone and need the security that a lasting relationship provides. This motivates you to seek a mate, but dating can be challenging at times. You so want things to work out that you can hang on even when you should move on. Have faith in the universe. Your ideal match may be only a date away. Love at first sight could be yours with a practical Virgo, your opposite sign, or one of the other earth signs, Taurus and Capricorn. You're in tune with Cancer and Scorpio, your fellow water signs. But life with a Gemini or Sagittarius could upset the stability you both need and desire.

Your wish is to always be surrounded by peace and harmony. Although you might achieve this in many areas, home life is unlikely to be among them. There you can expect a lot of activity, including neighbors and relatives dropping in on the spur of the moment. Your home is a place for communication, and you probably have bookcases, the latest technology, and more than a little clutter. Pisces parents are fond of their children and involved in their activities, but you may tend to be overprotective of them. You want to shield them from life's ups and downs, which is a natural instinct. But in the process you may actually do them a disservice. Learning by experience and testing their independence in a safe environment is often the best way for children to prepare for the imperfect life they'll experience as adults.

Acquaintances and the social scene aren't your style. You prefer a handful of best friends, some of whom are for a lifetime, and enjoy their company in small groups in comfortable, familiar surroundings. Even if you and someone close drift apart, you quickly pick up where you left off as though no time had passed. Among your friends is probably a soul mate or two. These are the people you lean on during difficult times and the ones who cheer your victories. You also learn a great deal about life from them.

Your Career and Money
Although you can do it if you must, a career behind a desk isn't your first choice. It becomes tolerable, and even desirable, if you have the opportunity to learn, share your knowledge, and possibly to travel. Once dissatisfaction sets in, however, you're quick to move on in search of the perfect career opportunity. This of course does not exist, which is something you learn with time and experience. In your day-to-day work life, you can have a significant and very positive impact on many people. You're the resident cheerleader, encouraging others, and exercising your leadership ability to bring out the best in yourself and coworkers. You also can do well as a manager.

You have excellent earning power, but also a tendency to splurge on impulse, especially for loved ones. Do yourself a favor: learn to live within a budget and make joint financial decisions with your partner. Both will go a long way toward creating the financial security you desire, as will regular savings and conservative, long-term investments. You could benefit from an inheritance or major gift from someone close to you, either a relative or friend.

Your Lighter Side

Chances are, you have a semisecret hobby. You might be a gourmet cook, or an outstanding musician, singer, artist, or photographer, or have an interest in graphic design. Explore this side of yourself this year by getting in touch with your exceptional creative energy. Or take your skills to the next level. It's also a great way to relax and recenter after a busy work day.

Affirmation for the Year

Financial security is my strength and my goal.

The Year Ahead for Pisces

Finances, home and family, your career, friendship, and knowledge are featured themes in 2012. All of these will occupy your time and attention at various times throughout the year, bringing gains in some areas and challenges in others.

The year begins with Jupiter in Taurus, the sign it transits through June 10. The daily pace will be hectic as Jupiter advances through your solar Third House, a placement that emphasizes quick trips, learning, and contact with siblings and neighbors. A community or neighborhood project could attract your interest this spring. If so, donate your skills and talents rather than your money. Take a similar approach if you plan to travel with friends or family, paying only your fair share of the costs. You'll also want to establish boundaries for calls, e-mail, and social media in order to better budget your time.

Jupiter enters Gemini June 11 to begin its year-long trip through your solar Fourth House of home, family, and domestic life. You could relocate under this influence, and rent or buy a new home. Be cautious, though, if you want to purchase property, as enthusiasm could encourage you to go for a larger mortgage. Do the opposite. Buy less and keep payments low. Jupiter here is also great for do-it-yourself home improvement projects, so take a close look at your place and let your creative mind generate low-cost ideas. Most of all, you'll enjoy time at home and with family, as well as entertaining friends.

Saturn changes signs later this year, spending most of 2012 in Libra, your solar Eighth House of joint resources. Here, Saturn emphasizes your partner's income, insurance, inheritance, taxes, and loans. This influence is one of the best for paying down debt and learning to manage your household with thrift in mind. It's important that both you and your partner are in agreement about your overall approach because this will increase your success in building financial security. Find the compromise that works for both of you.

Saturn also encourages you to examine your financial values and what matters most to you in a materialistic world. A luxury vehicle or a reliable one? A house full of the latest technology or only what satisfies your practical needs? Designer clothing for your kids or music and sports? Even if you've never considered these and similar questions, take advantage of this time to set the lifestyle pattern that's best for you and your family.

Saturn moves on to Scorpio, the sign it will occupy the next two and a half years as it transits your solar Ninth House. If you want to jump-start your career, develop a new one, or aim for a promotion, consider returning to school to begin or complete a degree or certification program. This could turn out to be just what you need to reach a career pinnacle when Saturn settles into your solar Tenth House in 2015.

Saturn in your solar Ninth House also favors travel, especially trips that emphasize learning about other cultures and visits to historical sites. You might also consider taking a vacation crash-course to enhance your cooking or creative skills. On another level, you can use this transit to deepen your spiritual journey through life by exploring and studying other belief systems.

Uranus continues its seven-year trip through Aries, your solar Second House. Like Saturn in Libra, this transit emphasizes money matters, but on a personal level: your income, spending habits, and generally how you manage your money. Take a close, honest, and realistic look at finances from a personal perspective. You'll find the results to be both surprising and enlightening. Then let Uranus motivate you to make necessary changes, including budgeting, the use of credit, savings goals, and how best to maximize your income in the short and long term.

Also, like the Eighth House, the Second House represents what you personally value—everything from security to possessions to your skills and talents. Examine this side of yourself, too, because these answers will help you form new attitudes and motivate you to maintain newly adopted financial habits. Take this a step further and tackle household clutter. Everything you toss out or sell helps to clear out old energy so you can attract an increased income. You could even earn some extra cash by holding a yard sale or taking unwanted items to consignment shops.

Neptune completes its time in Aquarius, your solar Twelfth House, February 2. Since it entered this sign in 1995, you've probably experienced periods where you preferred time alone to socializing and being with people. At the same time, this has given you the opportunity to look within, to access your inner voice, and to nurture your sixth sense. You also might have gained a greater appreciation for those less privileged by volunteering your time and effort for a good cause.

Neptune, your planetary ruler, begins its long journey through Pisces February 3. During the coming years, you'll reap the benefits of this inspirational planet as well as the faith it can generate, resulting in enhanced self-understanding and self-esteem. You'll become more at one with yourself, which will benefit the relationships in your life, possibly even more than what you personally gain from the experience. Despite these positives, you'll be more susceptible to people who talk a good game and have only their own best interests in mind. This of course means you need to be cautious about new people, especially those who make lofty promises or guarantees.

But Neptune is also known as the planet of illusion and confusion, so you can expect these feelings to take hold at times. It's all a part of the process of learning more about yourself and what you most want from life. Go easy on yourself and let your mind sort things out in its own time. Illusion eventually will be replaced by reality, and confusion by clarity.

Pluto occupies your solar Eleventh House as it advances through Capricorn. During its years here (until 2025), friends can change your life for the better in some way, and you'll do the same for them. You'll also attract new people into your life who are influential in the world, and others will appear just to help you achieve a specific goal or fulfill a wish. But there will be difficulties with some friends, and others may try to use you for their own ends.

You could take on a leadership position in a club, organization, or workplace team during these years, but some caution is necessary. Work hard at keeping things in perspective because it will be all too easy for your passion to become an obsession. You'll also need to remember to lead rather than dictate in any group activity. Prepare yourself by reading best-selling books that focus on leadership skills.

What This Year's Eclipses Mean for You

There are four eclipses in 2012, two solar and two lunar, and each is in effect for six to twelve months. Two of the eclipses are in Gemini, highlighting your domestic life, another focuses on your career, and the fourth is in your travel and education sector. All of these will influence your life this year and into 2013.

Jupiter, which enters Gemini, your solar Fourth House, June 11, will complement the May 21 solar eclipse in the same sign. Together, these influences increase the chance for positive developments in your domestic or family life, including a new house that will quickly become a home. The eclipse energy could motivate you to research your ancestors, and to create scrapbooks to preserve family memories. You also could welcome an addition to the family later this year or in 2013 as the November 28 lunar eclipse in Gemini re-energizes this solar sector.

June 4 will bring the year's first lunar eclipse, which will shine brightly in Sagittarius, your solar Tenth House. You'll be highly visible, thanks to this lunar energy, creating an opportunity to advance your career aims and elevate your status. Set your sights on a goal that could be attained this fall, and devise a plan to get where you want to go. This eclipse also encourages you to strive for a lifestyle that balances career and family time rather than overdoing one or the other.

The November 13 solar eclipse in Scorpio, your solar Ninth House, mirrors the influence of Saturn in the same sign after October 4. This will spark your spirit of adventure and initiate a quest for knowledge. Plan a winter or spring trip to a destination you've never before visited, and also check into online learning programs.

Saturn

If you were born between March 11 and 20, Saturn will contact your Sun from Libra before October 5. Saturn's energy will be focused on your Sun in June or July **if your birthday is March 11, 12, or 13**. Otherwise, Saturn will influence your life once between January and May, and again in August or September.

Money matters will require your attention during this transit, which could bring a decrease in family funds, possibly because of extra expenses or the increased cost of job benefits. This may or may not occur, but you'll want to plan ahead and get serious about putting your finances in order. Target debt reduction, building savings and retirement funds, and generally operating your household on a slimmer budget. Saturn is always about learning and responsibility, so make these your financial mission.

You'll also want to be sure your property and possessions are fully protected by vehicle and homeowner's or renter's insurance. Shop around if you need a new policy, and then read all the fine print before you sign. Then you can be confident you're covered should a claim be necessary.

During this time you could hear news about an inheritance, or an old financial matter could come to light or be settled. Check your credit reports for errors. If you're owed money, you may be able to collect it now. Conversely, it may be necessary to settle an old debt.

If your birthday is between February 19 and 28, you're among the first of your sign to have Saturn contact your Sun from Scorpio, your solar Ninth House. This favorable connection, which will occur after Saturn enters this sign October 5, will increase your stamina and determination, and have a steadying influence in your life. Saturn will again contact your Sun next year, so think of this first transit as only an initial step in your journey.

Seriously consider additional schooling that could help advance your career in a few years. Or enroll in a class to learn a foreign language or another subject that has always been of interest. Your goal, however you achieve it, should be to stretch your mind in order to explore new territory. You can also do this through travel, public television, reading, and getting acquainted with people from different cultural backgrounds.

Most important is individual growth. Get in touch with the world at large by exploring your life philosophy and how you fit into the bigger scheme of things. The more you question things, the greater your growth. Similarly, religion and spirituality are also associated with this sector. You may return to or reject the religion of your childhood, or embrace a new set of beliefs to guide your daily life. Examine the past to prepare yourself for the future.

Uranus
If you were born between February 19 and 29, Uranus will contact your Sun from Aries, your solar Second House of income, possessions, and spending. This transit won't necessarily affect your income. But it could, so the wise choice is to conserve resources. Be thrifty, avoid credit as much as possible, and save a higher percentage of your income. Take a close look at how you spend and on what, and then find ways to cut back where you can. Learn to be a better, thriftier shopper, and set up an savings plan at your bank.

This Uranus-Sun contact is great for disposing of unneeded and unwanted items, and you can probably net a profit from your discards. This is the practical, outer level of the changes occurring within as you sort through what you value personally, materialistically, and in your life as a whole. Define this first. Otherwise, you could toss out more than you intend just because of the urge to acquire new possessions, which could be strong—and expensive.

Neptune
If your birthday is between March 17 and 20, Neptune will contact your Sun from Aquarius, your solar Twelfth House, during January and the first few days of February, just as it did in 2011. Use this brief contact to review the past year and what you learned about yourself and your innermost desires. Reflect on the new truths you discovered and then decide how you can best incorporate them into your life as Neptune begins its transit of your sign.

If you were born between February 19 and 22, you'll have an extra special aura this year, thanks to Neptune's merger with your Pisces Sun. This magical combination is among the best for romance. But don't take things too seriously if you launch a dating relationship. What feels like true love may be only an illusion of the moment.

In addition to boosting your charm and powers to attract, Neptune will trigger your sixth sense. The more you listen the greater its strength, so nurture this side of yourself. Also take note of dreams, which can be insightful and even prophetic. Find an outlet to express your creativity, whether through art, music, or a favorite hobby.

But Neptune's influence can have you feeling as though you're in a fog, drifting and directionless, with ideas and plans shifting like the wind. Postpone major life decisions until next year, and be skeptical of anyone who tries too hard to convince you to make a major step, especially one involving money. Under this transit, it's as easy to be deceived by others as it is to experience moments of idealistic self-deception.

Pluto

If your birthday is between February 25 and 28, Pluto will contact your Sun from Capricorn, your solar Eleventh House. Group activities and friends will be prominent in your life this year, and you can be an effective leader in a teamwork setting, motivating others to do and be their best. In the process, you'll gain strength as a leader and deepen your knowledge of people.

You can also effectively tap Pluto's willpower and make it your own on a journey of transformation. Use it to slim down, maintain a moderate exercise program, change your diet, replace a bad habit with a good one, or almost anything else that will enhance your self-esteem.

A friend could transform your life this year, and you can do the same for others. It's also possible that someone you meet could become a valuable networking contact. But the possibility for manipulation also exists, so be wary of people who play games or try to push you into supporting their ego-driven interests.

Uranus in Aries, your solar Second House, will clash with Pluto in late June and mid-September. This could trigger a rift between you and a friend or organization. The issue could be related to finances or a strong difference in values. No matter how much you're pressured, don't mix money with friendship, especially if you're asked to cosign a loan. The odds are that you'll end up with the debt, or never be repaid if you lend money to a friend in need. Protect your resources and put you and yours first.

Pisces | January

Planetary Lightspots

Look forward to January 14. That's the date Venus enters Pisces. With it comes an increased ability to attract exactly what you want, from people to good fortune to money to success. You could hear good news within a week or so after Venus arrives in your sign, so share your wishes with the universe.

Relationships

Your social life gets a boost from the January 9 Full Moon in Cancer, your solar Fifth House, along with Mercury in Capricorn, your solar Eleventh House, from the 8th to the 26th. But you'll want to avoid seeing friends on the 14th and 20th, dates with potential for conflict. The 13th, however, is a good choice for a first date or a romantic evening with your partner.

Money and Success

You can be an effective communicator on the job the first week of January, thanks to Mercury in Sagittarius, your solar Tenth House of career and status. But you'll need to stay focused and remain calm on the 6th, when it might be tough to get your point across. Schedule an important talk or meeting for another date, if possible, and remind yourself not to be overly sensitive to the comments of others.

Planetary Hotspots

Expect periodic relationship upsets from January 23 to April 12 as Mars in Virgo, your solar Seventh House, travels retrograde. This can affect a committed relationship, family ties, and close friendships. But the retrograde period is not the time to end a relationship. A better choice is to try to objectively reflect on events and viewpoints that differ from yours. Then you'll be better prepared to make the best decision for you in late April or May.

Rewarding Days
3, 4, 13, 17, 21, 25, 30, 31

Challenging Days
1, 6, 7, 8, 14, 20, 22, 26

Pisces | February

Planetary Lightspots

You're at your most charming around the February 21 New Moon in your sign, and its alignment with Neptune enhances your ability to convince others to see things your way. Dream big as your symbolic solar year begins and then narrow your thoughts to the personal goals you want to achieve in the next twelve months. Make sure they're achievable and then put plans in motion.

Relationships

Again this month, relationships will be rocky at times with Mars still retrograde in Virgo, your solar Seventh House. But you'll also experience some uplifting moments as Mercury forms favorable alignments from your sign. Your words can inspire others around the 19th and at month's end, when you could also receive some very good news. Avoid controversial topics the first few days of February and again on the 22nd and 24th.

Money and Success

The work pace picks up under the February 7 Full Moon in Leo, your solar Sixth House. Balance busy days with evening exercise or time with a hobby. You could hear confidential job-related information near the Full Moon, or a coworker might share a secret. Don't share any of yours, however, because it's likely to be revealed later this month.

Planetary Hotspots

Unexpected expenses could arise after Venus enters Aries, your solar Second House, February 8. The 15th could be particularly challenging. A forgotten bill could come to light at that time or someone might ask you for a loan. Deal with the first possibility, and say no to the second. But planetary alignments could also bring you a small windfall around the 9th.

Rewarding Days

9, 13, 17, 21, 23, 26, 27

Challenging Days

3, 4, 10, 15, 22, 24

Pisces | March

Planetary Lightspots

Happy thoughts and good news accompany Venus in Taurus transiting your solar Third House after March 4. Connect with friends, socialize with coworkers, and share your upbeat optimism with everyone in your world. If you have the opportunity, get involved in a community project that offers the chance to network.

Relationships

The March 8 Full Moon in Virgo spotlights your solar Seventh House of relationships. Although you'll experience some uplifting moments with those you love, there is also increased potential for misunderstandings with Mars retrograde in this sector. Choose your words with care, and try to avoid difficult people, especially the first few days of March.

Money and Success

Even with retrograde Mercury, the March 22 New Moon in Aries could bring favorable financial news. But the cash could be delayed. You could profit through a small windfall, or find a sensational deal on clothing. If you shop, look for mismarked items at deep-discount sales.

Planetary Hotspots

Pay bills early this month and confirm that payments are received. With Mercury turning retrograde in Aries, your solar Second House, March 12, it would be all too easy for a payment to go astray, or be forgotten. Also avoid major purchases and financial decisions during this period. Retrograde Mercury slips back into your sign on the 23rd, so don't be surprised if some personal plans are stalled. Consider it an opportunity to review your goals for the next twelve months. Then you'll be able to move ahead with speed in mid-April.

Rewarding Days

11, 12, 16, 18, 21, 25, 26

Challenging Days

2, 3, 4, 7, 9, 13, 30

Pisces | April

Planetary Lightspots

Look forward to April 13. That's the date Mercury turns direct in your sign. Within days your life will begin to gain momentum as fresh energy triggers thoughts of all you want to do. Better yet, you'll feel as though you're making progress on the personal to-do list you developed (or should have) in March.

Relationships

Relationships also begin to return to normalcy after Mars in Virgo, your solar Seventh House, resumes direct motion on the 13th. Make a point to resolve any disagreements that occurred while Mars was retrograde, especially with partner and family. Prior to that, however, you'll want to go out of your way to avoid misunderstandings during the first week after Venus enters Gemini, your solar Fourth House, April 3.

Money and Success

The April 6 Full Moon in Libra, your solar Eighth House, highlights joint resources. If you haven't yet filed your tax return, the lunar energy will help you remedy that. Be sure to double-check all figures as Mercury will still be retrograde at that time. If you've already completed this task, the Full Moon could bring you a modest refund.

Planetary Hotspots

This month's hotspot isn't a single event. Rather, you'll experience aggravation in several sectors, mostly involving communication. A disagreement could end a friendship mid-month. But hold off if you have a change of heart later in April as the issues that caused the problem will always be present, even if under the surface. Focus on other friendships and look to widen your circle with people who are more compatible with you.

Rewarding Days

4, 8, 12, 14, 17, 21, 22, 27

Challenging Days

3, 5, 7, 9, 11, 15, 16, 24

Pisces I May

Planetary Lightspots

Need an excuse to dash out of town for a long weekend or vacation trip? It's yours, thanks to the May 5 Full Moon in Scorpio, your solar Ninth House. Make reservations for a summer getaway, or treat yourself to a relaxing few days this month. But go before the 20th, after which you'll be more in the mood to stay home.

Relationships

Relationships benefit from Mercury in Taurus, your solar Third House of communication, May 9–23. Easy planetary alignments favor memorable moments with your partner and siblings, as well as community and neighborhood friends. The 19th is a good choice if you want to host a barbecue for neighbors and their families. But month's end could bring domestic tension. Avoid sensitive subjects.

Money and Success

Finances could be tight in early May when difficult influences involving your solar Second House indicate restriction. This is also not the time to seek a loan, incur debt, or even to shop. It will be tough to find what you want and at a reasonable price. Particularly avoid an evening out with friends because you could end up with far more than your fair share of the bill or lose a valuable possession.

Planetary Hotspots

Venus in Gemini begins its six-week retrograde period May 15. You'll feel its influence most strongly in family and domestic matters, including periodic confusion and misunderstandings. This is not the time to begin a home improvement or decorating project even though you may have a strong urge to do this. If you do, the result won't be as expected or you'll decide to start over once Venus turns direct in June. Instead, use this time for planning.

Rewarding Days

1, 6, 13, 14, 15, 18, 19, 24

Challenging Days

3, 4, 8, 9, 16, 21, 23, 30

Pisces | June

Planetary Lightspots

Jupiter enters Gemini, your solar Fourth House, June 11. Good fortune will surround your family and domestic life for the next twelve months, and you'll create many happy memories of special times with loved ones and close friends. This month, Jupiter accents inspiration and optimism for the future when someone close to you shares words of wisdom.

Relationships

Venus travels retrograde until the 27th, before which it can trigger disagreements with family members. But this might be more your perception than reality. Listen closely to what others say. There may be far more truth and honesty in their statements than you're initially willing to accept. Later in June, Mercury in Cancer favors inexpensive social outings.

Money and Success

The June 4 Full Moon in Sagittarius, your solar Tenth House, could trigger conflict with anyone from a supervisor to a coworker to your partner (business or personal). Maintain a low profile, steer clear of controversial subjects, and don't let your temper take hold. It will be all too easy in the heat of the moment—even for you—to say or do something you'll later regret.

Planetary Hotspots

June 24 marks the date of this year's first Uranus-Pluto alignment. (The second is September 19.) With the energy coming from Aries and Capricorn, your solar Second and Eleventh Houses, money will be a key component. It also could involve a friend, lowered income, or a debt. In any case, this is not the month for major purchases or anything other than necessities. Save what you can.

Rewarding Days

1, 2, 9, 14, 15, 16, 19, 21, 25

Challenging Days

5, 6, 10, 11, 12, 20, 24, 27, 29

Pisces | July

Planetary Lightspots

The universe offers you a perfect stress reliever this month: home. Take advantage of favorable planetary alignments involving Venus and Jupiter in Gemini, your solar Fourth House, to relax and unwind at the end of the day. If you feel ambitious, use your creativity to redo a room on a budget. If you want to entertain friends, the 7th is a good choice.

Relationships

Both the July 3 Full Moon in Capricorn and the New Moon in Cancer on the 19th will trigger relationship difficulties. A friendship could end as a result, and the same is possible with a dating relationship. The issues are likely to be money and values or your or your partner's spending habits. But you'll also have some upbeat times, especially around the 22nd, when loving ties will become more so.

Money and Success

Mars enters Libra, your solar Eighth House of joint resources, July 3, the same date as the Full Moon. Expect finances to be on the agenda around that date. But try to remain calm even if you and your mate disagree about a purchase or how best to budget income. Use Mars instead to change habits that need changing and to generate extra income during the next seven weeks.

Planetary Hotspots

Your job will be the main area of life affected by Mercury after it turns retrograde July 14. Transiting Leo, your solar Sixth House, Mercury can trigger mix-ups with projects and instructions, misunderstandings with coworkers, and missed details. Double-check all your work, even if you think it's error-free. It's not. Also be prepared for indecision in some matters and delays on others.

Rewarding Days
7, 8, 12, 22, 23, 26, 27

Challenging Days
2, 4, 9, 17, 18, 24, 30

Pisces | August

Planetary Lightspots

The two Full Moons this month—August 1 in Aquarius, your solar Twelfth House, and August 31 in your sign—focus their energy on you and the value of taking it easy evenings and weekends. After working hard, it's the least you can do for yourself. Even better, get some exercise, spend time with a hobby and your kids, and also enjoy your own company and the comforts of home.

Relationships

You could experience some difficult moments with your children this month, including a battle of the wills. If you have a teen, expect a strong independent streak to emerge that will test your limits. Don't necessarily believe all your children tell you. Research the facts on your own, and also make a point to get to know your children's friends and their parents. You and your partner will be on the same wavelength after the Sun enters Virgo on the 22nd.

Money and Success

Your work life is upbeat this month, especially after Mercury turns direct in Leo, your solar Sixth House, on the 8th. Later, the August 17 New Moon in Leo adds extra incentive for high productivity and could even earn you a raise or small bonus. If you're job hunting, the New Moon could help you find a new position.

Planetary Hotspots

Although not to the level of last month, money matters will be challenging at times, with the most trying period being mid-month when several planets clash. Continue to monitor your budget and limit spending while finding free activities for summer fun. But there's also a chance you could earn some extra money during the last two weeks of August.

Rewarding Days

3, 4, 8, 9, 14, 18, 19, 22, 23

Challenging Days

6, 7, 13, 15, 20, 21, 24, 26, 28

Pisces | September

Planetary Lightspots

Your home will continue to be your haven this month as Jupiter advances in Gemini, your solar Fourth House. Be lazy and enjoy relaxing moments there, knowing you're surrounded by upbeat energy and your favorite people. Keep in touch with relatives, who will be especially supportive.

Relationships

The September 15 New Moon in Virgo puts other people in the spotlight as it activates your solar Seventh House of relationships. You'll have much contact with friends, family, coworkers, and most of all, your partner, and you'll be in tune with almost everyone. In addition to being one of the best months of the year for relationships, others will inspire you to pursue your goals with determination. If you're in a serious dating relationship, the lunar energy could prompt you to take things to the next level.

Money and Success

You'll be among the most popular coworkers as Venus transits Leo, your solar Sixth House, from September 6 on. A business trip is possible at month's end, or you could have an opportunity to attend a training class. If you have a desk job, add a few personal touches to your space such as family photos or a plant.

Planetary Hotspots

Uranus and Pluto clash again this month, just as they did in June. The most challenging days will be those around the September 29 Full Moon in Aries, your solar Second House. Finances will be the major thrust, with secondary emphasis on friends, groups, and legal matters. You could find yourself in a conflict involving insurance or an inheritance, or feel the pinch of reduced income and increased expenses.

Rewarding Days
1, 5, 6, 9, 14, 27, 28, 30

Challenging Days
2, 10, 11, 16, 19, 23, 24, 26

Pisces | October

Planetary Lightspots

A vacation or even a weekend getaway could provide just the change of scenery you need to unwind and refresh your spirit. It's a great way to use the positive planetary alignments in Scorpio, your solar Ninth House. But avoid the last week of the month, when weather delays are possible. If time away is impossible now, substitute with a quick community class that will enhance your creativity. You might even get the urge to return to school after Saturn enters Scorpio October 5.

Relationships

Love, romance, and togetherness are in the spotlight as Venus travels in Virgo, your solar Seventh House, October 3–27. Give loved ones extra time and attention, and plan an evening for two with your partner early in the month. A friendship could deepen considerably this month, or you might discover that someone you've known quite a while has romantic potential.

Money and Success

Finances are on the upswing this month, with the New Moon in Libra, your solar Eighth House, on the 15th. The week before you could hear long-awaited positive financial news, and possibly a raise or additional benefits for you or your mate.

Planetary Hotspots

Life calms somewhat after some challenging months, and you can look forward to days and even weeks that are mostly status quo. Mars, however, will stir things up after it enters Sagittarius, your solar Tenth House of career and status, October 6. Handle any upsets with finesse and charm and go out of your way to befriend those who aren't exactly your biggest supporters. Be skeptical, though, of anyone who tries too hard to win you over.

Rewarding Days

2, 3, 8, 12, 16, 21, 24, 30

Challenging Days

1, 4, 7, 11, 14, 25, 27, 31

Pisces | November

Planetary Lightspots

You'll be just as happy to stay home, especially as the November 28 Full Moon (lunar eclipse) in Gemini activates your solar Fourth House of family and all things domestic. Use this upbeat lunar energy to decorate your home for the holidays and also to host a December get-together for friends and coworkers.

Relationships

Your social life gets a holiday boost from Mars, which enters Capricorn, your solar Eleventh House, November 16. But you'll need to avoid some dates if you plan to see friends. The days near the 23rd and 27th could bring harsh words with a friend, and you'll also realize that buying gifts for a wide variety of people is far too expensive. That's okay. Plan now to bake cookies and other treats to give as gifts. Be sure to confirm dates, times, and places while Mercury is retrograde.

Money and Success

Venus in Libra, your solar Eighth House, through the 20th could bring a small windfall, but also an unexpected expense. Social outings with friends could be expensive, so check prices ahead of time and be prepared to suggest an alternative. Be alert on the 1st, when you could make a lucky find.

Planetary Hotspots

Despite the influence of action-oriented Mars in Sagittarius, your solar Tenth House, through November 15, career matters will stall as Mercury turns retrograde in the same sign on the 5th. It then slips back into Scorpio, your solar Ninth House, on the 14th before turning direct on the 26th. Travel will thus be prone to cancellations and delays. If you invite relatives to visit, be prepared for them to stay a while.

Rewarding Days
4, 9, 12, 20, 21, 25

Challenging Days
3, 5, 10, 16, 23

Pisces | December

Planetary Lightspots

Mars slips into Aquarius, your solar Twelfth House, on the 25th, where it will be until early February. Consider this a time-out, the chance to catch up with yourself and your life. You can also use this influence to clean closets and storage spaces and turn the discards into cash. The exercise will be therapeutic and could be lucrative.

Relationships

Both Mercury and Venus form favorable planetary contacts this month, first from Scorpio and then from Sagittarius. Together, they'll put you in touch with many people, including out-of-town friends and relatives. Organize a holiday get-together with coworkers after the 14th, when both planets will be in your solar Tenth House. And with Jupiter in your solar Fourth House, this month is a good one to entertain friends.

Money and Success

The December 13 New Moon in Sagittarius will have you in the career spotlight. It also could trigger a nice year-end bonus, and possibly talk of even greater things to come in 2013. Use the lunar energy for subtle self-promotion with all the right people, but don't believe everything you hear. Some people may stretch the truth in order to further their own interests.

Planetary Hotspots

December perks along until the last week of the month when the year's recurring themes are activated by the Full Moon in Cancer on the 28th. The lunar energy could trigger conflict with a friend or challenges with one of your children or a group you're involved in, and possibly finances. Help things along by taking charge and having faith in yourself.

Rewarding Days

2, 5, 9, 10, 15, 19, 22, 24, 29

Challenging Days

3, 7, 8, 14, 20, 28, 30

Pisces Action Table

These dates reflect the best—but not the only—times for success and ease in these activities, according to your Sun sign.

	JAN	FEB	MAR	APR	MAY	JUN	JUL	AUG	SEP	OCT	NOV	DEC
Move				23–25			5–8					
Start a class		26–28			9–19				4			
Join a club	9–19				9, 10							
Ask for a raise												20
Look for work								8–24				12–20
Get pro advice	12								14	12		
Get a loan									25	15		
See a doctor	10, 11						5	16, 17	12	9		31
Start a diet									12			3
End relationship											30	1
Buy clothes		4						31	1			
Get a makeover								13				1
New romance										16–26		1–9
Vacation	16–18											

2012
SUN SIGN
BOOK

Articles

Contributors

April Elliott Kent

Alice DeVille

Tim Lyons

Ivy Payton

Carole Schwalm

Bruce Scofield

Legend of the Five Suns
by Bruce Scofield

Early cultures such as the Egyptian, Hindu, Chinese, and Maya developed mythologies that offered nontechnical explanations for why we humans are here on Earth. It is natural to ask such questions, and large human societies tend to standardize such explanations, which over time may become doctrines of the dominant religions. Traditionally, our Western world view has been based on Middle Eastern mythology as written down by the Hebrews. Here the creator god first makes the world and then makes a human, Adam. But things are not right with Adam, and so the Creator makes a woman, Eve. But then the serpent tempts Eve, leading to expulsion from the Garden of Eden, and things get complicated.

After this fall from perfection, Adam, Eve, and their descendants have to learn to survive in the real world. The authoritative text of the Judeo-Christian religion, the Bible, recounts this story and then goes on to link these mythological early humans with historical personages. The Maya did the same thing in their creation epoch, the *Popol Vuh*. In this text the creator god made other gods who then made people, but the people had to learn on their own how to navigate the dark Underworld and better understand sacrifice and death, the two big themes of Mesoamerican civilization. When the hero twins of the *Popol Vuh* triumph over death, the narrative moves on to link the ancient mythology with historical family lineages. It appears this linking is a fine way to cement the authority or importance of one group over another.

The Bible describes the world as lying between Heaven and Hell. In Maya cosmology, we find a similar, though more detailed, description of a layered universe where the Earth plane is at the center, or between, the Underworld and the Heavens. The Earth plane itself is actually located on the back of a gigantic primordial crocodile that rests in an immense pool filled with water lilies. The Maya perceived the Earth as flat with four corners corresponding to the four directions, each with its own specific color.

> White — North
> Yellow — South
> Red — East
> Black — West
> Green — the Center

The sky was created from a two-headed serpent whose body was generated by the paths crossed by the Sun, Moon, planets, and so forth, which is probably the ecliptic used to measure the planets in astrology. The heavens, supported either by four skybearers or five trees (four in each cardinal direction and one in the center), were of thirteen levels, with one god assigned to each level. Beneath was the Underworld, called Xibalba, where one god was also assigned to each of its nine levels. In the *Popol Vuh*, the hero twins defeat the Lords of Xibalba, and thereby save humanity from their visitations.

The Aztecs were a culture that flourished more recently than the ancient Maya, yet their cosmology was similar. Their layered universe was also sometimes described as a primordial cosmic serpent, though the serpent was divided into three sections. Each section had a special domain: the head held the thirteen heavenly levels, the Earth was at the center, and the tail contained the nine levels of the Underworld. Like the Maya cosmos, each of these three sections had their own cardinal directions and all were connected at the center.

Once the general nature of the cosmos is mapped out, a culture needs to explain how the world we live in came to be. The Bible says God created all things. In Aztec mythology, Ometeotl, the first god, actually created itself. Ometeotl was not just a single god, it was a duality: both male and female, good and evil, light and darkness, fire and water, and so on. But Ometeotl only created so much, and then this dual god stepped out of the creation business. Ometeotl created or gave birth to four major gods, the four Tezcatlipocas, who each preside over one of the four cardinal directions. The correspondences are:

> East — White Tezcatlipoca; Quetzalcoatl, god of light, mercy and wind
> South — Blue Tezcatlipoca; Huitzilopochtli, god of war
> West — Red Tezcatlipoca; Xipe Totec, god of gold, farming and springtime
> North — Black Tezcatlipoca; Tezcatlipoca, god of judgment, night, deceit, sorcery, and the Earth

You can see that there is some confusion here, because one of the Tezcatlipocas goes by that name alone. But the important point is that these four gods created all the other gods and the world itself. The work of the first god, Ometeotl, was done. However, before the Tezcatlipocas could get anywhere with the work of creating other gods, nature, and finally people, they had to destroy Cipactli, the giant earth crocodile that kept destroying their creations. They did this by ripping her in half, an action that formed the Earth and sky. Her head, the symbol of the first of the twenty day-signs, is always depicted as having only an upper jaw. The four Tezcatlipocas next created the other gods, the most important of whom were the water gods: Tlaloc, the god of rain and fertility; and Chalchiuhtlicue, the goddess of lakes, rivers, oceans, and also beauty.

In Aztec mythology there was not a "single" creation, but rather a series of creations called "Suns." The first four Suns failed and were destroyed at the end of their time span. These four previous Suns are depicted in the center of the Aztec Sun Stone, the *Piedra del Sol*, as squares surrounding the central face. The first Sun was the jaguar Sun (Nahui Ocelotl), which was established by Tezcatlipoca. To complete the world, a great source of energy had to be created—the physical Sun. Tezcatlipoca, however, only managed to become half a Sun, making this first creation incomplete. During this first age, the gods created giant people from ashes, and gave them acorns to eat. But things did not go well, and a fight began between Quetzalcoatl and Tezcatlipoca. Quetzalcoatl, one of the original four gods, couldn't bear his enemy ruling the universe, so he knocked Tezcatlipoca, as the fiery Sun, out of the sky. In anger, Tezcatlipoca sent jaguars to destroy the giants and the world, so things sank back to the conditions that had existed at the beginning. This age is commemorated in the Sun Stone with the glyph of the day-sign Ocelotl (Jaguar) on the upper right.

Next, Quetzalcoatl took his turn at the steering wheel of creation and started the second age of the world, called the Wind Sun (Nahui Ehecatl). Soon this world became populated again, this time by humans of normal size. They lived on piñon nuts, and things went along fine for a while. Eventually, however, the people became corrupt, and the meddling Tezcatlipoca turned them into monkeys, probably out of frustration for his failure with the first Sun. Furious at this interference, Quetzalcoatl sent a hurricane to blow the monkeys away, and this ended the age. This age is commemorated in the Sun Stone with the glyph of Ehecatl, the form of Quetzalcoatl as a wind god, and the glyph of the day-sign Ehecatl (Wind), located on the upper left.

The next Sun was the Rain Sun (Nahui Quiahuitl). Tlaloc, the god of rain, took charge of this creation. He shone as the Sun, but for some reason refused to send rain in spite of the pleas of the people. Then, the ever-meddling and aggressive Tezcatlipoca stole Tlaloc's wife (Xochiquetzal), and Tlaloc was grief-stricken. Drought swept the Earth. Finally, in a rage, Tlaloc made it rain fire, which burned away this version of the world—except for a few humans who survived and were turned into birds. This age is commemorated in the Sun Stone with the glyph of the day-sign Quiahuitl (Rain), a symbol of Tlaloc, on the lower left.

Next the gods selected Tlaloc's sister Chalchiuhtlicue, the Water Goddess, to became the Sun (Nahui Atl). But Tezcatlipoca and Quetzalcoatl were filled with jealousy and they struck her down. As she fell, the sky opened up and water flooded the Earth, bringing a great destruction. The people who survived were turned into fish.

This creation is commemorated in the Sun Stone with the glyph of the day-sign Atl (Water), located in the lower right. This fourth world that was destroyed by a flood was the world before the one we live in now. It is interesting to compare this with similar myths from other cultures. Perhaps they all recall the rapid rise in sea level at the end of the last ice age.

Now, in the darkness between the Suns, Quetzalcoatl could not accept the destruction of his people, so he came up with a plan to restore humans in a new and better world. Along with his *nagual* (spirit twin) Xolotl the dog, he descended to the Underworld to collect the bones of the ancestors, the previous humans, from which he would make new people. To do this, he had to confront and trick the Underworld death god Mictlantecuhtli, which he did, and then he retrieved the sacred bones. Quetzalcoatl then ground up the bones and mixed them with corn and with his own blood. Human beings were the result of this combination.

People now existed, but there was no Sun for light because no other god or goddess wanted the job of being the Sun. This was a big problem because the next world could not come into being without a Sun. This crisis required a great meeting of the gods at the ancient city of Teotihuacan, which means "the place where men become gods."

In each of the four previous creations, one god had taken the toil of being the Sun: Quetzalcoatl, Tezcatlipoca, Tlaloc, and Chalchiuhitlicue. But each age inevitably ended because the gods fought amongst themselves and were not satisfied with the people they had created. Together the gods decided that the future, and possibly last, Sun would require the ultimate sacrifice. Two gods were chosen for this job: the haughty Tecciztecatl and the disease-stricken and lowly Nanahuatzin. A great fire was made, which burned for four days. When it came time for Tecciztecatl to jump into the fire, he failed four times out of fear. Frustrated, the other gods asked the weak Nanahuatzin to jump, which he did and succeeded in becoming a heavenly body. When Tecciztecatl saw that Nanahuatzin had jumped, his pride was wounded and so he jumped into the fire. Eventually, two Suns appeared in the sky. The gods became disturbed by what they saw because the second glowing disk, an undeserving Tecciztecatl, was shining equally to Nanahuatzin. So one of the gods took a rabbit and threw it in the face of Tecciztecatl. Tecciztecatl lost his brilliance, and the rabbit became permanently marked on his face—and the people of Mexico still say the Moon has the image of a rabbit!

But still the Sun did not move, and the gods came to accept that a very powerful sacrifice was needed—all of them needed to die so that people could live. The great god Ehecatl then singlehandedly sacrificed all the rest of the gods, and with a powerful wind that was blown from his mask he started the new Sun in motion. After this mass sacrifice, the Aztec gods had no real earthly power, because they only existed in the spiritual world. But the actions of the gods reminded people that they needed to repay the gods through their own sacrifices. As we know, the Aztec high priests took this very seriously and institutionalized a rather gruesome religion.

According to the legend of the Five Suns, the world is now in the fifth creation. In the Aztec Sun Stone, this is indicated by the face in the center, the image of the god Tonatiuh. He is the deity of the day-sign Ollin, which translates as "motion" or "earthquake." This age is said to end with destructive earthquakes. But when does the age end?

In a post-conquest document, "Legends of the Sun," some numbers are given that suggest the ages are measured in multiples of fifty-two, the number of years in an Aztec calendar round, what some call the Aztec century. The Harmonic Convergence of 1987 was justified by its orchestrators as being nine cycles of fifty-two years since the 1519 invasion of the Aztecs by Hernado Cortes. But nobody knows for sure what the official counting of the ages really was. The legend only tells us that there are five ages and that we're living in the last one, and that it will likely end with earthquakes.

All of this brings us to the present year, 2012. The Maya wrote many dates in stone and there is no question that their Long Count ends this year on December 21. Something to consider is that the 5,125-year Long Count is very close to one-fifth of the cycle of precession, which suggests the Maya looked at this approximately 26,000-year orbital cycle as composed of five ages—not unlike the Five Suns. The Maya didn't say any of this specifically, but if you consider that so many Maya things are just like those of the Aztec, it's possible that these similarities are really quite fundamental, and we could reasonably consider the Long Count to be essentially equivalent to the fifth Sun.

Does that mean the world will end in 2012? Not at all—the Maya had much longer periods of time and for them this fifth Sun was just one of many long blocks of time the world was passing through. Maybe it just marks a bumpy ride on the road to a better future.

References

Burland, C. A. *The Gods of Mexico*. New York: G.P. Putnam's Sons, 1967.

Duran, Fray Diego. *The Book of the Gods and the Rites and the Ancient Calendar*. Translated and edited by F. Horcasitas and D. Heyden. Norman: University of Oklahoma Press, 1971.

Markman, Roberta H., and Peter T. Markman. *The Flayed God*. San Francisco: Harper Collins,1992.

Miller, Mary and Karl Taube. *The Gods and Symbols of Ancient Mexico and the Maya*. London: Thames and Hudson, 1993.

Consider Green
if You Choose a New Career
by Alice DeVille

In our rapidly changing economic climate, over 10 percent of the United States population will look for opportunities to switch careers in 2012. People who were laid off from traditional jobs in recent months will perform many of these job searches. And while many of these new hires will feel lucky to have landed a new job, they will also feel dissatisfied with the transition position if it pays less than their former position, or if they feel underutilized in the new job. Hoping to tap into new and emerging networks, an increasing number of avid job hunters will look at career paths that have been designated "green." While looking at the realistic "Big Picture" that includes some of the obstacles to progress, this article broadly highlights career possibilities in green industries.

The Reality Check

It has been suggested that in the next decade it will be hard to distinguish between a green job and those that are viewed as traditional. Want the truth? When it comes to creating a green environment, interrelated industries are in different stages of implementation. Their challenge is to collaborate to bring green processes to the forefront. But first they must identify what resources are considered "renewable" and where they can be found. With a federally mandated renewable energy standard (RES), a percentage of each state's energy is supposed to be produced from "renewable" sources. The problem with such a mandate is that geographical locations vary, and some states do not have access to affordable renewable energy sources, meaning the legislation is inequitable.

Going "green" comes with a price. Organizations with big budgets can move more easily into the flow. Small businesses that are struggling to recover from the recession and do not have the deep pockets to pay for implementing new policies and proposals dictated by Congress are apt to feel an additional burden. The capital in these smaller firms takes too big a hit. Fewer jobs are generated, profits and employee benefits are reduced, job layoffs occur in some cases, and higher prices are passed on to consumers. These companies need to hire smart business managers and long-range planners to steer them toward profitability. And the case for phasing in the energy policy over time needs to be made to the government.

Astrological Indicators of Career Change

The trail-blazing spirit of transiting Uranus in Aries offers us a new beginning and the challenge to be pioneers in emerging fields of discovery in 2012. Transiting Neptune is also in a neophyte stage as it enters its natal home, Pisces, in early February, launching a journey that combines deep insight with spiritual integrity. Along with the stamina to work behind the scenes to create new definitions for the evolving changes, Neptune enjoys quiet time and reflection to identify key steps in career transition and to refine destiny. Jupiter in Taurus is a solid bet to work in tandem with Neptune to define the need for secure incomes and investments in new products. Saturn spends the first nine months of the year wrapping up its tour in Libra, the sign that seeks balance in life, in cooperative agreements, in partnerships, and in compromise. Pluto in Capricorn, the planet associated with transformation, could attract you to the interests of large enterprises or government agencies hiring staff for emerging initiatives.

If any of these transiting planets occupies your natal Second House (income and resources), Sixth House (daily work and productivity), Tenth House (career and status), and sometimes the Eighth House (partnership income and assets, income from a new source, or investment in a commodity), you could be among those seeking a new career. If you are aware of new green initiatives and feel the desire to join forces with organizations that set high performance standards, it will be up to you to articulate what type of position you would like in your search for greater career fulfillment. See your astrologer for a chart update to determine the best times for seeking new employment.

How Are Green Jobs Defined?

Green jobs are designed to have either a direct or an indirect positive impact on the environment. You hear about them mostly through the media. Although no universal definition for green jobs exists yet, government leaders at the first Meeting of the Middle Class Task Force headed up by Vice President Joe Biden defined green jobs as those that provide "products and services that use renewable energy resources, reduce pollution, conserve energy and natural resources, and reconstitute waste." It is much easier for individuals engaged in work suggested by this definition to connect the dots and see how their contributions improve the condition of the environment.

Part of your homework as a job seeker is to understand the array of industries that are creating green jobs and how to match them to your skills and interests. Although I have identified certain career fields that relate to specific Sun signs in the sections below, every profession has employees that represent of all signs of the zodiac.

Identifying Jobs within Industries

Organic Farming and Gardening

According to the U.S. Department of Agriculture's National Organic Program, demand for organic products continues to grow even though only about 1 percent of the world's farmlands are organically farmed. Organic foods are expensive largely due to transportation costs to get foods to the marketplace. Initiatives are in the works to create farms in urban centers so that food can be grown closer to the consumer base. Tailor-made opportunities go to the Earth signs Taurus, Virgo, and Capricorn, as well as Cancer, Libra, Pisces, and others with a natural green thumb. If you enjoy gardening and one of your goals is to reduce the use of nitrogen fertilizers to limit the effect of green house gases and toxic runoff, this field could host the perfect career for you.

Energy

Alternative energy jobs are those that derive energy from resources that are readily available on the planet and include: solar photovoltaics, onshore and offshore wind, municipal solid waste-to-energy, geothermal power, and sugar-based ethanol. Tony Soprano isn't the only one high on waste management. Waste is probably the most abundant renewable resource on the earth. Innovations in recent years have given way to biomass power, which creates electric power from organic material like manure, wood, crops, food, and garden waste in addition to reducing greenhouse gases. Waste-to-Energy (WTE) facilities burn both organic and manufactured waste in innovatively designed boilers that produce electricity to heat buildings.

Since the United States has well over 100 biomass power plants in several states, those of you with a scientific flair (Taurus, Virgo, Scorpio, and Aquarius) may target your search for appropriate positions. Examples include: agriculture specialists, microbiologists, research and development scientists at universities, chemists and biochemists for industry plants, and engineers. Construction workers are critical to designing and building bio-energy plants that also need mechanics, technicians, and equipment operators to run and maintain them. Some firms advocate cross-training in these disciplines. As the alternative energy field continues to grow, organizations will actively seek farmers and foresters to produce and harvest biomass, and waste-management employees will be needed to collect and move the waste materials.

Air Quality Management

Poor air quality impacts everyone, because it is dangerous to breathe. Jobs in this area include those that monitor air quality and hold others compliant. Of interest to individuals with a number of planets in Gemini, Sagittarius, Pisces, and Virgo are positions such as: air quality program manager, air quality consultant, air quality chemist, project manager, engineer, planner or air compliance specialist, as well as environmental air specialist or compliance officer. Remediation experts are needed to solve problems. Other related positions cover the gamut of designing and manufacturing air pollution control technologies. The American Lung Association campaigns to limit ozone emissions that can exacerbate lung disease and even cause premature death. One source of harmful ozone emissions comes from air purifiers that aggravate asthma and other respiratory conditions and can cause shortness of breath and coughing. Check out ALA to see how your medical, scientific, or service skills can serve its escalating needs.

Human Capital Management

Established companies need the full range of HR positions—benefits coordinators, employee development professionals, labor relations specialists, performance experts, planners, recruiters, safety coordinators, and savvy program and project managers to keep the goals in focus and the output high. If this is your area of expertise, look for advertised jobs in green companies or check in with a headhunter to narrow down your search. While the signs Aries, Cancer, Libra, Capricorn, and Aquarius often make their home in this profession, it may also be a match for you if you have two or more planets in the First, Fourth, Seventh, Tenth, or Eleventh House.

Green Building

Effective use of natural resources in building structures to improve air and water quality and create less waste will create new jobs in the construction field. The net effect is that people who live and work in these buildings are healthier, more productive, and balanced because the architecture, building supplies, materials, energy-efficiency, design, furnishing, and landscaping used in construction are much more sustainable over time. The field has numerous job openings and requires a vast array of specialists in disciplines related to these functions. Among the job titles you'll find are: architects, senior project or design managers, draftspersons, home performance retrofitters and specialists, construction managers, residential energy auditors, home energy consultants, interior designers, furniture designers, healthcare facilities consultants or designers, manufacturer's representatives, interiors project managers, landscape architects, grounds managers, landscape estimators, designers, and gardeners, and irrigation technicians. All Sun signs having multiple planets in the Second, Fourth, Sixth, and Seventh Houses please apply.

Publishing Design, Production, and Supply

Finding paper sources from sustainable forests is a critical part of greening the industry. Most publishers seek a variety of sustainable paper products for their green press initiatives because their products have a significant impact on landfills and on natural resources. Even fonts make a difference in how much ink it takes to create a product. The world would come to an abrupt halt without the use of paper and you wouldn't be reading this article. Smart choices and astute management reduce the industry's impact on the environment. This industry speaks to those of you with strong Third, Sixth, and Ninth house placements or the Sun sign Gemini, Virgo, or Sagittarius. Many excellent authors and editors come from these signs or have strong planets in these signs. The industry still needs talented writers. Fortunately, every Sun sign has its share of writers. Those of you with Mercury in Air signs, affiliated with fluency and flair with the written word, could be tapped for some plum assignments, so make your presence known. Other writing assignments in high-demand could come from Internet and mainstream firms looking for personnel to develop material for their social networks, apps, blogs, e-zines, how-to publications, and online newsletters. Salary varies, yet many freelance writers make a lucrative living searching the Internet for unique writing assignments. See how your expertise matches consumer demand and get on board with the electronic community.

Telecommunications

By now you have probably heard of the "smart grid," which refers to the electricity supply chain that touches all of us in a variety of ways through power generation, transmission, and distribution. The electrical infrastructure is undergoing a major overhaul, and it is going to take a number of enterprises and a lot of money to make the revisions we need to operate efficiently. A variety of service providers will evolve as smart grid transformation unfolds. Cable, telephone, and wireless companies are looking for ways to service the smart grid. They need a number of specialists to analyze demand, sell products, deal with logistics, develop and land contracts, service customers, offer training, and verify compliance. Internet providers and the technology industry are moving gradually into "cloud" computing as one way to improve IT systems and reduce costs. Special studies have been done to look at how the federal government can improve its system for purchasing and using these systems. The transition to the cloud is going to help start-ups and new businesses, especially smaller ones, control costs because they won't have to go out and buy several expensive servers. Businesses can go to Amazon and rent them on an as-needed basis. Always looking for the leading edge in technology, Microsoft is one of the first firms to come out with plans to make their business case for web-based or "cloud" computing. They and other partner firms looking to make a global difference will need personnel who understand the complex benefits of this emerging technology. Positions to consider include: business consultants, customer service representatives, cyber-security specialists, technical experts, and trainers. Perfect jobs for every techie wizard, especially Aries, Gemini, Leo, Virgo, Scorpio, and Aquarius—so scope it out!

Automobile Sales and Service

Auto makers are shifting to plug-in hybrids, electric, and hydrogen-fuel-cell-powered cars. They need sales personnel who are proficient in the latest technology and able to sell the public on the merits of these cheaper-to-operate vehicles. People with strong Gemini, Leo, Libra, or Sagittarius traits make excellent sales professionals. The long-awaited Chevrolet Volt went on sale in the fall of 2010 with a base price of $41,000, putting that car way out of range for the average consumer. Innovative technology is needed not only to keep costs at bay but also to give other manufacturers the incentive to compete in the market. As far as building and designing these vehicles, Aries people master the mechanical details and Aquarius types excel at the intricacies of computerized components.

Appliances Sales and Service

Home energy efficiency benefits everyone, homeowner or not, because it reduces the overall dependence on foreign sources for oil and natural gas. In the last two years, a survey by the Political Psychology Research Group at Stanford University noted that 80 percent of respondents favored government requirements to make new homes and office buildings more energy efficient. Most consumers have heard of the federal government's Energy Star for Homes Program that takes a neutral, bipartisan approach to rationalize saving energy. Homes and appliances that meet the strict requirements carry the Energy Star label. Tax incentives to purchase energy-saving replacement appliances, as well as to install them in new construction and in business environments, save consumers a significant amount of money in the long run. Industry hires in addition to sales include factory workers, designers, testers, and installers. Signs that work in this field include Leo, Virgo, Gemini, Cancer, Scorpio, and Aquarius.

Home Building or Improvement

Home builders have the opportunity to make a huge impact on reducing greenhouse gas emissions that cause global warming, but they don't necessarily sell that concept when marketing new homes. Why? Home builders believe that a large sector of the public is still skeptical about global warming. Instead, they build homes that use less energy, while making only minor changes in their construction practices. More new job openings are available for people who will plug air leaks and aid homeowners in holding down the costs of heating and cooling homes. Ditto for those engaged in home improvement and maintenance. Cancers, Capricorns, and Libras may find home building, sales, design, and improvement appealing as a transition career.

Charitable Work

Charities have long been known to use recycled clothing and household goods to improve the quality of life for those with limited resources. These charities need both salaried workers and volunteers to keep operating. Employers will need bookkeeping, customer service, human resources, inventory managers, receptionists, record-keepers, salespersons for outlet stores, and individuals who solicit donations for goods or cash. Other types of charities need a wide range of personnel to plan events and major fund-raising drives and to support their operations. Jobs in these fields might be ideal for service-oriented signs like Taurus, Virgo, Aquarius, and Pisces.

Education

Education is a means of providing indirect yet positive results and solid contributions to the green economy. The initiative needs individuals who are skilled at motivating and persuading people and organizations to take greener, more sustainable actions. Information about green laws and policies and how they are enforced is critical to making viable progress through public awareness. Readers with First-, Third-, and Ninth-House planets please apply, especially if you are Gemini, Leo, or Sagittarius or have planets in those signs.

Career Counseling

Career counselors from the high school level and beyond provide a valuable resource that helps students to identify "green collar" jobs. Headhunting firms need expertise in placing individuals in positions that get the job done. These positions are likely to be technical, nontechnical, and management positions for firms with established green-hiring practices. Due to budget constraints, organizations in emerging industries will take longer to hire for nontechnical positions that are normally comprised of individuals in financial management, human resources, marketing, and operations. Another reason for the delay in hiring nontechnical workers is that they are probably in the research and development phase of their transition and need all the scientists and technical specialists they can find to become competitive. You can count on an interview if you are a Gemini, Libra, Scorpio, or Aquarius or have many natal planets in the Third, Seventh, Eighth, or Eleventh House.

Your Personal Touch in the Green World

Now that you have considerable insight into green careers, you can make a difference in how you use resources by changing your behavior even before you change jobs. Consider conscientious options.

- When preparing the résumé for your green job, skip the print copy and submit it electronically along with your cover letter.
- Purchase recycled paper, count the pages you print each day, reduce that number, and use double-sided printing.
- If your organization has a recycling program, get some hands-on experience by volunteering to be the in-house czar in charge of properly disposing of employees' recyclable products from paper to phones to outdated electronic equipment.
- Turn off all electronic equipment at home, or at work, each night.
- Reuse packing material when preparing items for mailing. Allow adequate planning time to use ground shipping and you'll significantly reduce the carbon footprint and pay much lower prices than shipping by air.
- Sign up for training in green practices to improve marketability and gain a competitive edge among applicants.

By discovering where your skills are needed in a green organization, you will find the incentive and the money to fulfill your career dreams in the "green frontier."

Resources

McClelland, Carol. *Green Careers for Dummies*. Hoboken, NJ: Wiley Publishing Co., 2010.

Kerrigan, Kerry. "Green Ideas That Put Businesses in the Red." *Capital Business*: Volume 1, Issue 15:15.

Overly, Steven. "Tech Industry has Sky-high Hopes." WashTech, *Capital Business*: Volume 1, Issue 14:8.

Your Heart Connection
by April Elliott Kent

Growing up in the pre-DVD era, watching *The Wizard of Oz* on network television was a much-anticipated annual event in our household. I'm referring, of course, to the classic movie starring Judy Garland as Dorothy, a Kansas farm girl, who is magically transported to the extraordinary Land of Oz. There she meets a trio of friends who accompany her to see the Wizard, who they hope will grant their wishes.

As an astrological metaphor, it's tempting to think of this sweet story as a lunar tale, since young Dorothy spends most of the film looking for a way to return home. But I see the story a little differently. Maybe it's just those shiny, ostentatious ruby slippers that got Dorothy in so much trouble with the Wicked Witch, but I prefer to think of Oz as a story about the astrological Sun—a story of wishing to be something more than we think we are.

In astrology, the Sun symbolizes aspiration, the desire to reach our ultimate potential. But rather than earning our Sun sign's gifts from the outside world, what if we carry the seeds of their potential within us from the moment we're born? In Oz, Dorothy and her companions each wish for the very qualities that they already possess. The Lion laments his lack of courage, but shows bravery despite his fear; the wise Scarecrow doesn't believe in his brains, or the sentimental tin woodsman in his own tender heart. And Dorothy, of course, longs to return home to Kansas, unaware that the ruby slippers on her feet could take her there with three clicks of her heels.

Dorothy and her friends are far from alone in failing to recognize their innate gifts. How often have you heard someone say, "I'm not at all like my Sun Sign"? It's true that there's much more to astrology than the Sun's sign at your birth, and many other factors in your birth chart can overshadow the characteristics of that sign. But another reason it's often difficult to relate to Sun-sign astrology is that we're not necessarily born knowing how to "be" our Sun sign! It can be helpful, then, to think about your Sun sign not as a description of your personality, but as a blueprint for what you can potentially become.

The Tall Poppy

We live on a planet that owes its existence to the Sun, and our spirits open up to its warmth as a flower blooms on a sunny day. In yoga, we salute the Sun as the force that animates all life on Earth. And in astrology, the Sun holds a similar status: it is the animating force of the birth chart, and the sign it occupied at your birth tells us what brings you to life.

Some are born with a natural ability to celebrate the Sun's energy in their lives. Their dispositions are "sunny," open, and welcoming. Others cluster around them as they might surround a crackling fireplace on a cool evening.

But many of us are raised to think that calling attention to ourselves is selfish and unattractive. Where my husband comes from, they call this the "Tall Poppy Syndrome." Sometimes when people feel frustrated in their own lives, they try to "chop down" anyone else who succeeds in standing out from the crowd (the "Tall Poppy").

If you spent your life among smaller poppies, it might have been difficult for you to develop and embrace "solar" energy in your life.

So look to the Sun's sign at your birth as a map to hidden treasure. Your Sun sign's best qualities are already yours—just waiting, like Dorothy's ruby slippers, for you to step into them and walk the path with heart.

Aries (March 21–April 20)
If I Only Had the Courage

Aries is usually described as assertive and courageous. But what if you're an Aries who is a little shy, or who has trouble initiating action? Or perhaps you've known an Aries who covers up fear with aggression and bullying.

The most common misconception about courage is that brave people are not afraid. Of course they are; if they weren't, there would be no need for courage! As Eleanor Roosevelt once said, "You must do that which you think you cannot," and that is especially true if you were born with the Sun in Aries. To follow the path with heart, you must seek opportunities to test your strength, courage, and ability, and you need to do it every day.

You may, however, need to expand your concept of bravery. Courage is certainly found in soldiers, warriors, and firefighters, but it's not confined to the battlefield or to burning buildings. Courage is found, for most of us, in less spectacular but still difficult situations, such as the awkward conversation you're afraid to have with a coworker. Go ahead and have that conversation; you'll find you are braver than you think!

Taurus (April 21–May 20)
If I Only Had the Bucks

Wealth, comfort, and ease: Taurus is symbolized by the contented, well-fed bull. If you're struggling on your Taurus path, however, you may feel poor, even if you're not. You may deprive yourself of life's pleasures, or overcompensate by enjoying them too greedily.

It can be hard to appreciate all that we have; there always seems to be someone else who has more. Yet each of us came into the world with nothing at all, not even a stitch of clothing, and still found a way to get what we needed! You would think that transcending these humble beginnings would give all of us confidence, but the truth is, we misunderstand wealth. We imagine it lies in things that we can gather and use, but in fact, that path only leads to more cravings.

For Taurus, the path with heart celebrates the natural bounty of the physical world and the satisfaction of simply being alive. When you're feeling deprived, enjoy a beautiful painting. Listen to the song of the ocean's waves, enjoy the touch of a cat's fur, savor the taste of a chocolate bar, or let your nose linger over an obliging peony. No matter what your bank statement says, you are much wealthier than you know.

Gemini (May 21–June 21)
If I Only Had the Words

Gemini is known as the chatterbox of the zodiac, with an insatiable urge for information, new experiences, and fresh ideas. But what if you're a Gemini who "never has anything to say," hates talking on the phone, and rarely picks up a book?

In fact, some people born with the Sun in Gemini do talk a lot; but it's worth remembering that Gemini is the sign of communication, which requires listening as well as talking. Many Geminis are happiest sitting quietly on the sidelines at a party, observing everything and listening to every conversation at once, all of which they share with a dazzled partner on the drive home.

For Gemini, storytelling is the path with heart. You were born to listen to the world's stories and to retell them, and to pollinate the world with ideas as a hummingbird tends to a garden full of flowers. If you think you haven't got much to say, just open your ears and heart and listen to the world's stories; they will give you all the words you need.

Cancer (June 22–July 22)
If I Only Had a Home

The Wizard of Oz's Dorothy was, without a doubt, a home-loving Cancerian. Dorothy spends the entire film caring for her friends and her dog, and missing her aunt and uncle back home. Meek and timid, she only gets riled up when someone she loves is threatened.

You may be a Cancer like Dorothy, clinging to the familiarity of home and loved ones. Or you may be one of the rare Cancerians who makes do with rented furniture and microwaved meals. The truth is, while we think of home as a place where we live and people who share that place with us, that's only part of the story. For a Cancer, who is filled with the energy of the Sun, "home" is a state of being, and a quality of mind.

For Cancer, the path with heart lies in being the home that you're looking for, and giving others the comfort you seek. Give all that you can; the size of your home is limited only by the size of your heart.

Leo (July 23–August 22)
If I Only Had the Nerve

"Courage" was the wish of Oz's cowardly Lion. And while courage naturally belongs to Aries, it takes nerve—boldness and pure spunk—to follow Leo's true path: being true to yourself. "Oh, I'm not a typical Leo at all," you might protest. "I don't like all that attention." On the other end of the spectrum are Leos who take the negative stereotype of their sign to ridiculous lengths, preening and hogging the spotlight.

But limelight-hungry egotists and shy pussycats are miles from their hearts' true path. Leo shines when he is inspiring others through performing, creating, or simply by being the life of the party. Leo gives heart to every timid person who watches and thinks, "Hey, if she can do it, maybe I can, too." Watch a loving Leo on her heart's path, and you'll notice she spends as much time shining the spotlight on others as basking in it herself.

So do what you love. Do what makes you feel alive. You really do have a lot of nerve, Leo—celebrate it!

Virgo (August 23–September 22)
If I Only Had a Brain

"If only I were smart," moans the Scarecrow, the wisest, most resourceful fellow in Dorothy's merry band. Likewise, Virgo is often blind to his own sterling qualities. "I'm not a proper Virgo," declares my friend Beth. "My apartment is a mess, and my checkbook is never balanced." But an untidy Virgo often just has unreasonable standards of perfection, and grows disheartened when they can't be met. Why clean, when things will just get dirty again? Why tackle your checkbook if you can't balance your account to the penny?

If you're a Virgo who is too focused on life's imperfections, you may overlook your greatest gift: the ability to fix and soothe a broken, troubled world. It's true you have to notice problems before you can fix them, but you also need to know when to stop cataloguing the problems and start rolling up your sleeves! For Virgo, the path with heart lies in fixing problems. It takes a lot of skill, resourcefulness, and yes, brains to keep the world operating smoothly. Roll up your sleeves and tackle the problems one by one, and you'll find you're usually the cleverest person in the room—and a "real" Virgo after all!

Libra (September 23–October 22)
If I Only Had a Partner

Libra, the sign of relationship, has a sweet, refined, and harmonious reputation that is not entirely deserved. Because more precisely, Libra is the sign of balance, and one cannot balance sweetness with more sweetness. Behave too politely around a Libran and you're just begging for a fight.

So what if you're a Libran who has had trouble finding or maintaining a romantic relationship, business partnership, or even close friendships? Does that mean astrology is nonsense, or that you've failed as a Libra?

Neither. It means the key to having strong relationships is to know yourself first. Libra's heart path lies not in niceness, but in collaboration! An ideal relationship is one in which the partners' strengths are complementary, with each yielding gracefully to the other and neither feeling like a doormat. This balancing act requires a strong sense of self, so anything you can do to know yourself better (and spending time alone is a good place to start) is a step along your heart's true path. Your ideal partner is out there, and when you've embraced your true self, you will be able to recognize one another!

Scorpio (October 23–November 21)
If I Only Had the Strength

Interestingly, those born with the Sun in Scorpio nearly always announce that fact with pride, relishing their sign's racy reputation for intrigue, sexual magnetism, and emotional drama. Scorpios who don't reveal themselves are equally easy to identify, because they're the ones who refuse to tell you when they were born. Both reactions are usually born out of a desire to seem invulnerable and "cool."

But is that what Scorpio was born to be: a sexy, mysterious stranger with a pet snake and a full complement of body piercings, or someone who turns up their nose at all that is mysterious and magical in life, claiming that they're "not into all that stuff"?

For Scorpio, the path with heart lies in developing true strength, not just outer toughness. It takes fearlessness to merge in sexual and emotional intimacy with another person, to stand up for the weak and stand up to the strong, and to look mortality straight in the eye and say, "I'm not afraid of you." How can you move beyond your tough façade and develop inner strength? Simply by being as willing to confront your own normal, human weaknesses as you are adept at exposing the frailties of others—that is your heart's path to real strength.

Sagittarius (November 22–December 21)
If I Only Had the World

Though President John F. Kennedy (Sun in Gemini) was a wizard with words, a trip to Germany found him with his foot planted firmly in his mouth. "Ich bin ein Berliner," he declared, intending to show solidarity with the people of Berlin by claiming to be one of them. Unfortunately, he later discovered that "Berliner" was a colloquial expression for a kind of doughnut.

Such are the risks of treading upon foreign soil! You don't know all the cultural subtleties that betray foreignness. If you were born with the Sun in Sagittarius, the sign of foreign lands, you should appreciate that laughter, not embarrassment, is the only correct response to having made a *faux pas* like President Kennedy's.

Your heart's true path, Sagittarius, is to become a full-fledged, passport-bearing world citizen. You are designed to shine brightest among people who do not share your nationality, race, religion, creed, or political beliefs. Develop your spirit of adventure and ease with the unfamiliar by eating exotic foods, sampling cultural festivals, or learning a new language. Don't settle for a little corner of the world, when it's your birthright to enjoy the whole thing!

Capricorn (December 22–January 19)
If I Only Had Respect

Do you have a problem with authority figures? Are you constantly furious about the strict rules of your workplace and fed up with society's cruel and arbitrary laws? That kind of rebelliousness is fine if you're an Aquarian. But it's not quite right for you, Capricorn, because you were designed to be in charge.

I've known people born with the Sun in Capricorn who walk into a store to purchase something, only to get approached for help by fellow customers who assume Capricorn is the boss! You are designed to be looked up to, to remind others of our responsibilities, and to point out the ways in which we limit ourselves. Your heart's path is to be treated with respect.

To move toward your heart's path, build your authority and credibility. You do this every time you offer good advice, take the high road, and keep your word. So do these things without fail, in matters large and small; demonstrate respect for yourself and others, and you will find you receive all the respect you could hope for in return.

Aquarius (January 20–February 18)
If I Only Had a Friend

Aquarius is the odd flower in astrology's garden—a bird of paradise, spiky and colorful. As any gardener knows, the bird of paradise is also desperately hard to remove once it's taken root. Aquarius is considered eccentric and unpredictable, but here's his secret: Aquarius may enjoy shaking things up in your life, but he prefers to avoid too many changes in his own routines. And here's another secret: Aquarius wants to do things her own way, but she also wants to belong to a group of friends.

If you are an Aquarian and you pride yourself on your collection of buttoned-down oxfords, go out of your way to be radical and shocking, or shy away from social activities, then you have wandered away from your true path. You're not like anyone else, and that's exactly what makes you like everyone else, because each of us is utterly unique. For Aquarius, the path with heart lies in making everyone feel that they "fit in." Celebrate your weirdness, and love everyone else for theirs; that is the essence of friendship, and the surest way of making friends.

Pisces (February 19–March 21)
If I Only Had a Heart

There is, sadly, a certain kind of Pisces who gives up on life much too soon. It's all too difficult, the world is too rough a place, and they read once that Pisces is "supposed" to just drift through life and be spacey. And there's another kind of Pisces, too—the kind that is determined never to show even a moment's weakness, sensitivity, or vulnerability. "Everyone is a victim," growls this species of fish sarcastically, impatient with weakness in himself and others.

But Pisces, drifting and insensitivity, carry you far from your heart's true path. You shine brightest when you love the world—nothing more, nothing less. It takes a lot of courage and heart to love everything and everyone; it's a tall order indeed. But like the tin Woodsman, alleging his lack of a heart while rusting from his own tender tears, open the floodgates of emotion and you will find that you have all the heart anyone could hope for. Yes, it's scary—you may feel as though you'll drown in your own tears. But after all, you have fins to help you navigate the floodwaters—and a heart that is more resilient than you know.

The Mayan Long Count
by Tim Lyons

The Mayan Long Count that an end date of December 21, 2012, has engendered so much discussion and trepidation, began on August 11, 3114 BCE[1]—over three millennia before the people we now call the Maya developed their civilization. Though much of what we know of the Maya comes from inference, the following conclusions seem warranted:

- Their leaders (often referred to, these days, as "astronomer priests") seemed obsessed with time; they organized Mayan society with reference to that obsession.

- They made extremely precise measurements of time and the movements of celestial bodies, extending those measurements far into the past and future.

Unfortunately, most of the Mayan texts that might have contained interpretations of these measurements ended up in the bonfires of Bishop Diego de Landa, who, in one of the ironies of history, not only destroyed vast numbers of Mayan texts, but also, in his

Relacion de las Cosas de Yucatan (c. 1566), transmitted to the future much of what we know of the pre-conquest Maya. We find ourselves knowing the Mayan dates, but left largely to our own speculations in trying to figure out what significance the Maya attached to those dates. Though many such speculations have proven quite helpful—beginning with the pioneering work of such people as J. Eric Thompson, the later work of Frank Waters, and in our own era, people like John Major Jenkins, whose *Maya Cosmogenesis 2012* contains abundant material on Mayan calendric science and its connection to astronomical facts and Mayan architecture—we still might wonder what December 2012 means to us.

We can begin to understand the Long Count first by setting its start date into a larger historical context, and then by casting a horoscope for that start date. By looking at that horoscope and progressing it through time, particularly to December 21, 2012, we can discern something of the significance of the period, even if what we find has no necessary connection to Mayan notions. In an article of this length, we can't do an extensive analysis, but we can at least make a beginning, attempting to determine what it is that comes to an end on that date.

The Historical Context[2]

The Long Count start date falls in the middle of the Age of Taurus, a period that brought the consolidation (Taurus) of many of the intellectual explorations that took place during the preceding Age of Gemini. Two of the most important of these explorations involved written language and metallurgy, two developments that played indispensable roles in the kind of social organization that arose during the Age of Taurus—the kind of social organization we perhaps facilely call "civilization." Both of the explorations carry the markings of Gemini: tremendous curiosity and intellectual activity.

Metallurgy first appeared about 6,000 years ago, as the Age of Gemini gave way to the Age of Taurus. We can see it as a pre-eminently intellectual (Gemini) process, requiring objectivity and curiosity: people noticed that some materials became malleable, eventually liquefying when heated enough; they had to make careful observations, no doubt over many generations, driven by curiosity and without a clear sense of where that curiosity would lead.

The Gemini element led to Taurus, for the curiosity led to very practical, down-to-earth developments.

Written language, too, developed in stages. During the Age of Cancer, people settled into agrarian villages (during what some archaeologists now call the Neolithic Revolution), so parents had sufficient time and security for new approaches to child rearing, surely increasing, generation by generation, the intellectual acuity of the children and unwittingly providing the ground for the development of writing during the succeeding Age of Gemini. Like metallurgy, written language took definite form during the Age of Taurus, and it did so in relation to practical, down-to-earth matters.

One other Age of Gemini development demands attention: a marked separation between agrarian people and hunters, the separation reminding us again of the Twins. Though farmers and hunters can clearly develop a symbiotic relationship, with the hunters killing animals that would otherwise threaten crops and the farmers providing a steady supply of food during periods of scarce game, the split during the Age of Gemini eventually became an egregious one. The hunters, possessing the weapons and audacity necessary for the hunt, eventually emerged as what Lewis Mumford calls an aristocratic minority, eventually gaining control over large populations. A new ruling class developed, backed by violence and weaponry. We, therefore, can't separate the development of "civilization" from the dominance of the warrior class.

Taurus, of course, has to do with abundance, growth, and fertility. We see all of these during the Age of Taurus, as an agricultural surplus, resulting from newly developed large-field agriculture, gave people a heretofore unimagined security against want. Despite its obvious benefits, however, the surplus did prove to be a mixed blessing. Once people had a surplus, a managerial class developed in order to manage that surplus (Taurus), a process in which writing became necessary for the keeping of records. But though the class structure enabled a potentially helpful differentiation of function, it also led to many of the difficulties that arose over the next five millennia.

Eventually, people began to build larger cities, and surely one of the marks of civilization was bigness, both in crop output and building size. Within these larger cities people built central granaries.

The newly developing military class (the descendants of the hunt-ers) took control of this surplus. The central granary developed in tandem with the centralized temple; indeed, the temple served as a storehouse for the surplus. So we see the development, around the middle of the Age of Taurus, of all of these elements: large cities; central granaries and temples; gods demanding obedience; and a military class controlling city, granary, and temple. None of these developments could have taken place without the class structure.

Nor could the building of the pyramids, which required the work-ings of what Mumford called the mega machine, the first machine created by humans. On that machine, all succeeding machines, first with human parts and eventually with non-organic material, were modeled. That we have come to the end of the Long Count suggests that this form of social organization has outlived its usefulness— that human beings must develop new ways to live together, ways probably not based on a hierarchical, pyramid-shaped model, but on something more open and less machine-like.

We may interpret the Mayan Long Count horoscope as symbol-izing the birth of the new kind of social organization that arose in the middle of the fourth millennium BC, a mode of social orga-nization marked by bigness, class structure, military conquest, centralized bureaucracy, and ecological destruction. But though the Long Count horoscope symbolizes this process quite precisely, we shouldn't conclude that the various elements magically came together on August 11, 3114 BCE, or on any other specific date, for the process surely took many generations. One of the mysteries of the Long Count lies in how the Mayan astronomer-priests intuited a date that so nicely encapsulates that process through the astrologi-cal factors active on that day, a matter to which we now turn.[3]

The Horoscope for the Long Count

I have cast the horoscope for August 11, 3114 BCE, the most com-monly accepted date for the Long Count. Because a full analysis of all horoscope factors would take up more space than we have avail-able here, let's focus on two groups:

1. The various quincunxes: from Venus and Mercury to both Jupiter and the Moon; from Saturn to Uranus and (more loosely) Pluto. The first set forms a yod,[4] and the Saturn/

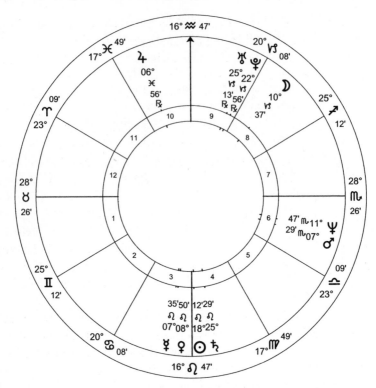

Uranus quincunx is one of the closest aspects in the horoscope (with an orb of aspect of only 17'). Through its conjunction with Saturn, the Leo Sun participates, though loosely, in this last quincunx.

2. The squares from the Mars-Neptune conjunction in Scorpio over to (again) the Mercury-Venus conjunction in Leo, forming a large and multiple square, with Mars making a pair of close squares and Neptune making squares with slightly wider orbs of aspect.[5]

Yods have a well-documented connection to imbalance and illness. The imbalance appears because signs in a quincunx relationship have so little in common, falling in signs of different elements and incompatible modes. At the same time, the sextile at the base suggests intellectual acuity. The quincunxes here link planets in Leo (fixed Fire) with planets in Capricorn (cardinal Earth) and

Pisces (mutable Water). In general, quincunxes result in ritualistic behavior patterns that bring planetary energies together unconsciously, often in a manner not healthy for the organism. For this reason, people work best with quincunxes not merely by gaining awareness, but by altering ritualistic imbalances embedded in the ongoing patterns of living.

A quincunx involving Leo and Capricorn suggests an imbalance related to authority, for though both signs have close connections to authority, the connections differ, Leo's having to do with kingship, Capricorn's with hierarchy. Interestingly, the two developed together back in the fourth millennium BCE, with the development of centralized, solar deities and of class structures and authority hierarchies surrounding the Sun-king. The uneasy relationship between the regal and hierarchical modes has generated a host of problems and potentials, but because of the quincunx aspect, we often don't see them clearly, perhaps because we see them simply as "parts of life."

The squares between Mercury and Venus in Leo to Mars and Neptune in Scorpio symbolize an uneasy union between delusion-based aggression (Mars-Neptune) and the aforementioned regality (Mercury-Venus in Leo), with the king's bureaucracy (Sun-Saturn in Leo; Leo/Capricorn quincunxes) serving as mechanism. Thus, Lewis Mumford tells us that the kings of the period, in order to ensure obedience, fell back on "force in ferocious, sadistic forms, repeatedly magnified into nightmarish extravaganzas of cruelty, as dehumanized as those we have witnessed in the last generation in the ingenious horrors, perpetrated by 'civilized' governments in Warsaw, Auschwitz, Tokyo, and Vietnam."[6]

We clearly see the marks of Scorpio and Leo in the violence, cruelty, and sadism ordered by the king, the solar deity. Neptune in Scorpio appears as delusions regarding power; Mars here could suggest cruelty perpetrated by the king's (Leo) warrior-army. Mumford tells us that "from the beginning, the balance of mechanized power seems to have fallen on the side of destruction," and that "insofar as the mega machine was passed on intact to later civilization, "it was in the negative form of the military machine—drilled, standardized, divided into specialized parts—that its continuity was assured."[7]

Now at the end of the Long Count, we must deal with the results: environmental degradation, a planetary illness symbolized by the quincunxes of the Long Count horoscope and inseparable from prevailing militarism. Our dominant mode of social organization has apparently caused a host of problems that resist easy solutions. We can trace these problems to their source: to the problematic linkage of centralized authority (what we could appropriately call "regality") and extensive bureaucracy, and then with the insistence on military might and aggression as a dominant mode of social expression. Now, we have social structures deemed "too big to fail" (in which group we can include not only corporations and banks, but militarized nation-states as well) that have wrought untold destruction; we have environmental destruction on a daunting scale; and we have endemic warfare carried on with apparently mindless cruelty. All these patterns developed first back in the fourth millennium BCE, the period of the Long Count's birth.

Time Analysis

In the astrological configurations discussed above, the area around 8–9 Aquarius, though untenanted, looms large: that area contains the trigger point of the yod,[8] so a transiting or progressed planet arriving there would "trigger" the yod into manifestation; it would also turn the natal square (Leo to Scorpio) into a t-square. With these ideas in mind, we can turn to the progressed horoscope for December 2012, where we find secondary progressed Saturn and Pluto in that area of the zodiac.[9]

If the natal yod symbolizes a fundamental imbalance expressed as an incubating illness, then the triggering of that yod could easily indicate the full manifestation of that illness: the present environmental crisis, a serious planetary fever (possibly suggesting the strong Leo—fixed Fire—in the natal horoscope) resulting from the kind of social organization already discussed. We see, too, the problematic role of militaries the world over, for the resultant fear and desire for security has done much to hinder, or even prevent, measures that might have dealt more effectively with the imbalance. The yod (imbalance, illness) and the square (military violence arising from delusion) intertwine, forming a knot difficult to untie.

Secondary progressed Saturn brings forward the natal Sun-Saturn conjunction and thus has to do with the regal hierarchies discussed above. The challenging aspects from SP Saturn (opposed natal Venus and Mercury; square natal Mars) suggest not only the resistance of those hierarchies to change, but also a marked increase in tension as a result. Secondary progressed Pluto could obviously suggest destruction, particularly when, together with SP Saturn, it squares the Mars-Neptune conjunction. The symbolism certainly suggests the threat either of nuclear conflagration driven by governments, or widespread destruction perpetrated by other Plutonic groups (the ones we often call "terrorists," who, along with many national governments, seem to qualify as "Plutonic"). At the same time, the ongoing conjunction between SP Saturn and SP Pluto could suggest a death-and-rebirth process involving the hierarchies themselves, resulting in a major change in social structuring. Plutonic war (e.g. driven by plutonium) or environmental catastrophe could obviously serve as triggers for such a change.

On the more hopeful side, we have SP Uranus, which by 2012 has moved almost exactly 60 degrees from natal Uranus, forming (with natal Uranus) a precise yod to natal Saturn. The sextile, pointing to the unprecedented intellectual development of humanity over the past few centuries, suggests an abundance of technical means available to solve the problems that beset us. But though we have the technical know-how (SP Uranus sextile natal Uranus), our social structures resist (quincunxes to Saturn) the necessary changes, perhaps because our quasi-ritualistic bureaucracies tend to perpetuate themselves at whatever cost.

The natal Saturn/Uranus quincunx certainly suggests an uneasy, and possibly illness-producing, imbalance between technical means developed via human brilliance (Uranus) and the aforementioned regal bureaucracy (Saturn in Leo conjoining the Leo Sun). Thus, an inner tension, developing over 5,125 years, manifesting in illness. Secondary progressed Uranus comes along and provides the means to deal with that tension, but with Saturn as the focal planet of the yod, the resistance comes from what needs changing: the social structure itself. The yod suggests that we have come to a fork in the road.

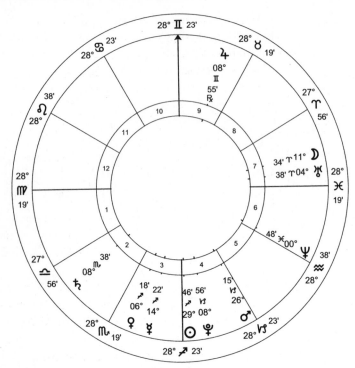

The Horoscope for December 21, 2012

What will follow? Though scholars disagree about whether the Maya saw the end of this Long Count as ushering in a new one (for this one, associated with the symbol ollin, concludes a series of five that seems to encompass what we call a Great Year), we should take at least a brief look at the horoscope for December 21, 2012. The following seem important:

- Yods appear again: one has Jupiter focal in Gemini; another has Saturn focal in Scorpio; and the two interlock, via the close quincunx between Jupiter and Saturn. The yod to Jupiter in Gemini has Venus in Sagittarius at the trigger point. The strong mutability suggests not the obdurate social forms of the previous Long Count, but something more fluid and disparate. The Jupiter/Saturn quincunx suggests a ritualized imbalance between expansion and order; this aspect may reflect difficulties related to population growth or resource depletion.

Of course, the yod to Saturn in Scorpio could suggest hierarchies clinging to power despite the strong mutability, even volatility (e.g., Moon in Aries conjoined Uranus) of the rest of the horoscope. But the horoscope does not have the daunting fixed square of the 3114 BCE horoscope.

• Whereas, in the previous horoscope we find an integrated Mars (square Mercury-Venus, conjoined Neptune, sextile Moon, trine Jupiter), in this one we find Mars unaspected. This could suggest highly organized (Capricorn) military aggregations not associated with the dominant social groupings. The symbolism certainly could suggest renegade but well-organized (Capricorn) para-military groups wreaking havoc throughout the globe. Of course, when we consider the harm done by the military mega-machine (to borrow Mumford's term), we might feel at least a little relieved at its demise. Further, our fears about Mars-related developments may have derived from the Leo-Scorpio afflictions of the Long Count horoscope. The new Mars has no afflictive aspects, and it appears in the sign of its exaltation. Perhaps we will see not roving paramilitary groups killing at random, but organized and unaffiliated groups performing necessary and valuable functions. Or perhaps we will see both.

• Finally, the horoscope has a square from Pluto in Capricorn to Moon-Uranus in Aries. The symbolism suggests radical insecurity, possibly coming from a breakdown of old social forms as a prelude to ways of organizing society, ways perhaps more malleable and less gargantuan. The Moon in Aries suggests pioneering new ways to find security; Uranus could suggest that new technologies born from human brilliance play an important role in this security.

A note of caution seems in order, though, particularly with regard to that concluding remark about technology. The Long Count ends just as we enter the Age of Aquarius. Despite human brilliance and the development of new technologies, we may find, as we enter an age ruled by a barren sign, an increasingly barren Earth. Whether we wish to or not, we may well need to rely on new technologies in order to make the adjustment.

End Notes

1. We can find, admittedly, some disagreements about the date. However, most scholars opt for either the 13th or the 14th, a difference that matters very little to this discussion. See note #4.

2. In presenting this historical material, I rely heavily on two sources: Lewis Mumford's *Technics and Human Development* (New York: Harcourt Brace Jovanovitch, 1966) and Arnold Toynbee's *Mankind and Mother Earth* (New York: Oxford University Press, 1976).

3. We first might note, here, a difference between our Great Ages and the Mayan version, for though both seem to add up to the Great Year (12x2,160=25,920, 5x5,125=25,625), for our Great Ages we have precise symbolism but no definite beginning date, whereas for the Mayan Long Count we have much less available symbolism but a very precise beginning date. The Mayans based their calendar largely the numbers 5 and 7, whereas we base ours largely on 3 and 4—an important matter, but one we must bypass for now.

4. I've set the horoscope arbitrarily for midnight, so we should consider the Moon's position as approximate. At precisely midnight, we would have found the Moon around 10 Capricorn, participating in a yod; in the hours after midnight, the Moon steadily moved out of orb. I should add, here, that even if we choose August 13th or 14th, we would still have a close quincunx from Saturn to Uranus and from Mercury and Venus to Jupiter. We would also have the square (see below) from Mercury and Venus to Mars-Neptune. The Sun would more closely participate in the Saturn-Uranus quincunx, but the Moon would have moved out of Capricorn.

5. Mercury's square of Neptune has an orb of 4d11A, certainly close enough for us to consider it a viable square. The closest aspect, Mars' square to Mercury, as an orb of 0d07S. If we use either August 13 or 14, the orbs from Neptune to Mercury, Venus, and Mars narrow.

6. Mumford, 184.

7. Mumford, 228.

8. I have borrowed the term "trigger" from Bil Tierney. See his discussion of yods in *The Dynamics of Aspect Analysis* (Reno, NV: CRCS, 1983).

9. Though in the horoscope of a human being, secondary progressed Saturn and Pluto don't generally play important roles unless they change direction, in the horoscope of a period of time lasting over 5,000 years, these progressed planets may play vital roles. (Also, some of the factors that play vital roles in natal horoscopy will play

little or no role in the Long Count's progressions. For example, the secondary progressed Moon will generally not play a role; ditto for most transits. Close study of transiting Neptune and Pluto in the Long Count horoscope shows that these transits do play an important role, and sometimes transiting Saturn and Uranus can serve as triggers, but a full study of this would take us well beyond the scope of this short essay.) Pluto had arrived in the trigger-area by the Renaissance; Saturn arrived in the nineteenth century, after which the two have moved more or less in tandem.

Yoga for the Sun Signs
by Robin Ivy

Mental clarity, physical tone, emotional balance, and spiritual connection are all benefits of a regular yoga practice. Yoga is at least 5,000 years old, yet it's a modern form of exercise and relaxation. In our technology-based world and fast-paced lives, yoga is restorative, working all the muscles and unifying mind, body and spirit. Encompassing control and surrender, the philosophies of a yoga practice can extend to our daily decisions and tasks. There are many styles of yoga, and for some of us one seems more compatible than another. However, in all forms of yoga, we benefit from conscious breath, physical movement, and meditation, or rest.

The Sun Salutation sequence is made up of postures that correlate with and can benefit everyone from Aries to Pisces. Sun Salutation is an asana central to the Hatha style of yoga. This sequence of postures, traditionally performed at sunrise, has origins in Hindu worship of the solar deity. As there are twelve signs of the zodiac, there are also twelve postures that form the Sun Salutation. Completion requires moving through the series twice, alternating left and right sides of the body and inhalations with exhalations. The entire body stretches backward and forward in turn, as well, indicating a connection to the signs Leo, ruler of the spine, and Aquarius, sign of the nervous system. Sun Salutation, in name and energy, has a natural connection to Leo and indeed does work the part of the body correlated to this regal and strong sign of the Sun. Integrated in the salutation are postures that energize, move and strengthen the Capricorn bones, Pisces feet, Cancer abdomen, Sagittarius hips, and Gemini wrists and hands among others.

Follow the sequence of Sun Salutations postures either by mentally picturing or physically acting out these descriptions and find your sign in the commentaries. If you are having difficulty with feeling energized in a certain area of your body, consider your connection to and the traits of the ruling sign for insight, and perhaps extra attention in your yoga practice.

Mountain Pose

Mountain pose, in name, relates to the element of Earth, sharing energy with Capricorn, Taurus, and Virgo. Capricorn, sign of the goat, metaphorically climbs and lives in the mountains. Mountain pose is a motivator, activating Capricorn ambition to start one's practice, and this posture activates the increase in blood flow to all parts of the body, encouraging Virgo flexibility. Mountains are timeless, and like fixed-sign Taurus, aren't going anywhere but instead remain constant! As you engage in the Mountain and Extended Mountain postures, meditate on your strong connection to the Earth and tap into your Earth-sign energy!

Pisces rules the feet, and close attention to the toes and rooting to the Earth with all parts of the feet are both key to Mountain. In Western culture, we probably don't pay enough attention to our feet, yet we use them more than almost any part of our body since they get us where we're going! Mountain is a great opportunity to tune in to the lower extremities and remember how much energy is released there!

Begin by bringing your feet and legs together, and spread your toes apart wide. Root your heels and feet to the ground and firm your legs. Then, roll your shoulders back and down and spread and lift your chest while your hands remain at your side, palms forward.

Extended Mountain Pose

Inhale through your nose and raise your arms up to the side, palms facing upwards. Extend your arms above your head to either side, and hold. Follow by bringing your hands forward in front of your chest and to prayer position.

Swan Dive to Forward Bend

The Swan relates to the Air signs. Libra's traits of grace and harmony are embodied in the Swan Dive. For Gemini, a sign with energy to burn, the cycle of Sun Salutation breaths begins with this first exhale, fueling the body for the remainder of practice. For Aquarius, sign of the central nervous system, the first forward bend begins to open the vertebrae, creating space and encouraging expansion. During your first Swan Dive, feel how the release of breath relaxes the nervous system while bringing a flow of blood to the brain, the place or intellect and thought and therefore, air!

Exhale through your nose while moving forward from the waist. Open your arms wide and fold into a standing forward bend. Touch your hands to the floor if you can or if not, to the front of the shins or ankles.

Standing Lunge

The action of a lunge is Mars' assertive Aries energy! This part of the salutation mimics the initial part of another posture called Warrior. Consider where you could make a breakthrough by taking an active stance in your life as you move into your first lunge.

This posture also engages the Sagittarius energy of the hips and thighs as it opens the pelvis and strengthens the glutes and quads. Lunge has the quality of the archer's stance as he aims his bow.

Inhale through your nose and place your hands next to your feet on the floor and step one foot back into a lunge. Keep the front knee directly over the ankle and keep the back leg firm. Now, exhale and bring the other foot back form to Downward-facing Dog position.

Downward Dog and Plank Pose

Downward Dog and Plank Pose work the belly and wrists, domains of Cancer and Gemini, respectively. The hands and wrists support us in both postures, helping move tension stored during daily tasks, including our use of computers, texting on our phones and other technology, as well as more strenuous physical work. Though it may not be comfortable for our hands, these postures are freeing and open up our hands and wrists to aid in the recovery process. Our hands are also integral to how we express ourselves, both in body language and through writing, so communication may flow more easily when our Gemini parts are open and activated.

Strengthening core abdominal muscles brings energy to the stomach, ruled by Cancer. Plank Pose is particularly good for the abdomen, requiring some strength and endurance as we hold ourselves up from the ground, engaging the core.

Both positions, done in a sequence, relate to how we support and nurture ourselves. Our hands and our core muscles need to be strong as do the complementary Gemini and Cancer traits of intellect and sensitivity, self-expression and ability to turn inward. The two postures encourage balancing and blending these energies and building both physical and emotional resilience.

Downward Dog

Exhale and bring the front foot back to align with the back foot and form Downward Dog. Spread your fingers and press your palms into the mat, they should be shoulder width apart. Now, lift your hips up toward the sky, lengthening your spine. Gently straighten your legs, pressing your heels down into your mat as far as you can go.

Plank Pose

Inhale and take your shoulders forward directly over your wrists, extending well with your arms to form the Plank Pose. Keep your thighs strong and firm, your feet flexed and your belly drawn in. Your body should look like a plank, at a slight angle from shoulders to feet with hips and abdomen level. Avoid the tendency to move your hips higher than the rest of your body.

Cobra and Knee-Chest-Chin

Cobra engages the entire spine, raising kundalini energy from root of the spine to crown of the head. Scorpio, the sign that governs the sex organs, and Cancer, sign of the abdomen and chest, are closely linked to this posture. The pubic bone presses to the floor sending energy through the lower charkas while the chest moves upward and forward opening the heart. The abdomen stretches fully as the front of the body raises from the floor. The Cancer and Scorpio parts of our body are awakened.

Cobra is also a Leo posture since the spine fully stretches and engages in back bend while the fourth chakra opens. Leo rules the back and heart.

Knees-Chest-Chin to Cobra Poses

From Plank, exhale and bend your knees to the floor and then lower your chest and chin to the floor. Keep your chest open and your elbows close to the side of your rib cage.

Inhale and raise your chest to begin Cobra pose. Roll your shoulders back and extend the shoulder blades down while pressing them in toward the chest. Your chest should be lifted and open and your elbows close to the body. Engage the muscles of the legs to firm your thighs. Your legs and feet should be well extended with toes pointed backward and tops of the feet to the floor.

Extended Child Pose to Downward Dog Pose

In Extended Child posture, the nurturing aspect of Cancer is at work. Bringing yourself to a place of safety and rest, this is a posture similar to a fetal position.

Exhale and tuck in your toes while bending your knees and pushing back to the Extended Child's position with head to the floor, bent knees and arms outstretched in front of the head.

From Child, move directly back into another Downward Dog. Pull the belly up and toward the back of the spine. Raise the hips toward the ceiling.

To complete the Sun Salutation, repeat in reverse the first three postures that began the series, using these instructions as a guide.

Standing Lunge

Inhale and bring the opposite foot forward in between your hands to the lunge position. On an exhale, bring the back foot forward to join the front foot so that your feet are together. Rest your hands on the floor, shins, or ankles, depending on your comfort level.

Reverse Swan Dive Transition

Inhale and lift your arms up to the side with palms facing upwards to the sky. Extend the arms above your head and bring to prayer position.

Mountain Pose

Exhale and return to Mountain Pose to close the Sun Salutation.

 og   og   og

Sun Salutation represents just one asana, or series of postures, that happens to integrate all and activate all the body parts, systems, and chakras. However, there are many forms of yoga to explore and practice. If Hatha does not strike a chord for you, you might try a form of hot yoga like Bikram, where the room is heated and a regular series of postures are practiced in each session. In some styles of yoga, poses are sustained, while in others a flow is created and we move from posture to posture more rapidly. Some signs, like the Fire signs, might prefer heat and a strenuous or athletic workout while others might find meditation and restorative poses more well-suited.

Whichever practice you choose, yoga's focus on the breath, on stretching and working the muscles and body systems, and on centering the self applies to all elements and signs of the zodiac. Awareness and attention to each part of the body helps bring us back into balance, cooling fires, heating where motivation might lack, releasing emotion, and grounding us solidly to the Earth.

Oil on Troubled Waters
by Carole Schwalm

Oil Spills are Neptunian, from their angelic side to the darkest of the dark. Astrologer Kim Rogers-Gallagher, in *Llewellyn's Daily Planetary Guide*, defines Neptune as a planet representing the capability of "compassion and sensitivity for beings and creatures less fortunate than yourself." Neptune symbolizes "charity or volunteer work because you realize we're all part of a bigger plan."

Organizations and volunteers immediately responded to wildlife in peril endangered by the Gulf oil spill. Hundreds of volunteers saved oiled birds and sea turtle eggs. Groups like the Coalition to Restore Coastal Louisiana, the National Audubon Society, the National Wildlife Federation, the Student Conservation Association, and the direction of the Department of the Interior and the U.S. Fish & Wildlife were on site. Call centers were established so people could alert wildlife volunteers of animals in peril. And people from all over the world donated money.

The combination of Aquarius and Pisces Neptune is very much a symbol of recovery and saving humanity from itself, through obligation and sacrifice. Human conservation efforts do work and will be increasingly necessary when, according to journal, "Science," one-fifth of the world's mammals, birds, reptiles and fish are in danger of extinction. Where wildlife may have naturally saved themselves, they can't when we join Mother Nature's normal disasters and soak habitats in oil, log and hunt and upset the balance of nature.

Neptune rules the ocean and oil, beaches, swamps frequented by waterfowl, and places where fish are, like the ocean and canals. All cry out for Neptunian "angels," now and in the future, because it takes years, even decades, to recover.

Crude Awakenings: The Dark Side of Neptune

Deepwater Horizon, Gulf of Mexico, April 20, 2010

Neptune rules chaos in general. Millions of barrels of oil spilled into the Gulf, and Deepwater started chaos and disorder of the balance of nature. Harry Roberts, professor of coastal studies at Louisiana State University, stated that four million barrels of oil in a spill can wipe out marine life and may alter the chemistry. In the Gulf, there are 1,200 species of fish, 200 species of birds, 1,400 mollusks, 1,500 crustaceans, 4 species of turtles, and 29 species of marine mammals. The yearly catch of blue crab alone is 50 million pounds. Ninety percent of sea life spawns off of the coast, and all are impacted by the oil spill.

Neptune rules and sudden collapses. It also rules oil explora-tion, hydraulics, and anything relevant to marine and submarine issues. Last but not least, Neptune rules addiction, like addiction to oil. All represent Neptune's dark side. There are 35,000 miles of pipeline in the Gulf alone, according to information available from www.worldphoto360.com. And there are miles and miles of pipeline in other areas, capable of collapse. There are oil tankers, oil storage units, all sitting targets for that matter. With Neptune, negatives aren't always visible immediately. Oil spills are literally accidents waiting to happen.

Other Neptunian sinister sides are bribery, conspiracy, and graft—all have a part in Neptunian deception. Neptune rules misinformation and/or mistakes that come to light later. British

Petroleum couldn't contain the well, but it did a stellar job of limiting information about the extent of the disaster. Neptune rules hidden things that operate so that effect isn't noticed. I needn't add, but I will, that oil-rich people have mega-millions to lobby and to control politicians and rulings, courts, and just about anything else.

Neptune rules asphyxiation and poisoning. In 1962, the last time Neptune was in a Water sign, Rachel Carson's *Silent Spring* was having a great impact on twentieth-century life. *Silent Spring* addressed the chemical industry. Neptune symbolizes forgetfulness, or failing to remember previous chaos.

To prove how little we learn from the past:

- 1.8 million gallons of chemical dispersants were used in the 2010 Gulf oil spill. The dispersants contain, among other things, bio-concentrates. The dispersants are toxic "to early-life stages of fish, crustaceans, and mollusks," according to an Exxon study. "They damage fish, then to the predator fish and up through the food chain to human eaters." Dispersants and petroleum toxicity are alive with carcinogens with known risks to humans, who also risk injuries to red blood cells, kidney and liver.

- The Exxon Valdez, destroyed plankton, a big part of the natural food chain. In the Valdez oil disaster, it is estimated that 250,000 seabirds, 2,800 otters, 300 seals, 247 bald eagles, 22 orcas, and billions of herring and salmon eggs died. In the Gulf War oil disaster in 1991, tidal flats were sealed in by tar. They still find oil in the marshlands.

John Muir said, "When we try to pick out anything by itself we find it hitched to everything else in the universe."

2012 and Beyond: Neptune in Pisces

The planet Neptune is in Pisces, the sign it rules beginning April 4, 2011. Then, a retrograde takes it back to degrees held April 20, 2010, when gallons, and gallons, and gallons of oil gushed out of BP's oil rig Deepwater Horizon.

Are more large "environmental disasters in the United States," and around the world, ahead? Yes, unless something is done the future will echo the past, while we are still trying to repair the previous disasters. Estimates with the Valdez are that it will take at least thirty years to recover. As of 2007, NOAA reported 26,000 gallons of oil remained in the sand on the shore, attributed to the Exxon Valdez (March 24, 1989).

In the Gulf War oil disaster in 1991, during the Iraq invasion of Kuwait, over eleven million barrels of oil were dumped in the Persian Gulf. The estimate is that recovery there will take hundreds of years.

We may never totally recover from Deepwater. University of South Florida's Ernst Peeples notes that six months after the disaster, scientists found no living fauna on the ocean floor where they have found oil. They also discovered dead animals at the bottom of the sea.

Neptune is in Pisces for fourteen years. Neptune rules oil and the sea, chaos and collapses. According to the *Huffington Post* in October 2010, the United States did the same thing, returning to deep-sea drilling with the same equipment six months later. Neptune recognizes no boundaries. That can't be negligence of laws that force companies to be responsible, can it?

How to Clean Oiled Birds

This process requires three people and three hours of patient, loving work. According to the Oiled Wildlife Care Network, first spray the bird with Dawn detergent. Then, gently wash the bird from beak to toe with swabs and Q-Tips. Then, rinse the bird with freshwater only to remove soap scum. Remove bird to a freshwater recovery tank. Give antifungal drugs if necessary.

When the bird has recovered, release where food sources haven't been damaged. The bird cannot return to the oil-spill habitats until the habitats are safely restored.

How to Rescue Sea Turtle Eggs

First, plan on spending long and hard hours, as Lorna Patrick did. Carefully and ever so gently remove the eggs one by one. Place the eggs in a special environment. Federal Express generously provides climate controlled trucks, and then will transport the eggs to another controlled environment at the Kennedy Space Center.

Maintain the eggs until the hatchlings can be relocated and/or released safely in a place where they aren't swimming in oil.

Resources

George, Llewellyn. *A to Z Horoscope Maker and Delineator*. St. Paul, MN: Llewellyn Publications, 1978.

Rogers-Gallager, Kim. *Llewellyn's 2011 Daily Planetary Guide*. Woodbury, MN: Llewellyn Worldwide, 2011.

Online Resources

PDNEV.blogs (De-oiling a pelican)

http://www.1.american.edu

http://www.whgme.com

http://www.earthshare.com

http://www.Victoriaadvocate

http://www.worldphoto360

http://www.grist.org

http://www.aolnews (Lauren Frayer)

About the Authors

Alice DeVille *is an internationally known astrologer, writer, and metaphysical consultant. She has been both a reiki and seichim master since 1996. In her northern Virginia practice, Alice specializes in relationships, health, healing, real estate, government affairs, career and change management, and spiritual development. Contact Alice at DeVilleAA@ aol.com.*

April Elliott Kent, *a professional astrologer since 1990, graduated from San Diego State University with a degree in Communication. Her book* Star Guide to Weddings *was published by Llewellyn in February 2008. April's astrological writing has also appeared in* The Mountain Astrologer (USA) *magazine, online journals, and Llewellyn's Moon Sign Book (2005–2011). April, a Leo, lives in San Diego with her husband and their two cats. Her website is: http://www.bigskyastrology.com.*

Robin Ivy *is a radio personality, educator, and astrologer in Portland, Maine. She fuses her passion for music and the metaphysical in "Robin's Zodiac Zone," a feature on her morning show on 94 WCYY in Portland. Visit Robin's website at www.robinszodiac zone.com.*

Tim Lyons *has been an astrologer for more than thirty years. He has contributed to two of Llewelyn's New World Astrology series (How to Manage the Astrology of Crisis, 1993; Astrology Looks at History, 1995), been a columnist for* American Astrology (now Your Daily Horoscope) *since 1990, and contributed numerous astrology articles to* Welcome to Planet Earth *and* The Mountain Astrologer. *He has also contributed to* The East West Journal, The Liguorian, Chrysalis, The Vajradhatu Sun, Bodhi Magazine, ETC, The Vocabula Review, *and various newspapers and given numerous lectures both in Colorado and elsewhere. He has a BA in English literature from Occidental College in Los Angeles and an MA in creative writing from The Johns Hopkins University in Baltimore. He works as a writing instructor at the University of Colorado and maintains an active astrology practice.*

Carole Schwalm *lives in Sante Fe, New Mexico. She has contributed to self-help articles and writes for America Online and other websites.*

Bruce Scofield *is a practicing astrologer who has maintained a private practice as an astrological consultant and conference speaker for over forty years. He is the author of seven books and hundreds of articles on astrology. He has served on the education committee of the National Council for Geocosmic Research since 1979 and was that organization's national education director between 1998 and 2003. He holds an master's degree in history and a PhD in geosciences and currently teaches at Kepler College and at the University of Massachusetts. Bruce Scofield and Barry Orr maintain a website, www.onereed.com, that contains articles and an online calculation program on Mesoamerican (Maya and Aztec) astrology.*